Nietzsche and Tocqueville on the Democratization of Humanity

Nietzsche and Tocqueville on the Democratization of Humanity

David A. Eisenberg

LEXINGTON BOOKS
Lanham • Boulder • New York • London

Published by Lexington Books
An imprint of The Rowman & Littlefield Publishing Group, Inc.
4501 Forbes Boulevard, Suite 200, Lanham, Maryland 20706
www.rowman.com
86-90 Paul Street, London EC2A 4NE

Nietzsche, Friedrich. *The Birth of Tragedy and The Case of Wagner.* Translated by Ronald Speirs. New York: Cambridge University Press, 2004. Reproduced with permission of the Licensor through PLSclear.

Nietzsche, Friedrich. *On the Genealogy of Morals and Ecce Homo.* Translated by Carol Diethe. New York: Cambridge University Press, 2017. Reproduced with permission of the Licensor through PLSclear.

Parts of chapter 3 reprinted from *Crisis and Renewal of Civilizations: The 21st Century Crisis of Ideas and Character,* "What Hath Man Wrought: Utopian Dreams and Delusions," 27–50, copyright (2015) ed. Marek J. Celinski, with permission from Nova Science Publishers, Inc.

Copyright © 2022 by The Rowman & Littlefield Publishing Group, Inc.

All rights reserved. No part of this book may be reproduced in any form or by any electronic or mechanical means, including information storage and retrieval systems, without written permission from the publisher, except by a reviewer who may quote passages in a review.

British Library Cataloguing in Publication Information Available

Library of Congress Cataloging-in-Publication Data Available

Names: Eisenberg, David A, 1978- author.
Title: Nietzsche and Tocqueville on the democratization of humanity / David A Eisenberg.
Description: Lanham, Maryland : Lexington Books, [2022] | Includes bibliographical references and index. | Summary: "This book provides an extended examination of Nietzsche and Tocqueville's political thought, with an eye to shedding light on history's democratic drift. It looks not only to a future that filled both thinkers with dread, but also to an aristocratic past that has been all but drowned beneath democracy's shallow waters"—Provided by publisher.
Identifiers: LCCN 2022014756 (print) | LCCN 2022014757 (ebook) | ISBN 9781793627872 (Cloth) | ISBN 9781793627896 (Paperback) | ISBN 9781793627889 (epub)
Subjects: LCSH: Nietzsche, Friedrich Wilhelm, 1844-1900—Political and social views. | Tocqueville, Alexis de, 1805-1859—Political and social views. | Democracy—Philosophy.
Classification: LCC JC233.N52 E37 2022 (print) | LCC JC233.N52 (ebook) | DDC 320.01—dc23/eng/20220518
LC record available at https://lccn.loc.gov/2022014756
LC ebook record available at https://lccn.loc.gov/2022014757

*For my parents, who gave me life—
and a good one to boot.*

Contents

Acknowledgments	ix
A Note to the Reader	xi
Introduction	1
1 Homo(genized) Sapiens	11
2 Aristocratic Man	91
3 The Revolutions	149
4 Democratic Man	235
Conclusion	289
Bibliography	295
Index	309
About the Author	311

Acknowledgments

The brevity of these acknowledgments should not bespeak a lack of appreciation so much as a lack of contact. In large part, the pages that follow were composed during days that had yet to dawn, amid monastic silences and crepuscular shadows. In my book, said silences and shadows are owed thanks.

Among the tangible objects of my gratitude, Jana Hodges-Kluck and Sydney Wedbush at Lexington Books merit special mention: the former for shepherding through a project that but for her commitment and care would be languishing still, the latter for her sedulous support in helping me negotiate a series of editorial hurdles that, in her absence, would hardly have been perceived, let alone cleared. It would be remiss of me not to thank the anonymous reviewer whose extensive and trenchant comments undoubtedly redounded to my benefit—and the reader's as well. I hope my gratefulness does not elude the reviewer's awareness as the reviewer's identity must my own.

Some of my musings on Rousseau in chapter 3 originally appeared in a chapter I contributed to an edited volume several years back: "What Hath Man Wrought: Utopian Dreams and Delusions" in *Crisis and Renewal of Civilizations: The 21st Century Crisis of Ideas and Character*, ed. Merek J. Celenski (2015). I am grateful for Nova Science Publisher's permission to reprint them here.

Last, to those select few who, while largely managing to escape the pre-dawn hours in which I wrote, could not evade the seemingly omnipresent specter that greeted them each morning on dawn's other side, I find myself deeply beholden. For their forbearance in abiding ever-shifting stacks of papers and piles of books, as well as a perpetually somnolent father, I am very thankful to my children (Adam, Alex, and Vivian). I would be lying if I said your existence did not greatly complicate this endeavor. I would not be lying if I said I would not have wanted it any other way. For putting up with the perpetual disorder and somnolence, my wife, Maureen, also deserves thanks, though she deserves thanks for so much more. But for you, I would be a fragment and pale shadow of myself. To the extent that this effort presupposes a sense of plenitude, it presupposes you.

A Note to the Reader

This book, like one of the primary works to which it is devoted, is not likely to be "precisely in anyone's camp."[1] Out of step with the times in which it was composed, it is unlikely to be embraced by bands of partisans or circles of scholars. As it does not seek to attract allies, it may yet prove, on that score at least, a success. Still, too academic for the general reader and not academic enough for the general academician, the book runs the risk of being less for all than for none.

For whom, then, is this book intended? Or to speak more like an editor, What audience does it target? That is the sort of pragmatic query that it would have been prudent to address before setting out to write this work, let alone completing it. If it behooves you, dear reader, to know upfront if this book is for you, permit me here to try to answer that question.

Apart from the obvious, namely those who have an interest in the book's central and eponymous characters, I would say, in the spirit of those characters, that this book is for those for "whom thinking is a *delight*"[2]—but not merely a delight. It is a book for those who, without necessarily seeking to be disquieted, know that sustained contemplation inevitably invites disquiet.

Ours is an age of crisis—or crises if one prefers. To the extent that we worry about such crises, we tend to do so with the apprehension that something may go terribly wrong. This book is animated more by the apprehension, what if everything should go terribly right? With that apprehension in mind, this book points to the perils that inhere in our day—that inhere in ourselves—on the understanding that it is good for us to see those perils[3] and that at present, we perceive them but dimly, if at all.

Should you choose to press on after reading this note, may the pages ahead serve to better illumine those perils and may they afford you some delight and disquiet along the way.

—D. A. E.
Paris

NOTES

1. Alexis de Tocqueville, *Democracy in America*, trans. Harvey C. Mansfield and Delba Winthrop (Chicago: University of Chicago Press, 2000), 15.
2. Friedrich Nietzsche, *The Will to Power*, trans. Walter Kaufmann and R. J. Hollingdale (New York: Vintage Books, 1968), xxii.
3. Tocqueville, *Democracy*, 519.

Introduction

Man quits history with the sort of ease with which Mark Twain gave up smoking: he has done it many times before. Tabling the countless apocalyptic prognostications that have never come to pass, there have been several occasions over the past two centuries or so when the cry went up—a cry of reason and relief—that the land without history had been espied and lay directly ahead. And yet, on the interminable seas of history, humanity drifts on. That man has been as successful in quitting history (or is it history that quits man?) as Twain was in quitting smoking ought to be plain. A mere three decades after Francis Fukuyama heralded history's end with much fanfare, history is still kicking; and, judging by the first two decades of the twenty-first century, is not about to stop anytime soon.[1] Beings that pride themselves so much on being rational should probably spend less time trying to previse history's end. Reason would seem to oblige as much. That humans are very unlikely to do so suggests that their pride might be misplaced.

It is worth wondering why man, or at least modern man, appears so bent on leaving history behind. An obvious rejoinder is that like smoking, history is no good for him. That may be the case, but to return to Twain, he loved smoking, in spite of the troubles it brought. It made him a better writer, if not a better man—a writer (Twain), if not a man (Clemens), fit to be immortalized.[2] Twain quit life before he quit smoking or rather, as a matter of necessity, he gave up both simultaneously.[3] Presumably, humans and history will go out in a similar fashion—in concert.[4] But barring some radical transformation, it is unlikely that man will be as enamored with history as Twain was with smoking. No doubt history and smoking enjoy limited analogizability—likely less than already has been exploited here—but if the reader will indulge but one more time: does not history, in spite of the troubles it brings (or perhaps because of them) make man better or more deserving of being immortalized? Is it not because man has history, because he lives in history, because he makes history, that he sets himself apart from all those creatures without history and renders himself a spectacle so singular and astonishing, that—to do him justice—an audience of divine spectators is needed?[5]

To return to that provisional answer proffered above, it is not enough to say that humans long for an end to history because history is bad for them. History no doubt is messy, littered with crimes and ravages, trials and tribulations, agonies and defeats, but it is only on account of it that man is worth his salt. To maintain that humans naturally want to live without that messiness is the tendentious claim of a particular type of human being, along the lines of claiming that all humans naturally long for comfort or equality or freedom. Why then the rush to reach history's end? Or to point more to the central concern of this book, what type of being desiderates history's end and the sempiternal rest that it promises? What can be gleaned about the character, about the nature, of those who look forward, however ambivalently, to an ahistorical future?

As ought to be apparent by now, this book is not a work of prophecy (or to speak more like a social scientist, it is not meant to be predictive). When history will end is a question that exceeds this author's ken and the scope of this work. (How it might end is a different question, one that is at least implicitly entertained in the pages that follow.) Rather, this book belongs more to psychology, not in the academic sense, but in the classical sense: it is an examination of the *psyche*, of the human soul, and more to the point, of the souls of different human types.[6]

A mere five paragraphs in and the reader, provided he or she has refrained from putting the book down for good or casting it to the flames, is likely to be on guard. "Man," "soul," "human types"—does this work belong to the twenty-first century or the first? (Of the common or uncommon era does not much matter.) That it is out of step with the times is evident. If it is not clear to which age it belongs, it is clear to which it is opposed: the present age—the age of democracy.

What distinguishes the age of democracy from the ages that precede it is the principle of equality. One hesitates to say the idea of equality. The idea of equality is coeval with society itself. What is singular about this age is that the idea has not only been widely, if not universally disseminated, but that it has been concretized. That is not to suggest it has been absolutized. In eradicating old inequalities, democratic man consistently finds new inequalities in need of eradication. His efforts are at once Sisyphean and Tantalean, as he futilely labors to roll back inequality, ever tantalized by the prospect that he will succeed in doing so. This age, centuries if not millennia in the making, has yet to reach its terminus. But it has a terminus toward which it speeds, razing everything in its path as it races to equalize man and level the world he inhabits.

This claim that the principle of equality sets this age apart is not likely to sit well with those who belong to it—the children of democracy. How can one posit equality as a defining feature of an age in which there remain so many inequalities, and often swelling ones at that? The pervasive and reflexive intolerance of inequality so indicative of the times is itself an indication that the present age is an age of equality. In an earlier day, people abided by inequality much more and were offended by it much less. If there are doubts on that score, may the following historical episode put them to rest.

The year is 1627, about a decade into the Thirty Years' War. La Rochelle, a Huguenot stronghold on France's west coast, had, through a series of revolts, earned the wrath of the Catholic King, Louis XIII, and his brilliant and implacable minister, Cardinal Richelieu. Late in the summer of '27, Royal forces commenced a siege that, owing to the city's redoubtable fortifications and provisions, would last for over a year. During that time, the city's population was reduced by more than 80 percent, dwindling from 27,000 at the start of hostilities to 5,000 at the time of its surrender. As provisions ran out, the city's inhabitants began consuming the domesticated animals within the city's walls—horses, dogs, cats—and when those were depleted, turned their attention to more pestilential ones—rats and mice. People boiled belts, boots, and other leather objects and consumed the resulting bouillon in a desperate bid to nourish themselves. At one point during the protracted siege, the Marquis de Feuquières, a lieutenant general in the royal army, was captured in a skirmish and immured inside the city. Throughout the entire time of his confinement, as the city's inhabitants succumbed to starvation and disease, victuals—including "roast duckling, green peas and strawberries, pastries and copious helpings of venison, lamb, and beef"—were carried into the city under a flag of truce and dutifully delivered to the Marquis. As Aldous Huxley, who recounts this incident in his book *Grey Eminence*, commented, "To us, the whole episode seems almost unthinkably odd; but in the seventeenth century, we must remember, it was axiomatic that a person of quality was different in kind from ordinary people and must be treated accordingly."[7] Today, a different axiom prevails: there are no different *kinds* of people; there is but a single humankind to which all people belong.

Few thinkers, if any, have apprehended the spirit of this age and the human type to which it belongs with greater profundity and perspicacity than Friedrich Nietzsche and Alexis de Tocqueville. The pairing likely will appear odd.[8] One, the vehement opponent of democracy; the other, democracy's staunch and admonitory friend. Tocqueville died when Nietzsche was 14. There is no record of Nietzsche having ever encountered Tocqueville's works[9] and no possibility of Tocqueville having encountered Nietzsche's, so that one only can speculate as to how each might have read the other. But although on the face of it odd, the pairing is not arbitrary. For notwithstanding the significant and oftentimes insuperable differences that separate their thoughts, their musings display considerable concord with respect to the democratic march of history and what it signified for humanity, a concord all the more remarkable given Nietzsche's inexorable disdain for democracy and Tocqueville's qualified reverence for it.[10] For both thinkers, democratic man is not superior to his aristocratic antecedent; the democratization of humanity is not synonymous with progress; and the democratic future, far from being a repository of hope and light, is a source of dread and terror for those who unflinchingly peer into it.

In no small part, what allows for this union of minds, particularly with regard to mankind's democratization, is their shared appreciation for the multiformity of man and the nigh ubiquitous disregard for human diversity in modern thought. In the classical age, it was common for thinkers to reflect on varieties of human beings—on contemplative souls and magnanimous souls and servile souls, and so on. This human variegation is neglected, if not repudiated in modern thought. One does not find in Hobbes, who not without reason considered himself the founder of modern political science, a distinction between types of human beings—between lovers of honor and lovers of pleasure and lovers of wisdom. Instead, human beings are depicted uniformly, monolithically. At bottom, all human beings are avaricious, self-interested, prideful, and pugnacious and what naturally motivates them all is but one thing: the fear of violent death and the desire to avoid it, that is, the desire for self-preservation. This reductionism is emblematic of modern thought. It is easier to solve the political problem when people are all alike than it is when people are substantively unalike. It is not incidental that the various political solutions proffered by modern thinkers tend to be of the one-size-fits-all variety. The heterogeneity with which humanity heretofore teemed will be displaced by an unmitigated uniformity: that is what humanity's democratization portends.

This impending uniformity distressed Nietzsche and Tocqueville, for it would amount to a prodigious diminution of the human spirit. In marginalizing or ignoring the aristocratic temper, modern thinkers misunderstood the temper of man simply. They took a certain type, that is, the democratic type, as being the paradigmatic or essential type and treated other types as atavisms that needed to be abandoned and consigned to the dust heap of history. But it was precisely in those cashiered types that Nietzsche and Tocqueville beheld a richness that, once discarded, would impoverish humanity en masse. It was moreover in the aristocratic type that both thinkers divined the genesis of man; the origins of a creature that transcended its animality. The danger that both thinkers beheld was this: because it is to *Homo demoraticus* that the age belongs and because this type considers itself to be the consummation of human evolution, other, nondemocratic types are looked upon as aberrations and retrogressions in need of amelioration or, that failing, annihilation. Along with suffering, strife, scarcity, and the like, "towering genius"—of which Lincoln spoke (and embodied)[11]—will be permitted no place in the democratic future. Pronounced differences offend democratic man; inequality he abhors above all else. This is why, as Tocqueville so incisively observed, people in democratic ages will willingly sacrifice their freedom on the altar of equality. The unconditional ascendance of democratic man will result in a contraction of the human spirit that will preclude, irrevocably, the possibility of human greatness. Man's democratization begets his animalization.

This danger, while apparent in the denouement to which modernity impatiently proceeds, cannot be appreciated fully unless one is acquainted with the agent that precipitates this procession, which is to say that one cannot discern the danger of mankind's democratization unless one discerns the nature of democratic man. And one cannot understand democratic man without an understanding of his opposing type. Just as a slave conceptually presupposes a master, and a proletarian a bourgeois, so too does democratic man presuppose another, namely an aristocratic other. To maintain that the democratic age signifies progress without a proper grasp of the age it superseded is little more than a self-serving prejudice, one that ought to have no place in an age that prides itself on having liberated itself from prejudice. (With misplaced pride, it seems, man brims.)

With a sense of probity that compels one to acknowledge unpalatable truths and a sensitivity to the tremendous distance that separates man from man, Nietzsche and Tocqueville plumbed the past and found the present wanting. Theirs were not the musings of reactionary minds; they understood as well as anyone that there could be no going back. But they also understood that the human type to whom the present and future belong is in many ways but a pale and insipid shadow of the type that anteceded him and that if left unchecked, the democratization of man would result in a world that, being the workmanship of those who oversee it, would itself be pale and insipid. This prospect saddened and chilled Tocqueville and nauseated Nietzsche.

The aim of this book is to fathom what inspired such dread in each of their souls and how mankind had arrived at such a portentous moment. It begins with an investigation of the modern project, whose principal architects, despite the scorn they heaped upon premodern thought, ultimately advanced that thinking insofar as they not only failed to call into question but persistently espoused the two most radical ideas to have emerged from Athens and Jerusalem: the supremacy of reason over instinct and the inborn equality of all human beings. Attention then is given to a type of man that the moderns either forsook altogether or purposefully sought to marginalize, namely the aristocratic type. Following this exposition of aristocratic man is an account of the revolutions that brought about his downfall, first in spirit and later in deed—the Socratic, Christian, and French revolutions. The final chapter is a dissection of the democratic man.

This is a book that is short on remedies and perhaps shorter still on hope, but bereft of neither. "Anyone who writes a book, however gloomy its message may be, is necessarily an optimist. If the pessimists really believed what they were saying, there would be no point in saying it."[12] In order to avoid a precipice, one must know that a precipice approaches. To that end, may this book have something to offer.[13]

A NOTE ON PRONOUN USAGE

Unless context explicitly indicates otherwise, the word man will be used capaciously to connote humankind or human being(s), that is, man *and* woman. The author acknowledges that such usage is out of step with the times; the author refuses to acknowledge that there is something discriminatory or misogynistic about such usage here.

There are a number of reasons—apologies, if one prefers—for maintaining the usage in this work.[14] In the first place, it is evident that originally (and until very recently), man was gender neutral and was used to designate mankind and comprehend indiscriminately those who belong to it. The claim that man is born with sin surely does not exempt the fairer sex. To suggest otherwise would be shamelessly misandristic. This inclusivity is supported by the word's etymological root: *manu* in Sanskrit denotes human being or the thinking creature.

Furthermore, this work traffics in the ideas of thinkers who routinely utilize the word in its broad sense. To be sure, perpetuating a practice simply because it is longstanding is a poor rationale. Such an approach would impede growth and preclude progress. Still, the alternatives would seem to be to accept the usage (the choice made); condemn, but countenance it; or correct it. Nietzsche's phrase, the last man, will illustrate the quandary well.

As with original sin, clearly the concept of the last man embraces woman. Nietzsche's vision of the future, chilling as it may be, is not one of a world destitute of bearers of last children. Given the plain meaning of Nietzsche's phrase and the well-established connotation of the word man, grounds for condemning it seem tenuous at best. As for correcting it, for one, doing so would be ponderous, and risibly so. When speaking of the last man, should one say instead the last human being? The last person? The last man and woman? What about children? They are neither men nor women. Would it not be wrong to exclude them? Are teenagers children, or do they merit a separate designation? The absurdity, one hopes, is apparent.

But absurdity aside, the last man not only has a ring to it but a significance that is not conserved in more voguishly inclusive language. The last man bespeaks a fundamental type of human being. The last person or people or human being brings to mind individuals who have overstayed their welcome at a dinner party or survived an apocalypse. This point bears stressing because, at some level, that is what this book is about—fundamental human types. Aristocratic man and democratic man are two types of human beings that are constituted or oriented differently; beings with discrepant values and longings and behaviors. That fundamental distinction, that essence, is not preserved when one speaks of aristocratic persons or democratic men and women.

Last, this book is a heterodoxy, in conflict with the idols of the day. It would be disingenuous and incongruous to bow to this pronominal piety—for no other reason than that it is a piety—in a book that calls into question so many of the pieties of the age. That such acquiescence might be expected or, worse yet, demanded should give all readers pause and impel them to wonder if the children of democracy really are more enlightened and tolerant than their benighted forebears.

NOTES

1. Francis Fukuyama, "The End of History?" *The National Interest*, No. 16 (Summer 1989), 3–18; *The End of History and the Last Man* (New York: Free Press, 1992). Though he has qualified his position on a number of occasions, Fukuyama has been reluctant to concede that history's death may have been reported prematurely. For qualifications, see *Our Posthuman Future: Consequences of the Biotechnology Revolution* (New York: Farrar, Straus and Giroux, 2002) and *Identity: The Demand for Dignity and the Politics of Resentment* (New York: Farrar, Straus, and Giroux, 2018); for his steadfast adherence to his initial claim, see "At the 'End of History' Still Stands Democracy," *The Wall Street Journal*, June 6, 2014, https://www.wsj.com/articles/at-the-end-of-history-still-stands-democracy-1402080661.

2. Twain, a prodigious smoker who smoked for the vast majority of his long life, found "cigar smoking to be the best of all inspirations for the pen." The following is Twain recounting one of the "few intervals" when he abstained from smoking: "My health did not improve, because it was not possible to improve health which was already perfect. As I never permitted myself to regret this abstinence, I experienced no sort of inconvenience from it. I wrote nothing but occasional magazine articles during pastime, and as I never wrote one except under strong impulse, I observed no lapse of facility. But by and by I sat down with a contract behind me to write a book of five or six hundred pages—the book called 'Roughing it'—and then I found myself most seriously obstructed. I was three weeks writing six chapters. Then I gave up the fight, resumed my three hundred cigars, burned the six chapters, and wrote the book in three months, without any bother or difficulty." Quoted in *Study and*

Stimulants: Or, The Use of Intoxicants and Narcotics in Relation to Intellectual Life, as Illustrated by Personal Communications on the Subject, from Men of Letters and of Science, ed. Arthur Reade (London: Simpkin, Marshall, and Co., 1883), 121–2.

3. Twain anticipated that his devotion to smoking would endure in the life to come. As he memorably quipped, "If smoking is not allowed in heaven, I shall not go." Quoted in Peter Krass, *Ignorance, Confidence, and Filthy Rich Friends: The Business Adventures of Mark Twain, Chronic Speculator and Entrepreneur* (Hoboken, NJ: John Wiley and Sons, 2007), 152.

4. History here obviously refers to a narrative or past to which human beings are indispensable, as the word's etymology intimates (the Greek *histor* (ἵστωρ) means "one who knows or sees; witness"). While one may speak of a history of time or tigers, those histories are possible only because humans have provided them. "In its amplest meaning History includes every trace and vestige of everything that man has done or thought since first he appeared on the earth." James Harvey Robinson, *New History: Essays Illustrating the Modern Historical Outlook* (New York: The Macmillan Company, 1912), 1.

5. Friedrich Nietzsche, *On the Genealogy of Morality*, trans. Carol Diethe (New York: Cambridge University Press, 2017), 58.

6. This understanding of psychology is in keeping with Nietzsche's, who referred to psychology as the "queen of the sciences, [which] the rest of the sciences exist to serve and prepare for." Nietzsche was critical of "all psychology so far" because "it has not ventured into the depths" of the human soul. For Nietzsche, "from now on, psychology is again the path to the fundamental problems." "The human soul and its limits, the scope of human inner experience to date, the heights, depths, and range of these experiences, the entire history of the soul *so far* and its still unexhausted possibilities: these are the predestined hunting grounds for a born psychologist and lover of the 'great hunt'". *Beyond Good and Evil*, trans. Judith Norman (New York: Cambridge University Press, 2014), 23–4, 43. Though he demurred at the charge, this understanding of psychology is also wonderfully conveyed in Dostoevsky's self-reflection: "They call me a *psychologist*; *this is not true*. I am merely a realist *in the higher sense*, that is, I portray all the depths of the human soul." Quoted in Mikhail Bakhtin, *Problems of Dostoevsky's Poetics*, trans. Caryl Emerson (Minneapolis: University of Minnesota Press, 1984), 60.

7. Aldous Huxley, *Grey Eminence* (London: Vintage Books, 2005), 169.

8. Its oddness is at least intimated by how seldom the pairing is made. Paul Franco paired the thinkers together in a fine article and commented in its very first sentence how odd it was to do so. Franco also surveyed the secondary literature and found "sustained analyses of the relationship between these two thinkers" (441) in very short supply. Paul Franco, "Tocqueville and Nietzsche on the Problem of Human Greatness in Democracy," *The Review of Politics* 76, no. 3 (2014): 439–67.

9. There is a lone reference to Tocqueville in Nietzsche's correspondence, but it is not clear whether Nietzsche actually read Tocqueville or if he simply was acquainted with the name. "I am just reading [Heinrich von] Sybel's chief work, in French translation (after studying the relevant problems in the school of de Tocqueville and Taine)." Nietzsche to Franz Overbeck (February 23, 1887) in *Selected Letters*

of Friedrich Nietzsche, edited by Christopher Middleton (Indianapolis: Hackett Publishing, 1996), 261. On this score, see Franco, "Tocqueville and Nietzsche on the Problem of Human Greatness in Democracy," 454–5, n. 30.

10. As Roger Boesche notes, in one of the rare sustained analyses of Nietzsche and Tocqueville, "although their reasoning proceeded in distinctly different directions, their conclusions were remarkably similar." Roger Boesche, "Hedonism and Nihilism: The Predictions of Tocqueville and Nietzsche" in *Tocqueville's Road Map: Methodology, Liberalism, Revolution, and Despotism* (Lanham, MD: Lexington Books, 2006), 127.

11. Abraham Lincoln, "The Perpetuation of our Political Institutions [The Lyceum Address]" in *Abraham Lincoln: Great Speeches* (Mineola, NY: Dover Publications, 1991), 7.

12. Joan Robinson, *Freedom and Necessity: An Introduction to the Study of Society* (New York: Pantheon Books, 1970), 124.

13. Something of the spirit of this effort is reflected in a letter Tocqueville wrote to Francisque de Corcelle (November 15, 1856) upon completing the first volume of *The Old Regime and the Revolution*: "I was unable to claim to paint a pleasant picture, only a likeness, persuaded as I am that the only opportunity nations, like individuals, have to heal is to first study the reality of their illness. Then it sometimes happens, it is true, that after having seen and known it, one succumbs to it, nonetheless. But without knowing it, one is certain not to heal. Few men would persist in their failings if they could have a clear view of them, see their source, and measure the results of them." Quoted in Robert T. Gannett, Jr., *Tocqueville Unveiled: The Historian and His Sources for The Old Regime and the Revolution* (Chicago: University of Chicago Press, 2003), 149.

14. For a lengthier and more learned defense of the usage, from which this apology borrows, see Jacques Barzun, *From Dawn to Decadence: 500 Years of Western Cultural Life 1500 to the Present* (New York: Harper Collins, 2000), 82–5.

Chapter 1

Homo(genized) Sapiens

For those who enjoy its blessings, democracy is something of a self-evidentiary good. While democratic regimes routinely are denounced by the very people who belong to and benefit from them, calls for the establishment of undemocratic regimes are in conspicuously short supply. Those who harangue about diversity and the need to respect cultures of all variegations appear to have no wish to supplant the democratic order that permits them to speak thus with any of the illiberal orders that, by their logic, merit commensurate esteem; rather would they remain in the land whose iniquities they daily rail against than relocate to a land whose far more veritable iniquities they daily ignore or, worse yet, excuse.[1] In short, remarks to the contrary notwithstanding, liberal democracy appears to be the favored regime, even among those who maintain that no regime should be favored.

Given the manifold and manifest advantages that democracy brings to a seemingly ever-expanding multitude, the preference for it is hardly any wonder. Nor is it surprising that those advantages would be taken for granted by so many who have never known a life without them. It might behoove those so disposed to consider the movement of migrants in the present day. Like the force of the sun on smaller bodies, the gravitational pull of liberal states is incontrovertible. Unlike the sun, their attraction is not mechanistic. Perhaps it is those bodies that do not shine that are most apt to absorb the radiance of the sun.

The curious thing about the multicultural stance is that while ostensibly it is a celebration of diversity, essentially it is a testament to conformity. Its central tenant might be reduced to nonjudgmentalism. Its principal position can be expressed apothegmatically as a slight revision of William Morris's dictum that no man is good enough to be another man's master. For the multiculturalist, no person (or people) is good enough to be another's judge. This is, in its own way, a judgment, much as the relativity of all truth is itself a non-relativistic truth. Tabling any logical inconsistencies that might inhere in the dictate to suspend judgment, what obtains here is the conceit that discrimination is wrong, not only in the negative, prejudicial sense, but in the positive, judicious sense as well.[2] And the reason is that, insofar as there is no objective ground upon which to stand, everyone is an equally poor, that is, incapable, judge. How one chooses to live his or her life is entirely one's own decision and—flagitious walks of life aside—no one is in a position to determine whether the choice one makes is right or wrong. All lives are equally choiceworthy. While this does superficially yield a tremendous amount of diversity, exhibited with the aid of tattoos and boundless sexual (re)orientations, the result is, in spite of appearances, a homogeneity rooted in the acceptance that there is no higher or lower. There is no standard by which to distinguish a life well lived from a life ill spent. Anyone who suggests otherwise has sinned against this very modern dogma and as a result, is condemned—inconsistently—for having broken the central commandment of the age: thou shall not judge.

Charges of uniformity are likely to rankle today's cosmopolites who, in response, proudly will roll up their sleeves and parade their identities to demonstrate how diverse they really are. Their resentment is likely to be exacerbated further by the claim that their homogeneity has very old, albeit still modern, roots, owing to their tendency to view the past as a repository of ignorance and injustice. (So much for suspending judgment.) It is true that individuality itself is a distinctly modern phenomenon, which is to say that conformity was the norm for much of human history.[3] To be different, to stand out, to be alone, was a wrong, not a right. But while communities demanded a degree of cohesion so as to better preserve themselves, that cohesion was internal and did not engender a suspension of the judgment of the sort on which those in the present age pride themselves. Indeed, the intracommunal demand for conformity suggested that there was a proper, good, true way of life and conversely, an improper, bad, false one. Those who defied the laws and customs of its people were not celebrated for their autonomy or individuality but were punished for their transgressions. Again, truth and right action were not relative, even if they were not, on a more objective basis, themselves true or right. This ubiquity of and need for a standard (or standards) of judgment prevailed not only within a given people but was even more pronounced among peoples. What followed from all this is that in an earlier day, interculturally, diversity was much more far reaching and genuine.[4] And it ought to go without saying that for the peoples of that earlier and much more precarious age, it was not something to celebrate.

What was vital to the erosion or overcoming of this diversity was the discovery or invention of humanity—of a commonality that bound disparate peoples together at some basic level. Humanity was not given.[5] What was far more apparent in a more primitive past were the distinct features—languages, customs, beliefs, garbs, and so on—that rendered different peoples incommensurable. Humanity is a generalization of the sort that permits people to navigate a world of inexhaustible variation. Perhaps a more authentic (i.e., truer) mode of apprehension would disclose the incalculable multiplicity of life instead of its persistent uniformity. The Heraclitian view may be more truthful, but also more difficult to manage. Order and stability are conducive to human thriving. To at least allow for this possibility is to acknowledge that human sapience may not develop in tandem with the so-called evolution of the species.

> Obviously, if we have to get out of the way of the traffic on Hollywood Boulevard, it is no good being aware of everything that is going on in the universe; we have to be aware of the approaching bus. And this is what the brain does for us: It narrows the field down so that we can go through life without getting into serious trouble.[6]

Perhaps, to paraphrase Spencer's dictum, it is the simple-minded that survive.

If the concept of humanity was needed to subsume human variegation, that subsumption does not follow necessarily from the concept. Or rather, it is possible to conceive of an underlying commonality and still maintain that there is an order of rank between human beings; that the distance between man and man is prodigious, if not insuperable. This is amply made plain in the teleological perspective that is indicative of classical thought. On that approach, everything in nature has a proper end toward which it naturally is directed, as the well-worn example of an acorn illustrates. By nature, an acorn strives to become a mighty oak tree. An acorn that fails to do so has failed to actualize its potentiality; it has failed to reach the end toward which nature impelled it; it is, in a word, deficient. And as with acorns, so too with human beings. According to Plato and Aristotle, the end toward which human beings are directed is the development of reason or understanding. Man is by nature a political animal not simply because he cannot live alone, but because it is only by communing with others that man's proper end is realized. Reason is discursive or dialectical; it advances not in isolation, but in concert, through dialogue and disputation.[7]

To accept that there is a nature common to man is not to accept that all men are common (or more to the point, equal), as classical thought attests. Just as human beings are not commensurately strong or fast or agile, not all human beings are commensurately wise. Just as many acorns fail to actualize their potentiality (they fail to become oak trees), many people fail to actualize theirs (they fail to become truly rational or enlightened human beings). While differences in height and physical strength may be tangential, to the extent that shortness or tallness is no impediment to advancing toward man's naturally given end, other disparities constitute distinctions that are more essential. This is what permits Plato to discourse at length about various types of human beings.[8] The orientation or composition of the souls of an aristocratic man and a democratic one—of those who extol virtue and those who glorify license—render the two distinct. Yes, both are human, but at some level, one is, in a manner of speaking, more human—or more completely human—than the other. There is something beastly or subhuman about licentiousness. The same cannot be said of virtue.

This understanding of human nature and the essential distinction between types of human beings was made more starkly by Aristotle in his discussion of slavery. Some humans, wrote Aristotle, are naturally slavish and their servility renders them unfit to rule themselves and fit to be ruled by others. To treat the slavish soul and the magnanimous one as being equal would be a perversion of justice and distortion of reality. It would be to treat as alike what are so manifestly and profoundly unalike. But though there is a fundamental distinction between the two, it should not be overlooked that in Aristotle's view, slaves were not inhuman.[9] For although the master rules over the slave no less than the male rules over the female and the father over the child, "the parts of the soul are present in all, but they are present in a different way."[10] It is on this understanding that Aristotle advocates freedom as a reward for slaves.[11] By serving their masters virtuously, slaves would be able to overcome their natural slavishness; they would transcend their brutishness and become more human. Indeed, in the classical world, manumission was not uncommon and there were several manners in which slaves could achieve it.[12] The slave was not condemned to a lifetime of servitude, nor did his temporary bondage amount to an everlasting ignominy. Hence, the likes of Epictetus and Terence could be found among the ranks of manumitted slaves. The irony, of course, is that slavery as an institution, where racial or biological necessity rendered the slave irredeemably subhuman, arose only with the advent of modern science and its political corollary, liberal democracy.

The human variegation—one might even fairly say, diversity (to employ that voguish and hallowed word)—that inhered in the classical view largely was effaced in modern thought. This resulted in no small part from the manner in which man was reconceived. The teleological understanding of the natural world—and humans with it—was repudiated during the Scientific Revolution. Purpose ceased to be a concern of modern science, which itself ceased to be a part of philosophy, as it became apparent that no purpose inhered in nature or at least, there was no scientific way of ascertaining that it did.[13] Science proved remarkably adept at calculating the movements of physical bodies and manipulating the material world to do as man bid, but what the point of all this movement was or that there even was a point proved beyond science's reach. It also is worth noting that it was philosophy, not science, that determined science's wherefore; that posited to what end matter was to be manipulated.

One reasonable conclusion to be drawn from this was that science was inherently limited, which is not to say flawed. Science was good at explaining how nature worked mechanistically, thereby permitting man to master it and prolong his own life, but was rather inept at explaining what one ought to do with that life, that is, how one ought to live. But because of the astonishing efficacy of science and the putative infallibility of the knowledge it provided, a conceit gradually materialized that genuine knowledge was scientific and that all other knowledge was not really genuine, that is, not really, or at all, knowledge. Science could explain the world in which man moved with a precision that other modes of apprehending simply could not match. That that explanation might prove vacuous was immaterial for those who championed the hegemony of science and displacement of those lesser modes.

What follows from the abandonment of a teleological view of nature is that there is no legitimate way to distinguish the good life from the bad; a life spent well from a life ill spent. A soul's health, on the Platonic understanding, is gauged by the degree to which that soul is in keeping with man's natural end. A soul is healthy, it is good, it is just, if its parts are properly arranged in accordance with the proper end given by nature. Because the natural and distinctive end of human beings is the development of reason, a soul is properly ordered if its spirited and appetitive parts are subject to, not masters of, the soul's rational part. It is on this understanding that different types of souls could be distinguished. There was a rank or hierarchy of human types determined by the extent to which those beings became more completely human. The life of the mind and the life of bodily pleasure were not equivalent for the very reason that one was the distinct way of man and the other indistinct from the ways of brutes. To pursue the latter at the expense of the former would be to disregard the end or purpose that nature oriented man toward; to prioritize the baser end at the expense of the higher. But if there are no natural ends toward which human beings are directed, a hierarchal ordering of the soul, and of human types with it, loses all legitimacy. The life of the mind and that of carnal pleasure are merely, to speak in contemporary terms, lifestyle choices, and by what standard can one say that one is higher or nobler than the other? This relativistic view may have been a later outgrowth of modernity, but its seeds were planted—wittingly or otherwise—at the start. As Plato indicated in the *Republic*, that sort of relativism inheres in the very nature of democracy.[14] Again, early modern thinkers may not have anticipated the relativizing forces they unleashed, but to the extent that they democratized humanity, unleash them they did.

Modernity's democratic bent can be traced back to Machiavelli, who inhabited that age of rebirth in which the modern world was born. Spawned by the rediscovery of the glories of antiquity, which had been lost to the West for a millennium, the Renaissance signified a period in which the classical world was celebrated and superseded with commensurate vigor, and perhaps no figure of that period embodies this approach better than Machiavelli. The Florentine's abiding reverence for ancient Rome and his disdain for the pale shadow of it that his contemporaries had become are evident. Yet, Machiavelli sought a break from antiquity, not a return to it. And to that end, he consciously pitted himself against his classical antecedents in a manner or to a degree that none of his forebears dared. The magnitude and sheer audacity of his undertaking can be inferred from the preface to his *Discourses on Livy*, where he likened himself to Christopher Columbus, and in doing so, intimated that he too had discovered something that would alter man's fate forever.[15] But whereas the Genoan happened upon a geophysical continent, the Florentine discovered a moral, or rather, amoral, if not immoral, one.

Formerly comprehending "the fairest part of the earth, and the most civilized portion of mankind,"[16] in Machiavelli's day Italy was riven by internecine strife and relentlessly preyed upon by foreign powers. To Machiavelli, it was clear that the political teachings of the past could not restore Italy to its former glory. The problem, as Machiavelli saw it, was that those teachings were divorced from reality and hence, were ineffectual in the real world—the only world that mattered. Past thinkers took their bearings from how human beings ought to be. On the teleological understanding, human beings ought to be wise or virtuous. But in Machiavelli's view, humans generally are predisposed to stupidity and vice, not wisdom and virtue—a verity that mocks man's noblest sentiments and designs. Earlier thinkers, be they Christian or pagan, posited an ideal for which people should strive. But that ideal remained perennially elusive and there was no indication that after a millennium and a half of such teachings, man had gotten any closer to reaching it; that humans had gotten at all better. Certainly, when compared to a first-century Roman, a Roman of Machiavelli's day fared poorly. If the heirs of Rome ever were to partake of the greatness it once embodied, a political teaching for *this* world would be needed; a teaching that took its bearings from how humans *are* rather than how they *ought* to be. The distinction between the two is substantive and enduring and—if the prior 1500 years were anything to go by—irreconcilable. A far more efficacious teaching would be grounded in human nature; not in some conjectural *telos*, but in the actual and verifiable behavior of human beings. In a world of enlightened individuals, it might make sense to be enlightened. But in a world of selfish brutes, it is better to be selfish and brutish. "For a man who wants to make a profession of good in all regards must come to ruin among so many who are not good."[17]

What follows from this teaching is that man is reduced to a lower common denominator. Classical thinkers like Plato and Aristotle were inegalitarian owing to the fact that they looked at human beings teleologically. Those who developed their reason in accordance with man's natural end were simply better human beings in the way that acorns that developed into oak trees were better acorns. In a land where all acorns failed to sprout, there would be no oak trees. In a land where all people failed to develop their rational capacities, there would be no genuine human beings—or at least all humans would be stunted. The ancients were hardly oblivious to human depravity. Nor were they naïve about what becoming a more complete human being entailed; about the tremendous burdens and commitments that were demanded of those who made the effort. As a result, they apprehended that the philosophically inclined, by their very nature, were fated to be *rarae aves*—in every age. But that did not entail that orienting man toward that higher end was unwarranted or pointless. To be sure, such teachings would not render all people virtuous, but in the absence of such teachings, there could be no virtue. There is nothing revolutionary in Machiavelli's discovery of the baseness of man, for it is no discovery at all. It is the acceptance of that baseness—the profession that the greater folly lies not in the corruptness of man, but in the effort to correct it—that constitutes the fateful foundation of Machiavelli's thought, a thought that has a decidedly leveling bent. As Leo Strauss noted, with Machiavelli, the aim of politics is effectively lowered.[18]

Consistent with that lowering is Machiavelli's elevation of the people—broadly and indiscriminately conceived. Measured against the great, who invariably are few, the people, who always are many, are more decent. For the former want to oppress while the latter only want not to be oppressed.[19] This gross oversimplification, so sympathetic to the many and antipathetic to the few, would become symptomatic of modern thought, even though from the start, its legitimacy was improbable. In view of a long succession of popular uprisings (the French Revolution not least among them) that made plain just how oppressive the many could be, this foundational conceit of modernity is not just dubious but insupportable. But in putting it forward—a teaching, incidentally, that could be said to be more imagined than real—Machiavelli effects a lasting inversion of the teachings of his classical antecedents. In the mind of a Plato or Aristotle, the many exist for the sake of the few; the lower for the sake of the higher. In the mind of Machiavelli and those who flocked to the continent he had discovered, the few exist for the sake of the many; the higher for the sake of the lower.

Machiavelli may have been instrumental in setting modernity in motion, but in many ways, the Florentine remains something of an anomaly, a thinker who belonged to two worlds.[20] In spite of the leveling implications of his political teaching and his embrace of man's baser elements, Machiavelli lauded human grandeur, both collectively (as in the case of the Romans) and individually (as in the case of a Septimius Severus). Machiavelli may have inversed the prioritization of his premodern predecessors, but he still distinguished between the few and the many; the great and the common. That distinction is nowhere to be found in the teachings of the self-proclaimed founder of political science: Thomas Hobbes.

The folly of those thinkers whom Machiavelli took to task for dwelling upon "imagined republics and principalities that have never been seen or known to exist in truth"[21] was not lost on Hobbes. How human beings behave and how they ought to behave are two separate matters and any teaching that gives greater weight to the latter at the expense of the former is not only bound to be misguided, but ruinous as well. The problem is, always was, and presumably ever will be that there is considerable disagreement on the question of how humans ought to behave.

> One and the same action is praised by some and criticized by others; a man now approves what at another time he condemns, and gives a different judgment of an action when he does it than when someone else does the very same thing. All these things are obvious signs that what moral Philosophers have written up to now has not contributed to the knowledge of truth; its appeal has not lain in enlightening the mind but in lending the influence of attractive and emotive language to hasty and superficial opinions.[22]

Hobbes's approach to this problem was at root Machiavelli's; that is, Hobbes's political teaching would be grounded in an understanding of human nature, not in its imaginary perfection or in the light of some speculative end toward which it was directed, but as it actually shows itself to be across time and space. It is in this sense that Hobbes thought himself to be scientific and declared to be the first political scientist. His philosophy would do for "the patterns of human action" what geometry had done for "the relations of magnitude in figures"—permit them to be known with certainty.[23]

Hobbes's method was to understand the political society in light of its constituent parts, that is, the individuals who comprise it. Because the ancients (mis)understood man to be a political animal, they thought it nonsensical to contemplate human beings who were uncoupled from society. What defined man was reason or speech, neither of which exists prior to or in the absence of human associations. A human without society is an abstraction; it is not really human. As Aristotle observed, beasts and gods can get on without society; humans cannot.[24] Hobbes thought otherwise. Or at least he thought humans could be understood—and perhaps best understood—in the absence of civil society (or in the light of its collapse).[25] His method is the inverse of Plato's. In the *Republic*, Socrates, in an effort to understand the nature of the human soul, constructs a city, on the understanding that the city is the soul writ large. To descry what a human is, Hobbes takes the opposite approach: he deconstructs the city.

In *Leviathan*, Hobbes indelibly described what life was like before the establishment of government.

> Whatsoever therefore is consequent to a time of war, where every man is enemy to every man; the same consequent to the time wherein men live without other security than what their own strength and their own invention shall furnish them withal. In such condition, there is no place for industry; because the fruit thereof is uncertain: and consequently no culture of the earth; no navigation, nor use of the commodities that may be imported by sea; no commodious building; no instruments of moving, and removing, such things as require much force; no knowledge of the face of the earth; no account of time; no arts; no letters; no society; and which is worst of all, continual fear, and danger of violent death; and the life of man, solitary, poor, nasty, brutish, and short.[26]

It is a state of perfect license, wherein each man has a right to all things; a state that, in Hobbes's famous formula, amounts to *bellum omnium contra omnes* [the war of all against all]. In such a state, not only do the inhabitants have a right to all things, they have a right to *do* all things. *Inter arma silent leges*—amid arms [i.e., in times of war], the laws are silent.[27] How deafening that silence must have been in man's natural state! Moreover, it is a state of equality, for although disparities in size, strength, agility, fortitude, and the like, exist, all men are equal insofar as each possesses the greatest power there is: the power to take the life of another.[28]

Hobbes's hypothetical leads him to the following conclusions: by nature man is an asocial being, committed to preserving himself at all costs; one who prioritizes his own good above the good of others and who, in an effort to secure and advance his good, will abide no restraint save for those that his physical limitations have imposed on him. Like Machiavelli before him, Hobbes finds his way to an amoral new world. Such a state cannot but result in a pervasive sense of fear owing to the exceeding precariousness of life and the prospect of violent death that lurks around every bend. In an effort to dispel this ubiquitous dread, atomistic humans who naturally are inclined to clash with one another come together to form civil society. Fear then is the catalyst for leaving the state of nature. But if it is a necessary cause, it is not a sufficient one, for it is safe to presume that the natural state of man is not at all that distinct from the natural state of a beast. Yet, man alone has transcended his natural condition. This can be explained by the fact that man alone has reason, a conceit that Hobbes was not prepared to abandon, though he did pave the way for the abandonment of it. (The logical inconsistencies of atomistic, antagonistic beings having the ability to develop reason, and, for that matter, speech would be damningly exposed in the following century by Rousseau.) If fear impels humans to quit their natural state, it is reason that permits them to do so.

In sum, on the basis of his hypothetical, Hobbes "obtained two absolutely certain postulates of human nature: one, the postulate of human greed, by which each man insists upon his own private use of common property; the other, the postulate of natural reason, by which each man strives to avoid violent death as the supreme evil in nature."[29] Armed with such apodictic certainties, Hobbes maintained that a perpetual peace was not beyond the reach of man. Political stability is ever tenuous and elusive because individuals elevate their private good above the common one. That the private good they seek sometimes is no good at all and that the pursuit of it at the expense of the common good often threatens to undermine both only lends further weight to Hobbes's position. There is to be found, in every community, an ineluctable conflict of interests, passions, appetites, ambitions, and so forth. Indeed, the fact that individuals will pursue their interests not only at the expense of others, but at their own as well, when sound judgment would oblige them to behave otherwise, betrays the feebleness of human reason. "Men are rather reasoning than reasonable animals, for the most part governed by the impulse of passion."[30] The words may be Hamilton's, but it is a Hobbesian sentiment if ever there was one.

Because humans are self-serving, poor ratiocinators, and directed—or misdirected—more by appetite than reason, the solution to this problem is not to correct human behavior but to constrain it. That was where all premodern thinkers erred: they endeavored to transform man into something he was not and apparently never could be. Man was more beast than angel; more brute than sage. If the matter had been open to question, it seemed to have been settled once and for all in Hobbes's day when, during the Thirty Years War, Christendom tore itself asunder with unbridled brutality. Talk of wisdom, compassion, humility, and whatever other lofty values the enlightened are apt to extol may stir the occasional soul, but it will not transform human nature. For far too long thinkers had been laboring to ameliorate the turpitude that inheres in the human breast with depressingly little to show for it. The solution to the problem of human corruptness is not to transfigure man but to accept that he was, is, and likely ever will be corrupt. Prioritize the is above the ought. That is the foundation for a more effectual teaching.

Once it is accepted that at some level humans are incurably degenerate, the aim should be to curb man rather than correct him. The means for effecting this is fear. In *The Prince*, Machiavelli famously argued that it is better for a prince to be feared than loved because fear more effectively directs or controls human behavior. "Men have less hesitation to offend one who makes himself loved than one who makes himself feared; for love is held by a chain of obligation, which, because men are wicked, is broken at every opportunity for their own utility, but fear is held by a dread of punishment that never forsakes you."[31] Fear is the key to Hobbes's promise of peace and stability for without it, men, who on the whole "are of evil character," and ever "bent on securing their own interest by fair means or foul,"[32] will not hesitate to sacrifice the common good for their private gain. For beings whose savagery is so deep-seated, fear is the only effective restraint. The people must be overawed or to employ Machiavelli's memorable formula, "satisfied and stupefied."[33] Saints and sages have tried in vain to correct human nature. Their folly stems from their inability to appreciate just how incorrigible a louse man really is. To paraphrase Kant, man is too crooked to be made straight.[34] But if he cannot be straightened out, his crooked ways can be held at bay or in check, not through education or moral improvement or spiritual purification, but through fear: on that basis, people will perform certain deeds and refrain from doing others.

One might be quick to dismiss the claim that there is anything novel or revolutionary about this teaching. Presumably, punishment and the fear of it have been integral to human communities for as long as humans have communed. Tabling the ways of primitive peoples and bringing the matter slightly closer to home, the Greeks and Romans were not exactly kindhearted pacifists ever eager to turn the other cheek. Punishments for transgressing the laws were steep and presumably, the threat of them instilled no small amount of fear. In the case of that world-conquering religion that did exalt meekness and counseled turning the other cheek (at least in principle if often not in practice), no small part of its success rested on the threat of eternal damnation, the prospect of which must have terrified and to this day terrifies still multitudes upon multitudes of people. It is true that a conception of hell gradually developed over time, but that only substantiates the point being made here. Part of the appeal for early Christians was the belief that the Second Coming would occur in their lifetimes. When it became increasingly apparent that Jesus would not be returning anytime soon, to sustain the religion, fear became increasingly vital.[35]

All this may be true, but it does nothing to confute the fact that Hobbes's teaching was revolutionary all the same. For one, Hobbes has no concern about the development of character or the cultivation of the soul. (His materialist and mortalist conception of the soul was not the least revolutionary aspect of that teaching.[36]) No doubt punishment and the threat of it was essential to the Greeks and Romans, but their fundamental concern was cultivating virtue. That is why education was of such importance to classical thinkers; by means of it, one became better or better developed in a holistic or teleological sense. For Hobbes, the lot of humanity is corrupt and there is nothing to be done about it or at least it would be more sensible to do nothing about it. Failure or refusal to accept this courts more problems than it solves. The extent to which modern thinkers would neglect the development of character was nicely illustrated by Kant, when he noted, "As hard as it may sound, the problem of setting up a state, can be solved even by a nation of devils (so long as they possess understanding)."[37] As for the prospect of eternal damnation (speaking of devils), Hobbes recognized the power of it, but thought that it was not powerful enough to check human misbehavior. Hell is abstract or, to push it further, imaginary. No one on earth has seen it; no one has suffered its torments. Imaginary republics are no more effective at fostering virtue than imaginary infernos are at arresting vice. "For the fear by which men are deterred from doing wrong is not caused by prescribing penalties but by inflicting them. For we gauge the future from the past, rarely expecting what rarely happens."[38]

What was needed to inspire fear and thereby ensure stability was a this-worldly power, not an other-worldly one; a power so great, so absolute, that people would not dare to defy it. Hobbes named this power Leviathan. Like the eponymous biblical beast,

Nothing on earth is its equal—
   a creature without fear.
It looks down on all that are haughty;
   it is king over all that are proud.[39]

Unlike its biblical namesake, Hobbes's Leviathan will not be confined to the pages of a religious tome and to the imaginations of those acquainted with it. Its power will be palpable to all those who bide within its bounds. It will deter people from transgressing, not by instructing or inspiring them to do right, but by rendering them too afraid to do wrong, for with its reach and wrath they will be well acquainted.

On the face of it, it is not evident how a thinker who advocates such a solution to the political problem can be considered a fountainhead of modernity, one of the defining features of which is its democratic bent. But the egalitarian underpinnings of the Hobbesian state are considerable and are worth touching upon not least because doing so will suggest that absolutism and democracy are, in spite of common conceits, not antithetical to one another.

While the state's power is absolute, it is not arbitrary. The state exists not to glorify or aggrandize itself, but to procure "the *safety of the people*"[40] and safeguard the rights of those who live under it, the fundamental right to life foremost among them. It was because life proved so difficult to preserve in the state of nature that individuals banded together and agreed to transfer their natural rights to an artificial sovereign. The absolute state is founded on the consent of the governed, who agree to give up their right to all things so as to enjoy the safety that comes with living under a sovereign whose power to protect the people is without limit. While the sovereign stands far above his subjects, the subjects are, vis-à-vis one another, equals. Indeed, the Hobbesian state is remarkably egalitarian; astonishingly so, given the age in which it was proffered. At a time when people were, on the basis of their social status, subject to different legal systems, Hobbes proposes a state with promulgated laws[41] that are succinct and perspicuous[42] and that bear upon all uniformly[43]—a state, moreover, wherein subjects are taxed equally,[44] public charities are established for those who cannot sustain themselves,[45] punishment is designed to be remedial and leniency is encouraged with respect to "crimes of infirmity,"[46] and people are free to do as they please whenever the law is silent (that is, when the posited law does not oblige or forbid certain actions).[47] It is this last point in particular that lends support to Strauss's claim that "if we may call liberalism that political doctrine which regards as the fundamental political fact the rights, as distinguished from the duties of, man and which identifies the function of the state with the protection or safeguarding of those rights, we must say that the founder of liberalism was Hobbes."[48]

The ostensible conflict between absolutism and liberalism might help explain why credit for siring liberalism more often goes to Hobbes's successor, John Locke, the champion of *limited* government. Absolutism may seem indefensible in classically liberal eyes, but it is important to bear in mind that for Hobbes, the state enjoys absolute power not for its own sake but for that of its people. If at heart humans are rapacious and pugnacious, any division or sharing of power is likely to invite discord, the very discord the state was erected to forestall. That argument may be no more convincing today than it was for John Locke in the seventeenth century, but it is an argument that is neither illogical nor illiberal. However unpalatable Hobbes's absolutism may be, the fact remains that the Monster of Malmesbury decisively colored modern political thought, particularly with regard to a teaching that was markedly unclassical, namely that—to quote that revolutionary and emphatically modern document whose espousers were intellectually indebted to that Monster—all men are created equal.

That "self-evident truth" is, of course, consistent with biblical thought; indeed, it is a truth that owes a tremendous and too often unacknowledged debt to that thought.⁴⁹ But in the minds of classical philosophers, there was nothing self-evident nor true about it. To be sure, the utter helplessness with which humans enter this world lends support to the view that we are all born equal. But to prop this ideal upon such physical or materialistic foundations runs into obvious problems. Certainly, it would enjoy little support among a people who, without qualms, practiced infanticide, as the Greeks did.⁵⁰ It also would appear incompatible with that modern and avowedly more humane form of infanticide, abortion, which in this more egalitarian and enlightened age, is not only practiced but celebrated. How else can one explain the ease with which those discovered to be genetically deficient are disposed of, but for a latent and physical inequality? Even if a classical philosopher could be persuaded that humans are born equal, the likely rejoinder would be, so what? A person's worth is not measured at birth but, if not at death, certainly at some point closer to that end of the continuum. It is not merely that people live, but *how* they live that matters. To bring this back to acorns, it is only in becoming an oak tree that an acorn, in a manner of speaking, distinguishes itself and demonstrates its merit. That is, one measures an oak by what it has become, not by the seed from which it sprouted. And again, as with oaks, so too with humans. For the ancients, it was not human equality but human inequality that was self-evidently true.

The modern approach, in keeping with Hobbes's, has been to define man not on the basis of some natural end, which, even if veritable, appears hopelessly elusive, but on that of man's natural beginning, which is far more evincible. Humans would be understood not in the light of some higher nature—about which there has been much disputation and little agreement—but in that of an elemental one that lends itself to greater concord (notwithstanding that discord is a central component of that nature). The ancients looked upon humans as political animals on the understanding that their higher nature only could be realized socially. If the development of reason or understanding is that distinctly human activity, and that activity is possible only in society, it follows that man is by nature social or political. The moderns argued that man by nature was asocial or apolitical on the understanding that society is a construct—an exceedingly complex one at that—and that in their natural and primitive state, human beings are simply incapable of constructing it.⁵¹

Hobbes's ambition to put an end to the perennial war of pens by placing moral philosophy on a more scientific footing proved foolhardy.⁵² With regard to questions of human nature, right and wrong, the proper construction of the state, and so on, modern thinkers would prove no less disputatious than their classical antecedents. The ink that flowed from Hobbes's pen had not long been dry when Locke, with superficial subtlety, decried those who championed absolute government, and the trenchancy of those remarks did nothing to spare Locke (or Hobbes) the withering critique leveled by Rousseau at their abortive returns to the state of nature. Even when a good deal of congruity existed between thinkers, say Hobbes and Locke or Rousseau and Kant, discrepancies in their teachings were substantial enough to render them irreconcilable, so that one was inclined to conclude that conflict was indeed endemic to the human condition and that sages are no more suited for perpetual harmony than are fools. The comfort afforded by Kant at the end of his *Universal History*, buoyed so greatly by the arrival of Hegel, must seem meager in the light of Marx's inversion of Hegel, to say nothing of the dreadful recrudescence of barbarism that occurred in the century that followed—much of it perpetuated in Marx's name, however spuriously. Indeed, even Kant's analogy can comfort no more as science itself, far from advancing in a linear and progressive manner, has been characterized by periodic upheavals in which the light that one generation shines on the natural world is, if not snuffed out, dimmed or deflected by the next.[53] "Nature and Nature's laws lay hid in night: God said, Let Newton be! and all was light,"[54] except light was not the wave it was thought to be and Newton's laws, it turned out, were not exactly binding.

In spite of their differences, on the whole, modern thinkers agreed—at least tacitly—on a matter of far-reaching significance, one that set them apart from their classical forebears: in studying man, it is the ordinary traits, not the extraordinary ones, that matter. Modern political philosophy is founded on a reduction of the human animal to a very common and uniform denominator. The precise value or measure of that denominator may be open to dispute, but that there is such a denominator and that, moreover, humans should be understood in the light of it, would appear not to be. Thus, in Hobbes's mind, man is reduced to a being that is avaricious and affrighted. Avarice and fear are the bedrocks of human nature. Upon these, "absolutely certain postulates" states should be constructed. By utilizing or exploiting the latter, sovereigns will be able to better control or channel the former. That there have been people who have mastered fear; who preferred to die in battle rather than preserve their hides in flight, and to do so, moreover, for some nonbiological end (pride, honor, virtue) would suggest that these attributes are not determinative. It would seem man is capable of transcending his base nature, which presumably he also shares with other beasts. Tellingly, this is not what distinguishes man in the eyes of Hobbes. Rather, it is the capacity for reason, which beasts do not have, that sets man apart. But here too, reason is conceived in a very egalitarian and reductive manner. On the classical understanding, reason was something that had to be cultivated and the reality was—and still is—that not everyone is commensurably cultivated on that score. Some simply enjoy, naturally it would seem, greater intellectual aptitude, just as some display innate musical or athletic talents.[55] But natural ability aside, the fact still remains that some devote more effort to cultivating it while others studiously neglect the cultivation of it. Hobbes presumably would not deny as much, just as Plato would not deny that an ignorant man is human. Where the two part ways is on the question of what such a distinction signifies. Are the wise man and fool more alike than unalike? Are they equals, and if so, in what way and with what consequences? Is the distance between man and man immense or, in effect, nil? For the ancients, reason—the advance of it—was something that distinguished human beings from one another. For Hobbes, reason—the mere possession of, or capacity for, it—is something that unites human beings together.

Hobbesian man is a rational agent whose ruling ambition is to preserve himself. In the state of nature, this invites doing whatever necessary to secure whatever advantages conduce to that end. But Hobbesian man, armed with reason, understands that in such a state, there can be no security; that his actions are self-defeating because the security he gains one day can be surrendered the next. Reason then compels him to not only quit his natural state but—once under the protection of an unnatural one—to perform certain duties.[56] Because reason frequently is subverted by passion, a Leviathan is needed. One might say, anticipating Kant, that if individuals were thoroughly rational agents, no state would be needed. To behave in a manner that compromises "the longest possible preservation of life and limb" is folly.[57] Any number of historical peoples might protest that to the extent that this is wisdom, it is a very utilitarian and bourgeois piece of it.[58]

Whatever quibbles Hobbes's successors had with him, and many were had, the reductive approach appears not to be among them. This is true not only for those who sought to refine his teachings but for those who aimed to repudiate them as well. To the former camp, Locke belongs. Locke was unambiguous in his denunciation of absolutism.[59] But though he thought the remedy worse than the disease, he was largely sympathetic to Hobbes's diagnosis of the human condition. Lockean man shares a good deal in common with his Hobbesian forebear. He is self-interested, atomistic, and enjoys—in that modern, egalitarian fashion—the capacity to reason. Where they part ways is on the question of human aggression. In Hobbes's natural man, one will find a will to do harm that ostensibly does not inhere in Lockean man. Locke is careful to distinguish two states, which Hobbes averred were one and the same, namely that of nature and that of war. The distinction is not trivial. If humans naturally are as malevolent and bellicose as Hobbes contends, so that their natural condition is invariably one of war, then an absolute and undivided sovereign may indeed be the appropriate remedy to correct or constrain human nature. Locke argues that a state of nature exists when there is no common arbiter to appeal to and that such a state should not be confused with a state of war, which exists whenever force is used without right. While the distinction between the two is not inconsequential, the line that separates a state of nature from that of war is ever so slender, for humans—without being the bellicose brutes Hobbes made them out to be—have a natural tendency to be fractious and when disputes arise in the absence of a neutral arbiter, they are very difficult to resolve peaceably. There is a natural tendency for the state of nature to devolve into a state of war.

Though not a state of war, Locke's state of nature is still insalubrious and like Hobbesian man, Lockean man is impelled to exchange his natural state for an artificial one. Locke's sovereignty is limited in part because the people it governs are limited. An absolute sovereign analogizable to a biblical beast is justifiable, to the extent that it is at all, on the grounds that it rules over belligerent knaves who need to be held in check. Lockean man is no angel, but nor is he some Hobbesian malefactor. Limited government not only will suffice to keep him in check; it will also better accord with the proper end of government. For Hobbes, that end is self-preservation. For Locke, the government's proper end is subtly and substantially different.

Lockean man also seeks to preserve life and limb in a state of nature that is fraught with uncertainty and danger. But because he is slightly more neighborly; because the will to do harm appears to be an aberration of his nature rather than an integral attribute of it, the real danger for Lockean man is not to his life and limb, but to his property, and it is the preservation of this that proves the principal impetus for him to leave behind his natural state. There was no property in the Hobbesian state of nature. For one, in the state of war of all against all, possession of anything must have been so precarious and fleeting that in no meaningful sense could one be said to have owned it. Moreover, and more fundamentally, no one has a right to anything because "*all things belong to all men* and there is nothing a man can call *his own* that any other man cannot claim by the same right as *his*";[60] what each person has in the state of nature is the right to "protect his life and limb as much as he can,"[61] and this entails not only "the right to all things,"[62] but the right to do all things.[63] If theft is the wrongful taking away of another's goods, there is no theft in the state of nature, because no one's goods are his own and, moreover, because nothing is wrongful. As in Ivan Karamazov's Godless universe, in Hobbes's state of nature, everything is permitted.

For Hobbes, then, "property and commonwealths came into being together."[64] Citizens of the commonwealth may have property rights vis-à-vis each other, but ultimately, the property belongs to the sovereign, not the subject. The conceit that individuals have an inherent right to their property is in Hobbes's view one of those pernicious doctrines that tend to result in the dissolution of the government.[65] All of this may logically follow from Hobbes's foundational premise and be defensible in light of it. And Hobbes devotes a good deal of space to arguing that absolute sovereigns have duties to their subjects; that it is not only the duty but in the interest of sovereigns to promote the prosperity of their peoples; and that besides, anything is better than the state of nature. Yet, it would seem reasonable to remain wary of his prescription, particularly since the sovereign must not be above or without the same base proclivities that provoke all people to tear one another apart. The will to do harm is never eradicated; it simply is controlled. But who or what controls a sovereign in whom absolute power reposes?

Misgivings of this sort are prominent in Locke's political teaching. Locke largely was sympathetic to Hobbes's political project but thought the central component of it was insupportable. In his opposition to absolutism, Locke posited doctrines that Hobbes argued tended to the dissolution of government, not least consequentially, that there is an individual right to property. For Hobbes, property cannot exist in man's natural state. For Locke, property cannot not exist. The reason is that everyone comes into the world with a piece of property, namely one's own body. Left at that, this teaching would not be all that distinct from Hobbes's: one's body is one's own and one enters civil society to protect it. But Locke's teaching is not so much about people's bodies but the world beyond them, the world that, in Hobbes's view, no one has a natural right to. Locke too accepts the supposition that originally the world was given to everyone in common and hence to no one in particular, which impels him to wonder "how any one should ever come to have a *Property* in anything."[66] Locke's answer is labor, which involves the use of the lone possession with which everyone comes into this world. Through labor, one mixes what is one's own with what is held in common, at which point the latter ceases to be held in common and becomes one's own. In this sense, property existed *before* the establishment of government and hence, man's right to it is natural.

Hobbesian man quits his natural state to preserve himself. Lockean man quits it to preserve not just himself, but his property as well. Not self-preservation, but comfortable self-preservation becomes the animating drive of man. Formerly a being who reached for the divine; who strove for virtue, and extolled wisdom and its perpetual pursuit, Lockean man is reduced to a property-loving animal. To be fair, that reduction entails an elevation of a sort that, by any sober reckoning, cannot but astound. Modern man, especially modern Western man, has transformed the world and surrounded himself with plenty and security in ways that could not have been imagined in an earlier age, and Locke, who contends that labor alone endues the world with value and invites the indefinite accumulation of wealth, not so much for the benefit of this or that person or class of people but for all mankind,[67] should be acknowledged for his part in this prodigious and unprecedented transformation. But Locke, no less than Hobbes, conceives of man in such a manner that human multiformity cannot but be curtailed considerably. For Hobbes, as dealt with above, anyone who jeopardizes life and limb is behaving contrary to reason. A Hobbesian world is one wherein nothing is prized above the preservation of self. It is difficult to envision what place lovers of wisdom, of honor, of justice can have in such a world. Locke's position is commensurately comprehensive and reductive. His claim, for example, that "Land . . . left wholly to Nature . . . is . . . *wast* [sic]"[68] permits no place for the view that nature possesses an intrinsic value, irrespective of what can be extracted from it. The natural world is reduced to matter; its worth is measured wholly by its utilizability. Modern man rapes the world his ancestors consecrated.[69]

The devaluation of the natural world brings with it a devaluation of man. If nature acquires its value through transformative labor, in what manner does human nature acquire its value? One might answer that man, being the workmanship of an omniscient and omnibenevolent Maker, has an inborn value and Locke pays more than lip service to this view.[70] But really, man's value is measured by the degree to which he can beget value; that is, by the degree to which he can add value to a valueless world by means of his labor. It is in being transformed that nature acquires its value; it is in transforming it that man acquires his. That is why, according to Locke, God favors "the industrious and rational."[71] It is they who do God's bidding; it is thanks to them that man's lot on this orb is made less miserable. And they make it less miserable not by ameliorating human nature, but by ameliorating nature simply. In the gospel of Locke, the industrious amount to redeemers: they redeem mankind from its fallenness and the misery that comes with it.

An awareness of man's fallen state had once served to temper human ambition. Man had been given a life without want, without suffering, without hardship and by defying the God who blessed him thus, had thrown it away. There was no going back and if ever again he was to taste an Edenic bliss, it would not be in this life. Man's sojourn in this world would be beset by sorrow and pain; he would wander through life as though it were a vale of tears. Such was his comeuppance.

But in addition to tempering man's ambitions, Christianity also instilled in him a sense of hope and longing that had been scarcely entertained prior to its advent. The promise of Jesus' Second Coming imbued history with a sense of purpose and direction it did not enjoy heretofore. For early Christians, the historical component was inconsequential insofar as they anticipated that Jesus' return would transpire in their lifetimes. As time passed, and it became apparent that Jesus was in no hurry to come back, history acquired a directionality, and a progressive one at that, to the extent that each day brought man closer to the end of time, however far off it may be. Human nature being what it is, it is not surprising that as time dragged on, man's faith in Jesus's return began to waver. Moreover, and more consequentially, the early modern era brought with it a number of discoveries that greatly upset the foundations upon which

Christian eschatology rested. That may have proved inimical to faith in the Second Coming, but the idea of progress endured; indeed, as man's power over nature increased, *that* faith only grew stronger. Thus the idea of progress was divorced from all divine support or agency, as exemplified so forcefully with communism, which promised to bring about, in the words of Moses Hess, "heaven on earth."[72] To be sure, that is a very late and, one might add, quixotic outgrowth of modernity, but the seeds of purely human progress were planted at the outset. It was Descartes who gave modern science its raison d'être by urging that we "make ourselves masters and possessors of nature" so that we may "enjoy the fruits of agriculture and all the wealth of the earth without labor" and what is more, "rid ourselves of an infinity of maladies of body as well as of mind, and perhaps also of the enfeeblement of old age."[73] A paradise of this world was at hand and it would be fashioned not by the hand of God but by that of Man.

Locke is no Cartesian, to say nothing of a proto-Marxist, but his project, no less than Descartes' (as well as, for that matter, Marx's), calls for the mastery and possession of nature. It is indicative of the modern approach and its reductive tendencies that progress is always measured materialistically. The natural world, replete with all the wonder and pulchritude it embodies, is God's gift to man so that he may exploit it for his own (material) comfort—a more *un*spiritual theism would be difficult to contrive. How could the adoption of such a worldview not result in a shocking loss of depth and, one might add, diversity? If suffering makes profound, might modernity, with its ambition to end all suffering, make man shallow?

In Locke's mind, "there cannot be a clearer demonstration" of the valuelessness of nature than the Americas of his day, where, in spite of being a land of tremendous bounty, the people know "not one hundredth part of the conveniences" that those in seventeenth-century England enjoy. The result is, as Locke memorably observed, that "a king of a large and fruitful territory there, feeds, lodges, and is clad worse than a day-labourer in England."[74] Tabling any quibbles about the overcrowding and squalor that characterized a good deal of London in the seventeenth century, as well as the ill consequences—pestilence chief among them—that members of the laboring class were acutely susceptible to,[75] to the extent that Locke's claim is true, its truth appertains exclusively to material well-being. That the native king of a large and fruitful territory may have a more abiding sense of belonging, a greater attachment to place, a stronger bond to kith and kin, a deeper soul or loftier ideals, in brief, that he might have a greater life satisfaction (to put it with undue insipidness) is, from the Lockean perspective, immaterial. One might contend that Locke's conceptualization of man does not homogenize him; that it still leaves room for different types to coexist, but as the tragic fate of America's Indians attests, such reasoning is dubious at best. The unremitting rapidity with which the natural world continues to bend before man's advance only serves to further substantiate that dubiety.[76] Even if God had not given the earth to the rational and industrious, it would appear it is theirs for the taking.

In Locke's philosophy, as with Hobbes's before him, there is no place for a typology of human beings, for the distance between man and man is essentially nil. Humans, at bottom, are lovers of material comfort and security. That very well may be true, but clearly they are more than that; and perhaps they are most or best when they sacrifice comfort and security for something loftier, something nobler, something less tangible.[77] Locke's appeal is to man's baser longings. Classical and Christian thinkers had no illusions or delusions about human degeneracy; they understood that humans were appetitive beings, but they taught that appetites should be restrained and sublimated. By prioritizing what is lower, one cannot but debase what is higher. Locke calls for the appetitive part of the soul to be unfettered. Avarice, a Christian sin, becomes a Lockean virtue—a virtue as indispensable and lofty as any, which is why not only are the "industrious and rational" given the earth, but the sovereign who "by established laws of liberty . . . secure[s] protection and encouragement to the honest industry of mankind" is godlike.[78] Locke's republic is the inverse of Plato's. In the Lockean city, the appetitive rule.

Locke's success is plain, as illustrated by his conspicuous impress on the most powerful, prosperous, and transformative country on earth.[79] In no small part, the success of his teachings rests on its broad appeal, an appeal that the political teachings of Plato or Aristotle or, for that matter Hobbes, simply could not match. Republics and principalities helmed by philosopher kings and absolute sovereigns are a much tougher sell than a limited government under which people are encouraged to heed their appetitive longings and the right to the fruits of their labors is sacrosanct. Locke's is a world designed not for sustaining the wisdom of the few, but for the comfort of the many. It is, unquestionably, a world of astonishing abundance. What it lacks is less evident.

One thinker who did not fail to detect the impoverishment of that world was Jean-Jacques Rousseau. In spite—or perhaps, in part, because—of the abundance that that teaching generated, Rousseau found it bankrupt, morally so. A teaching that rested on an avaricious atomism, where self-interest was not only accommodated, but venerated, was the sort of teaching that, in Rousseau's mind, lent itself to a world where the imbecilic lead the wise and "a handful of men [can] be glutted with superfluities while the starving multitude lacks necessities."[80] It was not just the gross inequalities that inhered in this world that troubled Rousseau, though trouble him they did; it was that the individuals who occupied it—the wealthiest not least among them—were themselves bankrupt. They live without virtue, without honor, without duty. Being neither beasts nor gods, they are obliged to exist side-by-side, but each has only his own interest at heart. Each lives wholly for himself, disinclined to sacrifice his personal welfare for the general welfare of the community to which he belongs and from which he cannot be apart.

> Always in contradiction with himself, always floating between his inclinations and his duties, [the modern individual] will never be either man or citizen. He will be good neither for himself nor for others. He will be one of these men of our days: a Frenchman, an Englishman, a bourgeois. He will be nothing.[81]

These rational and industrious laborers are but pallid specters of what man once was and what—with a new teaching—he might once again be.

Rousseau is, like Machiavelli before him, that curious thinker who has one foot in each world—the modern and premodern. While his reverential gaze is directed backward toward the Greek and Roman exemplars of yore, and, further back still, to primitive or natural man, he hastens humanity forward toward a revolutionary future of his own design. The ambiguity of his thought can be gleaned from his *First Discourse*, which was submitted to an essay competition offered by the Academy of Dijon. The essay topic: Whether the restoration of the sciences and arts has contributed to purifying morals. Put forward at the height and in the center of the Enlightenment, the presumptive answer was that of course they had, but Rousseau thought otherwise.[82] He reasoned that there was an inverse relationship between the sciences and arts on the one hand and morals on the other, so that the former's development entailed the latter's decline. Hardly a modern estimation! In his understanding of human nature, Rousseau also proves himself to be anomalously modern. The modern trend, it is being argued, has been to reduce man to a single type (in contrast to the classical conception of man). For Hobbes and Locke, humans are self-interested, atomistic creatures whose actions are determined by their fundamental desire—to preserve themselves, comfortably in Locke's case. This is true of man in the state of nature, as well as in civil society. In the cosmic scheme of things, humanity may be ephemeral, but within the time allotted to it, the nature of those who comprise it is, in a manner of speaking, eternal. Rousseau proffers a teaching that is radical and radically different, one that allows for the emergence of distinct types of human beings. But Rousseau does not signify a return. As proof of just how far he wandered from antiquity, to these new human types there is virtually no limiting principle.

Like Locke and Hobbes before him, Rousseau approached the political problem by returning to man's beginnings. Only by understanding whence man came could one posit a legitimate end toward which he should be directed. But it would be wrong to say that like his English predecessors he returned to the state of nature for, according to Rousseau, neither ever arrived there. "The philosophers who have examined the foundations of society have all felt the necessity of going back to the state of nature, but none of them has reached it."[83] Rousseau agrees with Locke—and thereby controverts the ancients—in accepting Hobbes's premise that man is by nature asocial. But in accepting this premise, Rousseau breaks from his early modern antecedents by thinking it through to its logical conclusion. Hobbes and Locke failed to achieve what they set out to do. While they purported to descry human beings as they existed before the founding of civil society, they ended up portraying a type of being that only could have come to be with the aid of civil society. "They spoke of savage man but described civil man."[84] Their *Homo natura* had all the trappings of *Homo civilus* to say nothing of *Homo economicus*.

When Hobbes claims that all men in the state of nature possess a will to do harm, there is nothing on the face of this that contravenes his understanding of man as being naturally asocial. With creatures that are reclusive and truculent nature teems. But when Hobbes provides the wherefore, it becomes clear that these earliest of beings are not in fact the earliest of humans or that humans by nature are not asocial. How else does one explain the natural and ubiquitous "will to do harm" that sometimes results from a *comparison* of talents and from vainglory and the demand for honor.[85] Pride, or *amour-propre*, which plays such a central role in Hobbes's political teaching, is indicative of social, not asocial beings.[86] The maladies that afflict the human condition that Hobbes endeavors to mitigate may be veritable, but if man is instinctively asocial, they are not congenital.

Amour-propre is not the only incongruity in Hobbes's teaching on natural man to which Rousseau draws attention. Far more damning for Hobbes's theory, and for Locke's as well, is the irreconcilability of man being concomitantly asocial and rational. In this respect, the classics were, at the very least, more consistent. If man is by nature a political animal (in the Aristotelian sense), then the fact that he is concurrently a rational animal necessarily follows, for only rational beings deliberate about right and wrong, good and bad, and "the just and unjust."[87] But if the presupposition that "man is an animal born fit for Society"[88] is erroneous; if civil society is invariably the product of convention and never can accord with nature; if, in short, man is by nature asocial, then it follows that man naturally possesses neither reason nor language.[89] But for both Hobbes and Locke, it was reason that distinguished man from beast and it was only by virtue of it that man was capable of quitting the state of nature and founding civil society: "The Natural Law is the dictate of right *reason* about what should be done and not done for the longest possible preservation of life and limb."[90] "The State of Nature has a Law of Nature to govern it, which obliges every one: and *Reason, which is that Law, teaches all Mankind, who will but consult it,* that being all equal and independent, no one ought to harm another in his Life, Health, Liberty, or Possession."[91] Hobbes and Locke's natural man finds himself in the paradoxical position of being confined to a state of nature he can quit only through the use of a faculty he, logically speaking, cannot enjoy. "It is impossible to understand the law of nature and consequently to obey it without being a great reasoner and a great metaphysician: which means precisely that men must have used, for the establishment of society, enlightenment which only develops with great difficulty and in very few people in the midst of society itself."[92]

Divested of all civilizational accouterments, man would not be the pugnacious being found in Hobbes's originary state nor the acquisitive, property-bearing one found in Locke's. Not only would he not possess the capacity to reason—a capacity needed to grasp the Law of Nature and quit his natural state—but there would be no Law of Nature to grasp even had he been endued with such a faculty. Man would be a beast among beasts. And though life comparatively speaking may be short, it would know nothing of the nastiness, poverty, and brutishness that characterized life in the Hobbesian state. Natural man would be free and equal, but not in the sense that each would be the executor of his own law and at liberty to snuff out his neighbor's existence. Nothing constrains him, save for his physical limitations, and he is obligated to no one, though a natural and latent sense of pity gives him a distaste for suffering and impels him to come to the aid of others in distress. For natural man, whose "modest needs are so easily found at hand"; who desires nothing that cannot be fulfilled; who has "neither foresight nor curiosity"; whose soul, in short, is "agitated by nothing,"[93] existence possesses a sweetness and affords a sense of contentment that is virtually unfathomable to civilized man. Given the Arcadian setting of man's natural state and the primitiveness of his faculties, one cannot help but wonder why, to say nothing of how, humans ever vacated it.

Rousseau's contention that civil society first began when someone, "having fenced off a plot of ground, took it into his head to say *this is mine* and found people simple enough to believe him" does little to resolve the matter for it is unclear why such a notion ever would enter the head of a being who inhabited a world where nature provided for all his needs to the extent that he never dreamed of wresting anything from her.[94] It is also unclear how such a creature, "wandering in the forests, without industry, without speech, without domicile, without war and without liaisons, with no need for his fellow men, likewise with no desire to do them harm, perhaps never even recognizing anyone individually,"[95] would not only be capable of fencing off a plot of land but also would happen upon others or have others happen upon him who would recognize that the plot he claimed for his own was indeed his.

Rousseau adduces a number of conjectures as to what could have prompted humans to depart their natural state and how their minds might have developed to such a degree that they would have been capable of doing so.[96] But whatever the conjecture, the fact remains that man's evolution was but an accident. It required "the chance combination of several foreign causes which might never have arisen and without which [man] would have remained eternally in his primitive condition."[97] Man did not so much quit the state of nature; he unwittingly stumbled out of it.

This answer invites more questions than it resolves. It would seem odd that a creature would have the capacity to stumble out of nature even if he was the hapless casualty of some cosmic accident. How does an accident within nature engender something unnatural? And why has no other animal transcended—accidentally or otherwise—its natural condition?

While it is correct to say that in Rousseau's state of nature man—or the creature that would become man (for at this point that creature not only is pre-social and pre-rational but also pre-human)—is an animal among animals, it would be wrong to understand him as just any animal. Man is unique among the animals and not simply because he is uniquely thumbed and postured. His difference is not physical but metaphysical. Man is that creature that is least constrained by its instincts or to put it differently, least defined by nature.[98] Man's being is becoming. He is free not just in the sense that no law binds him, but in the sense that he—alone among the beasts—has the capacity to (re)define himself. When stripped of all societal attributes, there were but two qualities that characterized this creature essentially, that distinguished him from the brutes with which he shared that irenic state: free will and perfectibility.

By the former, Rousseau meant that among the animals, man alone is not determined by instinct. "Nature commands every animal, and the beast obeys."[99] The reign of nature is, as it were, absolute, "so that a beast cannot deviate from the rule prescribed to it even when it would be advantageous for it to do so. Hence a pigeon would die of hunger near a basin filled with the best meats, and a cat upon heaps of fruits or grain, although each could very well nourish itself on the food it disdains if it made up its mind to try some." In contradistinction, man is undetermined by nature. He too is impelled by his instincts, but he can heed or oppose them;

> he is free to acquiesce or resist; and it is above all in the consciousness of this freedom that the spirituality of his soul is shown. For physics explains in some way the mechanism of the senses and the formation of ideas; but in the power

of willing, or rather of choosing, and in the sentiment of this power are found only purely spiritual acts about which the laws of mechanics explain nothing.[100]

In contemporary parlance, "what makes us the wise species—*sapiens*, remember, is Latin for 'wise'—is that our genes make brains that allow us to pick up things from one another that are *not* in our genes."[101]

As for perfectibility, "a term that Rousseau coined or at least was among one of the first to use,"[102] it signified an "almost unlimited faculty" that allowed man—both at the level of the individual as well as that of the species—to transform who or what it was. "An animal is at the end of a few months what it will be all its life; and its species is at the end of a thousand years what it was the first year of that thousand."[103] A crocodile is in the twenty-first century what it was two thousand centuries ago. Of man, the same could not be said. Formerly a being that wholly lacked speech and reason, man has become a being that, without speech and reason, would be wholly lacking. This is not a case of Galapagos finches developing beaks of different sizes, but is a constitutional change, if ever there was one. "[A] faculty which, by dint of time, draws [man] out of [his] original condition,"[104] perfectibility inescapably connotes a sense of progress, but for Rousseau, there was nothing intrinsically progressive about it. It is true that perfectibility accounts for man's virtue, enlightenment, and elevation, but it also accounts for his vice, errors, and degradation. Indeed, Rousseau goes so far as to suggest that it "is the source of all man's misfortunes."[105] One could argue, given the trajectory of human history, that imperfectability would be a more apt appellation for this distinctly human faculty. Whatever the name, the import of this novel understanding of human nature would be difficult to overstate. As Leo Strauss observed:

> Rousseau's thesis that man is by nature good must be understood in the light of his contention that man is by nature subhuman. Man is by nature good because he is by nature that subhuman being which is capable of becoming either good or bad. There is no natural constitution of man to speak of: everything specifically human is acquired or ultimately depends on artifice or convention. Man is by nature almost infinitely perfectible. There are no natural obstacles to man's almost unlimited progress or to his power of liberating himself from evil. For the same reason, there are no natural obstacles to man's almost unlimited degradation. Man is by nature almost infinitely malleable. In the words of the Abbé Raynal, the human race is what we wish to make it. Man has no nature in the precise sense which would set a limit to what he can make out of himself.[106]

History then is the saga of how humans *became* human; of the evolution, or as Rousseau would have it, the devolution of man, for in Rousseau's view, man's journey from ignorance to enlightenment has been declivitous. Man naturally is good; he is now corrupt. He knew only contentment in his natural state and is discontent in his social one. "Man is born free, and everywhere he is in chains. He who believes himself the master of others fails not to be a greater slave than they. How did this change come about? I do not know. What can make it legitimate? I do believe I can resolve that issue."[107] Rousseau's task is to legitimate civil society which in his eyes was unqualifiedly illegitimate. If nature was an exemplification of what was good, then by that measure, the civil society of Enlightenment Europe was anything but. That society was founded on the fundamental inequality between man and man;[108] its members were not citizens, but bourgeois whose want of virtue was reflected in their unceasing prattle about making money.[109] Bound by laws he does not prescribe and constrained by conventions he does not construct, a civilized man knows nothing of the sublime freedom of his natural state and the sweetness of life that accompanied it. In brief, as the Bible teaches, though, for very different reasons, man is fallen.

It is important to bear in mind that Rousseau's attack was not directed exclusively at those state of nature theorists who had failed to describe man as he was in his original state (though he clearly does single them out), but on the entire Enlightenment project. The underlying dogma of that project was wrong: the universal dissemination of reason was not an unqualified good. The road to salvation was not paved with reason(s). Man's natural state was good and man's natural state was ignorance. The acquisition of knowledge undermines man's natural goodness. "The development of the sciences and arts has added nothing to [man's] true felicity;" indeed, their development has hastened his moral degradation.[110] The question was how man could be returned to his natural goodness or that natural goodness to him? An answer to that question presupposes knowledge of man's original condition. Man must "manage to see himself as nature formed him" and learn to "separate what is original from what is artificial in the present nature of man."[111] But once secured, that knowledge hardly resolves the matter, for the way out of the contemporary morass is forward not back. Rousseau's influence on subsequent thinkers was nothing short of prodigious,[112] but as often is the case, a philosopher is greater than the sum of his epigones. The state of nature may have been an idyllic place, but it is one to which man cannot repair. Man can never again be the being he once was, a verity lost on Voltaire, who, upon reading the *Second Discourse*, penned a letter to Rousseau in which he quipped, "no one has ever been so witty as you are in trying to turn us into brutes: to read your book makes one long to go on all fours." [113] Rousseau shares this with the Hesiodic and Edenic traditions: he paints a picture of an ideal state, belonging to a remote past, to which man can never again return. As with the biblical state of nature, man has been banished from it—forever.

Rousseau's most radical and arguably most fateful teaching, though not his most celebrated, concerns the historicization of man.[114] Notwithstanding the magnitude of the early modern break from the ancients, no one before Rousseau was so daring as to suggest that humans were determined historically; or to put that differently, that humans, in essence, were undetermined.[115] For both Locke and Hobbes, man remained, by nature, the rational animal. Nature may not have prescribed ends toward which man was naturally directed as the ancients had maintained, but man essentially was determined by nature. To state it differently, even after the modern turn, it was still acceptable to speak of human nature. That is, until Rousseau arrived. For Rousseau, man is the undetermined being. If all those attributes that account for the deplorable condition in which civilized man now finds himself were acquired over time, then it follows that new traits can be procured, ones that, while not returning humans to their natural condition, can serve to bring about a new state that will reflect the qualities they once enjoyed in their original one. For Hobbes and Locke, the state of nature was not simply devoid of value. The nub of their teaching was not so much that man's natural state was worthless, but that it was inimical. Thus, insofar as he was a free, rational agent, man naturally was led beyond it to a rapprochement where his good could be secured, that is, to the establishment of civil society. Rousseau, in effect, inverts that teaching. Not the state of nature, but civil society, with its capricious constraints and egregious inequalities that are so indicative of advanced civilizations, is insalubrious for man's well-being; not the state of nature, but civil society must be transcended if man ever is to secure what is most important to him. For Hobbes and Locke, the state of nature is such that man cannot preserve what is most valuable to him (life, property). For Rousseau, civil society robs man of what is, or ought to be, most valuable to him—his freedom and equality.

The problem, as stated above, is that man cannot revert to his natural condition. The attributes that man acquired over the course of his long historical development cannot be jettisoned or willed away. Man cannot forego the use of reason or language nor can he become a solitary, ahistorical creature without ceasing to be human. He may not be a political animal by nature, but the historical process has fashioned him into one. As a result, civilized man cannot quit society as Hobbesian/Lockean natural man had quit nature. If civil society cannot be abandoned, then it must be remade. And it must be remade in the image, or at least with the image, of man's natural state. The state of nature becomes a standard to emulate, not a condition to scorn. That is not to say man should shed his vestments and take to the trees. Nor that he should forsake the arts and sciences and content himself with indulging his most primal urges. Man's natural freedom and the sweetness he enjoyed while living eternally in the present can never be restored. But that does not preclude civil society from being fashioned in such a way that man can enjoy a new freedom, a higher freedom, one that he prescribes himself; a society where he can build upon his natural equality and cultivate the natural sympathy he feels for his fellow human beings so that each individual finds himself a part of a community wherein he enjoys a newfound contentment of the sort that modern society consistently fails to afford.

The key factor of Rousseau's political teaching is the general will. It remedies the central fallacy upon which earlier thinkers had erected civil society, namely the inequality of man. The ancients had maintained that man is naturally unequal and that the best society would be the one that paid heed to man's natural inequalities (hence aristocracy—or monarchy, more uncommonly—was the best type of regime because it was ruled by the best people—or person).[116] Modern thinkers posited man's inborn equality but then set about constructing unimaginary republics of unequals. They propounded a regime where all yield to an absolute authority or where the primary function was to protect and perpetuate the inequality that results from the unequal acquisition of property. And while such theorists maintained that their regimes preserved the freedom of its inhabitants, they were misguided for where there is no equality, freedom is wanting, for the stronger will always be inclined to subjugate the weaker.[117] But if man is naturally equal and free, how does one transcribe what man enjoys naturally onto the conventional canvas that is civil society? As Rousseau posed the problem: "'How to find a form of association that defends and protects the person and goods of each associate with all common force, and by means of which each, uniting with all, nonetheless obeys only himself and remains as free as before'? Such is the fundamental problem to which the social contract provides the solution."[118]

The clauses of this contract "all come down to a single one, namely the total alienation of each associate with all of his rights to the whole community."[119] In Rousseau's formulation, the general will is the only legitimate basis of sovereignty. It is legitimate because the members who enter into it do so freely, of their own volition, and because each of its members is bound by it equally, so that no man is the better of another. In a sense, Rousseau's teaching restores to man those gifts with which he had been born but had squandered over the course of his eonian metamorphosis: freedom and equality.

Rousseau's teaching constitutes a remedy to and reversal of man's decline. By nature good, man has become evil. Man is fallen. He has fallen from the state of nature, much as he fell from the Garden of Eden and the Golden Age. Ever since the true founder of civil society "fenced off a plot of ground, took it into his head to say *this is mine* and found people simple enough to believe him," the history of man has been one of decline. "Crimes, wars, murders

... miseries and horrors"[120] sprung from that usurpation as if from the box of Pandora. But in contrast to the degeneration of man that is recounted in Hesiod's Five Ages, for Rousseau, human beings have the ability to stay and even reverse the decline that has characterized their history heretofore. Man's sin is not inherent, it is acquired. Moreover, and more importantly, it can be erased. Whatever depravities inhere in the breast of civilized man, they can be dislodged so that can man can be corrected, if not perfected. It is true that the natural goodness that originally belonged to man cannot be restored, but a higher goodness is within his reach.

> This transformation from the state of nature to the civil state produces a very remarkable change in man, by substituting justice for instinct in his conduct and by giving his actions the morality they previously lacked. Only then, when the voice of duty replaces physical impulse and right replaces appetite, does man, who until then had considered only himself, see himself forced to act on the basis of other principles and to consult his reason before listening to his inclinations. Although he deprives himself in this state of several advantages he derives from nature, he gains such great advantages from it—his faculties exercised and developed, his ideas enlarged, his feelings ennobled, his entire soul so greatly elevated—that if the abuses of this new condition did not often degrade him beneath the condition he left, he ought to be endlessly thankful for the happy moment that forever tore him away from it, and that, from a stupid and limited animal, made an intelligent being and a man.[121]

Again, there is something decidedly modern about Rousseau's teaching. He may panegyrize the past, celebrate the virtues of Sparta and the glories of Rome, call progress into question, but in the end, one finds an emphatically modern ambition reposing at the heart of his thought: mastery. Man may have been born free, but nature remains his master. While nature affords man the freedom to do as he pleases and "an unlimited right to everything that tempts him and that he can get,"[122] man does not establish what it is that pleases him. Though instinct does not determine him in the manner that it determines birds and felines, his freedom from instinct still only permits him to sate appetites that nature, not he, imparted to him. In this respect, he is but the slave of nature. "Moral freedom . . . alone makes man truly the master of himself. For the impulsion of appetite alone is slavery, and obedience to the law one has prescribed to oneself is freedom."[123] The freedom that man acquires in civil society founded upon the general will is not only a more veritable freedom, but a higher one. Once the hapless plaything of nature, man becomes his own master—and, in good modern fashion, hers as well.

Rousseau may set out to remedy man's condition, but he affords no simple nostrum. His teaching is one of remarkable austerity, an austerity that sometimes is lost on contemporary readers, but certainly was not lost on those students who put Rousseau's theoretical teachings into practice. Legitimate sovereignty, as Rousseau understands it, involves the complete subordination of the private to the public will, a virtually constant participation in public life (Rousseau disdained representative government), and the absolute proscription of dissent and non-conformity. It is on this last account that some of Rousseau's most chilling pronouncements were made. As Rousseau notes, "in order for the social compact not to be an empty formula, it tacitly encompasses the following commitment, which alone can give force to the rest: that whoever refuses to obey the general will be constrained to do so by the whole body, which means nothing else but that he will be forced to be free."[124] In the penultimate chapter of the book, while examining the articles of faith that belong to the civil religion, Rousseau points out that

> without being able to obligate anyone to believe them, [the sovereign] may banish from the state anyone who does not believe them. It may banish him, not as impious but as unsociable, as incapable of sincerely loving the laws, justice, and if need be of sacrificing his life to his duty. If anyone, after having publicly acknowledged these same dogmas, behaves as though he does not believe them, let him be punished with death. He has committed the greatest of crimes: he has lied before the laws.[125]

This rigor is a necessary ingredient to sovereign power: any abatement of the former would herald the degradation of the latter. For even when private interest and public duty have been reconciled—again, by completely sacrificing the former to the latter—the cultivation of virtue remains as necessary and, it would seem, as onerous as ever. This is true not only with respect to maintaining the integrity of a given community internally but to doing so externally as well, vis-à-vis other sovereign peoples. As presented in the *Social Contract*, Rousseau's political teaching does not augur the dawning of a halcyonian age. On the contrary, the legitimation of sovereignty precludes the possibility of universal peace and advances instead an age of perpetual strife. This follows from the requirement that the citizens of a given state participate actively in politics, which a bloated body politic would make all but impossible. Something along the lines of Corsica or Rousseau's native Geneva would fit the bill. As a result, the world would be populated by numerous state powers, each with its own articles of faith that no doubt would be in conflict, at least from time to time, with those of its neighbors. But even if a great international confederation possessed of a "united power" and "united will"—along the lines of what Kant touted[126]—were conceivable, one cannot overlook the fact that for Rousseau, the corruption of a people often results from the laxity that peace invites and that war, far from being deleterious, is salutary.

Long ago, Greece flourished in the midst of the cruelest wars. Blood flowed like water; and the entire country was covered with men. It seemed, states Machiavelli, that in the midst of murders, proscriptions, and civil wars our republic became more powerful. The virtue of its citizens, their morals, their independence did more to reinforce it than all its dissensions had done to weaken it. A little agitation gives vitality to souls, and what truly causes the species to prosper is not so much peace as freedom.[127]

(Rousseau does entertain the possibility of a perpetual peace elsewhere in his writings, particularly in the context of the union of European states proposed Abbé de Saint-Pierre. But he ultimately rejects such a prospect because its possibility is predicated on the supposition that human beings—rulers in particular—are rational actors, when in fact they are "insane," and though some may be endowed with good sense, "it is a sort of folly to remain wise in the midst of those who are mad.")[128]

This severity and the bellicosity that accompanies it render Rousseau something of an anomaly in modern thought, which as a rule is bent on softening the life of man, and therewith man himself. Indeed, Rousseau's exacting philosophy recalls the teachings of the *Republic* and reminds one of the austerities that inhered not only in that chimerical city founded in speech but in the actual regimes of antiquity (Sparta in particular), for which Rousseau's esteem is unmistakable. But lest one think that Rousseau's nostalgia for an age when politicians spoke endlessly of morals and virtue rather than business and money[129] suggests a desire to go back, Rousseau understood what so many of the reactionaries he opposed and the romantics he inspired could not: there can be no going back. As with all good moderns, for Rousseau, it is the future, not the past, toward which the longings of man are to be enduringly directed.

Rousseau, that solitary walking paradox who celebrated Lacedaemon and set the stage for Lenin,[130] at least allows for the possibility of a genuine diversification of man of the sort that his modern predecessors appeared so bent on consigning to the dust heap of history. Man, that curious creature who is at bottom a bottomless wellspring of potentiality, could make of himself whatever he wishes. Rousseau's philosophy was a protest against the domestication and demoralization of man that masqueraded as progress and enlightenment in his day. Yes, the general will calls for a uniformity and conformity of the sort that once made Sparta great, but its generalization, as opposed to universalization, would entail that there would be diverse peoples who esteemed differently and whose foundational lawgivers imposed on them distinct codes and values. There would be faiths and customs for which people would be willing to make tremendous sacrifices—the ultimate included—of the sort that are inconsistent with the values, or lack thereof, put forward by

Hobbes and Locke. Yet, in spite of his appeals to earlier paradigms, whether those of the state of nature or of ancient Greece and Rome, Rousseau did more to accelerate modernity than arrest it. A being whose defining traits are free will and perfectibility is one of boundless plasticity. What possibilities, what limitless possibilities inhered in the human breast! Such a revelation might have inspired a flowering of human cultures and human types on a scale that was scarcely imaginable heretofore; but instead, the opposite obtained. The homogenization of man continued apace and, as is modern man's wont, not without reason. Perhaps had Rousseau belonged to a different philosophical lineage, had he been part of another historical unfolding, his teaching would have engendered a diversification of human wants, ideals, values, morals, cultures, and the like. But it was to the Western tradition that Rousseau belonged, and one of the defining hallmarks of that tradition was the democratization, not diversification, of man. That history had been set in motion long before Rousseau and, for that matter, long before Hobbes and Locke as well. As will be argued below, it was, by the time those three set off for the state of nature, already underway for two millennia. One need not accept Rousseau's thesis regarding human nature to appreciate that humans are endowed with free will and that history is rife with accident and contingency. Still, if the democratization of humanity was not fated to advance in Rousseau's wake, that advance was, in view of the centuries that preceded Rousseau's hour upon the stage, logical, if not predictable. Therefore, it should come as no surprise that Rousseau, who was repulsed by the absolutism that Hobbes espoused, ushered in an absolutism far more uncompromising. Reduced to a tabula rasa, nothing prevented man, at least in theory, from being remade again and again. Belonging to a long tradition that celebrated human equality and increasingly championed a single mode of (correctly) apprehending reality, small wonder that, when deprived of any fixed and delimiting nature, man would not simply be generalized, but universalized.

Rousseau's successors did just that. Beginning most notably with Kant, Rousseau's teachings on the historicization and plasticity of man were appropriated and utilized not to promote greater diversity, but greater uniformity. Kant proved a peculiar man for the job. In a host of ways, the methodical, unerotic, unadventurous peripatetic of Konigsberg could hardly be more unlike the wandering Genevan. And yet, Kant was captivated by Rousseau all the same.

That captivation is well documented and was readily acknowledged by the Prussian sage.[131] Hume may have wrested Kant from his "dogmatic slumber,"[132] but Rousseau's influence was more lasting and determinative: there was an assimilation of the Genevan's philosophy, not merely a reaction against it, as was the case with the Scotsman's. Perhaps most consequentially, what Kant received from Rousseau was the concept of metaphysical freedom. However panegyrically Rousseau may have waxed about freedom in the state of nature, he ultimately subordinated it to an unnatural, even anti-natural, that is, metaphysical, freedom. Nature is the realm of necessity. Man's freedom in it is conditioned by nature to the extent that nature, not man, prescribes man's wants. Man transcends the natural realm by giving himself his own laws and determining his own wants. But the tension between natural and metaphysical freedom, so palpable in Rousseau's philosophy and personified in the solitary walker who can find no home in civil society,[133] is nowhere to be found in Kant's thinking. With Kant, nature is supplanted categorically; reason's triumph is complete.

The reduction of man to a rational agent may seem to hark back to early modern thinkers such as Hobbes and Locke, to say nothing of classical ones such as Plato and Aristotle. To be sure, neither Plato nor Aristotle qualified man in those terms, but insofar as they understood that the development of reason was the natural end of man, their views, on the face of it, might appear to be consistent with Kant's. But Kant's position was far more absolute. As stated above, for early moderns such as Hobbes and Locke, reason is in effect equated with common sense. Hence the relative ease with which man grasps the natural law,[134] a concept that historically has been a matter of considerable disputation on the part of very learned individuals. For classical thinkers, reason is something that is developed, a lifelong process that requires extraordinary discipline and diligence. It is true that reason is unique to man, but humans possess it as a potentiality. To actualize or advance reason so that one lives according to it and thereby lives a life in accordance with nature is uncommon. Healthy souls, on the Platonic understanding, are very few and far between.

Kant too understands reason as something that is developed, but its development takes place within the species, not the individual. On the classical understanding, the development of reason is deeply personal, which is not to discount the sociality of it. Reason is more than an accumulation of facts or the capacity to navigate and manipulate the physical world. It involves the ability to be master of one's affects, which unlike knowledge of physical laws, is not the sort of aptitude that can be handed down.[135] Kant's understanding is more in keeping with what is understood as science, particularly as it existed in Kant's day; that is, a body of knowledge that is cumulative and progressive. Aristotle was no intellectual slouch. But his truths, which were thought apodictic for a millennia, were errors that no child of the nineteenth century, to say nothing of the twenty-first, would be naïve enough to accept. In that sense, reason advances generationally. But it is not simply with respect to the material world that this advance occurs. As Kant wrote in the *Critique of Practical Reason* in what would turn out to be a felicitous inscription on his tombstone, "Two things fill the mind with ever new and increasing admiration and awe, the oftener and more steadily we reflect on them: *the starry heavens above and the moral law within.*"[136] In Kant's mind, just as the firmament above is well-ordered, subject to laws that permit the mind to grasp and predict the movement of its parts, man's inner world is subject to a law that dictates the proper course of his actions. It is true, for reasons spelled out below, that mercurial man does to that law what that Mercurial orb cannot do to Kepler's law of planetary motion: he violates it. But Kant has no illusion that such a law exists nor that one day man will be as bound to follow it as Mercury is bound to follow the laws of Kepler. With Kant, the reduction of man is nigh complete.

Modern science encourages if not obliges humans to see the world in a more uniform manner. How different an eclipse must have appeared in earlier times, not just different from its appearance to modern eyes, but different among the eyes of earlier peoples. The uniform understanding that modern science compels did not prevail prior to the objectification of reality. What modern man takes to be the same phenomenon—an eclipse, for example—presented itself in untold ways to minds that beheld the uniqueness of each and every natural event; minds that failed to detect any similitude among disparate events (or perhaps failed to impose a similitude on those events), thereby precluding the possibility of uniting and subsuming them under a single concept.[137] The variegation that must follow from such an outlook is no more. In spite of what postmodernists maintain, science is not whatever one makes of it.[138] An astrologer is no less subject to earth's gravitational pull than an astrophysicist. To be sure, one is free to dispute or deny what science claims, as flat earthers the world over demonstrate. Still, on the whole, science yields a more uniform view of the world—hence the modern world wherein lightning is not a divine portent and from which ghosts and ghouls have been banished. The world has been rendered explicable, superficially perhaps, but explicable all the same and explicable in the same terms for all. Kant's moral science does for man's inner world what modern science has done to his perception of the outer one: it undermines diversity and dispels ambiguity.

Kant's role in advancing the uniformization of humanity was momentous. Rousseau, again, had appeared to open new pathways with respect to the movement of modernity. There was no going back, but perhaps there were alternate courses to the ones charted by his early modern predecessors, which led to the corruption, diminution, and homogenization of the human spirit. A being without a fixed nature, that could be molded and remolded time and time again, presented unbounded possibilities. Moreover, Rousseau's political remedy, proffered to redress the gross inequalities and illegitimate bondage that characterized modern man's social condition (so at odds with his natural one), encouraged the prospect of a world populated by distinct and diverse peoples, however repressive and unforgiving the respective intracommunal conformity of those peoples may have been. Kant undid that prospect by appropriating the idea of a general will and universalizing it. Man's metaphysical freedom, predicated on the principle that bondage to nature and to other human beings is overcome when man subjects himself to a law he himself prescribes, would not be achieved disjointly by distinct communities, but universally by humanity en masse.

In universalizing the will, Kant concerns himself no more with human nature than Rousseau did when he generalized it. Indeed, Kant goes even further than his forerunner insofar as his point of departure in seeking out and establishing *"the supreme principle of morality"*[139] is not so much man but the rational being as such. That is, Kantian morality is equally binding for all rational beings, whether they are inhabitants of this planet or sojourners on another one. Morality is not grounded in human nature but in reason.

To found morality on anything other than reason, or the laws to which reason is bound, would render morality capricious and "exposed to all sorts of corruption."[140] For morality is no more capable of being established empirically than is physics: both require a metaphysical foundation upon which knowledge—whether of matter or morals—can rest.[141] Without an understanding of the fundamental principle of morality, all moral principles are apt to lapse into equivocation.[142]

> Everyone must admit that a law has to carry with it absolute necessity if it is to be valid morally—valid, that is, as a ground of obligation; that the command "Thou shalt not lie" could not hold merely for men, other rational beings having no obligation to abide by it—and similarly with all other genuine moral laws; that here consequently the ground of obligation must be looked for, not in the nature of man nor in the circumstances of the world in which he is placed, but solely *a priori* in the concepts of pure reason; and that every other precept based on principles of mere experience—and even a precept that may be considered universal, so far as it rests in its slightest part, perhaps only in its motive on empirical grounds—can indeed be called a practical rule, but never a moral law.[143]

Though the fundamental principle of morality only can be understood through pure reason, ultimately, and, one might add, curiously, it is nature's design, not reason's that makes such an understanding possible. Kant begins with the presupposition that not only does nature never furnish its organic beings with unpurposed parts, but that each organ it does provide is best suited to achieve the end for which it was designed. "In the natural constitution of an organic being—that is, of one contrived for the purpose of life—let us take it as a principle that in it no organ is to be found for any end unless it is also the most appropriate to that end and the best fitted for it."[144] However, intriguing Kant's proto-Darwinism may be, what here commands attention is his confutation of the Peripatetic and those who followed in his steps, who maintained that for man, the *sommum bonnum* is happiness. Nature, which furnishes no faculty in vain, would have hit upon a poor design if it had endowed man with the faculty of reason and posited happiness as his highest end. For even if one refuses to accept that there is an inverse correlation between reason and happiness demonstrated by the lack of the former resulting in the realization of the latter—that is, the conjunction of ignorance and bliss—it would seem that nature could have utilized a more fitting faculty for securing happiness, namely instinct. "For all the actions he has to perform with this end in view, and the whole rule of his behavior, would have been mapped out for him far more accurately by instinct; and the end in question could have been maintained far more surely by instinct than it ever can be by reason."[145] The question remains: wherefore reason?

Kant's teleological inclinations would be easy to discount given their incongruity with modern thought, which had done away with any teleological understanding of man and the cosmos to which he belonged. But there is something distinctly modern about Kant's teleology. The ancients, it will be recalled, were no detractors of man's rational faculty. In fact, it was the development of it that constituted the natural end toward which man is directed. The well-ordered soul is one where each part does its appropriate task, with the rational part overseeing the whole. It was on such grounds that Socrates's paradigmatically just regime reposed: the city in speech, itself a magnification of the human soul, was stratified on the understanding that different human beings are suited for different callings and that the highest calling—man's end, really—for which very few will be at all suited is the development of reason or to put it more anachronistically, the pursuit of wisdom, that is, philosophy. With Kant, reason ceases to be a mark of distinction, both universally (man has no privileged position, provided there are other races of rational beings out there in the cosmos) and particularly (the sage enjoys no privilege over the fool, provided it is a rational fool). As rational agents, all humans are endowed with the faculty of reason and thus subject to the laws that constrain it. Just as all bodies of mass are subject to the laws of gravity, so too are all rational agents subject to the laws of reason. Reason is not the great distinguisher, but the great leveler. The faculty that once served as a basis for the inegalitarian teachings so indicative of antiquity was now used to support the radical egalitarianism so indicative of modernity.

The question remains: why did nature endow man with the faculty of reason? Moreover, why did it permit this faculty to have a practical function in determining the actions of the will? Because instinct would have been a far more effective guide, Kant concludes that one cannot explain reason's practical function in directing the will as a means of achieving happiness, but only as a faculty for achieving the one unqualified good in the world: the good will as such. "[Reason's] true function must be to a *will* which is *good*, not as *means* to some further end, but in *itself*."[146] Man possesses reason for the purpose not of being a happy agent, but a moral one.

A moral agent—and only a rational agent can be a moral one—does good not from inclination, but from a sense of duty. His actions possess moral worth not on account of the aims they are intended to achieve nor the results they do, in fact, achieve, "but solely on the *principle* of *volition* in accordance with which" they are performed.[147] That principle is embodied in Kant's well-known categorical imperative which states: *Act only on that maxim through which you can at the same time will that it should become a universal law.*[148] The possibility of a categorical imperative, that is of an action being objectively necessary in itself without reference to some further end, presupposes that there is "something *whose existence* has *in itself* an absolute value, something which as *an end itself* could be a ground of determinate laws."[149] That something is man, or more properly speaking, not simply human beings, but all rational beings.

As an end in himself, the individual counts himself a member of a community that Kant designates the kingdom of ends. In it, the individual understands the intrinsic value—the *dignity*—not only of himself, but of every *person* that occupies that kingdom.[150] In doing so, he treats others never as means, but invariably as ends in themselves. By submitting himself to the categorical imperative, he acts only on those maxims that can be universalized and thus not only prescribes the universal laws to which all members of that kingdom are bound but subjects himself to those very same laws.

It is safe to say that no prior philosopher had put forward a more egalitarian moral teaching. Rousseau perhaps came closest, but given that his will was general, it remains particular in relation to the universal will promulgated by Kant. Were one to paint Rousseau's political philosophy in the rosiest of terms, absolving him of any responsibility for engendering Jacobinism, which applied with ruthless logic the lesson that man "shall be forced to be free,"[151] humanity still would be divided among republics that—in Lockean terms—would relate to one another as though they still belonged to the state of nature, long after the peoples of those nations had quit that primeval state.[152] Even were they not at war, presumably no republic would feel obligated to treat its neighbors as though they were their own kith and kin; to regard them as equals who were owed the same respect and fealty that the subjects of that republic showed one another. Nationalism, not cosmopolitanism, is the order of Rousseau's day.

With Kant, something very different results: a kingdom of ends that is universal in nature going so far as to embrace not just human beings, but all rational beings. Every rational agent belonging to this union, every *person* is an end in himself, possessed of an intrinsic, absolute value governed by universal laws that he concomitantly makes and subjects himself to so that what results is a profound and pervasive equality between person and person that would have seemed scarcely imaginable in Kant's day, to say nothing of the less egalitarian ages that preceded it. In arguing that rational agents were bound to obey the categorical imperative, Kant did not think that the categorical imperative would, in fact, be obeyed merely because it had been posited. For what the categorical imperative dealt with were not the insensate masses that would obey nature's laws regardless of whether Newton brought them to light, but beings, who were in a curious sense, hybrids composed of matter and spirit, motivated not only by reason but by instinct as well.[153]

The world according to Kant was divided into an intelligible realm and a sensible one; a world of noumena and phenomena. The former pertained to things in themselves; the latter to the appearances of those things. Though man can never know the noumenal realm, he has knowledge of it. Man is, in a way, an anomalous link between the two, belonging to both the sensible and the intelligible worlds: the former, insofar as he acquires information through the senses; the latter insofar as he is capable of pure spontaneous thought that "is not . . . independent of this or that experience, but . . . absolutely independent of all experience."[154] Were he to count himself solely a member of the sensible world, man would be governed wholly by the laws of nature. And were he to count himself solely a member of the intelligible world, "all [his] actions would be in perfect conformity with the principle of the autonomy of a pure will."[155] Because the intelligible world is the ground for the sensible one, Kant argues that it is the laws of the former that supersede those of the latter so that with respect to his intellect, man must obey the laws of the intelligible world, that is, he must comply with the categorical imperative and be a truly moral agent. It goes without saying that man has yet to abide by this logic. One could say that his ties to the sensible world are so great that he finds it impossible to ignore or sever them outright. To put it differently, man would have to cultivate his reason considerably before he could be a truly rational, and thereby moral agent. Thus, the kingdom of ends is but an ideal, which Kant readily admits.[156] But it is not some imaginary republic or utopia that has no place in this world. For Kant, its coming not only is possible but, one dare say, incluctable.

This eschatological longing is evident in Kant's 1784 essay, *Idea for a Universal History with a Cosmopolitan Purpose*. In it, Kant sets himself the not insignificant task of trying to descry "behind the senseless course of human events" "*a purpose in nature*" according to which the "history of creatures who act without a plan of their own" unfolds.[157] That in the particular, mankind acts in a manner that is "confused and fortuitous" does not preclude the possibility that in "pursuing their own ends," "individual men and entire nations are . . . unconsciously promoting an end which, even if they knew what it was, would scarcely arouse their interest."[158]

The teleological presuppositions so integral to Kant's ethical philosophy are no less integral to his political one, as the first proposition of his *Idea for a Universal History* betokens: *All the natural capacities of a creature are destined sooner or later to be developed completely and in conformity with their end.*[159] This can be substantiated, Kant maintains, by examining the external and internal (anatomical) constitutions of animals which reveal that there are no desultory organs; every organ fulfills the purpose for which it was designed. Whether the human appendix might have given Kant pause is perhaps immaterial, for the nub of his argument rests not so much on its empirical demonstrability but on what disposing of the teleological theory of nature would entail: "if we abandon this basic principle, we are faced not with a law-governed nature, but with an aimless, random process, and the dismal reign of chance replaces the guiding principle of reason."[160] Aimlessness and dismalness do not constitute grounds for refuting a truth any more than purposefulness and cheerfulness do for establishing it. The *principium contradictionis* may demonstrate that the universe cannot be ordered and devoid of order, but there is no reason why the universe cannot be devoid of order. An aimless universe may be a dismal universe, but that hardly renders it an impossible one. What it does result in is the complete undermining of Kantian philosophy—both political and moral.[161] With respect to the matter at hand, what is striking about Kant's political philosophy is not that it rests on teleological presuppositions, but that those presuppositions are used to support a position that is so at odds with the position of his philosophical antecedents, whose own teachings relied no less on a teleological understanding of nature and man's place in it. That understanding impelled the emblematically modern Kant to espouse a political teaching that was emphatically egalitarian; the ancients, one that was no less emphatically inegalitarian.

The reason for this can be gleaned in large part from Kant's second proposition which states that "*in man* (as the only rational creature on earth), *those natural capacities which are directed towards the use of his reason are such that they could be fully developed in the species but not in the individual.*"[162] The wise man, whom the ancients devoted no small effort to contemplating, is a chimera in Kantian philosophy. Only to a more primitive mind, one that had not yet grasped that wisdom can be achieved solely in the aggregate, never in the particular, could a wise soul seem possible. For the ancients, the best regime, ruled by the wise, was utopian not so much because wisdom was an impossibility, but because the likelihood of sages presiding over a *polis* either as a result of their own machinations or with the aid of an enlightened demos was virtually nil.[163] The wise man was not the impossibility, but his ascension to power, for all intents and purposes, was. But for Kant, the very notion that the goodness of a regime somehow could be measured by the wisdom of its rulers is erroneous. That is, to suggest that the best regime is possible at any given point in history, and that its reification occurs with the marriage of philosophy and political power is naïve, for not only is wisdom acquired at a very late date, but it is also acquired collectively. *Sub specie aeternitatis*, it is only the species that grows wise, never the individual.

If the development of reason is the end toward which man is directed (a claim both Kant and the classics make, though in markedly and unmistakably different manners), but that end is attainable only for the species and never for the individual, then the ideal political community—the best regime— would be egalitarian, not inegalitarian. Until reason is developed fully, all individuals will be found wanting. And once reason is fully developed, it will be developed altogether so that no one will be found wanting. At the end of the day (i.e., history), there is no rational basis for inequality.

At some level, this reasoning is overly simplistic. Rational basis or not, Kant understood that the social order is inegalitarian and will remain so for some time yet, and that a truly egalitarian state only would be achieved after considerable strife and struggle, through forces that promoted and exploited human inequality. Indeed, it is only by means of their antagonistic tendencies—their *unsocial sociability*, as Kant calls it[164]—that humans develop their higher faculties, reason chief among them, and are continually, albeit unwittingly, impelled toward the fully rational, egalitarian state. "Social incompatibility, enviously competitive vanity and insatiable desires for possession and even power"[165] are, however deplorable they may appear, gifts from nature for which man should be grateful and without which he never would be motivated to overcome his primitivism.

Though it is reasonable to deduce from the discord stirred by man's unsocial sociability that there is no justice or order to the cosmos or worse still, that there is order but it has been marred by "the hand of a malicious spirit who had meddled in the creator's glorious work or spoiled it out of envy,"[166] once one comprehends that the highest purpose of nature is the development of all natural capacities, one espies in such ostensible malevolence not only munificence, but wisdom. Man, who is enamored with unrestrained freedom, learns to impose limits on that freedom so as not to be destroyed by the mutually antagonistic inclinations lodged in his breast. Neither beast nor God, man is forced to discipline himself so that he may live among his own kind. By doing so, he establishes the conditions that conduce to cultivating his natural capacities. In this more humane social order, people compete with each other without destroying one another and thereby not only develop their faculties individually, but also allow for the progress they have achieved collectively to be preserved for, and expanded upon by, future generations.

Nature's goal is not simply to lead man from barbarism to civilization but to "*a civil society which can administer justice universally.*"[167] Because "man is *an animal who needs a master,*"[168] the problem of achieving such a civil society is both the most difficult and the last to be solved. For the master of man must himself be human and therefore will be naturally disposed to abuse his authority so that he in turn requires a master to restrain his own pernicious proclivities. A seemingly infinite regress is obviated by the gradual development[169] of man's rational faculty to the point where his moral behavior obeys the laws of reason and civil society becomes a kingdom of persons who exist as ends in themselves; that is, when man ceases to be an animal that needs a master or, to put it differently, when man becomes master of himself.

This last and most difficult problem to be solved, i.e., establishing the universally just state, is in fact subordinate to another problem which would seem to suggest that there is an even later and more difficult matter to be resolved.[170] "What is the use of working for a law-governed civil constitution among individual men . . . if the same unsociability which forced men to do so gives rise in turn to a situation whereby each commonwealth, in its external relations . . . is in a position of unrestricted freedom?"[171] An enlightened state that administers justice universally to its enlightened citizenry is fated to perish so long as it, on account of the advanced stage of its rational faculties, is obliged to abide by the demands of the categorical imperative while its unenlightened neighbors either fail to grasp or knowingly flout the moral law. Providentially, the same antagonisms that exist intra-nationally and goad a given people to create a civil society capable of administering justice universally also function internationally—on a much larger and more tragic scale but with the same beneficent denouement.

> Wars, tense and unremitting military preparations, and the resultant distress which every state must eventually feel within itself, even in the midst of peace—these are the means by which nature drives nations to make initially imperfect attempts, but finally, after many devastations, upheavals and even complete inner exhaustion of their powers, to take the step which reason could have suggested to them even without so many sad experiences—that of abandoning a lawless state of savagery and entering a federation of peoples in which every state, even the smallest, could expect to derive its security and rights not from its own power or its own legal judgment, but solely from this great federation (*Foedus Amphictyonum*), from a united power and the law-governed decisions of a united will.[172]

Thus, only when there exists "a great federation" of enlightened commonwealths, an "international state that embrace[s] all the peoples of the earth," in short, "a *world republic*"[173] where each state treats its neighbor as the people within a given state treat each other—that is, as ends and never as means—and where there reigns a perdurable peace that permits the full development of man's natural capacities can it be said that nature's hidden plan has been at long last realized.

That munificence or wisdom would be choice words to ascribe to the creator who designed such a plan might seem dubious. Would not a wiser and more munificent creator have spawned a species enlightened in its infancy rather than old age? Would he not have created beings fully capable of residing in Arcadia without having to struggle so long and suffer so much before reaching it? One often introduces a similar line of reasoning when calling into question the omni-benevolence of God, but Kant does not rely on some Spinozist argument to resolve the quandary. In Kant's mind, the conceivability of a more seamless design is immaterial. What matters is not so much the rationality of the design, but the advance of man's rationality. Humans who were spawned by nature with fully developed rational capacities would be found wanting when compared with those who developed their own capacities over the long course of history, for the former would be but the products of nature whereas the latter would transcend it, thereby becoming wise creators themselves and not the mere creations of one. For Kant, like Rousseau before him, what matters is that man becomes metaphysically free. "*Nature has willed that man should produce entirely by his own initiative everything which goes beyond the mechanical ordering of his animal existence, and that he should not partake of any other happiness or perfection than that which he has procured for himself without instinct and by his own reason.*"[174]

Born into this world a plaything of nature, man becomes the enlightened master of his own fate. In realizing nature's hidden plan, he transcends the natural world and fashions one that is wholly a reflection of his own essence as a rational agent. Though physically he remains bound by the laws of nature, metaphysically man obeys a higher law, one that he prescribes himself, and in doing so, elevates himself above the realm of natural necessity. The realization of nature's hidden plan brings about the "*perfect political constitution as the only possible state within which all natural capacities of mankind can be developed completely.*"[175] That state is characterized by a fundamental and universal equality where each individual, having developed fully his rational faculties, recognizes the innate, absolute value that inheres not only in himself, but in each and every rational agent with whom he coexists and treats them accordingly, that is, as ends in themselves and not as means for others. That understanding obtains not only for individuals but for the commonwealths that they belong to and is manifested in the peace that perdures in perpetuity.

That appears to be the great modern longing—an end to conflict. One should guard against concluding that this longing is innately human as opposed to innately modern. Throughout history, there have been many peoples for whom the unconflicted life was not worth living. Enlightened latecomers may be inclined to dismiss such peoples as primitive, retrograde, and barbaric (though multicultural pieties ought not to permit such deprecations), but even with Kant there is an awareness that conflict—unsocial sociability—has made man who or what he is. Without that conflict, humans would have remained dumb brutes, "as good-natured as the sheep they tended," and as valuable (or valueless) too.[176] What place remains, if any, for conflict in the kingdom of ends is unclear. Perhaps unsocial sociability is but a means to an end, one that is rendered useless once that end is reached. Still, if it has been a constitutional attribute of man, its obsolescence ought to at least give one pause. Whither man?

This problem becomes more pronounced with the great nineteenth-century systematizers who Kant felt assured nature would produce to complete the project he had adumbrated. For Hegel and especially for Marx history moves in such a manner that it not only negates itself but negates man in the process. For what remains of a being defined by its struggle—for recognition, for prestige, for the means of production—in an age without struggle? That, again, is the modern promise. The state, whether universal (Hegelian) or stateless (Marxist), portends a cessation to all conflict, for its realization entails the resolution of the perennial antagonisms with which history has been riddled.[177] Freedom—from want, from exploitation, from alienation, from nature, from man—will have been actualized. What will become of man at history's end is unclear. Perhaps, as Trotsky trumpeted, "Man will become immeasurably stronger, wiser and subtler; his body will become more harmonized, his movements more rhythmic, his voice more musical. The forms of life will become dynamically dramatic. The average human type will rise to the heights of an Aristotle, a Goethe, or a Marx. And above this ridge new peaks will rise."[178] Given communism's track record over the course of the twentieth century, a good deal of doubt on that score should not only be permitted but required. Even tabling the precipitous deterioration and widespread destruction of human life that routinely accompanied communism's advance, pop culture, twitter spats, and fast food do not exactly inspire confidence that the promise of reaching new peaks will be realized along the dialectical path, whether beaten by Marxists or Hegelians.

Rather than the mass elevation of man resulting in a world overrun by Aristotles, the more likely outcome of the modern project is a pervasive leveling of humanity, resulting in the reduction of man to a very common and base denominator. If the question of directionality remains open to debate—presupposing there is directionality, is history acclivitous or declivitous?—what seems beyond dispute is man's homogenization. The world over is to become Westernized, industrialized, democratized, and—Marxist grumbles aside—Christianized. It is a world that will be seen through an increasingly narrow and uniform lens. Perhaps that is progress; perhaps that is the product of enlightenment. Differences of opinion bespeak an insufficiency of knowledge. In a world where all are enlightened, opinions—orthodox ones, of course—necessarily will not differ. But the same would hold true for a people that was profoundly unenlightened. Whatever the case may be, there are ample signs to suggest that the present age is one in which enlightenment, rather than being on the march, is in retreat.[179]

Enlightened or otherwise, it is to an uncompromising conformity that modernity points. Those who imagine otherwise need only consider Kant's categorical imperative—that universal moral law that obliges those subject to it to perform the same actions even in the thorniest or most ambiguous of predicaments.[180] Ancient thinkers who plumbed the human soul discovered an inner realm that was wonderfully complex and enigmatic, a realm that modernity appears hell- (or heaven-) bent on smoothing and paving over. That complexity and enigmaticness were embodied in and exemplified by Socrates, that "world historical figure"[181] whose wisdom was ignorance, dialogic quests for answers often ended in states of aporia, and perfectly just regime rested upon injustices too numerous and egregious to evade notice.[182] Socrates may have exemplified the complexity of the human spirit to an unparalleled degree, but those complexities inhered in the breast of man qua man, not qua Socrates. Lovers of wisdom are rare birds to be sure, but there are all sorts of lovers who have made history and the being to whom history belongs, that is, man, estimable: lovers of virtue, honor, glory, beauty, justice, and so forth. What place is there for love at history's end?

To the extent that man's world is elevated, it is because it is propped on the shoulders of giants—giants of staggering intellect, vision, and devotion. This is not to discount the roles played by the multitudes of lesser stature. Philosophers do not sustain themselves in imaginary republics to say nothing of real ones. But what would man be were his history not littered with titans? There are no titans at the end of history. And Hegel concedes as much. "Once the state has been founded, there can no longer be any heroes. They come on the scene only in uncivilized conditions."[183] As for the prophetic vision of Hegel's intellectual expropriator, it too is devoid of titans, in spite of the aforementioned prognostications of one of his most celebrated disciples. Marx decried the division of labor for confining individuals to roles they did not freely choose. "Each man has a particular, exclusive sphere of activity, which is forced upon him and from which he cannot escape. He is a hunter, a fisherman, a herdsman, or a critical critic, and must remain so if he does not want to lose his means of livelihood." This division—along with the alienation and bondage it entails—is undone in communist society, where the means of production are controlled by no one and everyone is free to pursue his or her own interests. "In communist society, where nobody has one exclusive sphere of activity but each can become accomplished in any branch he wishes, society regulates the general production and thus makes it possible for me to do one thing today and another tomorrow, to hunt in the morning, fish in the afternoon, rear cattle in the evening, criticize after dinner, just as I have a mind, without ever becoming hunter, fisherman, herdsman or critic."[184] Such an idyll may have mass appeal, but it is not the sort of arrangement that begets genius. It is not by desultorily pursuing many walks of life, but by committing oneself to a lifelong pursuit that greatness is achieved.

The end of history appears to be populated less by elevated beings than by complacent ones. If it is an age that portends to be satisfying, the question that ought not to be shrugged off is, *for whom is it satisfying?* To the extent that it has been is in no small part because of the reductionist tendencies of modern thought, which would have it that at some level, all people find the same thing(s) satisfying. But surely no titanic soul would be at rest at the end of history. No Homeric Greek, no ascetic monk, no Comanche warrior, no lover of wisdom would find that state appealing. For whom then does history unfold? Hegel provides the answer, one that makes plain the underlying tenor of modern thought: the vassal.

Hegel, like Marx after him, and unlike Hobbes and Locke before, considers different types of human beings, the most consequential being those elemental and antithetical types: master and slave. The struggle between the two signifies not only the dawn of history, and man therewith, but is also the catalyst for the movement of history—a movement that terminates when the owl of Minerva spreads its wings with the falling of dusk.[185] As Hegel frames him in the famous section "Lordship and Bondage" in the *Phenomenology of Spirit*, the master is one who is impelled to subjugate another self-conscious agent and compels that agent to recognize his (the master's) subjectivity as being real or authoritative. What distinguishes those who are masters (paradoxically) by nature from all those who are not is that they alone are willing to risk their lives in a battle for prestige. In doing so, they esteem a nonbiological end above the biological ends nature prescribed and thereby transcend their natural animality and become human.[186] The slave, which definitionally a master presupposes, is in many ways the master's antithesis, preferring life to prestige or any other supranatural end for that matter. When faced with the prospect of death, the slave surrenders his own subjectivity and thereby becomes an object of the master. Having previously labored to satisfy his own desires, the slave now works for the sole sake of satisfying those of his master. Thus, the master has his wants met without having to labor to satisfy them. "The life of the masters, to the extent that it is not bloody Fighting, Fighting for prestige with human beings, is a life of pleasure."[187]

At first blush, it would seem that the master constitutes the apogee of human existence, not simply in this or that moment, but for all time. He assumes an almost godlike stature, commanding obeisance from those he lords over and having them fulfill his every wish so that his life may be one of uninterrupted leisure. But the master signifies an existential impasse; even in victory, he betrays his limitations. Though he now has his wants met, satisfaction eludes him. It was not, after all, pleasure that the master risked his life for, but prestige.

At one level, the Master has secured the recognition he sought: the slave unequivocally recognizes the master for what he is and acknowledges that not his own, but his Master's desires are authoritative. But "the outcome is a recognition that is one-sided and unequal."[188] Between master and slave, there can be no mutual recognition. Because the slave prefers slavishness to prestige; because he has not transcended his animality and therefore remains a thing, his recognition can be of no value to the master he recognizes. That is, the master is recognized by one he recognizes only as a slave or, in effect, not at all.

> And this is what is insufficient—what is tragic—in his situation. The Master has fought and risked his life for a recognition without value for him. For he can be satisfied only by recognition from one whom he recognizes as being worthy of recognizing him. The Master's attitude, therefore, is an existential impasse. On the one hand, the Master is Master only because his Desire was directed not toward a thing, but toward another desire—thus it was a desire for recognition. On the other, when he has consequently become Master, it is as Master that he must desire to be recognized; and he can be recognized as such only by making the Other his Slave. But the Slave is for him an animal or thing. He is, therefore, 'recognized' by a thing. Thus, finally, his Desire is directed toward a thing and not—as it seemed at first—toward a (human) Desire. The Master, therefore, was on the wrong track. After the fight that made him a Master, he is not what he wanted to be in starting that fight: a man recognized by another man.[189]

The master may have engendered humanity and set history in motion, but he advances neither. But just as mastery proves illusory for the one who risked his biological life for a nonbiological end, so too does slavishness for the one who refused to do so. As history will demonstrate, progress is the purview of the slave.[190]

In his initial encounter with the master, the slave underwent an experience that will account not only for his own elevation but for that of humankind.

When confronted with his own annihilation, the slave "[had] been fearful, not of this or that particular thing or just at odd moments, but [his] whole being [had] been seized with dread; for [he had] experienced the fear of death, the absolute Lord."[191] In this *pure universal moment,* the slave (without yet understanding it) caught a glimpse of nothingness, not his own particular nothingness, but the nothingness of man *universally.*

Such an insight is not available to the master who is immured in his own particularity. His point of view is the only subjectivity that counts as real: either it must stand as *the* point of view or it must perish with him. The slave, on the other hand, having experienced the nothingness of existence, remains unfixed. Unlike the master who can envision nothing beyond himself, the slave realizes that the master's position cannot exhaust the possibilities of human existence. While he recognizes the master as being human and is recognized neither by his master nor by himself as being the same, he comprehends that he can become human: humanity is greater than the sum of its masters. Moreover, whereas the master risked his life to become master, the slave chose not to risk his life not for the sake of becoming a slave, but for the sake of preserving his existence. Through his victory, the master became what he wanted to be. Through his surrender, the slave was constrained to be something he did not want to be. Thus, while the former has no desire to change, the latter desires precisely that—to change his position and transcend his slavish existence.

By making implicit in the slave an understanding of man as an unfixed being that can evolve, the moment of absolute dread affords a way beyond the existential impasse that resulted from the master's victory. But in and of itself, it cannot deliver the slave from his slavishness. The moment of absolute dread is but a moment, and an emphatically ephemeral one at that. With the celerity that it arrived, it passes away. Though the slave is transformed on account of it, he does not yet appreciate his transformation. What galvanizes him is not the dread that arose in that initial moment, namely that the master will annihilate him then and there, but rather the fear that the master can annihilate him at any moment. Whereas the slave initially bowed before the master because he feared his *immediate* death, he works for the master because he fears his potential death; that is, he labors on account of a fear that is *mediated.* Instinct impelled him to surrender to the master; a concept impels him to continue working for him.[192]

Not yet human when first confronted by his master, in laboring for him, the slave becomes human. By sacrificing his biological life for a nonbiological end, the master transcended nature and became human; by refusing to do the same, the slave remained sub-human. But the mediated fear that impels him to work is not mere impulse and by heeding it, the slave too transcends mere animality. Through labor, the slave not only transforms his own nature, but, as history will demonstrate, nature in toto.

The master too transforms nature, but he does so particularly. In the fight for pure prestige, the master transcends his animality. In winning that battle, he brings into his orbit another who acknowledges the validity of his world. But the master's triumph over nature is exceedingly limited. It pertains to his own sphere and nothing beyond. That is, his world exists only for himself and those he has enslaved. Beyond this limited circle, the master's subjectivity has no bearing; in effect, it has (or is) no reality. The victory not only is narrow but is moreover hollow. He contemns those who recognize him. His desires are met, but he is not satisfied. The world that is supposed to be a reflection of his own subjectivity remains alien to him, precisely because it is transformed not by himself, but by one he does not recognize. Conversely, the slave works to satisfy not his own, but his master's desires. But by working to satisfy his master's desires, the slave, not the master, transforms nature and shapes reality. As a result, the world bears the slave's impress, not the master's.

In the end, master and slave exchange positions. The master who sought independence by enslaving another is made dependent upon the very person he enslaved. The slave, who is dependent upon the master and forced to work for him, soon realizes his own independence through the very labor he is compelled to carry out. In a somewhat similar manner, the master, who risks his life for recognition, ends up being recognized by one he does not recognize and thus, is not recognized at all. On the other hand, the slave, who preserves his life by recognizing one who does not recognize him, ends up recognizing himself through *his* transformation of the world around him. Master becomes slave and slave becomes master. The recognition and autonomy the master vied for can be realized only by the slave. But whereas the master was concerned with asserting his own authority and securing recognition only for himself, the slave will do so for all humanity. It is the slave who transforms the world into a place of mutual recognition and universal freedom. History may have been inaugurated by the master, but it is the slave who crowns it.

By conceiving man dichotomously,[193] Hegel harks back to a premodern understanding of human beings. But seeing that history points to the unequivocal triumph of slave over master, Hegel is modern through and through. The arc of history has an unmistakably egalitarian bent, one that results in the reduction of man to a single type. In this regard, progress is at best ambiguous. To return to an earlier line of inquiry, for whom does history progress? For whom is it satisfying? The answer is the vassal, worker, common man, mass man, everyman—call him what one will. It is *his* wishes that history fulfills. But it is misguided to regard his wishes as man's simply or to assume that they exhaust the possibilities or constitute the pinnacle of human longing. Man became more than mere flesh and bone when he transcended his animality. That was achieved by masters, lords, elites, the few—call them what one will. It is hardly any wonder that so long as they remained in the driver's seat, history was but a succession of unremitting conflict (here taken in the broadest sense of that word, encompassing not just physical conflict, but spiritual and intellectual ones as well). But it is also no wonder that once history was wrested from the command of the few its movement would be in the direction of comfort, security, uniformity, and related goods that the many had prized all along. The end of history, then, signifies a return to man's beginnings and in the absence of all masters, man *qua* vassal possesses no impetus to transcend his purely animal desires. Granted, thanks to his long history and many advances, he would enjoy the means to sate those desires with an inimitable ease and efficacy, but his desires would still be animalistic and all those longings that had spurred him to transcend his animality would be lost. The terminus of man's millennial march forward would be a return to the beasts whence he came. In man's end is his beginning. Notwithstanding his occasional reluctance to pronounce such closure,[194] Hegel—along with the other thinkers who contributed the modern project that he consummated—doggedly prodded man down that paradoxically regressive road of progress.

> Perhaps it is possible to say that, if Hegel wanted to make the synthesis of ancients and moderns, of pagan master and Christian slave, of ancient warrior and modern worker, of the *polis* founded on the devotion of the citizens and the society founded on the satisfaction of the private persons, he ended up less with a true synthesis than with a tension between two poles or a precarious balance. It is perhaps possible to go even further and say that the balance reached tends, in the last analysis, to go in one direction. Taking the modern revolution and the emancipation of the passions as given, Hegel wants on these bases to restore the political organization and the human excellence which he blames the modern for endangering. But if it is true that his "state of civil servants" constitutes the formula which most rationally conforms to the essence of the modern state and the one which is most feasible, it is perhaps no less true to say that the reconciliation of ancients and moderns, as Hegel elaborates it in this formula and in his philosophy of history, represents in its essential elements a decisive consecration of modernity.[195]

It is not the least irony of a philosophic system that guarantees the resolution and therewith transcendence of the contradictions that inhere in the human breast, that one should find in the prospect that man one day will be satisfied completely something deeply unsatisfying.

This historical unfolding was championed by a succession of thinkers who failed to perceive what the ancients so percipiently discerned: the distance between man and man is even greater than the distance between man and beast.[196] It is to two modern thinkers who did plumb the chasm between man and man that this book now turns.

THE POINT OF DEPARTURE

Arriving circuitously at the point of departure, the fact that mankind's democratization is taken for granted by the people who enjoy a world that has been so thoroughly democratized is not exactly noteworthy. What is worth noting is that that democratization was taken for granted by a succession of thinkers who advanced that outcome at a time when mankind was so utterly undemocratized. All the thinkers dealt with above reduced man to a common denominator in order to ground their philosophic visions. Uniform drives and appetites were rendered paramount. On the face of it, Hegel appears the curious exception to this modern rule. Human beings were essentially dichotomous; master and slave belied the simple uniformity that was so prominent in the thinking of his modern predecessors. But insofar as the Hegelian system resolved that tension so that the outcome of the historical process was one where uniformity supplanted man's deep-rooted dichotomy and did so, moreover, in favor of the slave, Hegel's heterodoxy is, at the end of the day—or history—immaterial.

Again, what is curious about their thinking is that each in his own way took for granted the homogeneity of *Homo sapiens* at a time when heterogeneity was the norm. Human dissimilitude was profound and pervasive, not only inter-culturally, but—more germane to the matter at hand—intra-culturally as well. People were divided in a manner or to a degree that finds no parallel in the age of democracy—a verity all the more revealing given how divided people remain. Then, unlike now, it was as though, to borrow from Tocqueville, there existed distinct humanities or separate species of man. To claim that wealth determined which humanity people belonged to is to depreciate rather than appreciate the nature of that disjunction. To be sure, in myriad ways and with quotidian displays that partition was made plain, but it did not only extend outward. It was not wealth alone that permitted the members of the aristocracy to perch comfortably in luxury's lap. An aristocratic man was constituted differently. His distinction was constitutional.

This is not to say that human nature was a mere fiction. At bottom, man—and this is true of the lowliest of paupers no less than the loftiest of kings—possessed something that distinguished him from other beings. The ancients located this in speech or reason.[197] By nature, man was a political animal.[198] But an understanding of this did not prevent the ancients from distinguishing different types of human beings. Thus, Plato could discourse at some length about what separated, for example, the aristocratic soul from the oligarchic one[199] and Aristotle could distinguish the great-souled from the small-souled.[200] Neither Plato nor Aristotle averred that oligarchic souls and small souls were not human souls. Such souls simply were, when compared to aristocratic and magnanimous ones, wanting. In the nature of man, Plato and Aristotle described what Christianity would so roundly disavow: the inequality of souls.

One could contend that the discrepancy between the "is" and the "ought" that stands as one of the pivotal demarcations between classical and modern thought is inversed on this score. For the ancients took their bearings from the composition of mankind as it is (or at least then was), namely one that was ordered hierarchically, whereas the moderns took their bearings from how they surmised it *ought* to be, namely one that was devoid of hierarchies. It would seem that on this question, the moderns are guilty of that failing that they ascribed to the ancients and on account of which they felt compelled to confute them. To the extent that mankind has become more uniform, the moderns succeeded in bridging the divide between the "ought" and "is." But this almost would amount to a refutation of their animating principle. "Imagined republics and principalities" *can* be concretized. For what are the egalitarian republics of the present age but the imagined republics of an earlier one?

What is troubling is that in claiming to have taken their bearings from how man is and not how he ought to be, the moderns focused almost exclusively on the baser elements of human nature foregoing all consideration of more elevated ones. Those who comprised the first wave of modernity[201] reduced man to a drive that doubtlessly is prevalent, but need not be predominant. No student of history could plausibly maintain that self-preservation was the primary motive of the actors who composed it. Indeed, it would be fair to say that had that desire been predominant, there would be no genuine history to speak of. Those who comprised the second wave[202] jettisoned the idea of human nature and instead espoused the notion of metaphysical freedom. Man is but a blank slate, a being whose nature is becoming. But in their grand philosophies of history, the beings who make history (or whom history makes) are reduced to a very common level so that in the end, they become indistinguishable from one another. As presented in such systems, the only rational course for beings that are wholly unconstrained by nature is to aspire to ever greater equality and conformity—an eminently herd-like aspiration, if ever there was one.

The moderns aimed to reconfigure mankind in a manner that never before had prevailed; they promoted the rise of a type of man (the democratic) that had never held the reins and the suppression, if not outright elimination, of a type (the aristocratic) that had heretofore helped steer the course of history and to which they devoted scarcely a passing thought. What they aimed to bring about very well may deserve to be celebrated, but to do so without taking into account the moderns' reductive approach and the simplification of human nature that comes with it seems tendentious. Their one-sided exaltation of democratic man, glaring neglect of his aristocratic precursor, and failure to gauge the disparity between the two should give pause to all thoughtful souls who inhabit a world that bears the indelible impress of their speculations.

None of this was lost on Nietzsche and Tocqueville, who grasped the implications of this epochal upheaval. With peerless perspicacity,[203] they shed light on the character of democratic man, as well as that of his aristocratic antecedent, and revealed what the unequivocal ascendancy of the former over the latter would entail. To venerate the democratic revolution without giving their ideas and admonitions their due would be injudicious.

This need for caution was understood well by Tocqueville. As he wrote at the end of *Democracy in America*:

> No one on earth can yet assert in an absolute and general manner that the new state of societies is superior to the former. But it is already easy to see that it is different.
>
> There are certain vices and certain virtues that were attached to the constitution of aristocratic nations and that are so contrary to the genius of the new peoples that one cannot introduce them into their hearts. There are good penchants and bad instincts that were foreign to the first and that are natural to the second; ideas that present themselves to the imagination of the one that the mind of the other rejects. They are, as it were, two distinct humanities, each of which has its particular advantages and inconveniences, its goods and evils that are proper to it.
>
> One must therefore take care in judging the societies being born by ideas one has drawn from those that are no longer. That would be unjust, for these societies, differing enormously between themselves, are not comparable.[204]

As Tocqueville realized, and as any partisan of progress would affirm, one could not fairly judge the waxing democratic world according to waning aristocratic values, but Tocqueville also perceived what those partisans would be unlikely to concede—that the inverse was no less true. "Let us not hold our ancestors in contempt, *we do not have the right*. May it please God that we may recover, with their faults and prejudices, a little of their greatness!"[205] What further tempered Tocqueville's appraisal of democracy was the mood with which he surveyed it, which, as any careful reader of *Democracy in America* will note, was not exactly cheerful, nor for that matter, neutral.

> The entire book you are going to read was written under the pressure of a sort of religious terror in the author's soul, produced by the sight of this irresistible revolution that for so many centuries has marched over all obstacles, and that one sees still advancing today amid the ruins it has made.[206]

This "providential" march toward ever greater equality may have been fated and hence foolish to resist,[207] but Tocqueville did not exactly get in line. He knew better than to oppose the advancing ranks, but he could not bring himself to join them, at least not wholeheartedly. While he rightly is regarded as a friendly critic of democracy,[208] and arguably its greatest one at that, Tocqueville was not exactly a proponent of democracy. He understood that the democratic revolution was as incapable of being reversed as the ancien régime was of being restored, but ultimately, it was to that bygone world that his heart belonged. In a posthumously uncovered note penned around the time the second volume of *Democracy in America* was published, Tocqueville professed the following:

> Experience has proved to me that with almost all men, but certainly with me, one always returns more or less to one's fundamental instincts, and people never do well anything but what is in accord with their instincts. Let us therefore sincerely look for *my fundamental instincts and my serious principles.*
>
> I have an intellectual preference for democratic institutions, but I am aristocratic by instinct, that is, I despise and fear the crowd.
>
> I passionately love freedom, legality, the respect for rights, but not democracy. That is the base of my soul.
>
> I hate demagogy, the disorderly action of the masses, their violent and uneducated participation in affairs, the lower classes' envious passions, their irreligious tendencies. This is the base of my soul.
>
> I belong neither to the revolutionary party nor the conservative party. But in the end I hold more to the latter than to the former. For I differ from the second more by the means than the end, while I differ from the former by both means and end.
>
> Freedom is the first of my passions. This is what is true.[209]

Tocqueville could find solace in democracy's ineluctable advance thanks to his faith—the equivocality of it notwithstanding—in an "all-powerful and eternal Being."

> I let my regard wander over this innumerable crowd composed of similar beings, in which nothing is elevated and nothing lowered. The spectacle of this universal uniformity saddens and chills me, and I am tempted to regret the society that is no longer.

When the world was filled with very great and very small men, very rich and very poor, very learned and very ignorant, I turned my regard away from the second and attached it only to the first, and these delighted my view; but I understand that this pleasure was born of my weakness: it is because I cannot see all that surrounds me at the same time that I am permitted to choose in this way and to set apart among so many objects those it pleases me to contemplate. It is not the same with the all-powerful and eternal Being whose eye necessarily envelops the sum of things and who sees distinctly, though at once, the whole human race and each man.

It is natural to believe that what most satisfies the regard of this creator and preserver of men is not the singular prosperity of some, but the greatest well-being of all: what seems to me decadence is therefore progress in his eyes; what wounds me is agreeable to him. Equality is perhaps less elevated; but it is more just and its justice makes for its greatness and its beauty.[210]

For Nietzsche, who heralded the death of God, there was no divine or transcendent consolation at hand. An age where the distance between man and man is effaced is not more just than an age that embodies and cultivates that distance, however contrary to modern sensibilities that may sound. There is something misguided and mendacious about democratic justice, which in Nietzsche's mind almost amounts to a contradiction in terms. Equality is not "perhaps less elevated;" it is decidedly so. Nietzsche could find neither greatness nor beauty in an age that exhibited no genuine appreciation for either.

Though Nietzsche could not resign himself to man's democratization, his thoughts align with Tocqueville's on a number of principal points. Like Tocqueville, Nietzsche understood that the world governed by aristocratic values and the world governed by democratic ones were two distinct worlds with two distinct humanities. Nowhere is this more evident than in Nietzsche's distinction between master morality and slave morality, a distinction that is central to his moral and political philosophy. The "characteristic features of noble morality" have little or no correlation to "the morality of 'modern ideas,'" which makes it so difficult for a democratic man to empathize with his aristocratic antecedent.[211] The dissimilitude that makes empathy so difficult to come by invites condescension on the part of those born in democratic times for those who were not—an invitation that, Nietzsche repeatedly shows, is foolish to accept.

We modern men, very tender, very easily hurt, and offering as well as receiving consideration a hundredfold, really have the conceit that this tender humanity which we represent, this attained unanimity in sympathetic regard, in readiness to help, in mutual trust, represents positive progress; and that in this respect we are far above the men of the Renaissance. But that is how every age thinks, how it *must* think. What is certain is that we may not place ourselves in Renaissance conditions, not even by an act of thought: our nerves would not endure that reality, not to speak of our muscles. But such incapacity does not prove progress, only another, later constitution, one which is weaker, frailer, more easily hurt, and which necessarily generates a morality rich in consideration. Were we to think away our frailty and lateness, our physiological senescence, then our morality of "humanization" would immediately lose its value too (in itself, no morality has any value)—it would even arouse disdain. On the other hand, let us not doubt that we moderns, with our thickly padded humanity, which at all costs wants to avoid bumping into a stone, would have provided Cesare Borgia's contemporaries with a comedy at which they could have laughed themselves to death. Indeed, we are unwittingly funny beyond all measure with our modern "virtues."[212]

The tendency to judge the aristocratic world—and the past simply—by the standards of the present is specious.[213] History is not some linear progression that culminates in the modern world with modern man standing at the apex of existence or but a short remove from history's final consummation. It was particularly this conceit—the idea of a world historical process that inexorably moved from stage to higher stage only to terminate in the apotheosis of modern man—that Nietzsche found, at once, so absurd and, because of the unthinking fervor with which it was embraced, so pernicious.

Here and there one goes further, into cynicism, and justifies the course of history, indeed the entire evolution of the world, in a manner especially adapted to the use of modern man, according to the cynical canon: as things are they had to be, as men now are they were bound to become, none may resist this inevitability. The pleasant feeling produced by this kind of cynicism is the refuge of him who cannot endure the ironical state; and the last decade has, moreover, made him a present of one of its fairest inventions, a full and rounded phrase to describe this cynicism: it calls his way of living in the fashion of the age and wholly without reflection "the total surrender of the personality to the world-process." The personality and the world process! The world process and the personality of the flea! If only one were not compelled everlastingly to hear the hyperbole of hyperboles, the word, "world, world, world"—when one ought more honestly to speak of "man, man, man!" Heirs of the Greeks and Romans? of Christianity? to these cynics that seems nothing; but heirs of the world-process![214]

Despite modern man's conviction, despite his ecstatic feeling of pride, he enjoys no privileged vantage point that permits him to assay the course of history and, on the basis of the values of *his* age, condemn those who predate him. Again, the fact that today's thickly padded moderns—far more thickly padded now than when Nietzsche wrote, as unremitting cries for safe spaces and trigger warnings attest—would find the reality of an earlier age unbearably unnerving suggests that in some ways (perhaps many) they would be found wanting when measured against their less fragile forebears.

Where Nietzsche would part ways with Tocqueville is on the question of democracy's insuperability. For Tocqueville, there was no sense in opposing humanity's democratization because it was a "providential fact . . . [that] is universal . . . enduring . . . and escapes all human power; all events, like all men, serve its development."[215] One could hope to moderate the excesses of democracy,[216] as Tocqueville indefatigably endeavored to do, but one could not reverse or stymie its advance. Nietzsche agreed there could be no going back,[217] but he refused to concede that there was no way to get beyond the democratic age. Nietzsche did not treat the democratic revolution lightly. Like Tocqueville, he understood that there was something momentous and unprecedented about it; that it was not some transitory and incidental historical interlude. He foresaw, like Tocqueville, that "the democratization of Europe is irresistible."[218] But for Nietzsche—and this may signify the central disconnect between Tocqueville and Nietzsche, at least with respect to the matter at hand—it was not permanent. Rather the "democratization of Europe is, it seems, a link in the chain of those tremendous *prophylactic measures* which are the conception of modern times and through which we separate ourselves from the Middle Ages." Here is to be found one of Nietzsche's more approbative remarks on democracy: as a "prophylactic measure" it serves as a bulwark against "barbarians . . . pestilence . . . [and] *physical and spiritual enslavement*." Nietzsche likens the effort to erecting "stone dams and protective walls" that would protect mankind from such calamitous ills, first in a coarse and literal sense, but gradually in a loftier and more spiritual one. "We make it henceforth impossible for the fruitful fields of culture again to be destroyed overnight by wild and senseless torrents!" Never again will Europe be plunged into an age of darkness; never again will the cultural fruits upon which Europe reposes be lost to it. But democracy was not an end in itself; rather it was a stepping stone to something greater, a "collective preparation for the supreme artist of horticulture who will be able to apply himself to his real task,"[219] namely that of cultivating a higher culture, one that, presumably, democracy would be ill-suited for.

Nietzsche understood that centuries would be needed to prepare the groundwork for this cultural efflorescence and that, as a result, democracy would be the order of the day for some time to come. The democratization of Europe, and the world over, may be a fait accompli, but its permanence is not fated, even if the democratized cannot envision anything after democracy. "We must not hold it too much against those who are working on the present day if they loudly decree that the wall and the trellis *are* the end and the final goal; since no one can yet see the gardener or the fruit trees *for whose sake* the trellis exists."[220] If it is here uncertain for whose sake democratic man exists, what is clear is that, in spite of his ever-waxing self-absorption, he does not exist for himself.[221]

What also is, or ought to be clear, is that there is no historical process that impels mankind forward. Unlike Hegel and Marx, Nietzsche is not trying to discover the internal movement of history, as if it had some will of its own, but rather aims to bend history to *his* will. The world revolves not around the inventors of new noise—which Marx, with his reproach to philosophers for interpreting the world rather than changing it,[222] emphatically was—but around the inventors of new values. That is Nietzsche's supreme task—the revaluation of values. But it is a task that enjoys no guarantee of success. The gardener for whose sake the trellis exists may never show up; the fruit trees may never take root. Nietzsche prevised that the democratization of man could reach a point when its transcendence would cease to be possible. As Nietzsche's godless prophet declaimed:

> The time has come for man to set himself a goal. The time has come for man to plant the seed of his highest hope. His soil is still rich enough. But one day this soil will be poor and domesticated, and no tall tree will be able to grow in it. Alas, the time is coming when man will no longer shoot the arrow of his longing beyond man, and the string of his bow will have forgotten how to whir!
>
> "I say unto you: one must still have chaos in oneself to be able to give birth to a dancing star. I say unto you: you still have chaos in yourselves."
>
> "Alas, the time is coming when man will no longer give birth to a star. Alas, the time of the most despicable man is coming, he that is no longer able to despise himself. Behold, I show you the last man."[223]

Zarathustra's listeners are not last men nor, it is safe to presume, are Nietzsche's readers. Like the inhabitants of Motley Cow, those who inhabit the present age still harbor what is needed to give birth to a dancing star; they are still capable of overcoming themselves, so that man need not return to the beasts and prove the ebb to this great evolutionary flood that is life.[224] Indeed, it was precisely these concomitant ends—forestalling the advent of the last man and preparing the soil for the coming of a nobler one—to which Nietzsche devoted his life's work. Though plagued by debilitating physical ailments and prone to despair of unfathomable depths,[225] there were times when Nietzsche still managed to express an almost boundless hope.[226] But as with Tocqueville's *Democracy in America*, one finds that notwithstanding such expressions of hope and notwithstanding the almost incomprehensible willpower needed to overcome his many afflictions (both physical and psychological), at bottom, what animates Nietzsche's effort is a sort of religious dread—a sense of nausea that welled within his soul.[227] Unlike many of his epigones, Nietzsche realized that the death of God was not something to be taken lightly[228] and that the nihilism that threatened to consume modernity signified not just the death of God, but in a very real sense, the death of man as well.

Tocqueville did not proclaim God's death, but he clearly envisaged the prospect of man's. Understanding that humanity's democratization was a providential fact that could not be undone, its salvation depended on tempering the excesses to which democratic man is exceedingly susceptible. There was no returning to the aristocratic world and there was no superseding the democratic one.[229] The only question that remained was whether mankind would live in freedom or servitude. There is no doubt that Nietzsche heard the knell of the aristocratic world loud and clear, but the democratic world that was built upon its ruins was, in his eyes, neither providential nor permanent. Tempered or not, for Nietzsche, democracy presaged the degeneration of man. What was needed was not a tempering of the democratic spirit, but its overcoming; a revaluation of those values that had paved the way for the last man: "*All* sciences must, from now on, prepare the way for the future work of the philosopher: this work being understood to mean that the philosopher has to solve the *problem of values* and that he has to decide the *rank order of values.*"[230] But it is precisely an order of rank—not simply of persons, but also of values—that is so anathema to the democratic temperament. What was needed, then, was the very thing Tocqueville thought was no longer possible: a *new aristocracy.*[231]

The point here is not to pick sides, but rather to take seriously what those who carried out the modern project did not—namely that humanity is wonderfully and naturally heterogeneous and a prodigious distance separates man from man (particularly those of the aristocratic and democratic varieties). Without an understanding of the human type that has been displaced, as well as the type to whom the future putatively belongs, it is inapt to portray this change as progress. What is more, by better understanding man as he was, now is, and portends to be, one can better appreciate the fundamental alternatives with which humanity is confronted and will be better able to choose among them—to the extent that a choice still remains, if ever it did. For such a task, perhaps no guides are more indispensable than Tocqueville and Nietzsche.

NOTES

1. On Western intellectuals' exaltation of and devotion to repressive regimes, see, for example, Mark Lilla, *The Reckless Mind: Intellectuals in Politics* (New York:

New York Review of Books, 2016) and Paull Hollander, *From Benito Mussolini to Hugo Chavez: Intellectuals and a Century of Political Hero Worship* (Cambridge: Cambridge University Press, 2016).

2. "In the early days of my schooling, [discrimination] meant to make a proper judgment—and my teachers were possibly the last generation of pedagogues who believed that the inculcation of powers of discrimination was the noblest part of their job, so that some of their pupils, at least, might come to appreciate and, if possible, add to the finest traditions and achievements of our civilization. . . .

"Accordingly, a person who did not discriminate, who was undiscriminating, was a person without taste, morality, or intellect; undiscriminating, he was likely to be indiscriminate in his behavior. Discrimination was for these teachers the most important function of the mind; truth could not be distinguished from falsehood, beauty from ugliness, or good from evil, and the purpose of pegadgogy was to instill the correct prejudices. In the field of aesthetics, all that is necessary for kitsch to triumph is for men to fail to discriminate." Theodore Dalrymple, *In Praise of Prejudice: The Necessity of Preconceived Ideas* (New York: Encounter Books, 2007), 75.

3. Use of the word *individual* to denote "a single distinguishable person" can be traced back to the seventeenth century. Raymond Williams, *Keywords: A Vocabulary of Culture and Society* (New York: Oxford University Press, 1985), 162. Even in the ancient Greek world—Athens included—conformity was the norm. "In principle and to a substantial degree in practice, the citizen body was homogenous." Paul A. Rahe, *Republics Ancient and Modern: The Ancien Régime in Classical Greece* (Chapel Hill, NC: University of North Carolina Press, 1994), 16.

4. On a more mundane note, in a world where means of communication and travel were exceedingly limited, people inevitably were cut off from one another, which encouraged the diversification of human life, not only on the macro-level of empires and cities, but on a much smaller and more personal scale as well. The result was "a multitude of . . . little worlds. . . . [T]here was no typical single farm or community. In the same way that every life course was unique and colorful, different from any other at the time in ways that are not the case today, so it was with every piece of property, every farm, and every community. What was typical was the colorful mosaic-like quality of life: the richness and multiplicity of possibilities, the lack of uniformity." Arthur E. Imhof, *Lost Worlds: How Our European Ancestors Coped with Everyday Life and Why Life Is So Hard Today* (Charlottesville: The University of Virginia Press, 1996), 3–4.

5. "Common humanity and equality are not primeval facts that patiently await discovery. We should rather conceive them as inventions of novel and potentially disruptive ways of looking at human relationships. That all the people in the world constitute a single community is not an empirical fact. What it means is that people can be represented as members of the meta-community of an 'imagined humanity.'" Siep Stuurman, *The Invention of Humanity: Equality and Cultural Difference in World History* (Cambridge, MA: Harvard University Press, 2017), 1.

6. Aldous Huxley, *Huxley and God: Essays on Religious Experience* (New York: Crossroad Publishing, 2003), 45. Huxley, quoting the English philosopher C.

D. Broad, echoes this notion in *The Doors of Perception*: "'The suggestion is that the function of the brain and nervous system and sense organs is in the main *eliminative* and not productive. Each person is at each moment capable of remembering all that has ever happened to him and of perceiving everything that is happening everywhere in the universe. The function of the brain and nervous system is to protect us from being overwhelmed and confused by this mass of largely useless and irrelevant knowledge, by shutting out most of what we should otherwise perceive or remember at any moment, and leaving only that very small and special selection which is likely to be practically useful'. According to such a theory, each one of us is potentially Mind at Large. But in so far as we are animals, our business is at all costs to survive. To make biological survival possible, Mind at Large has to be funneled through the reducing valve of the brain and nervous system. What comes out at the other end is a measly trickle of the kind of consciousness which will help us to stay alive on the surface of this particular planet." Aldous Huxley, *The Doors of Perception and Heaven and Hell* (New York: Harper and Row, 1990), 22–3.

7. Stephen Greenblatt, *The Swerve: How the World Became Modern* (New York: W. W. Norton, 2011), 68–70.

8. See Books XIII and IX of the *Republic*.

9. Barbarians, the principal source of Greek slaves, were un-Greek, not unhuman: "the barbarian and the slave are by nature the same thing." Aristotle, *The Politics*, trans. Carnes Lord (Chicago: University of Chicago Press, 1985), 36 (1252b6–9).

10. Ibid, 53 (1260a9–13).

11. Ibid, 213 (1330a31–33). Indeed, in his own will, Aristotle stipulated that his slaves should be granted freedom provided his executors deemed them worthy of it. See Paul Millett, "Aristotle and Slavery in Athens," *Greece & Rome* 54, no. 2 (2007): 204–5.

12. William Linn Westermann, *The Slave Systems of Greek and Roman Antiquity* (Philadelphia: The American Philosophical Society, 1984), 25–7.

13. "Science could not acquire its wings until it had eliminated questions of purpose from its method. The establishment of quantitative correlations is the sole purpose of science and the sole guarantee that it can become predictive and verifiable." Stanley L. Jaki, *Angels, Apes, and Men* (Peru, IL: Sherwood Sugden and Company, 1990), 65–6.

14. See Book VIII. License, diversity, and equality are the defining features of democracy, wherein "each man would organize his life in it privately just as it pleases him." "Democracy ... would be ... a sweet regime, without rulers and many-colored, dispensing a certain equality to equals and unequals alike." Plato, *Republic*, trans. Allan Bloom (New York: Basic Books, 1991), 235–6 (557b, 588c).

15. Niccolò Machiavelli, *Discourses on Livy*, trans. Harvey C. Mansfield and Nathan Tarcov (Chicago: Chicago University Press, 2009), 5.

16. Edward Gibbons, *Decline and Fall of the Roman Empire*, vol. 1 (New York: Alfred A. Knopf, 1993), 3.

17. Niccolò Machiavelli, *The Prince*, trans. Harvey C. Mansfield (Chicago: Chicago University Press, 1998), 61.

18. Leo Strauss, "The Three Waves of Modernity" in *An Introduction to Political Philosophy* (Detroit: Wayne State University Press, 1989), 86.

19. Machiavelli, *Prince*, 39.

20. The dichotomous drift of Machiavelli's thought is reflected in the long-standing divide between scholars on the question of which world the Florentine belongs to. The view that Machiavelli pointed back (to antiquity) rather than forward (to modernity) is espoused by J. G. A. Pocock, *The Machiavellian Moment* (Princeton: Princeton University Press, 1975) and Quentin Skinner, *Machiavelli* (New York: Hill and Wang, 1981) (among many others). For the contrary view, see, for example, Leo Strauss, *Thoughts on Machiavelli* (Chicago: University of Chicago Press, 1995) and Harvey C. Mansfield, *Machiavelli's Virtue* (Chicago: University of Chicago Press, 1996). On the difficulty of pinning the Florentine down, see David Wootton, *Power, Pleasure, and Profit: Insatiable Appetites from Machiavelli to Madison* (Cambridge, MA: Harvard University Press, 2018), 37–65: "Of interpretations of Machiavelli there has been and will be no end. . . . Where readers of Thomas Hobbes, for example, have generally agreed on what Hobbes was saying, even if they disagreed about how to respond to it, there has been no consensus among readers of Machiavelli on how to interpret him, and his texts have been put to work to serve radically different purposes" (44).

21. Machiavelli, *Prince*, 61.

22. Thomas Hobbes, *On the Citizen*, ed. and trans. Richard Tuck and Michael Silverthorne (New York: Cambridge University Press, 1998), 5.

23. Ibid.

24. Aristotle, *Politics*, 37 (1253a).

25. Hobbes concedes that historically and strictly speaking, there may never have been a state of nature, though he also claims that such a state could be found in a number of places, for example, among the "savage people" of [seventeenth-century] America. Rather, the state is an "inference made from the passions" as they exist naturally in man. That is, the state of nature is deducible not from natural man but from civilized man and the validity of that deduction is demonstrated by the way people behave *in society*, for example, when they lock their doors at night, or arm themselves on journeys, or build forts and walls to defend their borders. Thomas Hobbes, *Leviathan* (New York: W.W. Norton, 2020), 90–1. Fredrick Copleston aptly characterized Hobbes's state of nature as "the state of affairs in which the individual is dependent for his security on his own strength and his own wits." Presumably, most people who have never toured a pre-societal state of nature have at one time or another been acquainted with this state of affairs. Fredrick Copleston, *A History of Philosophy: The British Philosophers (Part I: Hobbes to Paley)* (Garden City, NY: Image Books, 1964), 42. It is worth noting that while the state of nature very well may be an analytical construct, Hobbes appears to want to have it both ways; that is, Hobbes suggests that the state is not just a construct, wholly devoid of historical reality. The fact that in his mind, the natives of America live in such a state suggests as much. These primitive people have yet to be civilized and since man was not born civilized, the logical inference is that civilized man once was primitive man, that is, at some point in the past, the state of nature prevailed. Indeed, Hobbes affirms as much:

"Past centuries show us nations, now civilized and flourishing, whose inhabitants were then few, savage, short lived, poor and mean, and lacked all the comforts and amenities of life which *peace* and society afford" (*Citizen*, 30).

26. Hobbes, *Leviathan*, 89–90. To substantiate further the point made in the previous note, Hobbes's celebrated description of the state of nature where "the life of man [is] solitary, poor, nasty, brutish, and short" also does not square with the understanding that that state is nothing more than an analytical construct. The total absence of "industry," "commodious building," any "account of time," and "society" is not deducible from humans locking their doors at night and arming themselves when they travel.

27. The maxim, attributed to Cicero, is quoted by Hobbes, *The Elements of Law* in *Three-Text Edition of Thomas Hobbes's Political Theory*, ed. Deborah Baumgolden (New York: Cambridge, 2017), 140. Cicero's wording, from *Pro Milone*, is *silent enim leges inter arma* ("when arms speak, the laws are silent").

28. Hobbes, *Leviathan*, 87–8.

29. Hobbes, *Citizen*, 6.

30. Alexander Hamilton, Letter to James A. Bayard (April 1802), *Hamilton: Writings* (New York: The Library of America, 2001), 988.

31. Machiavelli, *Prince*, 66–7.

32. Hobbes, *Citizen*, 37.

33. Machiavelli, *Prince*, 30.

34. Immanuel Kant, *Idea for a Universal History with a Cosmopolitan Purpose* in *Kant: Political Writings*, trans. H.B. Nisbet (New York: Cambridge University Press, 1991), 46.

35. "For the first 500 years of Christianity, Christians and Christian theologians were broadly Universalist." Ken R. Vincent, "The Salvation Conspiracy: How Hell Became Eternal," *The Universalist Herald* (July/August 2006) (republished at https://christianuniversalist.org/resources/articles/salvation-conspiracy/). Vincent claims "that the main person responsible for making Hell eternal in the Western Church was St. Augustine (354-430 CE)." See also J. W. Hanson, *Universalism: The Prevailing Doctrine of the Christian Church During Its First 500 Years* (Boston: Universalist Publishing House, 1899), 271–81. Philippe Ariès argues that it was not until the twelfth and thirteenth centuries that fear of eternal damnation took hold in the popular mind. Prior to that, the understanding was that after death, the faithful would sleep until the Second Coming, "when they would awaken in . . . Paradise." The unfaithful would not be condemned to hell, but were simply consigned to an eternal sleep; "they would not awaken and would be abandoned to a state of non-existence." The idea that one would "be judged according to the balance sheet of his life" and punished or rewarded accordingly was good not only for regulating human behavior, but for recompensing the church. As the fear of divine judgment increased, so too did the sale of indulgences. Philippe Ariès, *Western Attitudes toward Death from the Middle Ages to the Present* (Baltimore: Johns Hopkins University Press, 1975), 31–2. On the remunerative benefits that the fear of hell brought, see Galen E. Foresman, "Hell as Punishment: Pitfalls for the Pit" in *The Concept of Hell*, ed. Robert Arp and Benjamin McCraw (New York: Palgrave Macmillan, 2015), 84.

36. David Johnston, "Hobbes's Mortalism," *History of Political Thought* 10, no. 4 (Winter 1989): 647.
37. Kant, *Perpetual Peace* in *Kant: Political Writings*, 112.
38. Hobbes, *Citizen*, 152.
39. Job 41:33–4.
40. Hobbes, *Leviathan*, 220.
41. Ibid, 179.
42. Ibid, 229.
43. Ibid, 226.
44. Ibid, 226–7.
45. Ibid, 227.
46. "But crimes of Infirmity; such as are those which proceed from great provocation, from great fear, great need, or from ignorance whether the fact be a great crime, or not, there is place many times for lenity, without prejudice to the commonwealth; and lenity when there is such place for it, is required by the law of nature. The punishment of the leaders and teachers in a commotion; not the poor seduced people, when they are punished, can profit the commonwealth by their example. To be severe to the people, is to punish that ignorance, which may in great part be imputed to the sovereign, whose fault it was, they were no better instructed." Ibid, 229.
47. Ibid, 147–8.
48. Leo Strauss, *Natural Right and History* (Chicago: University of Chicago Press, 1999) 181–2.
49. For a recent work that judiciously assesses that debt, see Larry Siedentop, *Inventing the Individual: The Origins of Western Liberalism* (Cambridge, MA: Harvard University Press, 2015).
50. "Exposing of newly born infants regarded as superfluous or undesired was practiced to a greater or lesser degree throughout the Greek world from earliest times." La Rue van Hook, "The Exposure of Infants at Athens," *Transactions and Proceedings of the American Philological Association* 51 (1920): 135. Although van Hook had his doubts, exposure of newborns in Classical Athens appears to have been common. See H. Bolkestein, "The Exposure of Children at Athens and the ἐγχυτρίστριαι," *Classical Philology* 17, no. 3 (July 1922): 222–39.
51. See, for example, Hobbes, *Citizen*, 24–5. "Infants and the uninstructed are ignorant of their [civil societies'] Force, and those who do not know what would be lost by the absence of Society are unaware of their usefulness. Hence the former cannot enter Society because they do not know what it is, and the latter do not care to because they do not know the good it does. It is evident, therefore that all men (since all men are born infants) are born unfit for society; and very many (perhaps the majority) remain so throughout their lives, because of mental illness or lack of training [discipline]. Yet as infants and as adults they do have human nature. Therefore, man is made fit for Society not by nature, but by training. Furthermore, even if man were born in a condition to desire society, it does not follow that he was born suitably equipped to enter it. Wanting is one thing, ability another."
52. Ibid, 5.
53. "The most unsettling shift in scientific self-understanding—about what science was and where it was going—began in the middle decades of the nineteenth

century, reaching its climax circa 1900. It was around that time that scientists began to wonder uneasily about whether scientific progress was compatible with scientific truth. If advances in knowledge were never-ending, could any scientific theory or empirical result count as real knowledge—true forever and always? Or was science, like the monarchies of Europe's anciens régimes and the boundaries of its states and principalities, doomed to perpetual revision and revolution?" Lorraine Daston, "When Science went Modern," *The Hedgehog Review* 18, no. 3 (Fall 2016), https://hedgehogreview.com/issues/the-cultural-contradictions-of-modern-science/articles/when-science-went-modern.

54. Alexander Pope, "Epitaph. Intended for Sir Isaac Newton" in *The Poems of Alexander Pope: A One-volume Edition of the Twickenham Text with Selected Annotations*, ed. John Butt (New Haven: Yale University Press, 1963), 808.

55. This truth is embodied in Plato's *Republic*, where a gold-souled child can be born to bronze-souled progenitors (415a-d).

56. "Every violation of natural laws consists in false reasoning or in stupidity, when men fail to see what duties towards other men are necessary to their own preservation." Hobbes, *Citizen*, 33–4.

57. Ibid, 33.

58. A Hobbesian rejoinder would be that fools rarely are fit to recognize their own folly nor apprehend the wisdom of others. To which a fool might retort, if this does pass for wisdom, enlightenment would divest mankind of its rich diversity and endue it with a numbing insipidity—an estimation that is not altogether foolish.

59. See, for example, John Locke, *Second Treatise* in *Two Treatises of Government*, ed. Peter Laslett (New York: Cambridge University Press, 2003), 328.

60. Hobbes, *Citizen*, 85.

61. Ibid, 27.

62. Ibid, 12.

63. Ibid, 27.

64. Ibid, 85.

65. Hobbes, *Leviathan*, 214.

66. Locke, *Second Treatise*, 286.

67. "Liberalism has always had in view the good of the whole, not that of any special group." Ludwig von Mises, *Liberalism* (Indianapolis: Liberty Fund, 2005), xxii.

68. Locke, *Second Treatise*, 297.

69. The imperative to conquer nature (or fortune) by force is integral to modernity and manifest at its outset. See Machiavelli, *Prince*, Chapter 25.

70. Locke's mistrust of the benefits of the microscope is in part predicated on the understanding that man's senses were designed by God and hence allowed man to see what he needed to see. To impute deficiency would be to impugn God. John Locke, *An Essay Concerning Human Understanding* (London: William Baynes and Son, 1823), 230–1. See also David Wootton, *The Invention of Science: A New History of the Scientific Revolution* (New York: HarperCollins, 2015), 235–6.

71. Locke, *Second Treatise*, §34.

72. "Under what sign does [the Christian] imagine the better future of the human species? Under the sign of heavenly joy in divine Salvation. But we experience this heaven on earth when we no longer live in self-seeking and hate but in love, in a

unified human species, in the communist society." Moses Hess, *A Communist Credo: Questions and Answers* in *Moses Hess: The Holy History of Mankind and Other Writings*, ed. and trans. Shlomo Avineri (New York: Cambridge University Press, 2004), 126.

73. René Descartes, *Discourse on Method*, trans. Laurence J. Lafleur (New York: Macmillian Publishing Co., 1956), 40.

74. Locke, *Second Treatise*, 297.

75. In Europe, for example, the poor were disproportionately affected by the plague. See Paul Slack, *The Impact of Plague in Tudor and Stuart England* (New York: Oxford University Press, 2003).

76. Brad Plumer, "Humans Are Speeding Extinction and Altering the Natural World at an 'Unprecedented' Pace," *The New York Times*, May 6, 2019, https://www.nytimes.com/2019/05/06/climate/biodiversity-extinction-united-nations.html; James E.M. Watson, et al., "Catastrophic Declines in Wilderness Areas Undermine Global Environment Targets," *Current Biology* 26 (November 7, 2016): 2929–34.

77. The Native Americans are a case in point. While their decimation in the face of European germs and guns may have been a foregone conclusion, their situation was made all the more pathetic by the spiritual enervation that accompanied their growing dependence on European comforts—comforts which they flourished without and languished with. For some reflections on this phenomenon see Tocqueville, *Democracy*, 308–9.

78. Locke, *Second Treatise*, 298.

79. Regarding Locke's influence on the American Founding, see, for example, Thomas L. Pangle, *The Spirit of Modern Republicanism: The Moral Vision of the American Founders and the Philosophy of Locke* (University of Chicago Press: Chicago, 1988); Paul A. Rahe, *Republics Ancient and Modern: Inventions of Prudence: Constituting the American Regime*, vol. 3 (Chapel Hill: University of North Carolina Press, 1994); Jerome Huyler, *Locke in America: The Moral Philosophy of the Founding Era* (Lawrence, KS: University of Kansas Press, 1995). For an opposing view, particularly with regard to Locke's influence—or lack thereof—on Jefferson, see Garry Wills, *Inventing America: Jefferson's Declaration of Independence* (New York: Vintage Books, 1979).

80. Jean-Jacques Rousseau, *The Second Discourse* in *The First and Second Discourses*, trans. Roger D. Masters and Judith R. Masters (New York: St. Martin's Press, 1964), 181.

81. Rousseau, *Emile or On Education*, trans. Allan Bloom (New York: Basic Books, 1979), 40.

82. For an account of this episode, see Leo Damrosch, *Jean-Jacques Rousseau: Restless Genius* (New York: Houghton Mifflin, 2005), 212.

83. Rousseau, *Second Discourse*, 102.

84. Ibid.

85. Hobbes, *Citizen*, 26.

86. Ibid, 71; *Leviathan*, 117. See also Leo Strauss, *The Political Philosophy of Hobbes: Its Genesis and Basis* (Chicago: University of Chicago Press, 1963), 11: "In four different arguments, Hobbes does not tire of designating the characteristic

difference between man and animal as the striving after honour and the positions of honour, after precedence over others and recognition of this precedence by others, ambition, pride, and the passion for fame."

87. Aristotle, *Politics*, 37 (1253a).
88. Hobbes, *Citizen*, 21–2.
89. "Reason is coterminous with language and language presupposes society: being presocial, natural man is prerational. . . . Since language is not natural, reason is not natural." Strauss, *Natural Right*, 270.
90. Hobbes, *Citizen*, 33 [emphasis added]. Hobbes defines right reason "in men's natural state" as "the act of reasoning . . . about actions . . . which may conduce to [one's] advantage or other men's loss."
91. Locke, *Second Treatise*, 271 [emphasis added].
92. Rousseau, *Second Discourse*, 94.
93. Ibid, *Second Discourse*, 117.
94. Ibid, 141–2.
95. Ibid, 137.
96. Ibid, 142–6.
97. Ibid, 140.
98. "Men, dispersed among the animals, observe and imitate their industry, and thereby develop in themselves the instinct of the beasts; with the advantage that whereas each species has only its own proper instinct, man—perhaps having none that belongs to him—appropriates them all to himself, feeds himself equally well with the most diverse foods which the other animals share and consequently finds his subsistence more easily than any of them can." Rousseau, *Second Discourse*, 105–6.
99. Ibid, 114.
100. Ibid, 113–4.
101. Kwame Anthony Appiah, *The Lies That Bind: Rethinking Identity* (New York: Liveright Publishing, 2018), 122.
102. John T. Scott, "Introduction" in *The Major Political Writings of Jean-Jacques Rousseau: The Two Discourses and the Social Contract*, ed. and trans. John T. Scott (Chicago: University of Chicago Press, 2012), xxxiii.
103. Rousseau, *Second Discourse*, 114–5.
104. Ibid, 115.
105. Ibid.
106. Strauss, *Natural Right*, 271.
107. Jean-Jacques Rousseau, *On the Social Contract* in *The Major Politics Writings of Jean-Jacques Rousseau*, 163–4.
108. "In [Rousseau's] eyes, modern man lives primarily in the element of society inasfar as he adopts the point of view of inequality in his relations with his fellow men. This is not particular inequality, economic or political, but simply inequality at large, an abstract and therefore omnipresent determination of social life." Pierre Manent, *An Intellectual History of Liberalism*, trans. Rebecca Balinski (Princeton: Princeton University Press, 1994), 78–9.
109. "Ancient politicians incessantly talked about morals and virtue, those of our time talk only of business and money." Rousseau, *First Discourse*, 51.

110. Ibid, 62.
111. Rousseau, *Second Discourse*, 92–3.
112. For a sense of that prodigiousness, see Allan Bloom, "Rousseau's Critique of liberal Constitutionalism" in *The Legacy of Rousseau*, ed. Clifford Orwin and Nathan Tarcov (Chicago: University of Chicago Press, 1997), 145–6.
113. Voltaire, *Voltaire in His Letters: Being a Selection from His Correspondence*, trans. S. G. Tallentyre (New York: G. P. Putnam's Sons, 1919), 149–50.
114. "The most famous innovation," Bloom contends, is the general will. Though earlier in his piece, he claims "Rousseau's great invention" is the *bourgeois*. Allan Bloom, "Rousseau: the Turning Point" in *Giants and Dwarfs: Essays 1960-1990* (New York: Simon and Schuster, 1990), 211, 222.
115. On this note, see Strauss, "Three Waves," 90, and *Natural Right and History*, 272–4.
116. Aristotle, *Politics*, Book III.
117. "For all peoples have a kind of centrifugal force by which they continually act one against one another and tend to grow at their neighbors' expense, like Descartes' vortices. Thus the weak risk being quickly swallowed up, and scarcely can any people preserve itself except by establishing a kind of equilibrium with all the others, which makes the pressure everywhere more or less equal." Rousseau, *Social Contract*, 196–7.
118. Ibid, 172.
119. Ibid, 172–3.
120. Rousseau, *Second Discourse*, 141.
121. Rousseau, *Social Contract*, 175 6.
122. Ibid, 176.
123. Ibid.
124. Ibid, 175.
125. Ibid, 271.
126. Kant, *Universal History*, 47.
127. Rousseau, *Social Contract*, 228.
128. Rousseau, *The Collected Writings of Jean-Jacques Rousseau (Volume 11): The Plan for Perpetual Peace, On the Government of Poland, and Other Writings on History and Politics*, ed. Christopher Kelly, trans. Christopher Kelly and Judith Bush (Lebanon, NH: University Press of New England, 2005), 49.
129. Rousseau, *First Discourse*, 51.
130. "In 1918, a few months after the October Revolution in Russia, a statue of Robespierre was erected near the Kremlin. Made of temporary materials, it soon fell to pieces, and was not replaced. The absence of a more permanent statue suggests that once the Russian Revolution was clearly established as a reality, it had less need to celebrate distant predecessors in far-away countries. That Robespierre was thus commemorated at all, in 1918, signifies Lenin's belief that his own movement, mediated through Marxism, was descended from the great French Revolution of 1789." R. R. Palmer, *The World of the French Revolution* (New York: Harper and Row, 1971), 261.

131. "Kant's biographers tell that his study, which was furnished with Spartan simplicity and lacked all decoration, had but a single ornament—on a wall hung the portrait of Jean-Jacques Rousseau. In other ways also the earliest accounts of Kant's life give varied evidence of his reverence for Rousseau as a person and his admiration for his work. Most familiar is the story that he who was a model of punctuality, and accustomed to regulate his daily routine by the clock, departed only once from this regular routine. When Rousseau's *Émile* appeared, fascinated by the study of the work in which he had become absorbed, Kant gave up his daily walk." Ernst Cassirer, *Rousseau, Kant, Goethe: Two Essays* (Princeton: Princeton University Press, 2015), 1. See also Cassirer, *Kant's Life and Thought* (New Haven: Yale University Press, 1981), 86–90.

132. Immanuel Kant, *Prolegomena to any Future Metaphysics* (New York: Macmillian Publishing Co., 1987), 8.

133. Jean-Jacques Rousseau, *Reveries of the Solitary Walker*, trans. Peter France (New York: Penguin, 1979), 93–104 ("Sixth Walk").

134. "The *State of Nature* has a Law of Nature to govern it, which obliges every one: and Reason, which is that law, teaches all mankind, who will but consult it, that being all equal and independent, no one ought to harm another in his Life, Health, Liberty, or Possessions." Locke, *Second Treatise*, 271. "The *Natural Law* therefore (to define it) is the Dictate of right reason. . . . By right reason in men's natural state, I mean not, as many do, an infallible Faculty, but the act of reasoning, that is, a man's own true Reasoning about actions of his which may conduce to his advantage or other men's loss." Hobbes, *Citizen*, 33.

135. For a modern appreciation of this, see Søren Kierkegaard, *Fear and Trembling*, trans. Alastair Hannay (New York: Penguin Books, 1985), 145: "However much one generation learns from another, it can never learn from its predecessor the genuinely human factor. In this respect, every generation begins afresh, has no task other than that of any previous generation, and comes no further, provided the latter hasn't shirked its task and deceived itself. . . . No generation can begin other than at the beginning."

136. Immanuel Kant, *Critique of Practical Reason*, trans. Thomas Kingsmill Abbott (Mineola, NY: Dover Publications, 2004), 170.

137. "The world appears to primitive man neither inanimate nor empty but redundant with life, and life has individuality, in man and beast and plant, and in every phenomenon which confronts man—the thunderclap, the sudden shadow, the eerie and unknown clearing in the wood, the stone which suddenly hurts him when he stumbles while on a hunting trip. Any phenomenon may at any time face him, not as 'It', but as 'Thou'. In this confrontation, 'Thou' reveals its individuality, its qualities, its will. 'Thou' is not contemplated with intellectual detachment; it is experienced as life confronting life, involving every faculty of man in a reciprocal relationship. Thoughts, no less than acts and feelings, are subordinated to this experience." H. and H. A. Frankfort, *The Intellectual Adventure of Ancient Man* (Chicago: University of Chicago Press, 1977), 6.

138. For some reflections on and rejoinders to the postmodernist view, see Wootton, *Invention of Science*, 580–91.

139. Immanuel Kant, *Groundwork of the Metaphysics of the Morals*, trans. H. J. Patton (New York: Harper and Row, 1964), 60.
140. Ibid, 57.
141. Ibid, 55–6.
142. Ibid, 73.
143. Ibid, 57.
144. Ibid, 62.
145. Ibid, 63.
146. Ibid, 64.
147. Ibid, 68.
148. Ibid, 88.
149. Ibid, 95.
150. For Kant, *dignity* is that which has an absolute, intrinsic value for which there is no equivalent or substitutable value. Dignity is, quite literally, priceless. *Persons*, as opposed to *things*, are ends in themselves precisely because they have dignity, or more strictly put, because they are capable of morality. "Morality, and humanity insofar as it is capable of morality, is the only thing which has dignity." Ibid, 96, 102.
151. Rousseau, *Social Contract*, 175.
152. Locke, *Second Treatise*, 365, 390.
153. "[A] rational being must regard himself *qua intelligence* (and accordingly not on the side of his lower faculties) as belonging to the intelligible world, not to the sensible one. He has therefore two points of view from which he can regard himself and from which he can know laws governing the employment of his powers and consequently governing all his actions. He can consider himself *first*—so far as he belongs to the sensible world—to be under the laws of nature (heteronomy); and *secondly*—so far as he belongs to the intelligible world—to be under laws which, being independent of nature, are not empirical but have their ground in reason alone." Kant, *Groundwork*, 120.
154. Kant, *Critique of Pure Reason*, trans. Norman Kemp Smith (Boston: Bedford/St. Martins, 1965), 43. Mathematics, which is concerned "with objects and with knowledge [that] solely . . . allow of being exhibited in intuition[,]" "gives us a shining example of how far, independently of experience, we can progress in *a priori* knowledge." Ibid, 46–7.
155. Kant, *Groundwork*, 121.
156. Ibid, 101.
157. Kant, *Universal History*, 42.
158. Ibid, 41.
159. Ibid, 42.
160. Ibid, 41.
161. This faith in reason and morality therewith is also evident in one of Kant's "proofs" of God where it is postulated that were there not "a wise Author and Ruler" that constituted the ground of morality, then we "would have to regard the moral laws as empty figments of the brain." Kant, *Critique of Pure Reason*, 639. The fact that moral laws may be just that renders this proof of God rather unconvincing. Of course, that is no "disproof" of God. In maintaining faith in reason, morality, and God, Kant

very well may have been more consistent than those who would remove God from the equation. Those who promulgate atheism with a perfervidity that appears incongruous in light of the prefix attached to the theism they disavow seem to have no trouble reconciling the purposelessness of nature with the order inherent in it. To maintain that out of chance and chaos there emerged a universe governed by immutable laws, in which a being capable of grasping those laws evolved, seems to require a leap of faith as great as, if not greater than, believing in something akin to a first mover or intelligent designer or omnipotent God.

162. Kant, *Universal History*, 42.

163. See Strauss, "Three Waves," 84–5; Pierre Manent, *The City and Man*, trans. Marc A. LePain (Princeton: Princeton University Press, 1998), 121–7.

164. Kant, *Universal History*, 44.

165. Ibid, 45.

166. Ibid.

167. Ibid.

168. Ibid, 46.

169. It is unclear just how gradual this development will be seeing that it presupposes the *immortality* of the species. Ibid, 44.

170. As with Hegel, there is a certain ambiguity regarding the sequence with which history's progressive stages unfold, particularly with respect to the putative final stage(s).

171. Kant, *Universal History*, 47.

172. Ibid.

173. Kant, *Perpetual Peace*, 105.

174. Kant, *Universal History*, 43.

175. Ibid, 50.

176. Ibid, 45.

177. "Society thus far, based upon class antagonism, had need of the state . . . for the purpose of forcibly keeping the exploited classes in the condition of oppression corresponding with the given mode of production (slavery, serfdom, wage-labor). . . . As soon as there is no longer any class to be held in subjection . . . nothing more remains to be repressed, and a special repressive force, a state, is no longer necessary. . . . State interference in social relations becomes, in one domain after another, superfluous, and then dies out of itself; the government of persons is replaced by the administration of things, and by the conduct of processes of production. The state is not 'abolished'. *It dies out*." Friedrich Engels, *Socialism: Utopian and Scientific*, trans. Edward Aveling (New York: Cosimo, 2008), 70.

178. Leon Trotsky, *Literature and Revolution* (New York: Russell and Russell, 1957), 256.

179. By way of evidence, America's decline in literacy ought to suffice. Americans read less and, unsurprisingly, read less well today than they did a generation ago. That hardly betokens progress. To paraphrase Madison, literacy is to enlightenment what air is to fire. On America's declining literacy see, for example, Bureau of Labor Statistics, U.S. Department of Labor, *The Economics Daily*, "People age 65 and older more likely than younger people to read for personal interest on the

Internet" (https://www.bls.gov/opub/ted/2018/people-age-65-and-older-more-likely-than-younger-people-to-read-for-personal-interest.htm); National Endowment for the Arts, "To Read or Not to Read: A Question of National Consequence," (https://www.arts.gov/sites/default/files/ToRead.pdf); National Endowment for the Arts, "Humanities Indicator: Time Spent Reading" (https://www.amacad.org/humanities-indicators/public-life/time-spent-reading). For some discerning and disquieting reflections on declining literacy's deleterious impact on cognitive functions see Maryann Wolf, *Reader Come Back: The Reading Brain in a Digital World* (New York: Harper Collins, 2018).

180. Consider, for example, Kant's dictate: "To be truthful (honest) in all declarations is, therefore, a sacred and unconditionally commanding law of reason that admits of no expediency whatsoever." This includes, to quote Benjamin Constant to whom Kant was responding explicitly, "tell[ing] a lie to a murderer who asked whether our friend who is being pursued by the murderer had taken refuge in our house." Kant, "On a Supposed Right to Lie because of Philanthropic Concerns" in *Grounding for the Metaphysics of Morals*, trans. James. W. Ellington (Indianapolis, IN: Hackett Publishing, 1993), 63, 65. For a defense of Kant from this charge, see Helga Varden, "Kant and Lying to the Murderer at the Door . . . One More Time: Kant's Legal Philosophy and Lies to Murderers and Nazis," *Journal of Social Philosophy* 41, no. 4 (Winter 2010): 403–21.

181. G.W. F. Hegel, *Lectures on the Philosophy of World History. Volume 1: Manuscripts of the Introduction and the Lectures of 1822–3*, ed. and trans. Robert F. Brown and Peter C. Hodgson with the assistance of William G. Geuss (Oxford: Oxford University Press, 2011), 384.

182. Consider, for example, the rustication of people over the age of ten. "It is not hard to understand that this step could be taken only through the slaughter of all parents, but even if we take the statement literally, we must note that Socrates has no pity or concern for the expelled citizenry and no hesitation in depriving them of their children. In order to establish a just city, the ultimate act of injustice is required." Stanley Rosen, *Plato's Republic: A Study* (New Haven: Yale University Press, 2005), 301.

183. G. W. F. Hegel, *Philosophy of Right*, trans. T.M Knox (New York: Oxford University Press, 1967), 245.

184. Karl Marx, *The German Ideology* in *Karl Marx: Selected Writings*, ed. David McLellan (New York: Oxford University Press, 1988), 169.

185. Hegel, *Philosophy of Right*, 13.

186. "All the Desires of an animal are in the final analysis a function of its desire to preserve its life. Human Desire, therefore, must win out over this desire for preservation. In other words, man's humanity 'comes to light' only if he risks his (animal) life for the sake of his human Desire. It is in and by this risk that the human reality is created and revealed as reality; it is in and by this risk that it 'comes to light', i.e., is shown, demonstrated, verified and gives proofs of being essentially different from the animal natural reality." Alexandre Kojève, *Introduction to the Reading of Hegel: Lectures on the Phenomenology of Spirit*, trans. James H. Nichols, Jr. (Ithaca: Cornell University Press, 1980), 7.

187. Kojève, *Introduction*, 46.

188. G. W. F. Hegel, *Phenomenology of Spirit*, trans. A. V. Miller (New York: Oxford University Press, 1977) 116.
189. Kojève, *Introduction*, 19.
190. "If idle Mastery is an impasse, laborious Slavery, in contrast, is the source of all human, social, historical progress." Ibid, 20.
191. Hegel, *Phenomenology*, 117.
192. Kojève, *Introduction*, 48.
193. "At every stage of history prior to its completion (assuming that to be possible), each human being is at once master and slave. . . . Needless to say, some individuals express more of the master than the slave in their nature. . . . But these individual 'types' are intrinsic to the nature of human spirit altogether." Stanley Rosen, *G.W.F. Hegel: An Introduction to the Science of Wisdom* (South Bend, IN: St. Augustine's Press, 2000), 155.
194. Consider for example Hegel's reflections on the place of conflict at the end of history. "In peace civil life continually expands; all its departments wall themselves in, and in the long run men stagnate. Their idiosyncrasies become continually more fixed and ossified. But for health the unity of the body is required, and if its parts harden themselves into exclusiveness, that is death. Perpetual peace is often advocated as an ideal towards which humanity should strive. With that end in view, Kant proposed a league of monarchs to adjust differences between states, and the Holy Alliance was meant to be a league of much the same kind. But the state is an individual, and individuality essentially implies negation. Hence even if a number of states make themselves into a family, this group as an individual must engender an opposite and create an enemy." Hegel, *Philosophy of Right*, 295.
195. Pierre Hassner, "Georg W. F. Hegel" in *History of Political Philosophy*, ed. Leo Strauss and Joseph Cropsey (Chicago: University of Chicago Press, 1987), 758.
196. This sentiment is taken from Montaigne who in turn attributes it to Plutarch. See Montaigne, "Of Inequality," *Essays*, trans. Donald M. Frame (Stanford: Stanford University Press, 1981), 189.
197. The Greek word *logos* (λόγος) signified both. For a brief discussion of the meaning and history of the term, see Christopher J. Rowe, "Logos," *The Oxford Classical Dictionary*, 3rd ed. (New York: Oxford University Press, 1996), 882.
198. See Aristotle, *Politics*, 37–8 (1253a2–1253a40). See also Strauss, *Natural Right*, 120–64, *passim*: "Man is by nature a social being. He is so constituted that he cannot live well, except by living with others. Since it is reason or speech that distinguishes him from the other animals, and speech is communication, man is social in a more radical sense than any other social animal: humanity itself is sociality. Man refers himself to others, or rather he is referred to others, in every human act, regardless of whether that act is "social" or "antisocial." His sociality does not proceed, then, from a calculation of the pleasures which he expects from association, but he derives pleasure from association because he is by nature social. Love, affection, friendship, pity, are as natural to him as concern with his own good and calculation of what is conducive to his own good. It is man's natural sociality that is the basis of natural right in the narrow or strict sense of right. Because man is by nature social, the perfection of his nature includes the social virtue par excellence, justice; justice and right are natural" (129).

199. See Book VIII of the *Republic*.

200. See Book IV of the *Nicomachean Ethics*.

201. The first wave consisted most notably of Machiavelli, Hobbes, and Locke. Strauss, "Three Waves," esp. 83–91: "Modernity started from the dissatisfaction with the gulf between the is and the ought, the actual and ideal; the solution suggested in the first wave was: to bring the ought nearer to the is by lowering the ought, by conceiving of the ought as not making too high demands on men, or as being in agreement with man's most powerful and most common passion" (91).

202. "The second wave of modernity begins with Rousseau" (89) and culminates in Hegel (and, by derivation, Marx). Ibid, esp. 89–94.

203. This is not to suggest that in the pantheon of philosophy, Tocqueville's rightful place is beside Nietzsche. For competing views on the question of whether or not Tocqueville was a philosopher, see Peter Augustine Lawler, *The Restless Mind: Alexis de Tocqueville on the Origin and Perpetuation of Human Liberty* (Lanham, MD: Rowman and Littlefield, 1993), 89–108 and Pierre Manent, "Tocqueville, Political Philosopher" in *The Cambridge Companion to Tocqueville*, ed. Cheryl B. Welch (New York: Cambridge University Press, 2006), 108–20. Manent argues that Tocqueville, by devoting his work to "the confrontation between 'aristocracy' and 'democracy'" and showing that "the debate between these two forms of humanity" has not, and cannot, be resolved, not only extended "the inquiry initiated by Greek philosophy," but did so at a time when, on account of the dogma of popular sovereignty, the conditions for such philosophic pursuits were less than favorable. In view of this, "How can we deny the name philosopher to the liberal sociologist who leads us out of the social cave?" (120). Manent's argument is compelling, but it is not clear that it can dispose of the fact that Tocqueville esteemed the political life above the philosophical. As Lawler notes, Tocqueville "preferred to be a political actor than a writer and, when he wrote, it was always on behalf of the political life. He wrote only when circumstances denied him a place on the political stage" (108). This would, on Nietzsche's understanding, amount to an inversion of the philosopher's "order of rank." Nietzsche, who looked upon philosophy as "the most spiritual will to power," argued that religion should be used by philosophers "as a means of securing calm in the face of the turmoil and tribulations of the *cruder* forms of government, and purity in the face of the *necessary* dirt of politics." By that measure at least, Tocqueville was no philosopher. Nietzsche, *Beyond Good and Evil*, 11, 54.

204. Tocqueville, *Democracy*, 675.

205. Alexis de Tocqueville, *The Old Regime and the Revolution*, vol. 1, trans. Alan S. Kahan (Chicago: University of Chicago Press, 1998), 179 [emphasis added].

206. Tocqueville, *Democracy*, 6. Regarding this sense of terror, Tocqueville spoke more candidly in a letter he drafted to Silvestre de Sacy (it is unclear if the letter had been sent): "I had become aware that, in our time, the new social state that had produced and is still producing very great benefits was, however, giving birth to a number of quite dangerous tendencies. These seeds, if left to grow unchecked, would produce, it seemed to me, a steady lowering of the intellectual level of society with no conceivable limit, and this would bring in its train the mores of materialism and,

finally, universal slavery. I thought I saw that mankind was moving in this direction, and I viewed the prospect with terror." Quoted in André Jardin, *Tocqueville: A Biography* (New York: Farrar, Straus and Giroux), 273.

207. Ibid, 6–7.

208. Peter Augustine Lawler, "Introduction" in *Democracy and Its Friendly Critics*, ed. Peter Augustine Lawler (Lanham, MD: Lexington Books, 2004), ix. "Tocqueville holds up a mirror to liberal democracy, and the image we see there has plenty of warts. But the hand that holds the mirror plainly belongs to a friend." Benjamin Storey, "Tocqueville on Technology," *The New Atlantis*, Fall 2013, https://www.thenewatlantis.com/publications/tocqueville-on-technology.

209. Quoted in *The Tocqueville Reader: A life in Letters and Politics*, eds. Olivier Zunz and Alan S. Kahan (Malden, MA: Blackwell, 2002), 219–20. Compare Tocqueville's "instincts" with those of his cousin (by marriage), René de Chateaubriand: "Democrat by nature, aristocrat by culture, I would quite willingly abandon my fortune and my life to the people, provided I had little to do with the mob." Quoted in Jean-Claude Lamberti, *Tocqueville and the Two Democracies*, trans. Arthur Goldhammer (Cambridge, MA: Harvard University Press, 1989), 264, n48.

210. Tocqueville, *Democracy*, 674–5.

211. Nietzsche, *Beyond Good and Evil*, 155.

212. Friedrich Nietzsche, *Twilight of the Idols* in *The Portable Nietzsche*, trans. Walter Kaufmann (New York: Penguin Books, 1982), 538–9.

213. "*Judge not.*—When considering earlier periods of history one must take care not to fall into an unjust condemnation of them. The injustice involved in slavery, the cruelty involved in the subjugation of persons and nations is not to be measured by our own standards. For in those days, the instinct for justice had not yet been so far developed. Who dare reproach the Genevan Calvin for having burned the physician Serveto? It was a consistent action that flowed from his convictions, and the Inquisition too was equally justified; only the views that then predominated were false and led to consequences that seem to us harsh because those views have become alien to us. And what, in any event is the burning of a single body compared with everlasting punishment in Hell for almost everybody!" Friedrich Nietzsche, *Human, All Too Human*, trans. R. J. Hollingdale (New York: Cambridge University Press, 2000), 54.

214. Friedrich Nietzsche, "On the Uses and Disadvantages of History for Life" in *Untimely Meditations*, trans. R. J. Hollingdale (New York: Cambridge University Press, 1997), 107–8.

215. Tocqueville, *Democracy*, 6.

216. Those excesses inhere in the very nature of democracy, an insight that was always central to Tocqueville's teaching. Curiously, in their fine introductory and interpretative essay, "The Third Democracy: Tocqueville's Views of America after 1840," Aurelian Craiutu and Jeremy Jennings are struck by the emphasis Tocqueville placed on the excesses of democracy in his later correspondence, an excess that contrasts sharply, in their view, with the stability of America's democracy that he highlighted in his earlier writings, particularly *Democracy in America*. But in Tocqueville's mind, that stability was anomalous and depended on the exceptional circumstances that America found herself in. America's stability did not result

from weeding out the excesses of democracy, but from keeping them at bay. From a Tocquevillian perspective, there is nothing remarkable about America's instability in the decade leading up to the Civil War. Indeed, Volume 1 of *Democracy in America*—the rosier of the book's two volumes, in which Tocqueville discusses the absence of great statesmen in America, tyranny of the majority, and "the most dreadful of all the evils that threaten the future of the United States" (namely slavery) (326)—anticipates such instability. Granted, with respect to democracy, slavery is an aberration and abomination. But the point still stands that the excesses of democracy are intrinsic to democracy, a verity Tocqueville apprehended in the 1830s and not for the first time in the final decade of his life. What renders Craiutu and Jennings' initial surprise all the more curious is that they seem to acknowledge as much later in their essay, where they list "four important conclusions" that Tocqueville drew in *Democracy in America*. The first is that "the instincts and passions of democracy ought to be constantly moderated and held in check because *democracy goes hand in hand with materialism, the tyranny of the majority, rampant individualism, and centralization.*" Aurelian Craiutu and Jeremy Jennings, "The Third Democracy: Tocqueville's Views of America after 1840" in *Tocqueville on America After 1840: Letters and Other Writings* (New York: Cambridge University Press, 2009), 28, 35 [emphasis added].

217. Ethological missteps aside, it was clear what Nietzsche meant when he whispered to the conservatives: "today too there are still parties whose dream it is that all things might walk backwards like crabs. But no one is free to be a crab. Nothing avails: one *must* go forward...." Nietzsche, *Twilight of the Idols*, 546–7. Interestingly and problematically, Mark Warren characterizes Nietzsche's political philosophy as "neoaristocratic conservatism." Warren is right to note that Nietzsche's "views on social and political matters are conservative in definitive respects," including his mistrust of political revolutions, opposition to the leveling tendencies of modern society, and stress on the importance of culture and customs in binding peoples together. Mark Warren, *Nietzsche and Political Thought* (Cambridge, MA: The MIT Press, 1998), 211–3. But in the end, Nietzsche's thought was more destructive than conservative. Destructive conservatism might be a more apt characterization of Nietzsche's political philosophy, one that points to the paradoxical nature of his philosophy and his task. When speaking of himself and his "children of the future," there is no irony or ambiguity to be found in the following declaration: "We 'conserve' nothing; nor do we want to return to any past periods." Nietzsche, *The Gay Science,* trans. Walter Kaufmann (New York: Vintage Books, 1974), 338. As Michael Allen Gillespie notes, Nietzsche's "task . . . was nothing less than the revaluation of all values, the complete transformation of European civilization." As Nietzsche "came to realize . . . to give birth to a new Europe, the old Europe had to be destroyed." ("If a shrine is to be set up, a *shrine has to be destroyed*: that is the law." Nietzsche, *Genealogy of Morality* (65–6).) That is a task that cannot be reconciled with conservatism, however one wishes to qualify it. Michael Allen Gillsepie, *Nietzsche's Final Teaching* (Chicago: University of Chicago Press, 2017), ix.

218. Nietzsche, *Human, All Too Human*, 376.

219. Ibid, 376–7.

220. Ibid, 377.

221. This truth often is lost on those who rely on Nietzsche's so-called middle period (*(Human, All Too Human, Daybreak*, and the first four books of *The Gay Science*) to render Nietzsche's thought compatible with democracy. David Owen, for example, cites Section 293 of *The Wanderer and His Shadow* ("Ends and Means of Democracy") as being a "positive articulation of [Nietzsche's] commitment to democracy." David Owen, "Nietzsche, Ethical Agency and the Problem of Democracy" in *Nietzsche, Power, and Politics: Rethinking Nietzsche's Legacy for Political Thought*, ed. Herman W. Siemens and Vasti Roodt (Berlin: De Gruyter, 2008), 159. It is true that on its own, the section suggests Nietzsche is favorably disposed toward democracy, but to deduce from it any meaningful commitment to democracy on Nietzsche's part is unconvincing. One just as easily could present Marx's condemnation of capitalism for putting an end to the "idyllic relations" that prevailed in the feudal era as evidence of his commitment to feudalism. It is not just "Nietzsche's own hostility to democracy in his later works" (Owen, 166) that makes this commitment to democracy untenable. Even in his middle and early periods, Nietzsche reaches a number of conclusions that simply cannot be reconciled with a commitment to democracy. It ought to suffice to adduce his benign and often favorable pronouncements regarding slavery. (Consider, for example, the "cruel-sounding truth" that he affirms in no uncertain terms: "*slavery belongs to the essence of culture.*" "The Greek State" in *Prefaces to Unwritten Works*, trans. and ed. Michael W. Grenke (South Bend, IN: St. Augustine Press, 2005), 48.) A reflexive adherence to independence leads Owen and other agonistic democrats (e.g., William Connolly, Bonnie Honig, and Alan Schrift) astray on this matter. In their view, democracy is good and Nietzsche thinks it is good, because, in his words, it "wants to create and guarantee as much independence as possible" (*Human, All Too Human*, 384). But for Nietzsche, "Independence is an issue that concerns very few people:—it is a prerogative of the strong" (*Beyond Good and Evil*, 30). Indiscriminatory independence of the sort that democracy promises is a symptom of decline; it "is one more proof of the degeneration of the instincts" (*Twilight of the Idols*, 546). And Nietzsche's posture on this is not confined to his later works. Thus, in the very same book that Owen relies on to demonstrate Nietzsche's commitment to democracy, one finds the following: "Subordination, which is so highly rated in the military and bureaucratic state, will soon become as unbelievable to us as the closed tactics of the Jesuits already are; and *when this subordination is no longer possible a host of the most astonishing operations will no longer be capable of achievement and the world will be the poorer*. It is bound to disappear because its foundation is disappearing: belief in unconditional authority, in definitive truth." (*Human, All Too Human*, 162) [emphasis added]. For a sound critique of contemporary "theoretical efforts to reconcile a radical Nietzschean *agon* with egalitarian political aspirations" (161–2), see Frederik Appel, *Nietzsche Contra Democracy* (Ithaca, NY: Cornell University Press, 1999), 159–70. See also Bruce Detwiler, *Nietzsche and the Politics of Aristocratic Radicalism* (Chicago: University of Chicago Press, 1990).

222. "The philosophers have only interpreted the world, in various ways; the point is to change it." Karl Marx, *Theses on Feuerbach* in *Karl Marx: Selected Writings*, 158.

223. Friedrich Nietzsche, *Thus Spoke Zarathustra* in *The Portable Nietzsche*, 129.

224. Ibid, 124. Gillespie shrewdly frames the last man in the context of the tightrope trope that Zarathustra pronounces in the prologue, where man is placed on an evolutionary continuum between ape and overman. "The last man thus is not the historically last man, the post-historical man that Hegel imagined, but the last man who is still man, that is, the last human possibility before the beast." *Nietzsche's Final Teaching*, 29.

225. Physically, Nietzsche suffered from, amongst other things, convulsive stomach pain, severe myopia, and crippling headaches. (In 1879 alone, he "experienced 118 days of severe illness—a 'lovely statistic', as he wryly commented to Elizabeth [his sister] on December 29.") David Farrell Krell and Donald Bates, *The Good European: Nietzsche's Work Sites in Word and Image* (Chicago: University of Chicago Press, 1997), 122. For an autobiographical account of his poor physical constitution see Friedrich Nietzsche, *Ecce Homo*, in *On the Genealogy of Morals and Ecce Homo*, trans. Walter Kaufmann (New York: Vintage Books, 1989), 221–5. For a biographical account, see, for example, Curtis Cate, *Friedrich Nietzsche* (London: Hutchinson, 2002). Cate provides the following illustrative and amusing anecdote: "Throughout the autumn and early winter of 1873 Nietzsche was almost permanently unwell, suffering not only from acute eye-aches every time he tried to read for more than an hour or two but also from nausea, stomach upsets and even vomiting—almost certainly due to his hyper-nervous condition in moments of difficult creativity. As his doctor friend, Professor Immermann, one day said to him, knowing in advance that it was an impossible prescription: 'Be more stupid and you will feel better'" (184). Regarding the psychological despair Nietzsche suffered, see, for example, his letter to Franz Overbeck on July 2, 1885, after completing the last part of *Thus Spoke Zarathustra*: "My 'philosophy', if I have the right so to call what mistreats me into the roots of my being, is *no longer* communicable, at least not by means of print. Occasionally I long to have a secret conference with you and Jacob Burkhardt, more to ask you how to avoid this distress than to relate news. . . . For me my life now consists in the *wish* that all things may be *different* from how I grasp them; and that someone would make *my* 'truths' unbelievable to me." Quoted in Karl Löwith, *Nietzsche's Philosophy of the Eternal Recurrence of the Same*, trans. J. Harvey Lomax (Berkeley: University of California Press, 1997), 193.

226. See, for example, the end of the Second Essay of the *Genealogy of Morality*, where Nietzsche proclaims that "the *redeeming* man . . . of the future [who] will redeem us from . . . nihilism . . . [and give] earth its purpose and humans their hope again . . . *he must come one day*" (66–7).

227. See, for example, *Ecce Homo*, 331. On Nietzsche's use of the word "nausea" more broadly, see Gudrun Von Tevenar, "Nietzsche on Nausea," *Journal of Nietzsche Studies*, vol. 50, No. 1 (Spring 2019), 58–78.

228. For a sense of the gravity that Nietzsche ascribed to the death of God (and not just His death, but His murder), as well as his prescience regarding the incongruous insouciance with which news of this portentous deed—"there has never been a greater"—would be received, see his celebrated parable, "The Madman" in *The Gay Science*, 181–2.

229. "Democracy is nonnegotiable, because it is triumphant; one could perhaps moderate its effect on the political level, but within its own principles, and not in recourse to opposite principles." François Furet, "The Intellectual Origins of Tocqueville's Thought," *The Tocqueville Review* 7 (1985/1986): 122.
230. Nietzsche, *Genealogy of Morality*, 34.
231. Nietzsche, *Zarathustra*, 315.

Chapter 2

Aristocratic Man

More than two centuries out from the great democratic upheavals that cleaved history, people today are far removed from the aristocratic age that preceded the age of democracy. This distance is exacerbated by the historical myopia that afflicts the futurally oriented, as the democratically inclined congenitally are. Access to that bygone world tends to be limited to the works—monumental, literary, artistic, and so on—that survived and captured it. While much can be observed through those windows, one should guard against reducing aristocratic man to the sumptuousness of his appetites or the splendor with which he surrounded himself. Of greater consequence, at least for present concerns, are the values that sustained his world and separated it from all peripheral ones. In his valuations and devaluations, aristocratic man distinguished himself from other human types, a phenomenon symptomatic of man vis-a-vis beast, for it is precisely as a creature that values that man sets himself apart.

> Verily, men alone gave themselves all their good and evil. Verily, they did not take it, they did not find it, nor did it come to them as a voice from heaven. Only man placed values in things to preserve himself—he alone created a meaning for things, a human meaning. Therefore he calls himself "man," which means: the esteemer.[1]

Valuing is part of the essence of life. "When we speak of values, we speak with the inspiration, with the way of looking at things, which is part of life: life itself forces us to posit values; life itself values through us when we posit values."[2] But while humans alone esteem, what they hold in esteem varies considerably across time and space.

> No people could live without first esteeming; but if they want to preserve themselves, then they must not esteem as their neighbor esteems. Much that was good to one people was scorn and infamy to another. . . . Much I found called evil here, and decked out with purple honors there. Never did one neighbor understand the other: ever was his soul amazed at the neighbor's delusion and wickedness.[3]

The rich heterogeneity of man is rooted in this distinctly human attribute, which is why no other species exhibits commensurate diversity. The diversity that does exist among animal species is determined naturally by geography, climate, and related environmental factors and while those factors have affected the development and diversification of man, that development and diversification is not reducible to those factors. The Mediterranean world in the fifth-century BC, for example, was dotted with distinct peoples whose interests, behaviors, beliefs, politics, and so forth, were appreciably different from one another. Had the Spartans and Athenians been more undifferentiated, presumably the peoples of that world would not have sown the seeds of their own demise by waging a decades-long war of attrition. Still, Athens and Sparta belonged to a broader culture and shared enough in common to put their differences aside and band together for the purpose of repelling the Persians,[4] whose own values were markedly unlike those of the Greeks. Today, in spite of veritable differences, Nordic countries and Lowland ones share enough in common to legitimate their inclusion in a union that—owing to a want of commonality—excludes the Eurasian behemoth, to say nothing of the Asian one. Those who count themselves as members of democratic, pluralistic societies, are likely to enjoy a greater sense of kinship among themselves than they would with those who live in societies colored by the Koran or Confucianism. Different peoples have their own tablets of good and evil, but there sometimes exists concord between them so that one can speak of something like Greek values or, in an even broader manner, aristocratic or democratic ones.

It would be difficult to overstate the importance of values to Nietzsche's philosophy. Perhaps the safest summation of Nietzsche's monumental philosophic endeavor can be deduced from the title he occasionally appended to his projected (but never realized) magnum opus: *Revaluation of Values*.[5] In the words of Nietzsche's Zarathustra: "The greatest events—they are not our loudest, but our stillest hours. Not around the inventors of new noise, but around the inventors of new values does the world revolve; it revolves *inaudibly*."[6] Nietzsche undoubtedly understood himself as such an inventor,[7] as one who would posit new values and help create a new tablet of good and bad and, in doing so, provide humanity what it heretofore had been lacking: a goal.[8] He would do what all genuine philosophers do and cannot but do—fashion the world in his own image.⁹ In revaluating the values that inhered in the Western tradition, particularly those that reposed in Athens and Jerusalem (Platonism and Platonism for the people, i.e., Christianity),¹⁰ Nietzsche aimed to forestall the denouement that mankind had been hurtling toward since the time of Copernicus,¹¹ when the highest values would devalue themselves,¹² the esteemer would cease to esteem, and "the nut of existence"—like man himself—would become "hollow."¹³

Tocqueville's ambitions were comparatively modest. He was more inclined to safeguard the Western tradition than overturn it; to preserve rather than uproot the values that stemmed from it. Though he almost certainly would have found many of Nietzsche's ideas abhorrent, he would have appreciated the prominence that Nietzsche assigned to the role of values in directing—or misdirecting—the destiny of man. Tocqueville's approach was similarly normative.¹⁴ The natural sciences have a great deal to say about what human beings are, but they cannot make sense of them essentially. Man is more than the mere sum of his physical parts, as Tocqueville aptly illustrated in *Democracy in America* in a wonderful footnote on Plymouth Rock:

> This rock has become an object of veneration in the United States. I have seen fragments of it carefully preserved in several towns of the Union. Does this not show very clearly that *the power and greatness of man is wholly in his soul*? Here is a stone that the feet of some miserable persons touched for an instant, and this stone becomes celebrated; it attracts the regard of a great people; they venerate its remnants, they parcel out its dust in the distance. What has become of the thresholds of so many places? Who cares about them?¹⁵

By imbuing the world around him with value, man distinguishes himself from beast. By establishing what should inspire reverence and what should arouse revulsion, humans distinguish themselves from one another.

At the risk of oversimplifying the matter, the role of values in Nietzsche's thought is paralleled by that of mores in Tocqueville's.

> I understand here the expression *moeurs* in the sense the ancients attached to the word *mores*; not only do I apply it to mores properly so-called, which one could call habits of the heart, but to the different notions that men possess, to the various opinions that are current in their midst, and to the sum of ideas of which the habits of the mind are formed.
>
> I therefore comprehend under this word the whole moral and intellectual state of a people.¹⁶

Tocqueville was not unmindful of the role that material forces played in directing the destinies of peoples any more than Nietzsche was.¹⁷ But people are shaped more by their mores than their physical surroundings. "One of the great general causes to which the maintenance of a democratic republic in the United States can be attributed"[18] is the mores of its people—mores unshared by the indigenous peoples who were displaced by the expansion of that republic. While the natural largess of the New World was integral to the stunning success of the Anglo-Americans, clearly that largess is not enough to account for it, seeing that the same natural bounty was at the disposal not only of the Native Americans but of other Europeans who had established footholds in the New World and did so, moreover, in advance of the English. It was not for opportunity that the French and Spanish were wanting.

As this might suggest, distinctions in mores often have a national basis. But on a deeper and broader level, one could speak of aristocratic and democratic mores. By appreciating the different tablets of good that hang over the aristocratic and democratic worlds, by examining the values and mores that circumscribe their horizons, one is better able to appreciate the animating impulses of each and to espy what the predominance of one (at the expense of the other) might spell for mankind. This sort of approach may be thought repugnant in the age of democracy, seeing that it rests on an anachronistic conceit, namely that there exists a substantive distinction between types of human beings. What likely will only serve to compound that repugnance is that the approach implicitly entertains the prospect that the mores that undergird the world of inequality may have value, and even more value, than those that undergird the world of equality. But on both scores, Nietzsche and Tocqueville do more than merely intimate as much. And given their uncanny ability to descry the distempers of democracy, dismissing them out of hand, however unpalatable their positions may be, would be unwise.

In light of the democratic prejudices that permeate the age, it would be fruitful to temper the anti-aristocratic sentiments that accompany them. Again, one should guard against inferring from the sumptuous appetites and extravagant fashions of the aristocracy that prodigal frivolity was its hallmark. To be sure, those appetites and fashions are at some level reflections of the values of its people (as appetites and fashions tend to be), but ultimately they are tangential phenomena and any effort to arrive at an understanding of the nature of the aristocratic world by means of them is liable to yield a gross mischaracterization of that world.

Similarly, the impulse to see aristocratic man as some malicious, merciless master also should be guarded against. The aristocratic soul is no more a bastion of cruelty than the democratic soul is one of kindness. That the aristocracy was capable of being ruthless and depraved is not a matter of dispute. But ruthlessness and depravity are human attributes and not—in any meaningful or definitive sense—aristocratic ones. If the crimes and ravages of the lower orders are less prominently on display in the annals of history, it can be explained in no small part because their dramas unfolded on a less prominent stage. At the very least, faith in the inherent goodness of "the people" should be obsolete in a world that has survived the horrors of the twentieth century—a century that, to a much greater extent than any that preceded it, belonged to them.[19]

Inhumanity may be endemic to humanity, a deep-seated trait that is alien to no man, be he of the aristocratic or democratic stripe. But human mastery—the mastery of others by others—is another matter. The desire, the capacity, the duty to rule others (in addition to oneself) is a distinctly aristocratic quality, a verity displayed in the order of rank that inheres necessarily in every aristocracy and of which democracy is so proudly devoid. This is not simply the logical result of being in power or, to put it differently, the case of might making right, but rather emanates from the very nature of aristocratic man. Presumably, in any given political order, there are rulers and ruled; those who command and those who obey—an elemental truth that Marxists struggled in vain to get their collective heads around. But the members of a genuine aristocracy are, definitionally, the best,[20] and their elevation is one that is evident not only to themselves but to the lower orders they lord over. What Chester Starr observed of ancient Greek aristocrats could be said of aristocrats simply: "They . . . had no doubt that they were the most important element in society and established its attitudes and values[. . . and] their claims normally were accepted, even cherished, by other, lower classes."[21]

This is antithetical to the spirit that animates democracy, where those who rule are elected and not destined to do so. It would not be inappropriate here to rehash the ancient critique of democracy that the people put in power by the unwise tend themselves to be unwise. But that critique is of no consequence in the age of democracy from which an order of rank, and the wise and the best with it, has been banished. No person, let alone a group of persons, is considered the better of another. People may be different, but the value of each is equivalent.

Laudable or not, the absence of an order of rank defies not only human history but human nature as well. Man the esteemer, the measure and measurer of all things, has distinguished himself from beast through his capacity to discriminate, to determine what has value and what does not. This distinction is lost in a world where one person's estimations cannot be counted higher or lower than another's. To maintain that every viewpoint is of equal value is to concede that every viewpoint is equally valueless. Aristocratic man posited values that reflected his own worth, that were emanations of his own strength, and that redounded to the glory of man as a whole. The noble ennobled. In the age of democracy, it is the many, not the few, who rule, and their strength inheres in numbers. The values of the multitude tend not only to be motley and cacophonous but also self-devaluing. Part of this stems from the contingency of those values. In an aristocratic age, values are fixed. They are grounded firmly in some authority, such as tradition, family, custom, or providence. The right of those who rule and the values they embody are questioned neither by the ruler nor the ruled. In democratic times, there is no authority. Or rather, the only authority is the people themselves. But people tend to be fickle, not firm. Democratic values are rootless and in flux. What is more, value—the ability *to* value—depends on an ability to discriminate. But discrimination is anathema to democratic man. Those who aspire to and demand greatness do not equate what is great with what is not. The inequality and intolerance that this mindset invites has no place in the democratic age where like and unalike are treated alike. While democratic man maintains that his indiscrimination is a mark of progress, it would be reasonable to counter that without discrimination there can be no progress. Without the impulse to assert his greatness, not only with respect to other beings but to his fellow ones as well, man would have remained sub-human.

This claim has an unmistakably Hegelian ring to it, and it is one that Nietzsche advocates without equivocation. With regard to the dawn of man, there is a congruity between the Master/Slave Dialectic and Nietzsche's hypothesis on the primordial founding of the state. According to Nietzsche, the origin of the "bad conscience"[22] is located in "the most fundamental of all changes which [man] ever experienced—that change whereby he finally found himself imprisoned within the confines of society and peace."[23]

> The first assumption in my theory on the origin of bad conscience is that the alteration was not gradual and voluntary and did not represent an organic assimilation into new circumstances, but was a breach, a leap, a compulsion, an inescapable fate that nothing could ward off, which occasioned no struggle, not even any *ressentiment*. A second assumption, however, is that the shaping of a population, which had up till now been unrestrained and shapeless, into a fixed form, as happened at the beginning with an act of violence, could only be concluded with acts of violence—that consequently the oldest "state" emerged as a terrible tyranny, as a repressive and ruthless machinery, and continued working until the raw material of people and semi-animals had been finally not just kneaded and made compliant, but *shaped*.

Nietzsche is quick to hammer home the violent nature of man's birth:

> I used the word "state": it is obvious who is meant by this—some pack of blond beasts of prey,[24] a conqueror and master race, which, organized on a war footing, and with the power to organize, unscrupulously lays its dreadful paws on a populace which, though it might be vastly greater in number, is still shapeless and shifting. In this way, the "state" began on earth: I think I have dispensed

with the fantasy which has it begin with a "contract." Whoever can command, whoever is a "master" by nature, whoever appears violent in deed and gesture—what is he going to care about contracts! Such beings cannot be reckoned with, they come like fate, without cause, reason, consideration or pretext, they appear just like lightning appears, too terrible, sudden, convincing and "other" even to be hated. What they do is to create and imprint forms instinctively, they are the most involuntary, unconscious artists there are:—where they appear, soon something new arises, a structure of domination that *lives*, in which parts and functions are differentiated and related to one another, in which there is absolutely no room for anything that does not first acquire "meaning" with regard to the whole.[25]

While the desire for recognition is not explicitly included among their motives, Nietzsche's primeval masters impose their worldview on their hapless subjects, assigning "a 'meaning' to everything in relation to the whole." Moreover, as with the Hegelian masters who initiate the dialectic of history and spawn humanity, their founding act is one of unmitigated force and violence. The contractual and consensual foundation of political society touted by the early moderns is conspicuously absent from Nietzsche's (and Hegel's) teachings. But there, in the dawn of history, the remarkable confluence of their ideas ends. On the movement, to say nothing of the goal of history, Nietzsche and Hegel are worlds apart. This is evident from the simple fact that for Nietzsche, there is no directionality to history, and certainly not a progressive one. But with respect to the elemental nature of man, the natural-born masters of Nietzsche's philosophy are not tragic figures mired in some existential impasse, as they are in Hegel's. Their reign may have ended, but their defeat was not fated. The equating of that defeat with progress is the mark of a tendentious and hubristic mind that presents history as an irresistible movement that culminates in those who presently pen it. Still, Nietzsche does not lament the going under of that originary master race. Those unconscious artists are not human paragons whose return Nietzsche conspired to bring about. It remains one of the more common misperceptions of Nietzsche that his aim was to supplant the age of Christian morality with one of godless immorality where cruelty was counted a virtue of the highest order and the lives of the people were ruled mercilessly by "some pack of blond beasts."[26] Though austere and decidedly inegalitarian, the members of Nietzsche's future aristocracy bear little resemblance to those who comprised that original ruling class, not least because the born organizers of the future will be endowed with a profound sense of the very thing those born organizers of yore knew nothing of: responsibility.[27]

It would be misleading to paint the original founders of the "state" as aristocrats, but two points should be borne in mind. First, their rule is natural.

Equality is something unnatural, a fabrication that is superimposed upon mankind only at a very late date. What is more, these masters not only rule by nature, but in doing so, they give form to a world that ever had been formless. Beings without direction, without purpose, without coherence, are suddenly organized into a larger whole and compelled to work toward something beyond what nature originally prescribed. Clearly, that was not what those instinctual masters set out to do, but their giving form and meaning to a world that knew neither was a manifestation of their own strength and not only a manifestation, but an affirmation as well. These are attributes that, while sublimated, inhere in aristocratic man. Second, without this ineluctable disaster that defied the organic rhythm that had characterized life heretofore, man would have remained sub-human. Had there never appeared those who command by nature, who were violent in act and being, man never would have evolved beyond his semi-animal condition. Axiomatically, enslavement offends the modern conscience, but without enslavement, there would have been no modern conscience; humans would have remained directionless and incoherent; that is, they would have remained sub-human. Without the inhumanity of slavery, there would be no humanity.[28] ("How much blood and horror lies at the basis of all 'good things'!"[29]) It is a claim that jibes not only with the thought of Hegel but that of Tocqueville as well.

Tocqueville's own musings on the origins of society bear the palpable impress of Rousseau.[30] In keeping with the general thrust of early modern thought, Tocqueville speculates that humans initially were pre-social. By nature, man is an apolitical animal. When humans left the forest and assembled for the first time, they did so

> not to enjoy life but in order to find the means of living. The object of their efforts is to find a refuge against the intemperance of the seasons and sufficient nourishment. Their imaginations do not go beyond these goods, and if they obtain them without exertion, they consider themselves satisfied with their fate and slumber in their idle comfort.[31]

During this "first age of societies," humans have "very few desires [and] feel hardly any needs but ones analogous to those of animals."[32] They sustain themselves solely through hunting and as a result lead a largely nomadic life.

What separates this earliest stage from the next is the discovery of agriculture. With that, people settle the land and take possession of it. And with the acquisition of property comes a condition that had been previously unknown to humans: inequality.

> While men were wanderers and hunters, inequality was unable to insinuate itself among them in any permanent manner. There existed no outward sign which

could permanently establish the superiority of one man and above all of one family over another man or family; and this sign, had it existed, could not have been transmitted to his children. But from the moment that landed property was recognized and men had converted the vast forests into fertile cropland and rich pasture, from this moment individuals arose who accumulated more land than they required to feed themselves and so perpetuated property in the hands of their progeny. Henceforth abundance exists; with superfluity comes the taste for pleasures other than the satisfaction of the crudest physical needs.
The origins of almost all aristocracies should be sought in this social stage.[33]

Tocqueville's account man's inception clearly lacks the bellicosity that inheres in Nietzsche's (and Hegel's as well). Though he does not speak of perfectibility or an innate sense of pity, Tocqueville's first humans resemble Rousseau's, in that for both thinkers, humans by nature are equal, placid, and virtually indistinguishable from the animals with which they coexist. In the beginning, life was idyllic. Even the transition from a nomadic world to an agricultural one appears to be organic, in stark contrast to the sudden and terrible violence that, on Nietzsche's telling, brought about the first settlement of man and overturned the untold ages that preceded it. But differences aside, Tocqueville and Nietzsche are in agreement that regardless of the sequence of events that resulted in the rule of some over others, without it, man forever would have remained a dumb brute. Equality is rudimental, a condition that is suitable for the sub-human. It is inequality that has distinguished and elevated man. As a goal then, equality very well may be a sign of regress, not progress.

This insight controverts the teachings of the early moderns and calls into question their respective remedies to the political problem. If equality and freedom are natural to the human condition, it really only applies in the case of the prehuman or subhuman condition. To find a political order with the aim of restoring or preserving that natural equality is, if not to return man to an earlier stage, to restore those conditions that obtained prior to the development of man's higher faculties, which is precisely what Nietzsche avers and Tocqueville, at the very least, apprehends. In some ways, this substantiates Rousseau's own musings on the political problem. Rousseau, who thought the state of nature proposition through to its logical conclusion—that is, to its beginning—realized that Hobbes and Locke's natural man bore too many of the trappings of civilized man. By nature, man is pre-rational and pre-social; he is sub-human. From this premise, Rousseau might have argued that using man's natural condition as a signpost to which modern man should look would be foolish, for notwithstanding the freedom and equality he enjoyed in his natural state, the being that existed before the advent of society was something fundamentally different from the being that emerged after it. No doubt, civilized man might have much to learn from his natural precursor, just as the seasoned adult might have much to learn from the unschooled child. But to suggest that the latter should somehow be the standard of measure for the former would appear to be a perversion of logic. For Rousseau, however, civilized man is a perversion of natural man. A civilized man never could return to his natural state, but he could fashion society so that it would approximate those conditions that had been lost to him since exiting the state of nature, thereby allowing him to meet the demands of his better, that is, original nature and the demands of the civil society to which he belongs and—save for those rarest of cases—cannot do without. In short, man could not reclaim his natural goodness, but that did not mean he could not become good.

Rousseau's egalitarianism had its exceptions, most notably with respect to the lawgiver who founds society and the solitary walker who flees it. But these exceptions did nothing to arrest or temper the ever-advancing drive for greater and greater equality, as the many revolutions that bear Rousseau's impress attest.[34] Rousseau accelerates the movement of modernity and thereby consigns—unwittingly, it would seem—solitary walkers to the dust heap of history. Why one ever appears upon life's stage is no doubt a mystery, but perhaps inequality is one of the preconditions for that appearance. The homogenization that modern thinkers courted, Rousseau not least among them, precludes, ironically, Rousseau and his ilk.

This apprehension is shared by both Nietzsche and Tocqueville.[35] In their minds, the democratization of man augurs a day when mankind will cease to advance in any meaningful sense of the word. To those who inhabit the present age, an age in which astounding leaps in science and technology are so routine that they no longer astound, this apprehension likely appears absurd to the point of being risible. But the question that always ought to attend such progress is, to what end? Both enthusiasts and skeptics alike would agree that the goal is to relieve man's estate[36] and approximate heaven on earth, thereby concretizing a world where evils such as pain, suffering, conflict, inequality, and the like have no place. Whether such aspirations are realizable is open to question. But supposing they were (and if they are not, it certainly will not be for want of trying), the consummation of the modern longing would do away with the very conditions necessary for man's higher development. That creature that had once been suspended between beast and God would cease to exist, not because he had ascended and approached the latter, but because his wants would be reducible to the former.[37]

If inequality is a necessary condition for the development of man's higher faculties, it is hardly a sufficient one. Inequality is not so much a virtue in itself as it is a precondition without which there can be no virtue. It does not signify to aristocratic man what equality signifies to democratic man: a sacrosanct good and end in itself. Rather, it is taken as a given, as a fundamental fact of life, and as part of the natural order that reflects the hierarchical character of the world that hierarchical beings inhabit.

But if inequality inheres necessarily in all aristocracies, it does not follow that every regime founded on inequality is an aristocracy. There are, after all, oligarchies and tyrannies, which should not be conflated with aristocracies, however, inclined the democratic mind may be to do so. And even regimes that extol equality and ostensibly are devoted to the actualization of it, often not only rest upon, but ruthlessly uphold, the most flagrant inequalities.[38] What distinguishes aristocratic man from other types is that he values something ineffable, something that is irreducible to material want and utilitarian longing. Above comfort, wealth, and privilege he prizes what distinguishes man, not only from other creatures but from his fellow ones as well. In doing so, he preserves the distance between man and man and not only safeguards what is highest in him, but moreover fosters its growth and perpetuation. "Every enhancement so far in the type 'man' has been the work of an aristocratic society—and that is how it will be, again and again."[39] This is a distinctly Nietzschean sentiment, one to which Tocqueville by and large subscribes.[40]

Nietzsche located the paragons of the aristocratic spirit in ancient Greece. Unlike some of Nietzsche's other youthful enthusiasms (e.g., Wagner and Schopenhauer), his reverence for "the best turned out, most beautiful, most envied type of humanity to date"[41] never waned. From his first work to his last, Nietzsche's veneration for that extremely rare model of a race and culture that had *become* pure[42] is unmistakable.

The root of that veneration, as well as the affirmational bent of his overall philosophy, can be traced back to his first book, *The Birth of Tragedy*. As he later observed in the 1886 preface, it was in the pages of that "arrogant and wildly enthusiastic book"[43] that

> he had placed the great question mark concerning the value of existence. Is pessimism *necessarily* a sign of decline, decay, malformation, of tired and debilitated instincts—as was the case among the Indians and appears to be the case amongst us "modern men" and Europeans? Is there a pessimism of *strength*? An intellectual preference for the hard, gruesome, malevolent and problematic aspects of existence which comes from a feeling of well-being, from overflowing health, from an *abundance* of existence? Is there perhaps such a thing as suffering from superabundance itself? Is there a tempting bravery in the sharpest eye which *demands* the terrifying as its foe, as a worthy foe against which it can test its strength and from which it intends to learn the meaning of fear?[44]

Nietzsche's answer concerning the value of existence is of consequence not only for an understanding of the tragic Greeks, but more broadly and foundationally, for that of aristocratic man. In descrying the origins of Greek tragedy, Nietzsche affirms that there is, in fact, a pessimism of strength, and that out of an overflowing health and a fullness of existence, a people can possess "an intellectual preference for the hard, gruesome, malevolent and problematic aspects of existence." That the Greeks harbored such predilections is disclosed in a myth about Silenus, the companion and tutor of Dionysus.

> An ancient legend recounts how King Midas hunted long in the forest for the wise *Silenus* . . . but failed to catch him. When Silenus has finally fallen in to his hands, the King asks what is the best and most excellent thing for human beings. Stiff and unmoving, the daemon remains silent until, forced by the King to speak, he finally breaks out in shrill laughter and says: "Wretched, ephemeral race, children of chance and tribulation, why do you force me to tell you the very thing which it would be most profitable for you *not* to hear? The very best thing is utterly beyond your reach: not to have been born, not to *be*, to be *nothing*. However, the second best thing for you is: to die soon."[45]

As the legend divulges, "the Greeks knew and felt the terrors and horrors of existence,"[46] and the "hidden ground of suffering and of knowledge,"[47] upon which it rested; and it was thanks to their experience of the Dionysian that they acquired such wisdom.

This wisdom did not come naturally to the Greeks, who were, Nietzsche contends, traditionally Apollinian. Each the son of Zeus, Apollo and Dionysus embodied divergent elements that engendered antagonistic impulses. Apollo, the sun god, in whom the Greeks "expressed the joyous necessity of dream-experience," is

> the god of all image-making energies, [and] also the god of prophecy. According to the etymological root of his name, he is the "luminous one," the god of light; as such, he also governs the lovely semblance produced by the inner world of fantasy. The higher truth, the perfection of these dream-states in contrast to the only partially intelligible reality of the daylight world, together with the profound consciousness of the helping and healing powers of nature in sleep and dream, is simultaneously the symbolic analogue of the ability to prophesy and indeed of all the arts through which life is made possible and worth living. But the image of Apollo must also contain that delicate line which the dream-image may not overstep if its effect is not to become pathological, so that, in the worst case, the semblance would deceive us as if it were crude reality; his image must include that measured limitation, that freedom from wilder impulses, that wise calm of the image-making god.[48]

Through the destruction of this repose, one comes to apprehend the essence of the Dionysian rapture. In contrast to his half-brother, Dionysus, the god of wine, inspires a state of intoxication and ecstasy wherein subjectivity dissolves[49] and the savagery that inheres in nature is unleashed.[50] Whereas Apollo embodies the realm of dreams, inspiring a self-restraint that is expressed artistically in sculpture, (Doric) architecture, and poetry, Dionysus embodies the realm of intoxication, inspiring a state of ritual madness where the individual is rent from the protective boundaries that help sustain the social order and delimit his place in it. Man feels himself united not only with his fellow beings, but with the whole of nature which, having "become alienated, inimical, or subjugated, [now] celebrates once more her festival of reconciliation with her lost son, [man]. Freely, the earth offers up her gifts, and the beasts of prey from mountain and desert approach."[51] This ecstatic state is exteriorized in dance and music, which, with its "emotional power of tone ... uniform flow of melody; and ... utterly incomparable world of harmony" confounds the measure of the Apollinian norm. "In the Dionysiac dithyramb man is stimulated to the highest intensification of his symbolic powers; something that he has never felt before urgently demands to be expressed: the destruction of the veil of maya, one-ness as the genius of humankind, indeed of nature itself. The essence of nature is bent on expressing itself." For this expression, "a new world of symbols" is needed.[52]

In those fits of madness, people unite in orgiastic festivals where all societal norms are dissolved. These festivals (Dionysia) were

> often characterized by ritual license and revelry, including reversal of social roles, cross-dressing by boys and men ... drunken comasts in the streets, as well as widespread boisterousness and obscenity ... The god's dark side emerged in rituals and aetiological myths concerned with bloodshed, madness and violence, flight and persecution, and gender hostility (as during the Agrionia).[53]

For some time, the Greeks were able to shield themselves from "these feverish excesses which must have reached them by every known land and sea route. What kept Greece safe was the proud, imposing image of Apollo, who, by holding up the head of the Gorgon to those brutal and grotesque Dionysian forces, subdued them." The Greeks preserved their spirit by honoring "the most Greek of Greek gods";[54] that "ethical divinity [who] demands measure from all who belong to him and, so that they respect that measure, knowledge of themselves."[55]

All this contrasted sharply with the license that was embodied in the Dionysian rapture. The grotesque and paroxysmal exhibitions of their barbaric neighbors were at first incomprehensible to the Greeks. "The dithyrambic servant of Dionysus can only be understood only by his own kind! With what astonishment the Apolline Greeks must have regarded him!" But through repeated encounters, these bizarre rituals became more and more familiar and the Greeks found themselves unable to ignore the "horror of realizing that all this was not so foreign to them after all, indeed that their Apolline consciousness only hid the Dionysiac world from them like a veil."[56]

> The Apolline Greek, too, felt the effect aroused by the *Dionysiac* to be "Titanic" and "barbaric"; at the same time, he could not conceal from himself the fact that he too was related inwardly to those overthrown Titans and heroes. Indeed he was bound to feel more than this: his entire existence, with all its beauty and moderation, rested on a hidden ground of suffering and knowledge which was exposed to his gaze once more by the Dionysiac. And behold! Apollo could not live without Dionysos! The "Titanic" and "barbaric" were just as much of a necessity as the Apolline![57]

What is remarkable is not simply that the Apollinian Greeks grasped the inherent Dionysian aspect of life (with its perennial cycle of death and rebirth and eternal substratum of chaos) nor that they embraced the Dionysian spirit rather than toil pertinaciously to keep it at bay, but that in incorporating it, they transformed it into something without peer or precedent. Rather than surrender to the Dionysian excesses as their neighbors had done or ward them off outright as the Spartans had done,[58] they appropriated the Dionysian spirit and sublimated it. Nietzsche calls the pacification of the Dionysian frenzy "the most important moment in the history of the Greek cult." And it is precisely this wedding of the Dionysian and Apollinian that accounts for "the immense gap which separates the *Dionysian Greek* from the Dionysian barbarian." The latter, who ritualistically reverted to "the condition of tigers and monkeys"[59] signified a retrogression of sorts, a return to a primordial age when man had not yet distinguished himself from beast. But in the hands of the Greeks, the Dionysian signified something quite different: "by a metaphysical miracle of the Hellenic 'Will', they [the Dionysiac and Apolline] appear paired and, in this pairing, finally engender a work of art which is Dionysiac and Appoline in equal measure: Attic tragedy."[60]

The birth of tragedy was a singular event; a peerless development by a peerless people, one that helps illumine the underlying character of aristocratic man.[61] Exposure to Dionysian delirium had brought with it the wisdom of Silenus—that at the bottom, nature is eternal, indifferent, and meaningless and that man is an "ephemeral wretch, begotten by accident and toil" whose existence has no higher meaning nor underlying significance. The opening to Nietzsche's *On Truth and Lie in the Extra-Moral Sense* imparts the sense of horror that must accompany this epiphany.

> In some remote corner of the universe, poured out and glittering in innumerable solar systems, there once was a star on which clever animals invented

knowledge. That was the highest and most mendacious minute of "world history"—yet only a minute. After nature had drawn a few breaths the star grew cold, and the clever animals had to die.

One might invent such a fable and still not have illustrated sufficiently how wretched, how shadowy and flighty, how aimless and arbitrary, the human intellect appears in nature. There have been eternities when it did not exist; and when it is done for again, nothing will have happened. For this intellect has no further mission that would lead beyond human life. It is human, rather, and only its owner and producer gives it such importance, as if the world pivoted around it. But if we could communicate with the mosquito, then we would learn that it floats through the air with the same self-importance, feeling within itself the flying center of the world. There is nothing in nature so despicable or insignificant that it cannot immediately be blown up like a bag by a slight breath of this power of knowledge.[62]

In the throes of the Dionysian rapture, man is shielded from the nothingness upon which existence—not just his own, but all existence—rests. Intoxicated beyond all measure, he dwells entirely in the moment—in an eternal now—heedless of what came before and what lies ahead. He is reduced to an animal that lacks the very qualities that distinguish man from the beast (foresight, reason, restraint). Perhaps it is in such frenzied stupors that happiness lies, but such excess cannot be endured indefinitely. What is more, if it is happiness that consumes man in such states, it is no human happiness. Whether beastly or divine, it is unfit for man. When "the rapture of the Dionysian state with its annihilation of the ordinary bounds and limits of existence" passes, as it must, man views his "everyday reality" with "nausea." Nietzsche likens the Dionysian man to Hamlet:

> both have gazed into the true essence of things, they have *acquired knowledge* and they find action repulsive, for their actions can do nothing to change the eternal essence of things; they regard it as laughable or shameful that they should be expected to set to rights a world so out of joint. Knowledge kills action; action requires one to be shrouded in a veil of illusion—this is the lesson of Hamlet, not that cheap wisdom about Jack the Dreamer who does not get around to acting because he reflects too much, out of an excess of possibilities, as it were. No, it is not reflection it is true knowledge, insight into the terrible truth, which outweighs every motive for action, both in the case of Hamlet and in that of Dionysian man. Now no solace has any effect, there is a longing for a world beyond death, beyond the gods themselves; existence is denied, along with its treacherous reflection in the gods or in some immortal Beyond. Once truth has been seen, the consciousness of it prompts man to see only what is terrible or absurd in existence wherever he looks; now he understands

the symbolism of Ophelia's fate, now he grasps the wisdom of the wood-god Silenus: he feels revulsion.[63]

The Greeks overcame this nausea with the aid of that "saving sorceress with the power to heal," art[64]—and more specifically, Attic tragedy. At the heart of Greek tragedy stood the satyr chorus. The satyr as it was conceived originally should not be confused with the romanticized depiction of him in modern times. He was not some hirsute flute-playing shepherd; nor was he, at least in Nietzsche's rendering, little more than a lascivious animal. Rather, he was "the archetype of man, the embodiment of his highest and most intense emotions."[65] The chorus acted as a sort of intermediary between the twice-born god and the audience that beheld him, and provided a metaphysical solace that at the bottom, "despite all changing appearances, life is indestructibly mighty and pleasurable."[66] Greek tragedy, "which discharges itself over and over again in an Apolline world of images,"[67] is ultimately the affirmation of life, replete with all its terror and meaningless suffering. The Greeks overcame the nihilistic underpinnings of existence not by denying them nor by striving to correct or escape them, but by embracing, and thereby, affirming them.

Perhaps nowhere is this better exemplified than in "the most suffering figure of the Greek stage, the unfortunate *Oedipus*."[68] Guilty of incest and patricide, Oedipus is an abomination that breaches the very foundations of the social order. What culture could look upon a person who violated its most sacred norms and not be consumed by loathing and disgust? Yet, in the minds of the Greeks, Oedipus was a noble figure whose heinous misdeeds did not merit his anathematization. Though the enormity of those crimes could permit no exculpation or even extenuation, they did not overshadow outright the good—paradoxical, to be sure—that Oedipus effected and the gratitude that was owed to him. The Greeks grasped that there was something gruesomely unnatural about the wisdom of Oedipus and for that matter, wisdom in general: "'The sharp point of wisdom turns against the wise man; wisdom is an offense against nature': such are the terrible words the myth calls out to us."[69] Therein lies the paradoxical nature of wisdom: man's elevation rests on dreadful contraventions of the natural order, the gravity of which can be gleaned from the proportionally appalling punishment those misdeeds demand. Oedipus, diviner of the Sphinx, whose indefatigable pursuit of the truth exposed his hideous transgressions (patricide and incest) and impelled him to gauge out his own eyes, evoked neither pity nor indignation nor a sense of resignation and despair among the Greeks. Instead, a very different lesson was divined: "The noble human being does not sin, so this profound poet [Sophocles] wants to tell us; every law, all natural order, indeed the moral world may be destroyed by his actions, yet by these very actions a higher, magical circle of effects is drawn which found a new world on the ruins of the old one that has been overthrown."[70]

The Greeks were not without an idea of progress,[71] but it was modest when compared with modern man's obstinate faith in it. What is more, for the ancients progress did not depend on the mastery and possession of nature upon which the modern project so squarely rests. Whereas modern progress points to a world without suffering, in the mind of the Greeks, the very price for progress is suffering. "Humanity achieves the best and highest of which it is capable by committing an offence and must in turn accept the consequences of this, namely the whole flood of suffering and tribulations which the offended heavenly powers *must* in turn visit upon the human race as it strives nobly towards higher things."[72] Prometheus's theft was a profanation, the severity of which was evinced by the ghastly comeuppance that was meted out to him. But the Promethean gift was one for which humans owed eternal gratitude and without which they never would have attained the heights that they have.[73] Man's elevation and privileged position presupposes a contravention of the natural order. Without transgressing nature, man would remain a beast among beasts. But it is because he violates the natural order and defies the gods that he must be punished. The ostensible indifference of life, the asperity of the gods, the perennial aguish that is man's inescapable lot—all is justified in man's providential fate. "'All that exists is just and unjust and is equally justified in both respects'."[74] It is not resignation and despair that life's interminable trials and tribulations invite, but joy and gratitude. The Greeks affirmed life for what it was—as that which continually overcomes itself.[75]

This spirit of affirmation was marvelously embodied in the Olympian deities, whom the Greeks birthed "from a most profound need." Having fathomed "the terror and horror of existence," the Greeks—"so sensitive, so vehement in [their] desires, so singularly capable of *suffering*"—"interpose[d] between [themselves] and life the radiant dream-birth of the Olympians." To share this existence—not an other-worldly one, but one emphatically of *this* world—with their gods permitted the Greeks to suffer the metaphysical horrors and terrors of life and, what is more, to do so cheerfully.

> Thus gods justify the life of men by living it themselves—the only satisfactory theodicy! Under the bright sunshine of such gods existence is felt to be worth attaining, and the real *pain* of Homeric man refers to his departure from this existence . . . so that one might say of them, reversing the wisdom of Silenus, that "the very worst thing for them was to die soon, the second worst ever to die at all." If a lament is ever heard, it sings of the short-lived Achilles, of the generations of men succeeding one another like leaves on the trees, of the demise of the heroic age. It is not unworthy of the greatest hero to long to go on living,

even as a day laborer. So stormily does the "Will," on the level of the Apolline, demand this existence, so utterly at one with it does Homeric man feel himself to be, that even his lament turns into a song in praise of being.[76]

The gods of Olympus constituted an aristocracy that stood above the people of Hellas but not beyond them. They coexisted, inhabiting the same order like "two castes [that] lived side by side, a nobler and mightier and one less noble; but both somehow belong together in their origins and are of *one* species, they have no need to be ashamed of one another. That is the element of nobility in Greek religiosity."[77] The Greeks felt themselves ennobled by the presence of the Olympic deities, but it was really they who ennobled their gods: those gods were merely the manifestations and exemplifications of their own grandeur.

> In the Greeks the "Will" wanted to gaze on a vision of itself as transfigured by genius and the world of art; in order that the Will might glorify itself its creatures too had to feel themselves to be worthy of glorification; they had to recognize a reflection of themselves in a higher sphere without feeling that the perfected world of their vision was an imperative or a reproach. This is the sphere of beauty in which they saw their mirror images, the Olympians. With this reflection of beauty the Hellenic "Will" fought against the talent for suffering and for the wisdom of suffering which is the correlative of artistic talent; as a monument to its victory, Homer stands before us, the naïve artist.[78]

In their affirmation and ennobling of life, the Greeks constitute paragons of the aristocratic spirit.

The root of that spirit is brought to light in Nietzsche's attempt to determine the value of morality and, more specifically, the origin of good and evil. This undertaking, which first began with *Human, All Too Human*, later bore fruit in *On the Genealogy of Morality*. The aim, as announced in the preface to that polemic, was to journey through "the vast, distant and hidden land of morality" which meant, "*discovering* this land for the first time"[79] for heretofore, a history of morality had been found wanting. That land had remained shrouded in the past because the few thinkers prior to Nietzsche who ever thought to search for it had all floundered on account of a shared defect, what Nietzsche calls the *family failing of philosophers*:

> All philosophers have the common failing of starting out from man as he is now and thinking they can reach their goal through an analysis of him. They involuntarily think of "man" as an *aeterna veritas*, as something that remains constant in the midst of all flux, as a sure measure of things. Everything the philosopher has declared about man is, however, at bottom no more than a testimony as to

the man of a *very limited* period of time. Lack of historical sense is the family failing of all philosophers.[80]

According to Nietzsche, the only ones who have attempted "so far to write a history of the emergence of morality" were the English psychologists. Scarcely inclined to laud anything English, Nietzsche here contests the charge that these psychologists, so fond of "pushing the *partie honteuse* [shameful parts] of [man's] inner world to the foreground," are little more than "boring frogs crawling around men and hopping into them" as though the human soul were but a swamp to which they naturally belonged. Instead, Nietzsche suggests that "these analysts holding a microscope to the soul are actually brave, generous and proud animals" who do not shrink from discovering the truth about man no matter how "plain, bitter, ugly, foul, unchristian [and] immoral" those truths may be.[81] But these saving graces notwithstanding, the English psychologists suffer the same condition that congenitally afflicts all philosophers: "the *historical spirit* itself is lacking in them."[82]

This lack can be gleaned from their abortive attempts to grasp how "the concept and judgment 'good'" originated. According to their "moral genealogy," the concept good finds its origin in those *unegoistic* actions that proved *useful* not for those who performed the action, but for those who were affected by it. The goodness of hospitality, for example, is determined by the stranger who benefits from it, not the host who extends it. In time, the reasons for esteeming these actions were forgotten, but because the habit of esteeming them remained, humans came to equate good with unegoistic so that unegoistic actions were felt to be good—"as if they were something good *as such*." Such genealogical explanations betray the prejudices of those who propound them. There is an unmistakably democratic, utilitarian, and, in short, English, bent to them. And they bear the imprint of that "fixed idea" that is nigh ubiquitous in the modern age: "the prejudice which takes 'moral', 'unegoistic', and '*désintéressé*' as equivalent terms."[83] In such logic, one can detect that congenital failing of philosophers: the measure of all things is *modern* man.

Nietzsche rightly regards this hypothesis as historically untenable. For one, the utilitarian spirit cannot be squared with the aristocratic one, in that an aristocracy is concerned above all else with the good of the few, not the many. The noble pursue their own good for their own sake, not selfishly or atomistically, but as members of a privileged group that embodies what is good and strives to preserve and cultivate it. If those who do not belong to that group benefit from those actions, that is an ancillary effect, not the principal objective of those actions. Indeed, one would be hard pressed to adduce a single aristocratic ethos in which the concept of utility enjoyed any particular prominence. It is hardly a matter of coincidence that as a school of thought, utilitarianism was not firmly established until the nineteenth century, when the democratization of man was well underway and, for all intents and purposes, a fait accompli.

To appreciate just how inconsonant utility is with classical virtue, one need only append it to the four cardinal virtues: wisdom, courage, moderation, and justice.[84] Obviously, courage can have useful consequences for others (in a phalanx, a courageous hoplite would be more useful than a craven one, not only to the other members of the phalanx, but also to the members of the city-state those hoplites were protecting), but on the classical understanding, the value of courage was ultimately relational to oneself. It was an integral part of a healthy soul in that the other virtues could not be sustained without it. And that ever was the primary aim—virtue or human excellence. To the extent that utilitarianism can get on without virtue, it is emphatically unaristocratic. One might frame the matter differently by wondering, in light of that emblematically modern and utilitarian equation—the greatest happiness for the greatest number—what the happiness of others is to the Homeric hero who risks his life in combat for *his* personal glory.[85]

None of this necessarily refutes the proposition that the origin of the good, found in those unegoistic actions that were reckoned good in the minds of those to whom they were done, was at some point forgotten, while the actions themselves continued to be esteemed. But it is not clear why the reasons for esteeming those actions would have been forgotten when the utility of those actions is ever apparent, as "a permanent part of our everyday experience." Equating the good with the useful, as Herbert Spencer did, would be more reasonable, although—according to Nietzsche—no more true.[86]

What is more, the very notion that the value of good originated with those to whom goodness was done stems from a modern bias regarding all questions of origin. It betrays a democratic conceit that Nietzsche gainsays elsewhere, namely that values are determined *reactively* rather than *actively*. This prejudice is especially prevalent in the realms of history and morality, but also in the ostensibly objective "fields [of] natural science and physiology,"[87] noticeably in the case of Darwinism and the outsized evolutionary role it ascribes to adaptation. But values, Nietzsche argues, were posited actively, not reactively. The concept of good was not determined by someone's reaction to external stimuli, but rather was an outgrowth of one's own strength, an affirmation of one's sense of power and all that flowed from it. According to Nietzsche's origin of the state and by way of extension, humankind, man was actively, albeit not consciously, shaped into the being that he is. Those natural born masters—forces of nature that appeared without reason, consideration, or pretext—happened upon a nebulous horde of semi-animals that they remorselessly worked until they were "not only thoroughly kneaded and pliant but also formed." Not only did such beings have no need for contracts, but it also follows that they did not need the semi-animals they acted upon to establish what was and was not good. (If the English approach were true, lions ought to be vegetarians.) Rather they themselves determined what was good, and did so not by sacrificing the ego, but by imposing it on others over and over and over again. Value was determined by those in power, not those who obeyed; by those who acted, not those who were acted upon.

> It has been "the good" themselves, meaning the noble, the mighty, the high-placed and the high-minded, who saw and judged themselves and their actions as good, I mean first-rate, in contrast to everything lowly, low-minded, common and plebeian. It was from this *pathos of distance* that they first claimed the right to create values and give these values names: usefulness was none of their concern! The standpoint of usefulness is as alien and inappropriate as it can be to such a heated eruption of the highest rank-ordering and rank-defining value judgments: this is the point where feeling reaches the opposite of the low temperatures needed for any calculation of prudence or reckoning of usefulness—and not just for once, for one exceptional moment, but permanently. The pathos of nobility and distance, as I said, the continuing and predominant feeling of complete and fundamental superiority of a higher ruling kind in relation to a lower kind, to those "below"—*that* is the origin of the antithesis "good" and "bad."[88]

Nietzsche's argument rests not only on demonstrating the untenability of the English genealogy but on establishing an etymological foundation for his own. By examining "the terms for 'good', as used in different languages . . . from the etymological point of view," Nietzsche discovered that "they all led . . . back to the same *conceptual transformation*—that everywhere, 'noble', 'aristocratic' in social terms is the basic concept from which, necessarily, 'good' in the sense of 'spiritually noble', 'aristocratic', of 'spiritually highminded', 'spiritually privileged' developed: a development that always runs parallel with that other one which ultimately transfers 'common', 'plebeian', 'low' into the concept 'bad'."[89] The concept of good results from an affirmation of the ego, not its denial. Those who ruled felt themselves to be good. The good was a reflection of their own merit and it was only after the concept had been established that the concept bad was created—as sort of an afterthought. Their natural supremacy elevated them far above the common kith and "from this *pathos of distance* . . . they first claimed the right to create values and give these values names." It is in that distance between man and man that the value of man in general finds its origins. The measure of man—and therewith of all things—is derived from human inequality. Or to put it differently, where equality prevails, there can be no measure.

Nietzsche concedes that "in most cases," the etymological origins of the words show that those who ruled "might give themselves names which simply show superiority of power (such as 'the mighty', 'the masters', 'the commanders') or the most visible sign of this superiority, such as 'the rich', 'the propertied.'"[90] While such cases do not controvert the "affirmational" character of the aristocratic spirit, they do little to validate the claim that that spirit undergirds what is distinct to and loftiest in man. After all, a lion in charge of a pride might—were it capable—designate himself "master" and "possessor." Or to speak of one who is capable, the despotic man, concerned above all else with the aggrandizement of his own power, might describe himself in such a manner.

But Nietzsche is quick to adduce words that display a far more nuanced tenor; words that do not merely convey a superiority of force or possessions, that is, phenomena that can be explained on the level of animality (inasmuch as animals distinguish themselves by their physical prowess or the territory they command), but rather convey a *"typical character trait"* that distinguishes man not only from animal but from his fellow man as well. Thus "the Greek nobility, whose mouthpiece is the Megarian poet Theoginis," call themselves the "truthful" suggesting that they possess or reflect reality, that they are the repository of truth. Truth and nobility were conflated so that the noble-born were distinguished from the *lying* common man, that is, those who somehow signified a diminution or perversion of reality. Nietzsche points out that in the Greek words *kakos* and *deilos*, cowardice is emphasized, in contradistinction to the Greek *agathos*. The well-born are good because they are brave, while the ill born are bad because they are wanting in bravery. With the Romans, Nietzsche traces the origin of the word good (*bonus*) back to the word for war (*duonus*), thereby showing "what made up a man's 'goodness' in ancient Rome."[91]

Such examples help to substantiate Nietzsche's point that "the noble mode of valuation . . . acts and grows spontaneously" as an affirmation of the natural world by those who felt themselves and their actions to be good. Those whom nature endowed with greater strength, health, power; whom nature, in effect, selected to predominate, in turn, affirmed the natural order by deeming good those things that reflected the goodness of nature and designating bad those things that were found deficient. Health and those who possess it are good; lack of health and those who lack it are bad. Such a mode of valuation, Nietzsche maintains, exhibits a greater degree of veracity and honesty than the reactionary mode because the measure of things relates to the world as it is. The noble did not invent an idea of happiness that they then aspired to achieve, but rather felt themselves to be happy and on the basis of that feeling fashioned a concept that reflected the goodness they felt. The value of good was rooted in and mirrored the natural order of things. It was created, but it was not created *ex nihilo*. Nature was its foundation. Those whom life affirmed, in turn, affirmed life.

As for the opposite realm, it is true that the aristocracy is apt to misunderstand those excluded from its ranks. But when the aristocratic mind errs in this regard, it displays neither mendacity nor malice. There is something superficial, even insouciant, about its misjudgments.

> When the noble method of valuation makes a mistake and sins against reality, this happens in relation to the sphere with which it is *not* sufficiently familiar, a true knowledge of which, indeed, it rigidly resists: in some circumstances, it misjudges the sphere it despises, that of the common man, the rabble; on the other hand, we should bear in mind that the distortion which results from the feeling of contempt, disdain and superciliousness, always assuming that the image of the despised person is *distorted*, remains far behind the distortion with which the entrenched hatred and revenge of the powerless man attacks his opponent—in effigy of course. Indeed, contempt has too much negligence, nonchalance, complacency and impatience, even too much personal cheerfulness mixed into it, for it to be in a position to transform its object into a real caricature and monster.[92]

Again, in its origin, the concept of bad is but an afterthought. Those who rejoice in the goodness of life do not dwell on its shortcomings. The object of the aristocratic man's contempt—in this case, the common man—is of fleeting concern. Objectionable as this may be to modern sentiments, exaggerating aristocratic man's lack of compunction would be unwarranted. In that harsher and earlier age, the oppressed were rendered fit for oppression, not by the aristocracy, but by nature. The baseness of the common man did not result from the aristocrat's debasement of him; rather that baseness preceded the judgment and, for that reason, merited it. The common man did not have to be made contemptible, he was found contemptible and he was contemptible because he lacked those qualities that made one good.

In assigning a value to things, aristocratic man establishes an order where hitherto there was none. To overstate the significance of this would be difficult. "The seigneurial privilege of giving names even allows us to conceive of the origin of language itself as a manifestation of the power of the rulers: they say 'this *is* so and so', they set their seal on everything and every occurrence with a sound and thereby take possession of it, as it were."[93] If what separates man from brute is the possession of speech or reason, then it is to aristocratic man, or at least his harbinger, that humanity owes its distinction. The advent of a mode of valuation wherein the ideas of good and, tangentially, bad were formed would constitute a signal moment that was at once natural and without precedent. In that event, by virtue of the gifts that nature bestowed on some, man would have become something different, something unknown, something without equal. A creature that esteems, that creates values—to do justice to such a spectacle "a divine audience was needed."[94]

It ought to go without saying that the values of the ruling class were *their* values, ones that glorified and perpetuated their privileged position and did so at the expense of all those who could not distinguish themselves in a world ordered thus. (The democratic mode of valuation would reverse this.) To the extent that the undistinguished possessed any value at all it was because the ruling class assigned a value—if only a negative one—to them. "Base people *were* only what they were *considered to be* . . . the only value the base person attributes to himself is the one his masters have attributed to him (creating values is the true *right of masters*)."[95] The world established by the masters was a world of intolerance and exploitation—qualities that, to varying degrees, inhere in all aristocratic orders and, as Nietzsche stresses, in all orders simply. But for aristocratic man, those qualities are not virtues or ends in themselves. As stated above, intolerance is not exalted in aristocratic orders the way that tolerance is in democratic ones. Intolerance comes naturally and, one might add, rightfully, to those whom nature has favored. As a discerning palate will not tolerate unpalatable foods, a discerning person will not tolerate unpalatable poltroons. To do otherwise would be to contravene the natural order and offend good taste. To Nietzsche's point, intolerance and exploitation are necessary to the operation of life and not just the operation, but its advancement well.

> Life itself is *essentially* a process of appropriating, injuring, overpowering the alien and the weaker, oppressing, being harsh, imposing your own form, incorporating and at least, at the very least, exploiting . . . Even a body within which . . . particular individuals treat each other as equal (which happens in every healthy aristocracy): if this body is living and not dying, it will have to treat other bodies in just those ways that the individuals it contains *refrain* from treating each other. It will have to be the embodiment of will to power, it will want to grow, spread, grab, win dominance,—not out of any morality or immorality, but because it is *alive*, and because life *is* precisely will to power.[96]

Decent denizens of the democratic age look back upon the past and behold something monstrous: a pitiless world that teems with intolerance, inequality, oppression, exploitation, and the like. But Nietzsche's argument is that it is the world in which those qualities have been removed (to the extent that they can be) that is monstrous and aberrational. Nietzsche suggests that the corrupt society is not the one in which exploitation inheres, but the one where the exploitative element has been removed, should such an exploit be possible. "'Exploitation' does not belong to a corrupted or imperfect, primitive society: it belongs to the *essence* of being alive as a fundamental organic function; it is a result of genuine will to power, which is just the will of life."[97]

What is also vital to keep in mind is that the aristocratic order does not suppress the lower order purely for the sake of doing so. It is true that the aristocratic class seeks to maintain its power, and to preserve the order that it established and that redounds to its advantage (as any ruling class, whether it be of the few or the many, does). But for aristocratic man, the end is not merely the maintenance of power (which could be said of the despotic man), but the preservation and propagation of what is noble. And so it has been that

> every enhancement so far in the type "man" has been the work of an aristocratic society—and that is how it will be, again and again, since this sort of society believes in a long ladder of rank order and value distinctions between men, and in some sense needs slavery. Without the *pathos of distance* as it grows out of the ingrained differences between stations, out of the way the ruling caste maintains an overview and keeps looking down on subservient types and tools, and out of this caste's equally continuous exercise in obeying and commanding, in keeping away and below—without *this* pathos, that *other*, more mysterious pathos could not have grown at all, that demand for new expansions of distance within the soul itself, the development of states that are increasingly high, rare, distant, tautly drawn, and comprehensive, and in short, the enhancement of the type "man," the constant "self-overcoming of man" (to use a moral formula in a supra moral sense).[98]

The instrumentalization of the lower order by the upper was effected with an eye to cultivating man's loftier faculties. Nature, or necessity, demanded as much. A people whose days pass in unremitting toil will have no opportunity to develop those traits that are, from a purely evolutionary standpoint, superfluous, but are, from a spiritual or philosophic point of view, precisely what accounts for man's singularity. Where leisure is found wanting, there can be no refinement. But while refinement requires leisure, leisure does not guarantee refinement, as the modern age—where designs to maximize leisure and the utter disregard for refinement go hand in hand—makes plain. A noble aristocracy, as opposed to a decadent one, does not exist for the sake of leisure, but rather makes use of its leisure for the sake of attaining something higher, something nobler.[99]

Referencing the city-states of ancient Greece and Venice, Nietzsche observed that the aristocratic commonwealth was an arrangement for breeding—for breeding a human type that embodied what a given people held to be best in man. After a long struggle in unfavorable conditions, a certain human type emerges, one that does not just preserve itself but imposes itself.

A tremendous range of experiences teaches it which qualities are primarily responsible for the fact that, despite all gods and men, it still exists, it keeps prevailing. It calls these qualities virtues, and these are the only virtues it fosters.

A type whose traits are few in number but very strong, a species of people who are strict, warlike, clever, and silent, close to each other and closed up (which gives them the most subtle feeling for the charms and nuances of association) will, in this way, establish itself (as a species) over and above the change of generations. The continuous struggle with constant *unfavorable* conditions is, as I have said, what causes a type to become sturdy and hard.[100]

Exploitation was required for such breeding, as was intolerance, but they were means, not ends. And that end, to reiterate, was not self-preservation. As with utility, that is a very modern value, the elevation of which would have struck all genuinely noble people as being ignoble. One might reimagine the *Iliad* by making the desire for self-preservation the animating desire of its heroes to appreciate how irreconcilable that quintessentially modern longing is with the aristocratic ideal (and, one might add, with heroism simply). To be sure, every people seeks to preserve itself, but the aristocratic world was not ordered for that purpose. It reached for something higher, often in spite of what the desire for self-preservation would have it do. (From a self-preservational point of view, the Greek's ten-year siege of Troy was an exercise in madness.) The real danger for the aristocracy did not come with conflict and the risk of defeat, but from forsaking its higher purpose and the decline and fall that inevitably followed. The case of Rome is perhaps the most celebrated. A more recent and no less telling case concerns *la noblesse française* of the *ancien régime*.[101]

For navigating the precipitous fall of the French aristocracy, Tocqueville proves an indispensable guide. Born into the nobility on the threshold of its collapse, Tocqueville's attentiveness to the splendor of the nobility as well as the dissolution into which it lapsed is without peer. Rightfully immortalized for *Democracy in America*, Tocqueville's last and unfinished work, *The Old Regime and the Revolution*, regrettably does not receive the consideration it deserves. At the risk of doing injustice to a mind as capacious as Tocqueville's, the substance of his thought revolved around the democratization of man—the result of a protracted and providential process that could not be arrested but could be moderated, and it was to that end that Tocqueville devoted his intellective endeavors. His central concern was not democracy in America or aristocracy in France, but rather the ineluctable movement from a rigidly hierarchical world to a world no less rigidly bent on destroying all hierarchies. To the future his thought turned,[102] but his intellect obliged him to probe the past, for one does not make sense of where one is going without apprehending wherefrom one came. In order to grasp the democratic upheaval into which he had been thrown, his gaze stretched from horizon to horizon—from an old world that was irrecoverable to a new world that was irrevocable.

What makes Tocqueville such an indispensable guide is not only his profound and often uncanny perspicacity but his abiding sense of probity as well, which is all the more rare and precious in view of the subject matter. Revolutions invariably have their partisans; and the more divisive the revolution, the more divided the partisans. Between the nobleman wed to the old order and the everyman devoted to the new, little love has been lost. But the uncommon liberality of Tocqueville's spirit permitted him to do justice to both and perceive the injustice of each.

> [Some] absolutely want to make me a party man and I am not that in the least. . . . They alternately give me democratic or aristocratic prejudices; I perhaps would have had one set of prejudices or the other, if I had been born in another century and in another country. But the chance of birth has made me very comfortable defending both. I came into the world at the end of a long Revolution, which, after having destroyed the old state, had created nothing durable. Aristocracy was already dead when I started life and democracy did not yet exist, so my instinct could lead me blindly neither toward one nor toward the other. I was living in a country that for forty years had tried a little of everything without settling definitely on anything; therefore I was not susceptible to political illusions. Belonging to the old aristocracy of my homeland, I had neither hatred nor natural jealousy against the aristocracy, and that aristocracy being destroyed, I did not have any natural love for it either, since one only attaches oneself strongly to what is living. I was near enough to it to know it well, far enough away to judge it without passion. I would say as much about the democratic element. No family memory, no personal interest gave me a natural and necessary bent toward democracy. But for my part I had not received any injury from it; I had no particular motive for either loving or hating it, independent of those that my reason furnished me. In a word, I was so thoroughly in equilibrium between the past and the future that I felt naturally and instinctively attracted toward neither the one nor the other, and I did not need to make great efforts to cast calm glances on both sides.[103]

Tocqueville's calm is especially invaluable today, centuries removed from the collapse of the *ancien régime*, when—on the question of equality—the partisan divide has been, for all intents and purposes, effaced, not because the partisanship on both sides has been tempered, but because the partisans on one side have been all but disposed of.

To the victors in this struggle, pause is not the sort of thing to be readily given, but Tocqueville perceived what appears to be lost on those who have won the day: one cannot duly comprehend the emerging democratic order without paying heed to the aristocratic order it overturned. Democracy signifies a repudiation of the aristocratic world and a proscription of the inequality that was integral to it. The people, in whose name and for whose sake democracy exists, embody values that diverge sharply from those that belonged to the aristocracy. Without having probed the aristocratic soul whose obsolescence had been fated, only a narrowness of mind could permit one to equate democracy with progress. Tocqueville appreciated this as much as anyone; so much in fact, that although he garnered consolation from the idea that democracy was more pleasing in the eyes of God, he could not simply equate humanity's democratization with progress. The passing of the aristocratic world, and aristocratic man with it, could not but be mourned by those who not only fathomed the inimitable glories of that world but recognized what conditions—or preconditions—were needed to bring them about. If the *ancien* order was irretrievably lost, if there was no returning to the past, it did not follow that admiration for that order had no place in the democratic age. On the contrary, so important was such an appreciation that without it, the democratic future could afford little more than small comfort(s).

Tocqueville was no philologist. That he was a philosopher is open to debate.[104] His treatment of the aristocratic order displays neither the breadth nor depth of Nietzsche's, though that owes more to the prodigious reach of Nietzsche's mind than the limitations of Tocqueville's. Nonetheless, their insights display considerable congruity with respect to the character of aristocratic man and, as will be seen later, his democratic successor as well. Both understood that the democratization of humanity did not just signify the emergence of a new political order, but a new human type and that this passage from old to new betokened a constitutional transformation of man—a transformation that captivated and disconcerted both thinkers. It was on the foundations of the aristocratic world that man rose to the heights that he did and the dismantling of that world very well could spell the demise of all that was lofty and noble in man. Moreover, Tocqueville provides a sensitivity that oftentimes is found wanting in Nietzsche's thought. If Nietzsche's musings on the aristocratic world tend toward mastery, power, intolerance, exploitation, cruelty, and so forth, Tocqueville's, while not ignoring such phenomena, underscore the moral principles that reposed in the aristocratic world, not only with respect to how they shaped the character of those who occupied its upper echelons, but how they impacted the lower orders that the nobility—the repository of those principles—lorded over. It would seem Tocqueville's aristocratic birth fostered in him a sympathy for the nobility, including its *noblesse oblige*, in a manner or to a degree that Nietzsche was not privy to.[105]

Like Nietzsche, Tocqueville understood aristocratic man as a glorified type, one that transcended the mere animality that abides in the human breast and, by virtue of doing so, elevated not only himself but all mankind. The aristocratic class "naturally conceives a high-minded idea of itself and of man. It willingly imagines glorious enjoyments for him and fixes magnificent goals for his desires." In extolling the aristocratic mindset, Tocqueville harbored no illusions about the severity that it was capable of nor the intolerance that was endemic to it. But while such features were not to be ignored or taken lightly, they should not eclipse the no less veritable truth that born from intolerance, cruelty, and exploitation, was a sublimity that distinguished man from all other creatures—himself included. As Tocqueville went on to note:

> Aristocracies often do very tyrannical and very inhuman deeds, but they rarely conceive base thoughts, and they show a certain haughty disdain for little pleasures even when they indulge in them; *this lifts all souls to a very high tone.* In Aristocratic times one generally makes for oneself very vast ideas of the dignity, power and greatness of man. These opinions influence those who cultivate the sciences as well as all others; they facilitate the natural spark of the mind toward the highest regions of thought and naturally dispose it to conceive a sublime and almost divine love of truth.[106]

Insofar as they partake of both the mundane and the divine, humans find themselves connected to, and hence suspended between, each. There is no divine spark in beast and no beast in God, but in man, both inhere. But humans can comport themselves in such a manner that they incline toward one end or the other so that they come closer to touching the divine or become more and more beastly. Aristocratic peoples, with their vast ideas of human greatness, facilitated the *natural* spark of the mind, encouraging it to ascend to the loftiest reaches. Thus, aristocratic man took considerable delight in theorizing, in exercising those faculties that distinguished man from beast and rendered him more accordant with the divine.

This is not to say that aristocratic man spurned praxis or contemned the pleasures of the body. As Nietzsche notes, "the chivalric-aristocratic value judgments are based on a powerful physicality, a blossoming, rich, even effervescent good health that includes the things needed to maintain it, war, adventure, hunting, dancing, jousting and everything else that contains strong, free, happy action."[107] Those predisposed for mastery delighted in physical strength and the exercise of it. The pleasures of the body were embraced, not eschewed. The Greeks, founders of the Olympics, extolled physical health and delighted in all sorts of athletic contests while flouting all that was unsightly and deformed.[108] But the end for aristocratic man was always something beyond physical pleasure or material comfort, whether it was glory or honor or virtue.[109]

Because the noble mind beheld human nature from an elevated vantage point, the lofty aspects of that nature enjoyed more prominence; what was base and common attracted little thought.[110] It is for this reason that aristocratic man preferred theory over practice and esteemed the pleasures of the mind and soul above those of the body. "There are," as Tocqueville notes, "several manners of studying the sciences."[111] The modern method, beginning most notably with Descartes and Bacon, has favored the practical side of science, making the mastery and possession of nature and the relief of man's estate its explicit and primary objectives. Such an approach would have struck those of a more aristocratic bent as being a perversion of science and an ignoble application of it. No doubt a science that prizes praxis can produce wonders that a more theoretically oriented science—such as existed in the classical world—never could envision, let alone affect, but the impulse to produce such wonders typically has little to do with wonder or any commensurately inspiring sentiment. Indeed, dispelling wonder from the world is, if not an express aim, then certainly a logical consequence of modern science. What one possesses and masters tends not to be an object or source of wonder.

In aristocratic times, those who "practice" science are motivated by an "ardent and inexhaustible love of truth" and derive pleasure from the mere pursuit and acquisition of knowledge without any regard for the practical application of that knowledge. Tocqueville draws attention to two thinkers—one ancient, the other early modern—who exemplify this spirit. In a passage that is at once panegyric and rueful, Tocqueville recalls a French thinker whose influence on his own thought was towering.[112]

> If Pascal had envisaged only some great profit, or even if he had been moved by the desire for glory alone, I cannot believe that he ever would have been able to assemble, as he did, all the powers of his intellect in order to better discover the most hidden secrets of the Creator. When I see him tear his soul away from the midst of the cares of life to tie it wholly to that search, prematurely breaking the bonds that hold it to the body, so as to die of old age before forty, I halt in bewilderment and understand that it is no ordinary cause that can produce such extraordinary efforts.[113]

Pascal's case is, in a manner of speaking, unorthodox. A child prodigy and mathematician of the first rank,[114] his brush with death resulted in a religious conversion after which the focus of his life became God, not science. Pascal was destined to be remembered as an uncommon thinker even if this conversion had not taken place, though it is not clear that his soul would have been riven in the manner that Tocqueville conveys. What is clear is that Pascal's understanding of science was aristocratic, in that he appreciated its fundamentally theoretical nature, or to put it differently, its practical limitations.[115]

A more mundane example of a mind that was anything but mundane is Archimedes, who in some ways epitomized "the learned of [aristocratic] times [who] are carried along toward theory" and who often "conceive an inconsiderate scorn for practice."[116] To bring this mindset to light, Tocqueville recounts a passage from the "Life of Marcellus" in *Plutarch's Lives*.

> Archimedes possessed so high a spirit, so profound a soul, and such treasures of scientific knowledge, that though these inventions [instruments of war] had now obtained him the renown of more than human sagacity, he yet would not deign to leave behind him any commentary or writing on such subjects; but, repudiating as sordid and ignoble the whole trade of engineering and every sort of art that lends itself to mere use and profit, he placed his whole affection and ambition in those purer speculations where there can be no reference to the vulgar needs of life; studies, the superiority of which to all others is unquestioned, and in which the only doubt can be whether the beauty and grandeur of the subjects examined, of the precision and cogency of the methods and means of proof, most deserve our admiration.[117]

"That," Tocqueville avers, "is the aristocratic aim of the sciences. . . . In Aristocratic centuries, enjoyments of the mind are particularly demanded of the sciences; in democratic, those of the body."[118] The aristocratic disposition naturally conduces to a loftiness of spirit and profundity of soul that no less naturally appear alien in democratic times, which is why Tocqueville feared that in those times, the inclination to venerate such loftiness and profundity, to say nothing of the capacity to sustain them, would become increasingly rare.

Naturally, this elevated disposition did not appertain merely to science, but to the entire worldview of aristocratic man. A fixed upper class that neither labored to achieve its wealth nor has any fear of losing it maintains "a sort of superb disdain for the little interests and material cares of life" and harbors "a natural grandeur of thought that their words and manners reveal."[119] As science in aristocratic ages tends to reflect man's higher nature, exhibiting a greater reverence for what is distinctly human (mind) than for what he shares in common with the beasts (matter), so too do the arts.

Thus, the painters of the Renaissance "ordinarily sought great subjects above themselves, or far from their times, that left a vast course to their imaginations." Their motive was not to depict life's prosaic moments, but its extraordinary ones; and not just depict them, but exalt them. In contrast, Tocqueville argues that the painters of his day were animated by a very different impulse. "Our painters often put their talent to reproducing exactly the details of the private life that they have constantly before their eyes, and they copy from all sides small objects of which they have too many originals in nature." Tocqueville does not dispute their talent: they succeeded marvelously in their endeavors, which, in their own way, surpassed the achievements of their Renaissance forebears. "[Jacques-Louis] David and his students" applied to the canvas not only their tremendous talent but their knowledge of human anatomy, which permitted them to paint the models before their eyes with striking precision. But their commitment to realism stunted their imagination. Raphael whose anatomic knowledge would have been found wanting by the standards of the nineteenth century, to say nothing of the twenty-first, did not aspire to merely delineate human physicality but to glorify it. "He wanted to make man something that was superior to man. He undertook to embellish beauty itself." In doing so, he bequeathed to humanity not an exact depiction of man, but an image of what he could and, one might contend, *ought* to be. Such art aims at elevating and glorifying man—there is "divinity in his works"—rather than merely portraying and explaining him.[120]

Without that loftiness of spirit, the aristocratic soul would cease to be aristocratic; indeed, it would, in time, simply cease to be. Or rather, it would become concretized and thereby, dehumanized; its bearer blind to its presence. In a world reduced to matter, what place is there for the immaterial? For the aristocratically inclined, whatever man and beast shared in common was of tangential import. Its commonness suggested as much. It was the ability to master and sublimate the natural drives, not to let them loose, that distinguished a man and set man apart. Restraint elevates and ennobles the human spirit; license debases and enslaves it. A celebration of what humans shared in common—with humans and animals alike—could not but result in the depreciation of man. For the glory of mankind reposed in and radiated from its pinnacles. Imposing and imperishable, those peaks stood as testaments to the heights that man could reach. By basking in their glory, the souls of those who never could ascend so high were lifted all the same. Those apogees of humanity not only rose far above the common lot but also stood few and far between. In the aristocratic mind, human greatness is ever the exception, never the rule.

No aristocracy was comprised exclusively of paragons, but as a rule, every aristocracy excluded the common from its ranks. This was true not only in terms of power, politics, and prestige, but in subtler ways relating to knowledge, art, and refinement. Thus science, for example, was the exclusive purview of the few, as the pursuit of it required leisure and aptitude, at least one of which the many tended to lack. It is true that in democratic times, science—at least the advanced pursuit of it—remains the purview of the few, as most remain incapable of comprehending its abstruse principles and arcane claims. But setting aside that in the modern age science is open to all, the fact remains that even those who have no capacity to pursue it still are shaped by its findings and privy to its discoveries; what is more, they accept what they learn—or are told rather—with sedulous credulity. In aristocratic times, science—and knowledge more generally—was not disseminated universally; it was not available to everyone. Nor for that matter was its impact felt by everyone; its purpose was not to satisfy the more pedestrian and vulgar aims of life or, to put it less caustically, to alleviate life's burdens. Science signified nothing to the common man, not only because he had no appreciation for or understanding of it, but because it had no bearing upon his existence. In the modern age, science bears upon everyone and, by subduing and manipulating the natural world, benefits everyone. In aristocratic times, science elevated only those who could pursue it—and those who could pursue it were decidedly few. And what it tended to elevate—to hark back to Tocqueville's earlier point—was the mind, not the body. Moreover, in modern times, the reign of science is so pervasive and absolute that even those who have virtually no comprehension of it cannot fail to apprehend its significance. Ignorance of the intricacies and complexities of modern science does nothing to attenuate the people's faith in science. Indeed, that ignorance is integral to their faith (and perhaps to faith simply). The authority of science is not to be questioned, not least by those who grasp so little of it. The mindlessness with which the refrain "trust the science" is parroted in the present age is a testimony to this. Science has displaced religion only to become a religion itself.

It bears repeating that in aristocratic times, it is not just affairs of the state that are administered by the few, but those of the mind as well. Intellectual and artistic standards are, like those who maintain them, elegant and elevated. Thus, the literature of "an aristocratic people in which letters are cultivated" must conform to fixed rules and principles that have been long and well established by the ruling class. These rules should not be conflated with the capricious decrees of modern-day totalitarian regimes. Reality is not procrusteanly contorted to conform to the reigning ideology.[121] Rather, a people that has never been preoccupied with material things will engender a literature that is rarified. Its writers will garner glory and fame, but never riches. Having passed their time in wealth, "they . . . naturally conceived a taste for studied enjoyments and a love of refined and delicate pleasures," which is reflected in their writings. "The least work will be groomed in its smallest details. . . . The spirit will always have a noble step . . . and writers will apply themselves more to perfecting than producing."[122] Writing is not an industry, but an art, in the truest and highest sense of the word. Because "readers are difficult and few,"[123] and because "everything is written for connoisseurs . . . the search for ideal beauty constantly shows itself."[124] This is manifested not only in the refinement of the written word but in the physical volumes that contained those words. Until the time of Guggenheim's invention, "books were rare and expensive and great difficulty was experienced in reproducing them and having them circulate."[125] Thus, (re)production tended to be limited to those writings exceptional enough to merit it. Indeed, this remained true even after the printing press was introduced.[126] What is more, the painstaking care with which books were assembled resulted in tomes of astonishing beauty, their outward splendor announcing the brilliance contained therein.[127]

In the age of democracy and moreover, mass production, where books are overproduced with little expense and in considerable excess so that everyone and anyone can find his or her way into print, the depreciation of the written word is inescapable. A book in aristocratic times possessed a weight, a measure, a value that finds no equivalent in the age of democracy. And this is not true merely of books and works of art, but of *les métiers en general*. The works produced by the artisans and the guilds to which they belonged take on an artistic quality in no small part because of the care and attention that went into producing them. Tocqueville observes that in "centuries of privilege . . . the exercise of almost all the arts becomes a privilege and that each profession is a world apart where not everyone is permitted to enter." A body of knowledge, perennially polished and perfected, is passed down among a select group from generation to generation; the members of that group, who comprise a given corporation, take extensive pride—"corporate pride"—in what they do. "In an industrial class of this kind, each artisan has not only his fortune to make but his status to guard." The artisan belongs to a corporation whose standards he must submit to and whose reputation he must uphold. It is not his private interest that governs, but rather the interest of the corporation and "the interest of the corporation is that each artisan produce masterpieces."[128]

Moreover, beyond corporate interest and pride, there is the interest of the buyer and in aristocratic ages, the buyer is sure to be possessed of great wealth and sophistication. "The men who compose [the aristocratic class] naturally draw from the superior and hereditary position they occupy the taste for what is very well made and very durable."[129] Demanding nothing less than perfection, the aristocratic buyer is "very difficult to satisfy" and because the artisan has no other market, he labors to do just that—satisfy. Objects of incomparable craftsmanship of the sort that are not likely to be replicated in an age of mass production and consumption are the result. "When it was only the rich who had watches, they were almost all excellent. Scarcely any but mediocre ones are made any longer, but everyone has one."[130]

The unequaled works—of art, literature, craftsmanship, and so on—that were produced in aristocratic times presupposed a world of unequals, where a select class strove to perpetuate the glory its members embodied. By its very nature, human distinction is reserved for the few. A titan enjoys no prominence in a world of titans. But in the aristocratic world, the divide that separated man from man was not only extensive, but it was also fixed. One was born noble, or one was not.[131] No doubt a consequence of this arrangement was that ignoble souls remained part of the nobility and noble ones were forever cut off from it—an unsavory and unjust reality of the aristocratic order, which Socrates seeks to remedy in the *Republic*.[132] But this injustice—a double injustice, perhaps (inequality and immobility)—should not blind one to the fact that every political order, however fair it purports to be, cannot root out injustice. One reason why is that every regime, whether aristocratic or democratic, rests on general rules. But there are always exceptions to those rules. That being the case, injustices of this sort tend not to be voluntary or rather, for their own sake. A progressive tax unjustly deprives some of their earnings but does so to affect what is presumed to be a more equitable distribution of wealth. A fixed aristocracy unjustly deprives some of the opportunity to enter into its ranks but does so to ensure that the very high standards it has cultivated will be preserved. Those standards were not established overnight; they were cultivated across untold generations. When ranks become confused, so too do the standards that distinguish high from low. The absence of high art—or the inability to distinguish high art from low—in the present age might serve to substantiate this verity.[133] "From the inaccessible heights to which it had withdrawn,"[134] an aristocracy jealously maintained the rank between man and man so as to better preserve the glory, not just of the few, but of all who fell within its embrace.

That fixity of the aristocratic order and the glory that radiated from it were reflected in the manners of its people, a topic that may seem trifling at first blush. But Tocqueville maintains that the value peoples attach to manners—"[people] become accustomed to everything except living in a society that does not have their manners"—renders them deserving of "serious examination."[135] While aristocratic manners at times could appear ridiculous, what they ultimately exhibited was "a natural grandeur of thought" that came almost naturally to those who had no need to fret about "the little interests and material cares of life." Tocqueville stresses that "genuine dignity of manners consists in always showing oneself in one's place, neither higher nor lower."[136] It was disgraceful for a member of the upper class to be boorish just as it was preposterous for a member of the lower order to be (or try to be) genteel. Of course, a noble was eminently capable of being boorish:

> the interiors of courts have made it sufficiently evident that great external appearances can hide very base hearts. But if the manners of aristocracy did not make virtue, they sometimes adorned virtue itself. A numerous and powerful class in which all the external acts of life seemed at each instant to reveal the natural loftiness of sentiments and thoughts, the delicacy and regularity of tastes, the urbanity of mores, was no ordinary spectacle.

The manners of aristocracy placed beautiful illusions over human nature; and although the picture was often deceptive, one felt a noble pleasure in regarding it.[137]

In a manner of speaking, aristocratic man painted with the brush of Raphael. In this way, he appeared more divine, even if his brushwork could not always conceal the fact that at bottom, he was all too human.

This favorable portrait of an aristocratic man is likely to ruffle more than a few democratic feathers. To democratic hearts and minds, the greatness of the aristocracy and the oppression of all those who did not belong to it rested on a fundamental distortion of reality; on a lie, and an ignoble one at that. No man—and certainly no class of men—is naturally the superior of another. But it is not clear that an age so firmly wed to the natural sciences and the materialistic and ultimately nihilistic view of the cosmos sustained by them enjoys any privileged claim to truth and honesty. In a cosmic void devoid of meaning, are not the reigning values of the day no less arbitrary than those of an earlier day; are they not but the convenient fictions of *its* ruling class, namely the people themselves? Might not human equality be the lie, a lie that needs no adjectival qualifier (what remains of nobility and ignobility in the age of democracy?), particularly when the foundational ground for that equality—*Imago Dei*: the creation of man in the image of God—has been eroded.

The nihilistic consequences of this devotion to equality can be gleaned not only in the overcoming of the distance between man and man but in the distance between man and beast as well. Democratic man takes an almost perverse pride in the knowledge that he shares a distant primatial ancestor with bonobos and orangutans. His fixation on genes does much to sustain his faith in human equality (after all, dissimilarity among beings that share 99.9 percent of their genome cannot amount to much), but it also does much to obscure what distinguishes humans from animals (mice, cats, and cattle not least among them).[138] Whatever insight into reality this affords, surely it does nothing to elevate man nor does it do anything to nurture those qualities that heretofore had rendered him such an extraordinary being. Nor does it do away with the need for fictions. Humans cannot carry on in the absence of meaning, which modern science does nothing to provide. Thus, the choice appears to be not between truth and falsehood, as an enlightened modern would have it, but between lie and lie—one that says humans partake of the divine and one that says they are but animals. To borrow again from Tocqueville's imagery, it is either in the light of Raphael's brilliance or David's realism that man appears.

On the face of it, the aristocratic elevation of man did nothing for the vast orders that were excluded from the canvas or relegated to some periphery of it, a slight that democracy promised to redress. (Mankind's democratization may result in the overall devaluation of man, but at least in principle, it marginalizes no one.) In aristocratic times, it was not mankind that ascended toward the divine, but only some very small fraction of it. One could contend, as Nietzsche did, that man's glorification requires that the majority personally know nothing of glory. "A high culture is a pyramid: it can stand only on a broad base; its first presupposition is a broad and soundly consolidated mediocrity."[139] Part of this is simply a question of labor, upon which every society relies. Agriculture may be a precondition for higher society, but it is hardly sufficient. An aristocracy of farmers is a contrariety that would seem to preclude its existence outside a utopia.[140] But it is not just a question of leisure. Every aristocratic order presupposes that some lives—some types of life—are elevated and that not everyone is capable of living at such heights. "As one climbs *higher*, life becomes ever harder; the coldness increases, responsibility increases."[141] A life that is distinctively human because of its spiritual or intellectual orientation and devotion is the sort of life for which not everyone is suited. The majority is constituted in such a manner that it finds its happiness in sating pleasures of a more materialistic and animalistic bent. When the pyramid is leveled, the pleasures of the body are not baser than those of the mind. In a society that cannot distinguish high from low, there can be no high culture and the glory of man cannot but fade.

None of this, of course, is going to impel democratic man to give up *his* privileges. Even if all this were true, the glory of a few cannot justify the oppression of the many. The extent to which that objection is invalidated by the tendentious values of those who make it—"inequality is bad because it is bad *for us*"—can be tabled for now. What is worth considering are the lengths to which Tocqueville went to demonstrate that notwithstanding the oppression and inequality that inhered in and permeated the age of aristocracy, it was a time when people—not just those of the upper class, but people of all ranks—partook of a contentment not readily encountered in the modern age and where people, attached by bonds far less tenuous than those that connect democratic peoples, experienced a sense of community and belonging that is all but unknown in this, ironically, more humanitarian age.

Tocqueville has been charged with idealizing the *ancien régime*, a charge that is not wholly without merit.[142] But while Tocqueville's sympathies for the old order were patent, he was not oblivious to its shortcomings. Tocqueville occupied a curious moment in history, a sort of transitionary time when the old order was effectively moribund, but the new order had not yet fully materialized. He straddled a rift that sundered history, dividing an aristocratic past from a democratic future. Tocqueville described the character of the new order that was centuries if not millennia in the making and understood that there could be no going back. But his familial roots, which also stretched back centuries into that world whose ruins he found himself cast upon, rendered him acutely sympathetic to all that was passing before his eyes. The rancor that animated those who celebrated the destruction of the *ancien régime* and the indignation that consumed those whose world had been destroyed did not cloud Tocqueville's judgment. He perceived what the democratic upheaval portended with greater sagacity and probity than those of his day, on whichever side of the political divide they stood.

Thus, Tocqueville could draw attention to the brutal callousness of the aristocracy without condemning it outright. In a poignant example, Tocqueville cites a letter from the Marquise de Sévigné, penned at the time an onerous tax was being imposed upon the lower classes of Brittany. The letter, which begins with the marquise playfully chiding her daughter, quickly turns to "the news from Rennes." Without the least hint of sympathy, the mother relates the tribulations of the "miserable people" who have been expelled from the town "without knowing where to go, having neither food nor any place to lodge." She writes of a fiddler who was broken on the wheel and quartered with his pieces "exposed in the four corners of the town" and dryly notes that the hangings will begin tomorrow after which she promptly turns to news of the weather. It was as though she were recounting a play for which she did not care very much and not the actual torment of human beings which she personally beheld.

Tocqueville had no illusions about what happened to the lower classes of Brittany in the year 1675. "These tumultuous movements were repressed with an unexampled atrocity." But notwithstanding the gross insensitivity exhibited in the letter of the marquise, Tocqueville understood that Madame de Sévigné was not a "selfish and barbaric creature." It was not an active antipathy for the lower orders that compelled her to relate their sufferings as she did, but rather the inability to comprehend their suffering. "Madame de Sévigné did not clearly conceive what it was to suffer when one was not a gentleman."[143]

This peculiarity was not limited to the marquise but was symptomatic of the entire aristocratic world. In a society that was so rigidly stratified, where "each caste [had] its own opinions, sentiments, rights, mores and separate existence," an active sympathy between members of different classes was essentially infeasible. The thoughts and feelings that were indicative of the upper class were so distinct from those of the lower classes that "they scarcely believe[d] themselves to be a part of the same humanity."[144] Thus, "when the chroniclers of the Middle Ages, who all belonged by their birth or their habits to the aristocracy, relate the tragic end of a noble, it is with infinite sorrow; whereas they recount the massacre and tortures of men of the people all in one breath and without a frown."[145] In aristocratic societies, "men were prodigiously unalike"[146] and it is only among people who are alike that there can be any "real sympathy."[147]

The want of sympathy should not be understood as anything akin to "an habitual hatred or systematic scorn" for the people on the part of the ruling order. Aristocratic man failed to comprehend the suffering of the common man; he was not bent on exacerbating it nor was he keen on reveling in it. While the notion of a common humanity could find little traction in a hierarchical world where humans were chasmically divided, there were to be found personal bonds that enjoyed far greater depth and durability than those that link individuals in this age of equals. This was true not only of intra-class relations but inter-class ones as well.

In part, this truth can be glimpsed from the fact that the aristocratic world had no word for individualism, a neologism that belongs to an age when—paradoxically it would seem—people would become more alike than ever before. The reason is that members of the aristocratic world belonged above all to a group.[148] Subordination of the self to something larger was so vital that to be severed from your group was viewed as a punishment of the most severe kind. One was banished from the family; ostracized from the community; "sentenced to individuality."[149] The liberation, and moreover, the celebration of individual selfhood is an emphatically modern phenomenon.

While the rigid stratification of the aristocratic world no doubt offends modern sensibilities, that world was ordered in such a manner that the members of it—whatever their station may have been—were linked to one another as constituent parts of a larger whole. "Aristocracy had made of all citizens a long chain that went from the peasant up to the king."[150] This chain transcended not only class but time, uniting in the present ages that had set with ones that had yet to dawn, thereby rendering "all generations, so to speak, contemporaries."

> A man almost always knows his ancestors and respects them; he believes he already perceives his great-grandsons and loves them. He willingly does his duty by both, and he frequently comes to sacrifice his personal enjoyments for beings who no longer exist or who do not yet exist.
>
> In addition, aristocratic institutions have the effect of binding each man tightly to several of his fellow citizens.
>
> Classes being very distinct and immobile within an aristocratic people, each of them becomes for whoever makes up a part of it a sort of little native country, more visible and dearer than the big one.
>
> As in aristocratic societies all people are placed at a fixed post, some above the others, it results also that each of them always perceives higher than himself a man whose protection is necessary to him, and below he finds another whom he can call upon for cooperation.
>
> Men who live in aristocratic centuries are therefore almost always bound in a tight manner to something that is placed outside of them, and they are often

disposed to forget themselves. It is true that in these same centuries the general notion of *those like oneself* is obscure and that one scarcely thinks of devoting oneself to the cause of humanity; but one often sacrifices himself for certain men.[151]

These attachments, including the willingness to sacrifice oneself for those to whom one is attached, are exemplified in the relationship between lord and vassal. Originally, the vassal's primary virtue was his military service. He swore allegiance to a lord, promising to follow him into battle; to fight and, when the occasion demanded, fall beside him. An indelible ignominy awaited the vassal who returned from a battle his lord did not survive. In exchange for his military allegiance, the lord afforded his vassal protection and sustenance. (The English word "lord" derives from the Old English term *hlaford*, which means literally "the giver of the loaf.") Over time, the system of vassalage evolved considerably, with the purely militaristic foundations giving way to a more complex and nuanced *raison d'être*. In addition to protection and sustenance, a lord conferred upon a deserving vassal a *beneficium* in the form of money, rights or, not least importantly, a fief—the inheritable land that was managed by the vassal, though ownership of it ultimately was retained by the lord.[152]

Tocqueville devotes some attention to the more developed system of vassalage and what it signified for the relationship between those who occupied the upper and lower classes. As he notes, vassals not uncommonly were commoners, but they were closely connected to their lords and intimately involved in their day-to-day affairs. If following their lords into battle was still a chief function of vassals, it was not, as Tocqueville put it, "the principle condition of their tenure." Thus, for example, a vassal often played a prominent role in the lord's court, "the mainspring of feudal government," where he helped govern those who fell under the lord's aegis. Periodically, a vassal would be obligated to sit beside the lord (or his judge) and serve as a sort of assistant arbiter in the trials and lawsuits that were brought to the court, meting out punishment and enacting justice in the cases that came before them. For Tocqueville, this is a telling instance of how "the rural class was drawn into contact with the nobility and daily joined with them in the conduct of affairs."[153] Naturally, class distinctions were not effaced, but those distinctions made possible the cohesion of the aristocratic world—a world to which the lower classes were no less integral than the upper.

What to modern eyes appears as an oppressive and exploitative system proves to be far more symbiotic. This was true not only with regard to the relationship between lord and vassal (who could boast considerable privilege and prestige for one not of the nobility) but with respect to the more common peasants as well. Before the advent of the nation-state, to say nothing of the welfare state, the maintenance of public order and care for the people fell upon the particular lord in whose compass that populace lay. During this time, there was nothing akin to patriotism: Fidelity to one's lord preceded love of one's country.[154] While a peasant's life in relation to his lord's was one of abject privation and servility, it would be wrong to conclude that lords did not care for their peasants, however incongruous that may sound to modern ears. "The nobles, placed at an immense distance from the people, nevertheless took the sort of benevolent and tranquil interest in the lot of the people that the shepherd accords to his flock; and without seeing in the poor man his equal, they watched over his destiny as a trust placed by Providence in their hands."[155] It was in the noble's interest to protect and care for his flock. After all, the people residing on his land tilled it not only for their own sake but for their master's as well; the master's protection of and care for them redounded to their mutual benefit. This, of course, did not entail lifting peasants out of the poverty in which they were mired, but it went far beyond simply keeping bandits at bay (though—it should be noted—in an age pervaded by lawlessness and from which a central authority was absent, the order and security that lords did provide was, in itself, an inestimable benefit). As Tocqueville observed, "in the old feudal society, if the lord had great rights, he also bore great burdens. It was up to him to help the poor within the bounds of his domain." To illustrate the sort of burdens and obligations that fell upon feudal lords, Tocqueville draws attention to the Prussian Code of 1795, which includes the following: "the lord must see that poor peasants receive an education. He must, insofar as possible, feed those of his vassals who do not possess any land. If some of them fall into want, he is required to come to their aid."[156] This aspect of the aristocratic age—the nobility's care for and responsibility to the peasantry—tends to be discounted in, if not outright interdicted from, democratic man's collective conscience. Those who hold equality to be sacrosanct find it difficult to see past the egregious inequalities of earlier times.

None of this is meant to make light of the terrible hardships that must have attended life for the peasantry.[157] All the same, however paradoxical it may seem, the very people who oppressed the peasants cared for them—genuinely and considerably.[158] Indeed, sometimes care and oppression went hand in hand: "the peasant of the fourteenth century was both more oppressed and more helped [than the peasant of the eighteenth century]. The aristocracy sometimes tyrannized him, but never abandoned him."[159] The encumbrances with which peasants were saddled seemed less onerous the more they were cared for. Tocqueville notes that this is not much different from how the people viewed their government in his own day or, one might add, in any day: "one bore the burdens it imposed in consideration of the guarantees it offered."[160] But parallels of this sort can do little to overlay the yawning fissure that separates the *ancien régime* from post-revolutionary France. History had been cleaved in 1789. Tocqueville may never have tasted the sweetness of living for which Talleyrand pined,[161] but that did not prevent him from apperceiving the resplendence that radiated from the aristocratic world. It will forever remain a testament to the breadth of Tocqueville's mind and the magnanimity of his soul that he was capable of bridging the divide that severed the aristocratic age from the democratic. While clearly a friend of the latter, he was clearly not an enemy of the former. He beheld the grandeur and glory of aristocratic man and realized that while his reign entailed the oppression of large swaths of mankind, the virtues embodied in the aristocratic world shone down upon and uplifted all who inhabited it.[162]

NOTES

1. Nietzsche, *Zarathustra*, 171.
2. Nietzsche, *Twilight*, 490.
3. Nietzsche, *Zarathustra*, 170.
4. Herodotus, *The Histories*, trans. Audrey de Sélincourt (New York: Penguin Books, 1996), 497–8.
5. On Nietzsche's intention to write a magnum opus, see Thomas H. Brobjer, "Nietzsche's Magnum Opus," *History of European Ideas* 32, no. 3 (2006): 278–94.
6. Nietzsche, *Zarathustra*, 243.
7. Nietzsche, *Ecce Homo*, "Why I Am a Destiny," 326–35.
8. Nietzsche, *Zarathustra*, 172.
9. Nietzsche, *Beyond Good and Evil*, 11.
10. Ibid, 4.
11. Nietzsche, *Genealogy of Morality*, 115; Nietzsche, *Will to Power*, 8.
12. Nietzsche, *Will to Power*, 9.
13. Nietzsche, *Zarathustra*, 171.
14. Resisting the positivistic inclinations of his century, Tocqueville maintained that what defined modern society *essentially* was not its industrial or economic or scientific makeup, but rather its democratic constitution. The significance of Tocqueville's insight has less to with the institutional or structural composition of democracy than it does with the spirit that animates it. In this regard, see Raymond Aron, *Main Currents in Sociological Thought*, vol. 1 (New Brunswick, NJ: Transaction Publishers, 1998), 240–3. On the nebulousness of Tocqueville's conception of democracy, see James T. Schleifer, *The Making of Tocqueville's Democracy in America* (Indianapolis: Liberty Fund, 2000), 225–39: "Tocqueville's very failure precisely to define démocratie accounts, in part, for the brilliance of his observations. If he had at one time fixed definitively upon a single meaning, all of the others would have been more or less lost from sight. His vision would have been at once restricted, his message narrowed, and his audience diminished. His extraordinary ability to imagine and to consider so many different uses, to revolve the idea so continuously in his mind, led to the richness and

profundity of his insights" (239). Jean-Claude Lamberti echoes Schleifer's judgment. As Lamberti notes, "Readers—and even more—commentators on Tocqueville frequently complain about his imprecise terminology, noting that the term 'democracy' is never rigorously defined, despites its central place in the work." But like Schleifer, Lamberti is not one of them. "Although Tocqueville is not very systematic in his use of terminology, his intuition of the essential is so powerful that the variety of uses of the term 'democracy' rarely creates a serious ambiguity for the attentive reader; it seems rather to contribute to the richness and vigor of Tocqueville's thought." Lamberti, *Tocqueville and the Two Democracies*, 15, 17.

15. Tocqueville, *Democracy*, 34 [emphasis added].

16. Ibid, 275.

17. See, for example, Nietzsche's ruminations on the significance of climate and geography or, on a more micro scale, the influence of diet in *Ecco Homo*, 692–8.

18. Tocqueville, *Democracy*, 274.

19. Of course, the upheavals that littered the twentieth century were not needed to demonstrate that the many are no more angelic than the few. Tocqueville clearly apprehended as much, though, as he noted in *The Old Regime and the Revolution*, it appeared many of his countrymen at the time of the Revolution had "completely forgotten" the episodes from their own past (e.g., the Jacquerie) that announced this truth. Tocqueville, *Old Regime*, 229.

20. Etymologically, aristocracy is rooted in the ancient Greek *aristos* (άριστος) meaning "best, noblest."

21. Chester G. Starr, *The Aristocratic Temper of Greek Civilization* (New York: Oxford University Press, 1992), 4.

22. The second essay of *On the Genealogy of Morality*, "'Guilt', 'bad conscience' and related matters" is devoted in large part to this phenomenon. For a brief, but insightful analysis of the bad conscience, see Thomas Pangle, "Nihilism and Modern Democracy in the Thought of Nietzsche" in *The Crisis of Liberal Democracy: A Straussian Perspective*, ed. Kenneth L. Deutsch and Walter Soffer (Albany: State University of New York Press, 1987), 192.

23. Nietzsche, *Genealogy of Morality*, 56.

24. With respect to the racial overtones of Nietzsche's use of Aryanism and blond beasts that recur in his writings, Hugo Drochon makes the important observation that "Nietzsche . . . is more interested in *values* than he is in *race*. . . . [T]he blond beast is a metaphor for a lion, the noble king of the jungle, and the Ayran and Celtic races just so happen to be the historical conquering races of Europe, but may take on other non-Aryan attributes in other circumstances (Arabian or Japanese). There is therefore both a literal and figurative aspect to Nietzsche's account of the blond beasts of prey: while historically the European conquerors were blond (literal), Nietzsche then uses this theory and applies it to the rest of the world (figurative)." Hugo Drochon, *Nietzsche's Great Politics* (Princeton: Princeton University Press, 2016), 84.

25. Nietzsche, *Genealogy of Morality*, 58–9.

26. For a refutation of such notions, see Walter Kaufmann, *Nietzsche: Philosopher, Psychologist, Antichrist* (Princeton: Princeton University Press, 1974), especially part III. While Kaufmann's assessment is comprehensive and oftentimes

compelling, it ultimately goes too far in mollifying Nietzsche's philosophy. Nietzsche hated anti-Semites and would have abhorred Nazism, but it is baseless to suggest, as Kaufmann does, that Nietzsche did not glorify war and spoke of it merely in metaphorical terms. Kaufmann wanted to reconcile Nietzsche with the spirit of the age, which essentially are irreconcilable. Thus, by way of example, one finds Kaufmann blithely impugning Nietzsche for being "surely wrong" on what was for Nietzsche "the fundamental problem of 'man and woman'." See Kaufmann's note (31) in *Beyond Good and Evil* (New York: Vintage Books, 1966), 167. Kaufmann not only belonged to, but was, in the memorable words of Connor Cruise O'Brien, "the king of the gentle Nietzscheans." Connor Cruise O'Brien, "Nietzsche and the Machiavellian Schism" in *The Suspecting Glance* (London: Faber and Faber, 1972), 59. Curiously, given his criticisms of those thinkers who seek to depoliticize and democratize Nietzsche in an effort to make Nietzsche's views more consonant with their own, Hugo Drochon mollifies Nietzsche's musings on war, arguing "that what Nietzsche has in mind is fundamentally a war of spirits, an intellectual warfare to determine what type of man should be bred." Drochon, *Nietzsche's Great Politics*, 176. What renders Drochon's verdict even more curious is that it is reached on the very same page where he quotes the following passage from *Ecce Homo*: "The new faction in favour of life that takes on the greatest task of all, that of breeding humanity to higher levels (which includes the ruthless extermination of everything degenerate and parasitical)." The ruthless extermination of everything degenerate and parasitical hardly sounds like a cerebral joust. Even if Drochon is right on this score, he surely is wrong when he writes, "Nowhere does Nietzsche ever suggest that massacres should be committed" (176). In Nietzsche's unpublished notes, which Drochon relies on heavily, one finds the following: "The consequences of my teachings must rage furiously: but on its account uncountably many shall die." (Quoted in Gillespie, *Nietzsche's Final Teaching*, 213). For a deeper and more faithful treatment of the significance of war in Nietzsche's thought see Thomas Pangle, "The 'Warrior Spirit' as an Inlet to the Political Philosophy of Nietzsche's Zarathustra," *Nietzsche-Studien: Internationales Jahrbuch für die Nietzsche-Forschung* 15 (1986): 140–79; Stanley Rosen, *The Mask of Enlightenment: Nietzsche's Zarathustra* (New York: Cambridge University Press, 1995), chap. 2; Gillespie, *Nietzsche's Final Teaching*. While glorifications of strife do not riddle Tocqueville's thought as they do Nietzsche's, the Frenchman was not oblivious to the virtues of war. "I do not wish to speak ill of war; war almost always enlarges the thought of a people and elevates its heart. There are cases where only it can arrest the excessive development of certain penchants that equality naturally gives rise to, and where, for certain deep-seated maladies to which democratic societies are subject, it must be considered almost necessary." Tocqueville, *Democracy*, 620–1. For some critical and unsympathetic reflections on Tocqueville's restrained bellicosity, see Boesche, "The Dark Side of Tocqueville: On War and Emoire" in *Tocqueville's Roadmap*, 109–25. Compare Tocqueville's musings on this matter with those of Rousseau's in *On the Social Contract* (quoted above p. 42). It also bears mentioning that Nietzsche's praise of war was hardly unqualified. See, for example, Nietzsche, *Human, All Too Human*, 177–8.

27. "The philosopher as *we* understand him... as the man with the most comprehensive responsibility, whose conscience bears the weight of the overall development of humanity" is, like those original, instinctual masters, "predestined for command." The philosopher is the "complimentary person in which the *rest* of existence justifies itself." Nietzsche, *Beyond Good and Evil*, 54, 99. On "the long story of how *responsibility* originated" and its culmination in the "sovereign man" whose "mastery over himself also necessarily gives him mastery over circumstances, over nature, and over all more short-willed and unreliable creatures," see *Genealogy of Morality*, 37–9. Strauss, who grasped just how comprehensive this responsibility is, referred to it as "cosmic." Leo Strauss, "Note on the plan of Nietzsche's *Beyond Good and Evil*" in *Studies in Platonic Political Philosophy* (Chicago: University of Chicago Press, 1986), 188.

28. Much of this logic concerning the origin of the state and man's emergence from his semi-animality is echoed in Nietzsche's youthful musings on the Greek state. There Nietzsche argues that the state and the slave (that "blind mole of culture") with it were the products of nature's "pitiless rigidity," which yielded conquerors who instinctually overcame weaker individuals and, in binding them together, gave them "an affinity" they hitherto lacked. As is the case in the *Genealogy of Morality*, the emergence of the state is "sudden, violent, [and] bloody." Friedrich Nietzsche, "The Greek State," 50–1. See also *Beyond Good and Evil*, sec. 257.

29. Nietzsche, *Genealogy of Morality*, 39.

30. Rousseau was one of three French thinkers Tocqueville spent time with each day, the other two being Pascal and Montesquieu. Alexis de Tocqueville to Louis de Kergorlay, November 12, 1836, quoted in Tocqueville, *Democracy*, xxx.

31. Alexis de Tocqueville, *Memoir on Pauperism*, trans. Seymour Drescher (Chicago: Ivan R. Dee, 1907), 39–40.

32. Ibid, 40.

33. Ibid, 40–1 [emphasis added].

34. In this regard, it might be worth reflecting on the American and French Revolutions. Equality was central to the one Rousseau inspired, tangential to the one he did not. While the American framers celebrated man's inborn equality, they emphatically rejected the leveling and, in a manner of speaking, late-born equality espoused by Rousseau. Hence, as Madison argues in *Federalist 10*, "the first object of government" is "the protection of different and unequal faculties of acquiring property, [from which] the possession of different degrees and kinds of property immediately results." James Madison, *Federalist* No. 10, in *The Federalist Papers*, ed. Clinton Rossiter (New York: Mentor, 1999), 46. Consider also the utter absence of the word "democracy" from America's foundational documents. "The honest and serious students of American history will recall that our Founding Fathers managed to write both the Declaration of Independence and the Constitution of the United States without using the term 'democracy' even once. No part of any one of the existing forty-eight State constitutions contains any reference to the word. Such men as John Adams, Madison, Hamilton, Jefferson and others who were most influential in the institution and formation of our government refer to 'democracy' only to distinguish it sharply from the republican form of our American Constitutional System."

Clarence E. Manion, *The Key to Peace* (Chicago: The Heritage Foundation, 1951), 49–50.

35. "The possibility of such a human type, the theoretical type, is, according to Tocqueville, most threatened in democracy, and it must be vigorously defended if humanity is not to be grievously impoverished." Allan Bloom, *The Closing of the American Mind* (New York: Touchstone, 1988), 251.

36. Francis Bacon, *The Advancement of Learning*, in *Essays, Advancement of Learning, New Atlantis, and Other Pieces*, ed. R. F. Jones (New York: Odyssey Press, 1937), 214.

37. As Gillespie perceptively notes, "Ultimately, the descent into animality can only be achieved by the elimination of the wealth of contradictory drives and impulses that make man the lord of the earth. Nietzsche in this sense sees the desire for inner peace as a diminution of life itself." *Nietzsche's Final Teaching*, 212.

38. This was the rule rather than the exception wherever communism took root. By way of example, in the Soviet Union in 1935, the party elite and their families enjoyed "the newest products from abroad" including "the latest automobiles, pedigreed dogs, wines and radio sets. . . . Paris dresses, silks and perfumes" for the wives and "expensive toys" for the children. That same year, "when rationing was abolished, butter appeared in the so-called commercial stores at 25 rubles per pound. That equaled the earnings of a worker for five days." Alexander Orlov, *The Secret History of Stalin's Crimes*, quoted in Paul Hollander, *The End of Commitment* (Chicago: Ivan R. Dee, 2006), 34.

39. Nietzsche, *Beyond Good and Evil*, 151.

40. See, for example, Tocqueville, *Democracy*, 220: "Almost all the peoples that have acted strongly on the world, those who have conceived, followed, and executed great designs, from the Romans to the English, were directed by an aristocracy, and how can one be astonished at that?" See also Tocqueville's article, "Political and Social Condition of France," *London and Westminster Review* 3, no. 1 (April 1836): 137–69: "Liberty may be conceived, by those who enjoy it, under two different forms: as the exercise of a universal right, or as the enjoyment of a privilege. . . . [The] aristocratic notion of liberty produces, among those who have imbibed it, an exalted idea of their own individual value, and a passionate love of independence; it gives extraordinary energy and ardour to their pursuit of their own interests and passions. Entertained by individuals, it has often led them to the most extraordinary actions; —adopted by an entire people, it has created the most energetic nations that have ever existed" (165–6). For an interesting discussion of this passage and the significance of it in Tocqueville's thought, see Pierre Manent, *Tocqueville and the Nature of Democracy*, trans. John Waggoner (Lanham, MD: Rowman and Littlefield, 1996), chap. 2, esp. 18–20. As Manent notes, Tocqueville goes on to suggest that the modern, democratic idea of liberty is the correct idea, thereby implying that the aristocratic idea is false. But it is precisely the false idea that has produced wonders the likes of which the world has seen only rarely whereas the correct idea, which has gained ascendency for the first time in the present age, portends to engender an interminable stagnation and irreversible diminution of the human spirit. This suggests a problem that was central to Nietzsche's thought

though does not appear to have entered Tocqueville's, namely what the value of truth is.

41. Friedrich Nietzsche, *The Birth of Tragedy*, trans. Ronald Speirs (New York: Cambridge University Press, 2004), 17.
42. Friedrich Nietzsche, *Daybreak*, trans. R. J. Hollingdale (New York: Cambridge University Press, 1997), 149.
43. Nietzsche, *Birth of Tragedy*, 6.
44. Ibid, 4.
45. Ibid, 22–3.
46. Ibid.
47. Ibid, 27.
48. Ibid, 16.
49. Ibid, 17.
50. Ibid, 20.
51. Ibid, 18.
52. Ibid, 21.
53. Albert Henrichs, "Dionysus" in *Oxford Classical Dictionary*, 481.
54. W. F. Otto quoted in ibid, 122.
55. Nietzsche, *Birth of Tragedy*, 27.
56. Ibid, 21.
57. Ibid, 27.
58. Ibid, 27–8.
59. Ibid, 20.
60. Ibid, 14.
61. Tracy Strong argues that "for Nietzsche tragedy was not an aristocratic or elitist activity" and that "in his earliest considerations" on the subject he chose to "highlight its democratic element approvingly." Tracy B. Strong, *Friedrich Nietzsche and the Politics of Transfiguration* (Urbana, IL: University of Illinois Press, 1999), xviii. It is true that there is a democratic element to tragedy insofar as the metaphysical solace it offers is, at least in principle, open to all. The Dionysian wisdom that tragedy manifested obtained for everyone. One might also glean a democratic element in the fact that, as Nietzsche points out, at an Attic tragedy, "there was fundamentally no opposition between public and chorus." Greek theaters were designed so that "everyone quite literally [could] *overlook* the entire cultural world around him, and ... imagine, as he looked with sated gaze, that he was a member of the chorus" (*Birth of Tragedy*, § 8). But Strong's emphasis of the democratic element of tragedy is problematic for several reasons. For one, while Attic tragedy conveyed the wisdom of Dionysus, it did so in a sublimated, Appolinian manner. Dionysian wisdom may have been open to all, but tragedy itself was the invention of a singular people, and not just any people, but a positively aristocratic one. What is more, Nietzsche specifically dispels the notion that tragedy arose out of the people. "This idea [that the chorus represents the people] had no influence on the original formation of tragedy, since its purely religious origins preclude the entire opposition between prince and people .... Even with regard to the classical form of the chorus familiar to us from the works of Aeschylus and Sophocles, we regard it as blasphemous to speak of the premonition

of a 'constitutional popular assembly'" (*Birth of Tragedy*, § 7). Moreover, according to Nietzsche's judgment, tragedy declines at the very moment it becomes democratic. With Euripides, the knell of Greek tragedy is sounded, precisely because he democratized it: "Thanks to [Euripides] people from everyday life pushed their way out of the audience and on to the stage; the mirror which once revealed only great and bold features became painfully true to life, reproducing consciously even the lines which nature had drawn badly" (*Birth of Tragedy*, § 11). The problem with the "left" Nietzsche that Strong champions has nothing to do with Nietzsche's esotericism and whether or not it is "elitist" or "democratic" in nature (xxii). Nietzsche, without being esoteric, makes plain his irreconcilability with the left, both on a personal and philosophical level. Personally, it was his nausea over the rabble that was always his greatest danger (*Ecce Homo*, "Why I am so Wise," #8), hardly the sentiment of a leftist philosopher. Philosophically, Nietzsche maintained that the *small* man must recur eternally (an epiphany that paralyzed his godless prophet with disgust) (*Zarathustra*, 331); that "every enhancement so far in the type 'man' has been the work of an aristocratic society—and that is how it will be, again and again, since this sort of society believes in a long ladder of rank order and value distinctions between men, and in some sense needs slavery" (*Beyond Good and Evil*, 151); and that "because [life] requires height, it requires steps and contradiction," as well as "war and inequality" (*Zarathustra*, 213). Again, none of these are the thoughts of a man on the left. Nor, for that matter, are any of these thoughts conveyed subtly, let alone esoterically. This is not to suggest that Nietzsche is a man of the right or a conservative of whatever stripe. (see Chapter 1, note 217 above.). But attempts to reconcile Nietzsche with liberalism, of which there is no shortage, require the distortion or abandonment of tenets that are central to liberalism or Nietzsche so that either one or the other (and possibly both) is lost in the effort. Those attempts embrace—at least tacitly—the utilitarian approach of Michel Foucault. "For myself, I prefer to utilize the writers I like. The only valid tribute to thought such as Nietzsche's is precisely to use it, to deform it, to make it groan and protest." Michel Foucault, "Prison Talk" in *Power/Knowledge: Selected Interviews and Other Writings, 1972–1977*, ed. Colin Gordon (New York: Pantheon, 1980), 53–4. There is no doubt that Nietzsche's thought can be deformed for liberal ends—or any number of other ends for that matter. But it is a little disingenuous to maintain that the only valid tribute to his thought is to twist it into something it is not. It is also naïve to think that his thought can be deformed to support liberalism without deforming liberalism in the process. For efforts to liberalize Nietzsche see, for example, William E. Connolly, *Identity/Difference: Democratic Negotiations of Political Paradox* (Minneapolis: University of Minnesota Press, 2002); Lawrence J. Hatab, *A Nietzschean Defense of Democracy* (Chicago: Open Court, 1995); Bonnie Honig, *Political Theory and the Displacement of Politics* (Ithaca: Cornell University Press, 1992); David Owen, *Nietzsche, Politics, and Modernity: A Critique of Liberal Reason* (London: Sage Publications, 1995); Paul Patton, "Nietzsche, Genealogy, and Justice" in *Nietzsche and Political Thought*, ed. Keith Ansell-Pearson (London: Bloomsbury, 2013), 7–22; Alan Schrift, ed. *Why Nietzsche Still? Reflections on Drama, Culture, and Politics* (Berkley: University of California Press, 2000). On Nietzsche's incompatibility with liberalism, see Keith Ansell-Pearson, *An Introduction to Nietzsche as Political Thinker* (New York: Cambridge University Press, 1994), 9–12; 39–44. As Pearson neatly puts it, "Nietzsche's aristocratic conception of politics . . . is . . . the only overt or explicit politics which it is possible to associate with him." Ibid, 148. That position is echoed by Frederick Appel: "One of my central claims is that Nietzsche's radically aristocratic commitments pervade every aspect of his project, making any egalitarian appropriation of his work exceedingly problematic." Frederick Appel, *Nietzsche Contra Democracy*, 5. As Gillespie notes with respect to the eternal recurrence—the doctrine that, in Gillespie's view, "gives everything in [Nietzsche's] thinking its meaning and purpose"—"practically, the doctrine is a complete rejection of the modern, liberal/democratic/socialist life, a rejection of the notion of rights, of human dignity, of the value of work, of the nation-state, of peace, and of what he sees as the somnambulant consumerism of the 'last man.'" Gillespie, *Nietzsche's Final Teaching*, 17, 20. See also Detwiler, *Nietzsche and the Politics of Aristocratic Radicalism*.

62. Friedrich Nietzsche, *On Truth and Lie in the Extra-Moral Sense* in *The Portable Nietzsche*, 42.

63. Nietzsche, *Birth of Tragedy*, 40.

64. Ibid.

65. Ibid, 61. On Nietzsche's novel and problematic rendering of the satyr, see M.S. Silk and J.P. Stern, *Nietzsche on Tragedy* (New York: Cambridge University Press, 1981), 146–9.

66. Nietzsche, *Birth of Tragedy*, 39.

67. Ibid, 44.

68. Ibid, 47.

69. Ibid, 48.

70. Ibid, 47. On this note, consider how the misdeeds of the noble Greeks appeared in the eyes of their Olympian deities: "as foolishness, *not* sin!" What is more, in trying to make sense of their misdeeds, the Greeks found that their gods were somehow complicit. "In this way, the gods served to justify man to a certain degree, even if he was in the wrong they served as causes of evil—they did not, at that time, take the punishment on themselves, but rather, as is *nobler*, the guilt." Nietzsche, *Genealogy of Morality*, 65.

71. See, for example, Ludwig Edelstein, *The Idea of Progress in Classical Antiquity* (Baltimore: Johns Hopkins University Press, 1967).

72. Nietzsche, *Birth of Tragedy*, 49–50. This claim elicits a comparison with the Edenic, "Semitic myth of the fall," but Nietzsche is quick to differentiate the two. "What distinguishes the Aryan conception is the sublime view that *active sin* is the true Promethean virtue," as opposed to the passive sin found in Genesis "where the origin of evil was seen to lie in curiosity, mendacious pretense, openness to seduction, lasciviousness—in short, a whole series of predominantly feminine attributes" (50).

73. Ibid, 49.

74. Ibid, 51.

75. "And life itself confided this secret to me: 'Behold', it said, 'I am *that which must always overcome itself*'." Nietzsche, *Zarathustra*, 227.

76. Nietzsche, *Birth of Tragedy*, 24.

77. Nietzsche, *Human, All Too Human*, 65.
78. Nietzsche, *The Birth of Tragedy*, 25.
79. Nietzsche, *Genealogy of Morality*, 8.
80. Nietzsche, *Human, All Too Human*, 12–3.
81. Nietzsche, *Genealogy of Morality*, 10–1.
82. Ibid, 11.
83. Ibid, 11–2.
84. See Plato, *Republic*, Book IV, esp. 105–25 (427d–445e). It is true that ultimately Epicureanism equates virtue with utility insofar as virtue is good to the extent that it is useful for securing the only genuine good, pleasure. But in view of the fact that there is no place for politics in Epicurus's philosophy, and seeing that it lends itself to individualism (if not crass hedonism), there is something, if not egalitarian, then decidedly unaristocratic about it. For a relevant discussion of Epicureanism, see Strauss, *Natural Right and History*, chap. 4, esp. 109–11. See also René Guénon, *Crisis of the Modern World* (Hillsdale, NY: Sophia Perennis, 2004), 17: "A word that rose to honor at the time of the Renaissance, and that summarized in advance the whole program of modern civilization is 'humanism'. Men were indeed concerned to reduce everything to purely human proportions, to eliminate every principle of a higher order, and, one might say, symbolically to turn away from the heavens under pretext of conquering the earth; the Greeks, whose example they claimed to follow, had never gone as far in this direction, even at the time of their greatest intellectual decadence, and with them utilitarian considerations had at least never claimed the first place, as they were very soon to do with the moderns."
85. Walter Donlan, *The Aristocratic Ideal and Selected Papers* (Wauconda, IL: Bolchazy-Carducci Publishers, 1999), 4. "The Homeric hero in war was inspired by a single purpose: to win personal glory and honor (*timē, kydos*) for himself by means of valorous deeds performed on the field of battle. Accordingly, the goal of every activity, practically without exception, was the recognition of self by peers as a good warrior."
86. Nietzsche, *Genealogy of Morality*, 12–3. None of this is to say that peoples of earlier times failed to see the good in the useful. Clearly a useful weapon or chalice or citizen was preferred to the useless one. But while the utility of something was not scorned, it hardly constituted the measure of a thing's goodness, to say nothing of the origin of the concept good. Perhaps nothing discloses this disdain for, or at least indifference to, utility more effectively than pre-modern science, which so deliberately subordinated practice to theory and not—as would be the case with modern science—vice versa.
87. Ibid, 13.
88. Ibid, 11–2.
89. Ibid, 13.
90. Ibid, 14. The following passage from Gerald Else's *Aristotle's Poetics: The Argument* neatly affirms Nietzsche's etymological contention: "Greek thinking begins with and for a long time holds to the proposition that mankind is divided into 'good' and 'bad', and these terms are quite as much social, political and economic as they are moral. . . .

"The dichotomy is absolute and exclusive for a simple reason: it began as the aristocrats' view of society and reflects their idea of the gulf between themselves and the 'others'. In the minds of a comparatively small and close-knit group like the Greek aristocracy there are only two kinds of people, 'we' and 'they'; and of course 'we' are the good people, the proper, decent, good-looking, right-thinking ones, while they are the rascals, the poltroons, the good-for-nothings—in short, everyone else. It is inherent in the idea and the terminology of the division that there cannot be any third class." Gerald F. Else, *Aristotle's Poetics: The Argument* (Cambridge, MA: Harvard University Press, 1957), 75.

91. Nietzsche, *Genealogy of Morality*, 14–5.
92. Ibid, 20.
93. Ibid, 12.
94. Ibid, 58.
95. Nietzsche, *Beyond Good and Evil*, 157.
96. Ibid, 153.
97. Ibid.
98. Ibid, 151.
99. One of the fundamental modern longings is for a society where toil no longer is required, as Marx's promise of an age where anyone can be a hunter and fisherman and farmer and critic over the course of any given day attests. What this prospect portends is that man will engage in such activities recreationally and *ipso facto* superficially. The result would be a world filled with mediocrities and dilettantes. There would be no genius to speak of. The aim of the modern project is to free man from the burdens of labor, but only so that he will be free from all burdens, not so that he will take on new ones. There is no ambition to develop man's higher faculties. On the contrary those who inhabit the contemporary age increasingly argue that there are no higher faculties. Man has become the master and possessor of nature not to ascend to the gods, but to return to the beasts whence he came. In this regard, it is also worth noting that leisure is the goal of modern man, not aristocratic man. Rest and relaxation is the aspiration of the former, cultivation and overcoming that of the latter.
100. Nietzsche, *Beyond Good and Evil*, 158–9.
101. Ibid, sec. 258.
102. "This book [*Democracy in America*] is not precisely in anyone's camp; in writing it I did not mean either to serve or to contest any party; I undertook to see, not differently, but further than the parties; and while they are occupied with the next day, I wanted to ponder the future." Tocqueville, *Democracy*, 15. On this score, see François Furet's perceptive remark: "Before *Democracy in America*, European culture had conceived of America as the childhood of Europe, the image of its own beginnings, and had dwelt on the process of settling and clearing, on man's conquest of untamed nature. Tocqueville's book, proceeding by deduction, as it were, from the central hypothesis about equality, turned that image inside out like a glove. America, he told the Europeans, is not your childhood, it is your future." François Furet, *Interpreting the French Revolution* (New York: Cambridge University Press, 1986), 14.

103. Letter to Henry Reeve (March 22, 1837) in Alexis de Tocqueville, *Selected Letters on Politics and Society*, ed. Roger Boesche, trans. Roger Boesche and James Toupin (Berkeley: University of California Press, 1985), 115–6.

104. See Chapter One, note 203 above.

105. In spite of what appears to have been little more than wishful thinking, Nietzsche's blood was neither Polish nor noble, a claim he tenaciously clung to "to the end of his life." R. J. Hollingdale, *Nietzsche: The Man and His Philosophy* (New York: Cambridge University Press, 1999), 6–7.

106. Tocqueville, *Democracy*, 436 [emphasis added].

107. Nietzsche, *Genealogy of Morality*, 17.

108. "Athletics turn up everywhere in Greek literature and art, partly because the aristocratic way of life heavily stressed physical prowess." Chester G. Starr, *The Ancient Greeks* (New York: Oxford University Press, 1979), 33. Greek contempt for the ill formed went far beyond "exposing physically defective infant[s . . . which was] a routine practice in Ancient Greece." Cynthia Patterson, "'Not Worth the Rearing': The Causes of Infant Exposure in Ancient Greece," *Transactions of the American Philological Association* 115 (1985): 113. By way of evidence, consider the ceremony of the *pharmakos*. In Ancient Greece, a *pharmakos* (ritual scapegoat) "was a human embodiment of evil who was expelled from the Greek city at moments of crisis and disaster." Typically, a *pharmakos* was "a criminal or a slave or *an excessively ugly or deformed man* . . . a cast-off from society." Todd M. Compton, *Victim of the Muses: Poet as Scapegoat, Warrior and Hero in Greco-Roman and Indo-European Myth and History* (Washington, DC: Center for Hellenic Studies, 2006), 4 [emphasis added].

109. "'Warrior' and 'hero' are synonyms, and the main theme of a warrior culture is constructed on two notes—prowess and honor. The one is the hero's essential attribute, the other his essential aim. Every value, every judgment, every action, all skills and talents have the function of either defining honor or realizing it. Life itself may not stand in the way. The Homeric heroes loved life fiercely, as they did and felt everything with passion, and no less martyr-like characters can be imagined; but even life must be surrendered to honor. The two central figures of the *Iliad*, Achilles and Hector, were both fated to live short lives, and both knew it. They were heroes not because at the call of duty they marched proudly to their deaths, singing hymns to God and country—on the contrary, they railed openly against their doom, and Achilles, at least, did not complain less after he reached Hades—but because at the call of honor they obeyed the code of the hero without flinching and without questioning." M. I. Finley, *The World of Odysseus* (New York: The Viking Press, 1978), 115.

110. It bears noting that classical philosophy, which tended to be aristocratic, viewed the cosmos and man's place in it teleologically, whereas modern philosophy, with its overtly democratic underpinnings, spurned all teleological considerations and scoured man's origins for his essence. The one viewed humans in light of their perfection, the other in light of their lowest common denominator.

111. Tocqueville, *Democracy*, 435.

112. See note 30 above.

113. Tocqueville, *Democracy*, 435–6.

114. "Among the contemporaries of Descartes none displayed greater natural genius than Pascal. . . . At the age of fourteen he was admitted to the weekly meetings of Roberval, Mersenne, Mydorge, and other French geometricians; from which, ultimately, the French Academy sprung. At sixteen Pascal wrote an essay on conic sections; and in 1641, at the age of eighteen, he constructed the first arithmetical machine, an instrument which, eight years later, he further improved." Walter William Rouse Ball, *A Short Account of the History of Mathematics* (London: Macmillan and Co., 1908), 282.

115. The mathematical mind deals with matters that are "never seen in practice and are quite outside ordinary experience." Blaise Pascal, *Pensées*, trans. A. J. Krailsheimer (New York: Penguin Books, 1995), 183. On this score, see Barzun, *From Dawn to Decadence*, 214–20: Pascal provides "a warning against SCIENT*ISM*. . . . The clue to the fallacy of SCIENTISM is this: geometry (in all senses of the term) is an ABSTRACTION from experience; it could not exist without the work of the human mind on what it encounters in the world. Hence the realm of abstraction, useful and far from unreal, is thin and bare and poorer than the world it is drawn from" (218).

116. Tocqueville, *Democracy*, 436.

117. Plutarch, *Plutarch's Lives*, vol. 1 (New York: Modern Library, 1992), 420.

118. Tocqueville, *Democracy*, 436–7.

119. Ibid, 579.

120. Ibid, 443. As Tocqueville notes elsewhere, "Equality does not destroy imagination . . . but limits it and permits it to fly only while skimming the earth." Ibid, 571. In working *toward a psychology of the artist*, Nietzsche also favorably singles out Raphael, referring to him as an artist who "said Yes . . . and *did* Yes." For Nietzsche too, art—of the aristocratic or as he might put it, affirmational variety—does not simply reflect and represent the world, it idealizes and transfigures it. "In this state [that of the true artist], one enriches everything out of one's own fullness: whatever one sees, whatever one wills, is seen swelled, taut, strong, overloaded with strength. A man in this state transforms things until they mirror his power—until they are reflections of his perfection. This having to transform into perfection is—art. Even everything that he is not yet, becomes for him an occasion of joy in himself; in art man enjoys himself as perfection." Nietzsche, *Twilight of the Idols*, 518–9.

121. As was the case, for example, with the theory of relativity in Nazi Germany and in Stalin's Soviet Union: in the former, because Einstein was a Jew and in the latter, because "Marx had said the Universe was infinite, and Einstein had got some ideas from Mach, who had been proscribed by Lenin." Paul Johnson, *Modern Times: The World from the Twenties to the Eighties* (New York: Harper Colophon, 1985), 453. In like fashion, Mao dismissed the science of genetics and championed Lysenkoism, because "Lysenko's theories meshed perfectly with Mao's obsession with class struggle. [Mao] readily believed that plants from the same 'class' would never compete against each other for light or food." Jasper Becker, *Hungry Ghosts: Mao's Secret Famine* (New York: The Free Press, 1996), 68–9.

122. Tocqueville, *Democracy*, 447.

123. Ibid, 450.

124. Ibid, 451.

125. Ibid.

126. "Like their modern counterparts, 15th-century publishers only financed the kind of book they felt sure would sell enough copies to show a profit in a reasonable time. We should not therefore be surprised to find that the immediate effect of printing was merely to further increase the circulation of those works which had already enjoyed success in manuscript, and often to consign other less popular texts to oblivion. By multiplying books by the hundred and then thousand, the press achieved both increased volume and at the same time more rigorous selection." Lucien Febvre and Henri-Jean Martin, *The Coming of the Book: The Impact of Printing: 1450-1800* (London: NLB, 1976), 249.

127. "There is no reason to be surprised by this care for solidity and the quality of materials used in binding, which arouses admiration in the trade today. At that time a manuscript or its successor, a printed book, was so comparatively rare and costly an item of merchandise that it merited care in its preservation and adornment. From the invention of printing right up to the 18th century, although the readership increased, the book was still the preserve of a small and favoured elite. In days when paper was made by hand and books printed on hand presses, the book was still seen as a precious object, which it was important to preserve, and therefore had to be bound carefully." Ibid, 104.

128. Tocqueville, *Democracy*, 439.

129. Ibid, 440.

130. Ibid, 441. James Ceaser takes exception with this point, proffering it as an instance where Tocqueville's otherwise penetrating perspicacity failed him. "On first reading this statement in the sixties, it seemed remarkably prescient. A cheap Bulova at that time could not compare with an eighteenth-century Swiss masterpiece. But today a ten-dollar digital Casio is more accurate than its old Swiss counterpart, even if its snappy plastic encasement may not quite measure up on aesthetic grounds." James Ceaser, *Liberal Democracy and Political Science* (Baltimore: Johns Hopkins University Press, 1990), 29. But while at one level doubtlessly true, Ceaser's argument does more to prove Tocqueville's point than refute it. For what is a ten-dollar Casio if not mediocre? And conversely, what is an eighteenth-century Swiss masterpiece if not excellent? The greater precision of the one belies its mediocrity as the comparative imprecision of the other does its excellence. Ceaser's point is revealing because it betrays the modern disposition that prizes order and utility above depth and beauty. On Ceaser's reading, a well-insulated split-level home in Kalamazoo is better than a drafty chateau in Normandy.

131. "It was not through merit that one was born noble, free, or slave, and therefore no one should seek to change his condition." Pierre Riché, *Daily Life in the World of Charlemagne* (Philadelphia: University of Pennsylvania Press, 1978), 99. "Men were born into a status, participated in the society in relation to that status, and were more or less bound to a set of rights and duties defined by that status." Seymour Drescher, *Dilemmas of Democracy: Tocqueville and Modernization* (Pittsburgh: University of Pittsburgh Press, 1968), 26.

132. Plato, *Republic*, Book III.

133. Roger Scruton, "The Great Swindle," *Aeon*, December 17, 2012, https://aeon.co/essays/a-cult-of-fakery-has-taken-over-what-s-left-of-high-culture.
134. Tocqueville, *Democracy*, 590.
135. Ibid, 578.
136. Ibid, 579.
137. Ibid, 581.
138. Lydia Ramsey and Samantha Lee, "Humans share almost all of our DNA with cats, cattle and mice," *The Independent*, April 6, 2018, https://www.independent.co.uk/news/science/human-dna-share-cats-cattle-mice-same-genetics-code-a8292111.html.
139. Friedrich Nietzsche, *The Antichrist*, in *The Portable Nietzsche*, 646. As Nietzsche put it elsewhere, "So that there is a broad, deep, and fertile soil for the development of art, the monstrous majority, in the service of a minority, must be slavishly subjected to life's necessities *above* and beyond their individual requirements." Friedrich Nietzsche, "The Greek State," 48.
140. As Marc Bloch noted, "farming was no proper occupation for a gentleman." To the extent that nobles from the sixteenth century on did involve themselves with farming, it was in a supervisory role. Marc Bloch, *French Rural History: An Essay on its Basic Characteristics*, trans. Janet Sondheimer (Berkeley: University of California Press, 1956), 143–4. See also Peter Laslett, *The World We Have Lost: England before the Industrial Revolution* (New York: Charles Scribner Son's, 1965). "A gentleman never worked with his hands for his living" (12).
141. Nietzsche, *Antichrist*, 646.
142. See, for example, Hugh Brogan, *Alexis de Tocqueville: A Life* (New Haven: Yale University Press, 2007), especially his chapter on Tocqueville's *Ancien Régime*, "Writing Revolution" (525–84), where Brogan likens Tocqueville's final work to "mythmaking" (570) and a "medley of fiction and wishful thinking," though, extraordinarily for all that, it still managed *not* to be "a work of bad history" (574). Brogan's biography, almost universally praised, is something of a maddening affair for anyone who considers Tocqueville a thinker of depth and integrity, for upon reading it, one is left with the impression that Tocqueville's musings were the product of an embittered heart rather than a noble mind. To Brogan, Tocqueville was little more than a reactionary, "one of a defeated class, [who] could not forget or pardon defeat . . . [and who] yearned for his birthright, by which, he felt, he was entitled to be part of the government of France" (573). This last charge appears particularly unwarranted seeing that Tocqueville ran for *elected* office more than once. Indeed, in his first effort (in 1837), he invited, if not ensured, his defeat by, as a matter of principle, refusing the help of his cousin, Count Louis-Mathieu Molé, who was Prime Minister at the time and was eager to grant Tocqueville his so-called birthright. (On this score, see Lamberti, *Tocqueville and The Two Democracies*, 129.) In 1839, Tocqueville managed to convince the electors of Valognes what Brogan apparently never could appreciate, namely that he was not "an aristocrat in disguise: [As he told his compatriots,] in all of France and, I daresay, in all of Europe, there is not one man who has demonstrated more publicly that the old aristocracy is dead forever" (from André Jardin's far more judicious biography of Tocqueville (295)). Brogan's reading of Tocqueville

is often misleading and prejudicial. Thus, for example, Brogan observes the following: "Yet there is one especially important difference between [Tocqueville's first work and his last]. In 1835 the tone is buoyant; democracy is on the march, young Tocqueville is not afraid of the future or especially enamored of the past. In the *ancien régime* his mood is quite other" (569). That the 1835 work, so buoyant in tone, "was written under the pressure of a sort of religious terror in the author's soul, produced by the sight of this irresistible [democratic] revolution," appears to have eluded Brogan, which is somewhat surprising given that Tocqueville's arresting revelation is provided in the work's opening pages. As for the young Tocqueville who was not afraid of the future or especially enamored of the past, he had this to say: "The spectacle of this universal uniformity saddens and chills me, and I am tempted to regret the society that is no longer." Granted, that sentiment was written at the end of the second volume of *Democracy in America*, published five years after the first, but it belonged to the same work, the same period, the same mind. (On the matter of the change of tone between *De Democritie et l'Ancien Régime*, Jardin observes: "His conception of the slow movement of civilization had not essentially changed, but his experience of the world and of men had made it more complex and in certain respects more somber" (483).) In the end, one suspects that the democratic revolution that so troubled Tocqueville's soul, is a matter with which Brogan can find nothing troubling—which is why he considers Tocqueville's idea of tyranny majority, an idea Brogan misunderstands miserably, a "bugbear" (263); why he reprehends Tocqueville for his abuse of socialism (e.g., 468–9, 499); and why of Marx, who makes several appearances in a biography on Tocqueville, nary a critical word is said. Of Tocqueville, on the other hand, there is no shortage of disparaging remarks. "What is obvious today," according to Brogan, is that Tocqueville's "own political and economic opinions were as ill-founded as those which he so passionately resisted" (500). What is less obvious is why Brogan would pen a 700-page biography of a man whose only real claim to celebrity was his meditation on the democratization of mankind when the political opinions he promulgated were, according to Brogan, so obviously ill-founded. Brogan's biography does enjoy at least two redeeming qualities. First, as history, it admirably brings to life the world that Tocqueville inhabited. Second, insofar as he treats Tocqueville's ruminations as reactionary and renders the Norman noble wholly the product of his times, Brogan reduces a great mind to a prosaic one. By doing so, Brogan emblematizes the character of historians who belong to the democratic age. For a critical review of Brogan's work, see Daniel J. Mahoney, "A Noble and Generous Soul," *The Claremont Review of Books*, vol. VII, no. 3 (Summer 2007): https://claremontreviewofbooks.com/a-noble-and-generous-soul/. "If Brogan succeeds in recovering Tocqueville's world, however, he is woefully unsuccessful in capturing his thought." For the generalizing and leveling tendencies of historians in the age of democracy, see Tocqueville, *Democracy*, 469–72. Those tendencies were understood well by Nietzsche, who sought to combat them. See, for example, Nietzsche, "On the Uses and Disadvantages of History for Life." "The time will come when one will prudently refrain from all constructions of the world-process or even of the history of man; a time when one will regard not the masses but individuals, who form a kind of bridge across the turbulent stream of becoming. These individuals do not carry forward any kind of process but live contemporaneously with one another; thanks to history, which permits such a collaboration, they live as that republic of genius of which Schopenhauer once spoke; one giant calls to another across the desert intervals of time and, undisturbed by the excited chattering dwarfs who creep about beneath them, the exalted spirit-dialogue goes on. It is the task of history to be the mediator between them and thus, again and again, to inspire and lend the strength for the production of the great man. No, the goal of humanity cannot lie in its end but only in its highest exemplars" (111).

143. Tocqueville, *Democracy*, 536–7.
144. Ibid, 535.
145. Ibid, 536.
146. Ibid, 587.
147. Ibid, 536.
148. "Early societies were made up of groups rather than individuals. A man on his own counted for very little." Bloch, *French Rural History*, 150. "Each member of [aristocratic] society conceived of himself not as an individual or a citizen, but as a member of one or more communities within the hierarchy which both bound and protected him." Drescher, *Dilemmas of Democracy*, 26–7.
149. Nietzsche, *Gay Science*, 117.
150. Tocqueville, *Democracy*, 483.
151. Ibid, 483.
152. Edward Peters, *Europe and the Middle Ages* (Upper Saddle River, NJ: Prentice Hall, 1983), 170.
153. Tocqueville, *Old Regime*, 154–5.
154. Tocqueville notes that "the very name of patriotism is not old in our idiom" and that the word *patrie* is found in French authors only from the sixteenth century on. *Democracy*, 592. "The word 'patriotism' appeared in England in 1726 and in France in 1750." Aira Kemiläinen, "The idea of patriotism during the first years of the French Revolution," *History of European Ideas* 11
 (1989): 11.
155. Tocqueville, *Democracy*, 8.
156. Ibid, 123.
157. For an understanding of those hardships, not the least of which was famine—the peasants' "ever present companion"—see Bloch, *French Rural History*. The peasant rebellions, which form "a long and tragic chain" that stretches through European history, were reactions, as well as attestations, to those hardships. Bloch analogizes those torrents of discontent to strikes in capitalist societies. As he notes, "A social system is characterized not only by its internal structure but also by the reactions it produces; a system based on authority at times may result in the sincere performance of mutual obligations, at others in a brutal outbreak of hostility on both sides." Bloch, *French Rural History*, 26, 169–70.
158. "Tocqueville constantly pointed to the cardinal fact that a durable society was able to exist for centuries despite the fact that a relative handful of individuals monopolized wealth and power. This was due to the fact that both the dependent and the protector felt bound by a shared relationship of community . . . . Each member knew

his rights and obligations—what was expected of those above as well as those beneath him." Drescher, *Dilemmas of Democracy*, 27. It is the absence of this care—of a sense of obligation that those on top feel towards those beneath—that prompts Tocqueville to characterize the "manufacturing aristocracy . . . rising before [his] eyes" as being "one of the hardest that has appeared on earth." Tocqueville, *Democracy in America*, 532. Tocqueville seems to have been of the view that any aristocracy that may materialize in the age of democracy—be it industrial or, what he could not have prevised, digital—would be fugacious; that is, that democracy ultimately would prevail. As he reflected in his notes, "All newly born societies begin by organizing themselves as aristocracies. Industry is now subject to this law." Quoted in Lamberti, *Tocqueville and the Two Democracies*, 183. Whatever ambiguity may surround the long-term viability of an aristocracy in the age of democracy is in some ways immaterial, for as Seymour Drescher astutely observed, "What Tocqueville feared most was not the threat to equality, but the threat to liberty. What most vitally concerned him was neither industrial serfdom nor an industrial aristocracy, but industrial centralization." Drescher, *Dilemmas of Democracy*, 85.

159. Tocqueville, *Old Regime*, 182.

160. Ibid, 117.

161. "*Celui qui n'a pas vécu au dix-huitième siècle avant la Révolution ne connaît pas la douceur de vivre.*" ("Those who haven't lived in the eighteenth century before the Revolution do not know the sweetness of living.")

162. "In the aristocratic community each felt himself part, not of universalized and equal rights and duties, but only of a shared value system. It was psychologically gratifying as well to the extent that each member of society could vicariously participate in the power and glory of its highest members, who themselves were considered vicars, not incarnations, of divine power." Drescher, *Dilemmas of Democracy*, 27.

Chapter 3

The Revolutions

The fall of the Bastille was "a prologue to a farce or tragedy; or perhaps both."[1] However one wishes to qualify the French Revolution, the fact remains that the *ancien régime* went the way of the Bastille: dismantled, for good. So seismic, so sweeping, so portentous, was the Revolution that the adjectival qualifier affixed to it is as apt to describe as it is to obscure. For although the Revolution was conspicuously French, it transcended France. It was much more than a political upheaval and, unlike prior political revolutions, it affected far more than those who were politically upheaved. It was, as Tocqueville observed, a political revolution that behaved like a religious one.[2] It would rent not only the Continent but history. "1789 became the birth date, the year zero of a new world founded on equality."[3] There could be no going back.

The French Revolution, like any revolution, did not erupt *ex nihilo*. The democratic torrents that welled from it—that were blazoned in the immortal words appended to it (*liberté, égalité, fraternité*)—had been gathering steam long before the Revolution let them loose. Had those currents not continually gathered steam across the centuries, 1789 would be a date confined to anonymity or remembered for something altogether different. The French Revolution merely made plain for all to see what had been advancing for some time.

For how long precisely one cannot say. It is the sort of question that the man of science, himself a product of humanity's millennial democratization, will be inclined to dismiss because, by its very nature, it permits no conclusive answer. The catalytic properties of ideas—and one never should lose sight of the fact that humanity's democratization is the product of an idea or many, for that matter—exhibit such tremendous ambiguity that those who demand certitude are likely to deny their relevance, if not validity, altogether.

The question of when humans began to walk upright is worth taking up, first because it is of evolutionary significance in the Darwinian sense, but also because it holds out the promise that one day—thanks to fossil records and other tangible findings—an answer, however broad, will be secured so that little room will be left for debate. When was the democratization of man first afoot? How can one determine the date of that? What proof could settle that matter and put it to rest? And is that not the aim of modern science—of modern man, really: to settle all matters and, once and for all, allay unrest?

For the more philosophically minded, it is the very search itself that matters.[4] The success of that search can be measured in part, not by the end that is reached (for finite and fallible beings such as man, there can be but one end), but by the dead-ends avoided. Therein lies the merit of Nietzsche and Tocqueville's musings on the nature of democratic man: they put one on the right track. The French Revolution looms large in Tocqueville's later thought, much as the American Revolution, broadly conceived, did in his earlier thought. As was the case with his youthful undertaking, Tocqueville was concerned less with the historicity of events, than with understanding the causes—the immaterial ones not least among them—that brought them about. To take up *The Old Regime and the Revolution* as a way of acquainting oneself with the Revolution would be a despairing endeavor, perhaps one that could be loosely analogized to reading Machiavelli's *Discourses on Livy* as an introduction to ancient Rome. This has less to do with the complexity of Tocqueville's arguments or the density of his prose (which is a model of eloquence and clarity)[5] than with the fleeting attention he devotes to the major events of the Revolution (the Tennis Court Oath, the storming of the Bastille, the September massacres, the Terror, etc.). As an introduction, Tocqueville's final work is more liable to befuddle the reader than enlighten him. But any acquaintance with the unfolding of the Revolution would be deeply enriched by Tocqueville's disquisition precisely because he illumines the wherefores for and consequences of it. As Tocqueville writes in the preface: "The object of this book is to understand why this great revolution, which was simultaneously taking shape all over Europe, broke out in France rather than elsewhere, why it was so natural a product of the society it was going to destroy, and how, finally, the old monarchy could fall so suddenly and so completely."[6] And it is an object that Tocqueville secures with characteristic acuity, though not without escaping criticism.[7] In disinterring the Revolution's roots, Tocqueville wrestled with the problem that consumed him throughout the course of his intellectual life, namely how to preserve human greatness in view of the leveling tides that portend to submerge all peaks beneath democratic waters. In his youth, he had sailed to America to espy man's future, exploring that country which had, at the time, taken democracy to its furthest limits. In his waning years, he turned to his own country, reflecting on the most far-reaching event of France's long and rich history. *The Old Regime and the Revolution* was not just about France any more than *Democracy in America* was about that eponymous nation. The insights contained in each work, like the revolutions that convulsed each country, transcend national boundaries and appertain to humanity en masse. All revolutions invite excess, whether they are revolutions in thought or deed. One could not hope to temper the excesses of the democratic revolution, as Tocqueville so ardently desired to do, without first grasping the nature of that revolution. And one could not hope to achieve that simply by studying the revolution's more salient tumults. The French Revolution may have cleaved history, but in the broader context of man's democratization, it was as much a consequence as it was a catalyst. The democratic revolution had been sparked long before those egalitarian upheavals flared up in the waning years of the eighteenth century.

Nietzsche, who faulted earlier thinkers for their want of historical perspective, had no illusions about the significance of the French Revolution, especially in terms of man's democratization.[8] But like Goethe, whom he unwaveringly esteemed, Nietzsche had not been deceived by the spectacle that "seduced even the noblest of spirits."[9] The Revolution was ruinous, not just for the aristocracy, but for humanity, for its animating principle—"the doctrine of equality"—was poison; indeed, in Nietzsche's mind, "there is no more poisonous poison anywhere."[10] Still, Nietzsche understood that the Revolution itself was merely an outgrowth; that its roots ran deep—unfathomably deep for the Revolution's devotees. The poison that the Revolution spilled was not of its own concocting; it had been coursing through mankind for centuries, millennia even, going back to the dawn, not of civilization, but of Western civilization. Because in general the historical sense is stunted and because sound and fury tend to captivate even the brightest minds, the significance of the French Revolution often is inflated; its derivativeness overlooked. But to return to that wonderful proclamation of Nietzsche's godless prophet, it is not the loudest, but the stillest hours that shape and reshape man and alter history's trajectory.[11] With respect to the advent of democratic man, Nietzsche had in mind two hours, both of which transpired long before the banner of equality was planted among the ruins of the *ancient régime*. The first was when Socrates "brought philosophy down from the heavens [and] placed it in cities";[12] the second, was when God brought himself down and sacrificed himself for his wayward children.

Of these two hours, it was the significance of the second that was not lost on Tocqueville. Christianity is conducive to democracy,[13] so much so that democracy would seem to be the natural and inevitable corollary to it. Other roads to the democratization of humankind undoubtedly could be conceived and might have been taken, but once a religion whose foundational tenet is the equality of souls becomes ascendant, humanity, in effect, is fated to be democratized. Christianity's ascendance can be explained, in part by its universal appeal.[14] For Tocqueville personally, that appeal had its limits. But while Tocqueville's own comportment toward Christianity remained ambivalent up until the moment he drew his last breath,[15] he had no doubt about the puissance of faith and the indispensable part Christianity played in democratizing man. Nietzsche, of course, was also without doubt regarding the impact of Christianity, but when it came to reckoning the value of Christianity, the two hardly could be more divided. One would scour Tocqueville's writings in vain to find anything remotely akin to Nietzsche's animadversion at the end of *The Antichrist*:

> I call Christianity the one great curse, the one great innermost corruption, the one great instinct of revenge, for which no means is poisonous, stealthy, subterranean *small* enough—I call it the one immortal blemish upon the human race.[16]

But the disparity in their views on Christianity mirrors the disparity in their views on democracy; neither should obscure the consonance of their views on mankind's democratization and the indispensable role Christianity played in effecting it.

As for that earlier hour, when Socrates strutted and fretted upon life's stage, Tocqueville effectively has nothing to offer.[17] The revolutionary and originary part that Socrates played in democratizing man appears to have eluded him. For a brief while then, Tocqueville will be obliged to remain silent.

THE SOCRATIC REVOLUTION

The democratizing influence of Christianity is evident, even if many today remain studiously oblivious to it. A universal God is a good place to start, but Christianity universalized that God in a manner or to a degree that greatly exceeded what its Jewish forebears had accomplished. In spite of its universal divinity, Judaism remained the religion of a particular people. Christianity embraced all people, barring no one from its ranks, and moreover, posited as a foundational tenet the equality of souls. Those are the sort of principles of which democratizations are made. What is more, and doubtlessly related, Christianity went on to embrace humanity not only in spirit, but in fact, infiltrating the greatest empire the world had known, surviving its collapse, and advancing triumphantly across its ruins, leaving no corner of Europe—and, in time, the globe—untouched. Perhaps with respect to mankind's democratization, no force was more prodigious than this. Yet, the democratizing movement of history had been set in motion prior; that movement, like the civilization in which it was initially carried out, had twin foundations, fraternal, rather than identical. And the subsequent-born one was Christianity. Without discounting its influence, in the end (and beginning), Christianity in many ways was derivative, not simply with respect to the first great monotheistic people, from which Christianity, in a manner of speaking, appropriated its most famous teacher and many of its teachings,[18] but with respect to that other pillar of Western Civilization—Athens.

Nietzsche draws attention to the derivative character of Christianity by designating it "Platonism for 'the people'."[19] That derivativeness, of course, runs deeper; for if Christianity—with its subordination of the earthly realm to a heavenly one and its postulation of an eternal truth to which all other "truths" must conform—is a perversion and simplification of Plato's thought, then it owes its existence to that human being without whom Plato (qua Plato) never would have been: Socrates.[20]

Christianity hardly seems the ineluctable outcome of Socrates' thought nor does humanity's democratization follow as neatly from Socrates' teachings as it does from Christ's.[21] But as Nietzsche argues, Socrates effected a transformative break from the aristocratic mindset that animated his Greek antecedents. In reconceiving the nature of virtue and knowledge, as well as the means to their procurement, Socrates could not but court a creeping uniformity, one that would, in time, minimize the vast expanse that had separated man from man.

This break was visible on the Greek stage. With the Euripidean drama, the knell of Greek tragedy was sounded. It was Euripides, Nietzsche contends, who brought the common man onto the Greek stage, transforming him from a spectator into a spectacle. Previously a stomping ground for demigods, the stage now became a place where "everyday life could be represented" and where "bourgeois mediocrity" had been given "its chance to speak." Moreover, it was for the common man that Euripides composed his plays, as he sought to promulgate his wisdom to the greatest number.[22]

These anti-egalitarian sentiments aside, Nietzsche's deeper claim is that Euripides aimed to bring to light what had ever remained veiled. The Greeks had harbored a reverence for concealment and mystery, as intimated by "Heraclitus's famous formula 'Nature loves to hide'."[23] That reverence entailed an appreciation for the limits of human knowledge and the recognition that there is something unnatural, perhaps supernatural, about wisdom. It is not light alone that attends the pursuit and acquisition of knowledge. Some stones are better left unturned, a lesson so strikingly conveyed by Sophocles through the tragic figure of Oedipus. With Euripides, this mindset is driven from the Greek stage. Regarding himself as "the first sober [poet]," Euripides saw it as his responsibility to impugn his irrational precursors. "Euripides undertook to show the world the opposite of the 'unreasoning' poet . . .

his aesthetic principle [was] 'Everything must be conscious in order to be beautiful.'"[24]

But with respect to the democratizing movement of history, Euripides was more effect than cause. He serves to validate the charge put forward by Nietzsche in *On the Genealogy of Morality* that artists ever "have been the valets of some morality, philosophy, or religion."[25] However far beneath him he felt his two great dramaturgical forerunners to be, there was one person who always towered above and stood behind him: Socrates.[26]

For Nietzsche, Euripides is "the poet of aesthetic Socratism,"[27] the supreme law of which is "to be beautiful, everything must be reasonable."[28] This constituted an inversion of values, distinct from, but no less radical nor consequential than the one that Christianity subsequently affected. With Socrates, reason, which enjoyed no privileged place prior to him, assumes a position so commanding that before it all else must bend.

It is the rotting society that revolts. The revolution brought about by that ugly plebeian[29] was possible only among a people with "tired instincts,"[30] that is, only *after* the Greeks had begun to decline. In a more robust age, Socrates's dialectic machinations would have been to no avail and the outsized role of reason that he advanced would have been dismissed out of hand. But an age that declines thirsts—knowingly or not—for an elixir; for new values to supplant the old and that is what Socrates promised with "the equation of reason, virtue and happiness: that most bizarre of all equations, which, moreover, is opposed to all the instincts of the earlier Greeks."[31]

A truly happy, "well-turned out human being" instinctively performs certain actions and refrains from others: "virtue is the *effect* of his happiness."[32] Virtue does not beget happiness; rather, virtue is begotten by a people who already are happy. "As long as life is ascending, happiness equals instinct," not virtue. When life is in decay, as it was in fifth-century Athens, one seeks to combat the instincts with the aid of reason. "Rationality at any price; the war against the instincts is not a cure but merely another disease. To have to fight the instincts, that is the formula of decadence."[33] Reason, which reigns supreme not only in Socratic thought, but across much of the Western tradition Socrates helped engender, was a faculty of little repute in the minds of those who preceded him.

> Before Socrates, dialectic manners were repudiated in society: they were considered bad manners, they were compromising. The young were warned against them. Furthermore, all such presentations of one's reasons were distrusted. Honest things, like honest men, do not carry their reasons in their hand. It is indecent to show all five fingers. What must be proved is of little worth.[34]

The Homeric heroes, unlike the Platonic one, had no need of dialectics. Achilles was esteemed because of his virtue, which neither he nor Homer had any need of justifying rationally. Not reason, but instinct (or nature) was the foundation of virtue. One might say that Achilles was naturally predisposed to virtue. The virtuous were first and foremost the strong, the healthy, the powerful, in short, those whom nature endowed with the capacity to rule. This harks back to the aristocratic mode of establishing values taken up above. The ruling class was the measure of all things. Life was imbued with values that reflected the vigor of those who imbued it. The order of rank that separated high from low was established as an affirmation of life; it displayed a lust for, and overabundance of, life on the part of the ruling class. Good and bad were not determined by the degree to which they conformed to the dictates of reason, but the degree to which they reflected and moreover promoted the instincts of those who commanded. "Good and bad is for a long time the same as noble and base, master and slave. . . . In Homer, the Trojan and the Greek are both good. It is not he who does us harm but he who is contemptible who counts as bad."[35]

This aristocratic, pre-Socratic mode of valuation was done naturally and instinctually, but the unconsciousness of it did not detract from the value of it, that is, until Socrates entered onto the stage. What Sophocles had said of Aeschylus—that "he did the right thing, although he did it unconsciously"[36]—no longer can be said after the Socratic revolution. "To be good everything must be conscious"—that is the mode of valuation with which Socrates altered the course of history.

> The sharpest words in favor of that new, unheard-of esteem for knowledge and insight were those spoken by Socrates when he said that he was the only man of his acquaintance who confessed to *knowing nothing*; on his critical wanderings through Athens, by contrast, when he called on the greatest politicians, orators, poets, and artists, he encountered the same illusion of knowledge everywhere. He registered with astonishment the fact that all those famous men lacked even a secure and correct understanding of their profession, and performed it only by instinct. "Only by instinct": the phrase goes to the heart and center of the Socratic tendency. With these words Socratism condemns existing art and existing ethics in equal measure; wherever it directs its probing gaze, it sees a lack of insight and the power of delusion, and it concludes from this lack that what exists is inwardly wrong and objectionable. Socrates believed that he was obliged to correct existence, starting from this single point; he, the individual, the forerunner of a completely different culture, art, and morality, steps with a look of disrespect and superiority into a world where we would count ourselves supremely happy if we could even touch the hem of its cloak in awe.[37]

The sublimation of reason and the depreciation of the instincts constitute a reorientation of man (or perhaps a reconstruction), the likes of which never had been seen before nor arguably since. It would be difficult to overstate the significance of the Socratic Revolution, a significance that Nietzsche communicates with customary brilliance.

> Consider for a moment how, after Socrates, the mystagogue of science, one school of philosophy follows another, like wave upon wave; how an unimaginable, universal greed for knowledge, stretching across most of the cultured world, and presenting itself as the true task for anyone of higher abilities, led science on to the high seas, from which it could never again be driven completely; and how for the first time, thanks to this universality, a common network of thought was stretched over the whole globe, with prospects of encompassing even the laws of the entire solar system; when one considers all this, along with the astonishingly high pyramid of knowledge we have at present, one cannot do other than regard Socrates as the vortex and turning-point of so-called world history.[38]

The Socratic Revolution results in the transfiguration of man—not the Greeks or Western man, but man simply. It alters man's very nature; or rather, it compels man to prioritize the elements of his nature in such a manner that he sees himself and the world around him in a radically different light. Humans had once seen themselves essentially as political animals or as children of God made in their Father's image. But all that has given way to the understanding that it is reason that sets humans apart. Remove God and politics from the equation, and what is left? Man, the rational animal. There is nothing Homeric or Shakespearean about a world populated thus, though in the minds of these rational animals, that is unlikely to count as a rebuke. While such animals are not oblivious to the glories of the past, those glories cannot atone for the dearth of the reason that pervaded those earlier times. And wherever reason does not prevail, ignorance and madness do.[39] But modern man's self-coronation is, if not delusional, misguided; his crowning achievement is not so much that he has figured it all out, but that he has simplified himself and the world he inhabits. The world rendered familiar and man with it too—that is what he grasps and that is the source of his self-satisfaction.[40] Man has lowered his sights and, by virtue of doing so, has hit the mark. Man, the reductionist animal.

Rational inquiry may be central to the Socratic method, but what his dialectical investigations frequently result in is not wisdom, but bewilderment or *aporia*. While such a denouement would seem to suggest the inherent limits of reason, as would, for that matter, Socratic wisdom itself (which is, of course, Socratic ignorance),[41] one cannot ignore the fact that even in adumbrating its limits, Socrates endowed reason with a power it did not enjoy prior, one that in time would overshadow all other approaches to apperceiving the world. What cannot be grasped rationally simply cannot be grasped.

This applies not only to the philosopher or scientist, but to man *qua* man. With the Socratic revolution, democratic man takes what constitutes not his initial steps, but his first great leap.

That man's democratization might have been achieved by other means no doubt is possible, but clearly to that end, reason conduced wonderfully. Equality is a fabrication that man has superimposed upon the world around him so as to better navigate and feel more at home in it (a verity of which both Nietzsche and Tocqueville were cognizant[42]). Left to his own devices—to his instincts—inequality would be the order of the day. To see things as they are is to perceive the singularity, the incomparability of life's phenomena. In Blake's immortal words: "If the doors of perception were cleansed, everything would appear to man as it is, Infinite. For we have closed ourselves up "til we see all through the narrow chinks of our cavern."[43] As Nietzsche has it, the fundamental fact of all life is not will to equality or even will to (self-)preservation, but will to *power*.[44] Without any sublimation of that will or moderation of it, life is characterized by inequality, struggle, discord, and the like. In such a world, the equality of persons has no place. To contend that everyone in the state of nature is equal because everyone has the capacity to take the life of another is merely a clever turn by a being far removed from that state who applies to it a measure that has no place in it. Anyone who found himself transported to the state of nature would find such a logical deduction absurd, however, sound it may seem in the realm of reason. So long as one survived, one would be aware that he was not the equal of another but that there was an above and a below and that one's survival to some extent depended where on the continuum one found oneself.

Reason then allows man to imprint the idea of equality upon reality. But the turn from instinct to reason does not render the hypostatization of equality a fait accompli. There is nothing that necessitates that the advent of equality dovetail with that of reason. Plato's thought, wherein the elevated role of reason and the intrinsic inequality of human beings go hand in hand, attests as much. By way of a more modern illustration, one might consider those revolutions—the French and Russian come readily to mind—that were predicated on a perverse and fanatical commitment to reason and equality, and in the end, bastardized both. But if the turn to reason does not guarantee the democratization of man, it greatly lends itself to it. In no small part, this is because of the nature of reason itself. As Nietzsche recounts the origin of scholars, he notes that the Jews had a remarkable propensity for employing reason and that this propensity could be understood in light of their unparalleled history.

> A Jew . . . in keeping with the business circles and the past of his people, is least of all used to being believed. Consider Jewish scholars in this light: All of them have a high regard for logic, that is for *compelling* agreement by force of

reasons; they know, with that they are bound to win even where they encounter race and class prejudices and where one does not like to believe them. For nothing is more democratic than logic; it is no respecter of persons and makes no distinction between crooked and straight noses.[45]

When reason prevails, the character of the individual becomes a matter of ancillary import. Reason in the hands of the ignominious man is no less legitimate than reason in the hands of the magnanimous one. In this way, the turn to reason facilitates a leveling of man that was not feasible in the time when instinct reigned.

Socratism lent itself to the democratization of man in another way, one that had more to do with the unifying goal of reason than its leveling character. This goal is central to what Nietzsche calls the spirit of science: "the belief, which first came to light in the person of Socrates, that the depths of nature can be fathomed and that knowledge can heal all ills."[46] Science itself predates Socrates.[47] It is enough to cite the names of Thales, Anaximander, and Pythagoras to appreciate as much. In his youth, Socrates displayed a keen interest in the study of natural phenomena and had those youthful pursuits proved more satisfying to him, it is not just his story or Greek history that would have unfolded very differently. A profound discontent with the philosophic musings of his predecessors impelled Socrates to embark on his celebrated second sailing,[48] after which he returned and with him brought philosophy down from the heavens into the city. It is on account of this undertaking that Nietzsche refers to Socrates as *the mischief-maker in science*:

> Philosophy separated itself from science when it posed the question: what kind of knowledge of the world and life is it through which man can live happiest? This took place in the Socratic schools: by having in view the objective of happiness one applied a ligature to the arteries of scientific research—and does so still today.[49]

By making happiness the aim of knowledge, Socrates severed his thought from the original understanding of science and in doing so, begot a new spirit of science, one that endures to this day.

The staying power of that spirit is all the more remarkable in view of the fact that modern science has all but divorced itself from the Socratic quest, that is, philosophy. So effective and final has this divorce become that knowledge of the former confluence between science and philosophy and the former's genesis in the latter has been largely forgotten.[50] The divorce was not initially mutual nor, for that matter, purposive. To be sure, a conscious and concerted effort to supersede the inherited wisdom of the ancients was made by thinkers like Descartes, Bacon, and Hobbes. But their aim was not to dispense with natural philosophy, so much as give it a firmer footing. Hence one finds, well into the eighteenth century, the conflation of philosophy and science, a conflation that would no longer be permitted in the following century.[51] But the effort to place philosophy on a more secure footing rendered philosophy immaterial. The elevation of *praxis* in general, and the mathematization of nature in particular, yielded a new understanding of science, one that made a separation from the traditional notion of science (i.e., natural philosophy) all but inevitable. The disjunction between modern science and classical science can be traced to one field in particular: physics.

> Prior to the victory of the new physics, there was not the science of physics simply: there were Aristotelian physics, Platonic physics, Epicurean physics, Stoic physics; to speak colloquially, there was no metaphysically neutral physics. The victory of the new physics led to the emergence of a physics which seemed to be as metaphysically neutral as, say, mathematics, medicine, or the art of shoemaking. The emergence of a metaphysically neutral physics made it possible for "science" to become independent of "philosophy" and in fact an authority for the latter. It paved the way for an economic science which is independent of ethics, for sociology as the study of nonpolitical associations as not inferior in dignity to the political association, and, last but not least, for the separation of political science from political philosophy as well as the separation of economics and sociology from political science.[52]

Again, this disjunction was not exactly purposive. Those early modern thinkers who labored to make philosophy less fallible did not anticipate that their success would render philosophy, by and large, dispensable. But once methodological considerations became more important than metaphysical ones, such an outcome was all but fated.

> The emancipation of science from an overarching entity called "natural philosophy" is one defining characteristic of the Scientific Revolution. The key point is that, in earlier times, knowledge of nature was held to make sense only in the framework of a comprehensive view of the world and man and how these are connected.
> The new science claimed to provide an understanding of reality that did not owe its warrant to whether or not it fitted in with an all-encompassing insight into the order of the world but only to the extent to which it satisfied inherent criteria of a methodical nature: quantitative precision, and, above all, susceptibility to empirical checking on the level of detail.[53]

Yet, despite this divorce and the rise of modern science and fall of philosophy that it precipitated, the spirit of science—that finds its origins in Socratism and sees knowledge as a panacea for life—lives on. For in spite of all its pretensions to objectivity, science rests upon a number of presuppositions that it cannot substantiate scientifically (for example that truth is better than untruth; that knowledge is salubrious for human beings; that, in brief, science is good), and these faiths were not set down in the seventeenth and eighteenth centuries, when science ostensibly became autonomous, but rather two millennia prior, when the spirit of science first emerged.

This insight regarding the nature of science is central to Nietzsche's thought and it was central from the start, as he discloses in his prefatory attempt at self-criticism where he looks back on that book in which his "youthful courage and suspicion vented itself"[54]—*The Birth of Tragedy*. "What I got hold of at that time was something fearsome and dangerous, a problem with horns but not necessarily a bull, but at any rate a *new* problem; today I would say that it was the *problem of science itself,* science grasped for the first time as problematic and questionable."[55] One might be quick to rejoin that what was a new problem then is a trite one today. To be born in the aftermath, no matter how far removed, of the Great War, which deeply shook man's faith in science and progress,[56] is to be born in a time when the problematic nature of science is as bright as day. Even tabling all consideration of the potentially calamitous consequences of modern warfare, one still is confronted with a litany of dangers for which modern science, to varying degrees, is responsible; a litany that is hammered home starting at a very early age—global warming, environmental degradation, mass extinction, overpopulation, genetic engineering, human cloning, and the obsolescence of man that artificial intelligence portends, to name but a few. But the potentially deleterious effects of science do not get to the root of the problem; indeed, they do not even point to it. Even if every danger that science courts were neutralized, science would still remain problematic and questionable. To put it differently, to find solutions to the popular problems that science poses would not resolve the problem of science.

Nietzsche was less concerned about science going off the rails than it staying on track. It was not the missteps and unanticipated consequences of science that troubled Nietzsche but its animating faith—a faith that, notwithstanding all the prodigious strides science has made across the centuries, remains unchanged. That faith is the Socratic faith, the faith that Socrates gave to man, the faith "that the depths of nature can be fathomed and that knowledge can heal all ills."[57] It is a faith that has not merely survived for two and half millennia, but in that time has grown more and more indomitable. Nietzsche recognized that the achievements of modern science dwarfed those of earlier times[58] and that the discoveries of modern scientists irrevocably altered man's understanding of the cosmos and his place in it.[59] But Nietzsche maintains that in spite of all that, the spirit of science remains unchanged. And that spirit signifies a radical shift in man's relation to the world and himself.

Prior to Socrates, before the Greeks began their decline, "the finest, most beautiful, most envied race of men ever known"[60] had no need of a panacea, certainly not of the sort Socrates peddled. That is not because the Greeks were bereft of learning and blissful in their ignorance. A culture that boasts the poetry of Homer and Pindar; the tragedy of Aeschylus and Sophocles; the philosophy of Parmenides and Heraclitus belongs to no dark age. (To the extent that ignorance and barbarism belong together, neither belonged to the Greeks. Barbarism was a Greek coinage, and it signified that which was un-Greek.[61]) Their pre- or un-Socratic wisdom was predicated on the awareness that in essence, life was not intelligible, that "at the very foundation of existence," everything was "fearsome, wicked, mysterious, annihilating and fateful."[62] What for Nietzsche is so remarkable is that when confronted with the unintelligibility of existence, "the Greeks of the best, the strongest and bravest period"[63] did not attempt to flee into some beyond, nor did they aspire to master and correct nature; rather, through art—the tragic art specifically—they embraced life (its horrors included) and celebrated it.

The Greek worldview was profoundly pessimistic. Having apprehended the wisdom of Silenus, perhaps it could not have been otherwise. At bottom, existence was chaos, devoid of purpose and bereft of rhyme and reason. The despair and ruin that such an insight naturally invites was held at bay by the Greeks. They did not resign themselves to this reality so much as sublimate it. To do so, what was required—and what the Greeks, who for centuries flourished in body and soul, knew no shortage of—was exuberance, strength, and "an excess of plenitude."[64] The Greeks made plain that there can be a pessimism of strength: "An intellectual preference for the hard, gruesome, malevolent and problematic aspects of existence which comes from a feeling of well-being, from overflowing health, from an *abundance* of existence."[65]

For a people constituted in this manner, myth and tragedy were of far greater importance than science and logic. The former, not the latter, allowed the Greeks to navigate the void into which they had been tossed. This is of no small consequence precisely because the Greeks had science at their disposal. But whatever value the Greeks conferred upon science, ultimately it had little impact on their understanding of the world and their place in it. The theogonies of Homer and Hesiod did far more to mold the Greek's perspective than did the mechanistic cosmology of Anaximander. Strange as it may sound to those born into a world that science has so imperiously constructed, myth and poetry had a far greater bearing on the lives of the Greeks than did reason and science. As Nietzsche put it, "that which Thales and Anaxagoras know would normally be termed out of the ordinary, miraculous, difficult, divine, but useless, because to them it had nothing to do with humane goods."[66] Scientific knowledge had no bearing on the human world; or rather, its import was tangential. Those committed to the acquisition of it were concerned above all about the world of nature, not that of man. To a Greek devotedly wed to his *polis*, what did it matter that the first element was water or that atoms were indivisible? The uselessness of such science was comically lampooned by Aristophanes, but only because by then, it had become involved with humane goods.

The focus of Aristophanes's pasquinade and the person responsible for making humane goods the object of science is, of course, Socrates. In the *Phaedo*, Socrates recounts his second sailing when he redirected his thinking and in so doing, redirected the course of history. He recalls to Cebes that when he was young, he had "an extraordinary passion for that branch of learning which is called natural science [for he] thought it would be marvelous to know the causes for which each thing comes and ceases and continues to be."[67] However, his passion soon waned when it became clear to him that the speculations of natural philosophers did little to slake his intellectual thirst. Indeed, not only did they fail to yield the answers he sought; they left him more befuddled than he had been before so that he unlearned what he thought he once knew.[68] Specifically, Socrates recounts his encounter with Anaxagoras, whose theory that mind "produces order and is the cause of everything" delighted the young Socrates because he had found an authority on causation that was after his own heart. However, his initial enthusiasm was quickly dashed and the reason why is revealing.

> I assumed that he [Anaxagoras] would begin by informing us whether the earth is flat or round, and would then proceed to explain in detail the reason and logical necessity for this by stating how and why it was better that it should be so. I thought that if he asserted that the earth was in the center, he would explain in detail that it was better for it to be there; and if he made this clear, I was prepared to give up hankering after any other kind of cause. I was prepared also in the same way to receive instruction about the sun and moon and the other heavenly bodies, about their relative velocities and their orbits and all the other phenomena connected with them—in what way it is better for each one of them to act or be acted upon as it is. It never entered my head that a man who asserted that the ordering of things is due to mind would offer any other explanation for them than that it is best for them to be as they are. I thought that by assigning a cause to each phenomenon separately and to the universe as a whole he would make perfectly clear what is best for each and what is the universal good. I would not have parted with my hopes for a great sum of money. I lost no time in procuring the books, and began to read them as quickly as I possibly could, so that I might know as soon as possible about the best and the less good.[69]

Socrates surveyed the musings of his predecessors and found them wanting. They disclosed nothing about the best and the less good. This much his predecessors likely would have conceded, at least with respect to their natural and cosmological investigations. In this regard at least, Socrates's gripe is nugatory. What do the best and less good have to do with the study of nature? Atoms are neither good nor bad; they simply are.[70]

Atomism exemplifies why the Socratic quest could find no satisfactory outlet in the scientific speculations of the pre-Socratics.[71] There is an irreconcilability between Socratism and Democratism, one that Nietzsche, who regards Democritus as a sort of pinnacle of pre-Socratic thought, draws attention to.

> Of all the more ancient systems, the Democritean is of the greatest consequence. The most rigorous necessity is presupposed in all things: there are no sudden or strange violations of nature's course. Now for the first time the collective, anthropomorphic, mythic view of the world has been overcome. Now for the first time do we have a rigorous, scientifically useful *hypothesis*. As such, materialism has always been of the greatest utility. It is the most down-to-earth point of view, it proceeds from real properties of matter, and it does not indifferently leave out the simplest forces, as is done by [accounts of] mind or that of final ends by Aristotle. It is a grand idea, this entire world of order and purposiveness, of countless qualities to be traced back to externalizations of *one force* of the most basic sort. Matter, moving itself according to general laws, produces a blind mechanical result, which appears to be the outline of a highest wisdom.[72]

The influence of this grand idea on Nietzsche's own thought is not difficult to detect. As Nietzsche had it: "The total character of the world is in all eternity chaos—in the sense not of a lack of necessity, but of a lack of order, arrangement, form, beauty, wisdom and whatever other names for our aesthetic anthropomorphisms."[73] That an investigation into the nature of things would have nothing to say about the best and the less good is no reason for impugning it any more than the inability of mathematics to determine which regime is best (and which less good) would constitute grounds for its impugnment. The best and less good were human constructs that at most could be imposed on the natural order, but could not be found to inhere in it.

Whatever he might have thought about Nietzsche's insight into the total character of the world, it is clear that for Socrates, a philosophy that fails to move beyond that is useless. (It is worth noting that with that claim, Nietzsche would agree. Had he been a pre-Socratic, perhaps Nietzsche might have reasoned otherwise. But in a post-Socratic world, philosophy cannot but be concerned with the best and less good.[74] A cosmic void, devoid of meaning and purpose, is no place for man, even if he has no other place to repair—a reminder that in spite of his own atheism, Nietzsche was no proselytizer of it.) If philosophy had no bearing on the life of man, if its principal

164   Chapter 3

contribution was to determine the material cause of all things (be it water or air or *apeiron*), then it was, in Socrates's mind, useless.

> Astronomy [Socrates] considered among the divine secrets, which would be nonsense to investigate. There is indeed advantage to knowing the motion of the celestial bodies as a leader of sea and land journeys and night-watches—one may learn this much from navigators and watchmen—but everything beyond is wasting valuable time. Geometry is necessary insofar as it puts everyone in the position properly to carry out buying, selling, and measuring land—a man with normal attentiveness learns this without a teacher—but silly and worthless if it leads to the study of juxtaposed mathematical diagrams.[75]

Nietzsche presents Socrates as the first utilitarian philosopher. "Socratic philosophy is absolutely *practical*: it is hostile to all knowledge unconnected to ethical implications."[76] On this understanding, the personage portrayed in *The Clouds* is the anti-Socrates. The question no longer is what is being, what is matter, what is motion, to say nothing of from which end does a gnat toot,[77] but what is justice, what is courage, what is the good.[78] For the first time, philosophy is intended to impress its stamp on the character of *human* life. "[Socrates] is the first philosopher of life and all schools deriving from him are first of all philosophies of life."[79]

The ramifications of the Socratic revolution were not lost on Nietzsche. Thanks to it, everyone in a sense is either a pre- or post-Socratic.[80] What renders it so pivotal is not that it overturned an existing moral order, but that it provided the basis for a new one—a moral order grounded in reason and knowledge. "*Knowledge* as the path to virtue differentiates his philosophical character."[81] Prior to that turning point in so-called world history, tradition and religious prescription constituted the path to virtue. The virtue of the Spartan hoplite was not founded on reason, but on his obedience to the laws of Lycurgus and the customs of Lacedaemon. One was educated in virtue, but not in the sense of acquiring more knowledge about it. One learned the laws and customs, was shamed or otherwise punished for transgressing them, performed the ancient rituals, and so forth.[82] But at no point was knowledge understood as a precondition for virtue. One did not need to know what courage was to be courageous. But when Socrates brought philosophy down from the heavens, all that changed forever.[83]

The Socratic revolution is not significant simply because an ugly plebeian singlehandedly "dare[d] to negate the nature of the Greeks which, whether as Homer, Pindar, or Aeschylus, as Phidias, as Pericles, as Pythia and Dionysus, as the deepest abyss and the highest height, is certain of our astonished worship,"[84] but because he did so in such a manner that he engendered a new tradition that to this day endures. One still may extol the world of Homeric heroes, but one does not honor the virtues of those heroes by adopting them. But everyone, to some degree or other, honors that Platonic hero by aping him in his quest for reason and grounding one's own views—one's own life—in it. To espouse a position without being able to defend it rationally is essentially to forfeit the position. So ingrained has this understanding become that it appears senseless to contend otherwise. Post-Socratic man cannot help but be rational.[85] Socrates rendered reason a tyrant,[86] one that continues to dictate to this day.

Implicit in Socrates's rationalistic approach, with its most bizarre of all equations (reason=virtue=happiness), is that virtue can be taught. Before the revolution, virtue was reserved for those whom nature predisposed for it. No doubt custom and rearing played their parts, but it was one's natural disposition that inclined one toward, and made one fit for, virtue. And nature, as is her wont, distributed her gifts parsimoniously and—as those who received less are apt to contend—unfairly. Achilles and Odysseus were the exception, not the rule, and their inimitability had nothing to do with their ability to explicate their virtues rationally. According to the Socratic equation, Achilles and Odysseus were not paragons of virtue.[87] By supplanting instinct with knowledge, the entire moral order of the Greek world was overturned.

> Socrates becomes the critic of his times: he investigates how far it behaves from dark drives and how far it behaves from knowledge, thereby yielding the democratic result that the lowest manual laborer stands higher than the statesman, orator, and artist of his times. A carpenter, coppersmith, navigator and physician are taken, and their technical knowledge is tested—[each] can cite the persons from whom he learned the means. In contrast, everyone had an opinion concerning [the questions], What is Justice? What is piety? What is Democracy? What is law? Yet Socrates found only darkness and ignorance. Socrates claims the role of a learner, but he persuades his interlocutors of their rashness.[88]

Nature is no egalitarian. Reason redresses her callous indifference and renders man fit for equality. Socratic philosophy "is *for everyone* and *popular* because it holds that virtue may be taught. It does not appeal to genius and the highest powers of knowledge."[89] Rather it appeals to the faculty of reason, a faculty of which every able-minded member of humankind is said to partake. In doing so, for the first time, a "purely human ethic resting on principles of knowledge . . . is *sought*."[90] Socrates likely would have objected to the categoricalness of Kant's imperative, but the path from the Athenian gadfly to the Königsberg peripatetic is not difficult to trace.

It was reason, after all, that the modern thinkers employed to overcome the distance between man and man. Reason directs humans to the same end—an end characterized by equality, comfort, security, and so forth. Any resistance to that movement is dismissed as irrational. And the irrational is—in the post-Socratic world—by its very nature, wrong. Even those thinkers who did not give reason its due; who subordinated reason to other qualities—nature, for example, or the sentiments—tended to be instruments of the democratizing forces of history rather than the masters or inquisitors them. Reason may enjoy an equivocal role in Rousseau's thought, but there is nothing equivocal about the uniformity that Rousseau advances in the name of the general will. The shadows that at times obscure the path from Socrates to Kant have been altogether dispelled once one reaches Rousseau. From there, the road to Königsberg is straightforward.

Reason proves the great unifier and leveler, and it is Socrates who unleashes its astounding equalizing force. It is not simply the universality of the faculty in question that promotes this end, but the universality of the measure or standard it establishes. Wherever reason prevails, everyone is placed on the same footing to the extent that whatever may have justified inequality heretofore—power, heredity, divinities, customs, and so on—becomes irrelevant in a world governed by reason. The inequality that arose naturally from nature's favoring of some above others is corrected by the Socratic turn to reason. What does one's physical prowess or thirst for life or lust for rule or will to power matter in an age of reason? Without reason on one's side, the jig is up; the game, lost.

Socrates may have set man's democratization in motion, but it is reasonable to conclude that he did so unwittingly. A philosophy that celebrates the hierarchy of the human soul—and for that reason, of human souls—is repugnant to a mindset that brooks no hierarchies. But if Socrates did not aim to democratize man, he did endeavor to overcome the instincts that naturally brought about and sustained human inequality. He may not have opposed the instincts in the name of equality, but he did oppose them on the grounds that life lived according to them was deficient. Reason is a corrective; an antidote to the instinctual life. It counters the natural drives and desires that aristocratic man embraced and in the absence of no longer could be.

If the aristocratic mindset is, by its very nature, affirmational, the Socratic mindset is anti-aristocratic. An aristocratic man embraces life because it is good; Socratic man repudiates life because it is lacking. The unexamined life is not worth living.[91] How at odds that estimation is with the tragic view that prevailed before Socrates, which had it—as the figure of Oedipus serves to remind—that it is the examined life that is not worth living. To what extent the examination of life has made it worth living can be tabled for now. What bears drawing attention to is how antithetical the aristocratic and Socratic mindsets are to one another. The one is fundamentally affirmational; the other, Nietzsche argues, negational. The essence of the Socratic struggle is negative; it is "the struggle *against* desire, drives, anger and so on [which ultimately] directs itself against a deep-lying ignorance."⁹² This negative aspect inheres in the daemon that guides Socrates and hence, inheres in Socrates himself.

> We are offered a key to the essence of Socrates by that wonderful phenomenon known as the 'daimonion of Socrates'. In particular situations, when his enormous mind began to sway uncertainly, he was able to get a firm hold on things again thanks to a divine voice which made itself heard at such moments. Whenever it appears, this voice always *warns* him to *desist*. In this utterly abnormal nature the wisdom of instinct only manifests itself in order to *block* conscious understanding from time to time. Whereas in the case of all productive people instinct is precisely the creative-affirmative force and consciousness makes critical and warning gestures, in the case of Socrates, by contrast, instinct becomes the critic and consciousness the creator—a true monstrosity *per defectum*!⁹³

In a world governed by instinct, Socrates was an aberration. He was a wrench thrown into the works of Greek culture, at a time when life was lived "so prodigally, so exorbitantly" and "history move[d] so fast!"⁹⁴ It is true that by the fifth century, the instincts already were in decay: 'people with tired instincts . . . let themselves go—toward happiness' as they put it, toward pleasure, as they did it—and who kept mouthing old, magnificent words (words that they had absolutely no right to use any more, given the lives they were leading).'⁹⁵ Indeed, it was only onto such stage that a monstrosity like Socrates could have entered. But his divine quest did not follow logically nor inexorably from the decay of Greek instinct. One just as well could imagine the emergence of a new instinct or restoration of an old, rather than the war against instinct that Socrates declared and, in time, won.

> When one finds it necessary to turn *reason* into a tyrant, as Socrates did, the danger cannot be slight that something else will play the tyrant. Rationality was then hit upon as the savior; neither Socrates nor his "patients" had any choice about being rational: it was *de rigeur*, it was their last resort. The fanaticism with which all Greek reflection throws itself upon rationality betrays a desperate situation; there was danger, there was but one choice: either to perish or—to be absurdly rational. The moralism of the Greek philosophers from Plato on is pathologically conditioned; so is their esteem of dialectics. Reason-virtue-happiness, that means merely that one must imitate Socrates and counter the dark appetites with a permanent daylight—the daylight of reason. One must be clever, clear, bright at any price: any concession to the instincts, to the unconscious, leads *downward*.⁹⁶

The triumph of reason over instinct was not a remedy to the decadence into which the instincts had lapsed, but merely another expression of it.

The most blinding daylight; rationality at any price; life, bright, cold, cautious, conscious, without instinct, in opposition to the instincts—all this too was a mere disease, another disease, and by no means a return to "virtue," to "health," to happiness. To *have* to fight the instincts—that is the formula of decadence: as long as life is *ascending*, happiness equals instinct.[97]

The development of reason may have hastened decay instead of arresting it, but in the struggle between reason and instinct, there can be no dispute about the victor, however pyrrhic the victory may be. As Nietzsche would put it elsewhere, slave morality does not constitute an ascendancy, but it has become ascendant. "The people have won."[98] Likewise, Socratism won and it won not only the day, but the history and, one might add, soul of the West. Since the time of Socrates, notwithstanding periodic regressions, reason has advanced inexorably, surpassing and suppressing all "lesser" modes of apprehension along the way.

It was to Athens that Socrates confessed he had been appointed by the god,[99] a testimony to the wisdom of that god, for where else but Athens could that divine mission have been carried out? Still, by its very nature, that mission was one that was not circumscribed by any *polis*. It belonged to no city, but the city of man. Its universality distinguishes it from the older philosophic efforts of those tyrants of the spirit[100] who drew breath and inferences before Socrates.

> The entirety of older philosophy still belongs to the time of unbroken ethical instincts; Heraclitus, Anaxagoras, Democritus, Empedocles—each breathes Hellenic morality, yet each according to a different form of Hellenic ethics. We now arrive at a search for the purely human ethic resting on the principles of knowledge; it is *sought*. To those of earlier times, it was there as a vital breath of air. This sought-after, purely human ethic conflicts with the traditional Hellenic *custom* of ethics: again, we must resolve custom into *an act of knowledge*.[101]

If in this secular age of reason one is eager to dismiss the divine nature of Socrates' mission, it would seem that its transcendently humanistic character is beyond dispute.

The success of the Socratic revolution can be gauged in no small part by the fact that its banner was carried aloft not only by its adherents but also by those who consciously sought to sever philosophy from its ancient and antiquated roots. That is not to suggest that the modern project does not signify a substantive shift in man's relation to the world and to himself. If nothing else, its lowering of the aims of philosophy, and of man therewith, indicates as much. But if one understands the Socratic revolution as the turn to reason (from instinct) for the sake of correcting life, then it is clear that the modern project has merely accelerated that revolution, not changed its course. The philosophers who advanced the modern project elevated the role of reason and did so for the sake of easing man's lot. Likewise, modern science, which has divorced itself from philosophy and parades as the only legitimate source of knowledge, betrays its debt to the discipline for which it exhibits not the least bit of gratitude by essentially carrying on its mission. Granted, modern science has nothing to say about virtue or the good life and purposefully neglects the sorts of queries that spurred Socrates' dialectical investigations, but still, it is not the impartial, value-neutral method it purports be. For at the bottom, it too seeks to effect what Socrates sought, namely the correction of life, and to this end it utilizes the same instrument wielded by the Athenian gadfly—reason.

THE CHRISTIAN REVOLUTION

With regard to the broader democratic revolution, the Socratic revolution proved to be a necessary cause, not a sufficient one. The turn to reason lent itself to humanity's democratization without predestining it. Nor, for that matter, did Socrates ever intimate that the ultimate aim of his divine mission was the abolition of all social hierarchies, even if he did spend his days questioning existing ones. One never should lose sight of the fact that the ancients—and this goes not simply for the pre-Socratics, but for the post-Socratics as well—were consistently inegalitarian and not in spite of reason, but on account of it. To maintain that humans, in contradistinction to other animals, are endowed with reason is not to say that all humans enjoy that faculty in equal measure. The turn to reason may have leveled the playing field to a degree that would have been scarcely imaginable in a world governed by instinct, but it did not exactly eradicate inequality. To put it in more contemporary terms, equal results do not follow from equal opportunities. Indeed, the unequal capacity to reason validated societal inequality. To be governed by a fool was contrary to nature—and reason.[102]

Democratic man's debt to Athens is incalculable; yet, for his democratization, a greater debt lies elsewhere. Not by reason alone was the democratic revolution carried out. While that revolution in time left no terrestrial recess untouched, it was, in its origins, an emphatically Western revolution. Its animating principle was not so much that humans are rational beings but that they are, intrinsically, equal ones. And that principle emanates not from Athens, but Jerusalem. It is not a Socratic doctrine, but a Christian one. "The most profound and vast geniuses of Rome were never able to arrive at the idea of [human equality] . . . [I]t was necessary that Jesus Christ come to earth to make it understood that all members of the human species are naturally alike and equal."[103] As Nietzsche put it in customarily caustic fashion, "The poison of the doctrine of 'equal rights for all'—it was Christianity that spread it most fundamentally."[104] While the acerbity of Nietzsche's quip is inconsistent with Tocqueville's thought, the tenor certainly is not.

> The most noteworthy innovation of our modern moral teaching, to me, consists in the tremendous development in the new form that is now given to two principles which Christianity had first put in grand evidence: the equal rights of every man in the goods of this world, and the duty of those who have more to help those who have less. The revolutions that displaced the old European ruling class, the general extension of wealth and education which has made individuals more and more alike have given an immense and unexpected impetus to the principle of equality, which Christianity had established in the spiritual rather than in the tangible material sphere. The idea that *all* men have a right to certain goods, to certain pleasures, and that our primary moral duty is to procure these for them—this idea, as I said above, has now gained immense breadth, and it now appears in an endless variety of aspects. This first innovation led to another. Christianity made charity a personal virtue. Every day now we are making a social duty, a political obligation, a public virtue out of it. And the growing number of those who must be supported, the variety of needs which we are growing accustomed to provide for, the disappearance of great personalities to whom previously one could turn with these problems of succor, now makes every eye turn to the State. Governments now are compelled to redress certain inequalities, to mollify certain hardships, to offer support to all the luckless and helpless. Thus a new kind of social and political morality is being established, a kind which the antique peoples hardly knew but which is, in reality, a combination of some of their political ideas with the moral principles of Christianity.[105]

While both revolutions were of such scope and force that they effectively yoked mankind in toto, the Christian was fated to be the more consequential with respect to mankind's democratization. Socrates leveled man before reason; Christ before God. One could evade the former, but not the latter (until God was killed, but by then it was too late. He had been rendered an inextricable part of the equation.). The equality of man was explicit in the Christian doctrine; the inequality of man at the very least implicit in the Socratic one. It bears mentioning that while Nietzsche held both accountable for man's degeneration, he did not hold them equally accountable. It was for the later revolution that he reserved his most vitriolic invective; his assessment of the first was considerably more nuanced. Thus the pen that time and time again was taken up against that ugly plebeian could be used to transmit the following:

> If all goes well, the time will come when one will take up the memorabilia of Socrates rather than the Bible as a guide to morals and reason . . . . The pathways

of the most various philosophical modes of life lead back to him; at bottom they are the modes of life of the various temperaments confirmed and established by reason and habit and all of them directed towards joy in living and in one's own self; from which one might conclude that Socrates' most personal characteristic was participation in every temperament. Socrates excels the founder of Christianity in being able to be serious cheerfully and in possessing that *wisdom full of roguishness* that constitutes the finest state of the human soul. And he also possessed the finer intellect.[106]

Nietzsche, who meditated on the nature of philosophy as few others have,[107] aligned naturally with Socrates, notwithstanding his indictment of him. He was a friend of reason no less than Socrates and one could argue even more so in that he perceived just how deleterious an excessive faith in, or reliance on, reason could be. Christianity was a different matter, one that Nietzsche had little tolerance for. However pernicious Socrates' effect may have been, it was the teachings of Christ, not Socrates, that spelled the end of antiquity.

Tocqueville, at the risk of understating it, saw things differently. For one, as noted above, he had virtually nothing to say about Socrates. But that aside, Tocqueville viewed Christianity as an advance and placed it far above the pagan world it conquered.[108] What Nietzsche indicted as "the immortal blemish of mankind"[109] and held to be responsible for the overall degeneration of man, Tocqueville considered an "admirable moral system"[110] that effectively elevated all of humanity. One need only consider their dispositions toward the Gospels to appreciate just how diametrically opposed their views on Christianity were.[111] But this glaring disparity notwithstanding, Tocqueville, no less than Nietzsche, appreciated just how decisively instrumental Christianity was in shaping the West. Both grasped that "Christianity is the great source of modern morality"[112] (however disinclined modern man, in his self-professed maturity, may be to acknowledge this fact), and that modern democracy cannot be understood without taking into account the role Christianity played in fostering a democratic brotherhood of man.

The fundamental contribution that Christianity made to the West, at least with respect to impressing upon it its democratic character, is mankind's subsumption and unification under God.

> The realm of duties had been limited [in the pagan world]. Christianity broadened it. It had been limited to certain citizenries; Christianity extended it to all men. It had been restricted and confirmed the position of masters; Christianity gave it to the slaves. Thus Christianity put in grand evidence the equality, the unity, the fraternity of all men.
>
> Christianity and consequently its morality went beyond all political powers and nationalities. Its grand achievement is to have formed a human community beyond national societies.[113]

As Nietzsche observed, "Christianity was not 'national', nor was it a function of race."[114] Rather its appeal was to all humans by virtue of their being human. "For there is no distinction between Jew and Greek; the same Lord is Lord of all and bestows his riches upon all who call upon him."[115] "[God] made from one [man] every nation of men to live on all the face of the earth."[116] "There is neither Jew nor Greek, there is neither slave nor free, there is neither male nor female; for you are all one in Christ Jesus."[117] The revolutionary character of such sentiments has all but vanished in the two millennia since they were first pronounced—a testament to the success of that revolution and the sheer scale of Christianity's triumph. But it is modern man's myopia, not his wisdom or maturity, that prevents him from appreciating just how extraordinary such teachings were and how remarkable they remain.[118]

Therein lies Christianity's singular contribution to mankind's democratization. It was not monotheism, which was primarily a Hebraic creation. As the example of the Hebrews shows, the existence of but one God does not entail that all peoples are equal in His eyes. Yahweh was the God of the Jews, not of humanity, and it certainly was not the aim of the Hebrews nor the will of their God, to proselytize mankind. Thus, while monotheism naturally facilitates man's democratization, it does not guarantee it.[119] In essence, Christianity is democratic to a degree that finds no equivalent in other religions. The connection between Christianity and democracy is not tautological, but symbiotic. The theological equality of all human beings before God lends itself to the establishment of a political equality of all human beings before the law or the state. As Tocqueville observed, "Christianity, which has rendered all men equal before God, will not be loath to see all citizens equal before the law."[120] This is not to suggest that Christianity singlehandedly affected man's democratization. Reflecting on the prior seven hundred years, Tocqueville observes that virtually every great event has "turned to the profit of equality." These include "the Crusades and the wars with the English[, which] decimate[d] the nobles and divide[d] their lands; the institution of townships[, which] introduced democratic freedom into the heart of the feudal monarchy; the discovery of firearms[, which] equalized the villein and the noble on the battlefield"; and the invention of the printing press.[121] But if the gradual development of the equality of conditions required great events and tangible innovations, it also required a theological (or theoretical) foundation that was conducive to it. Printing, for example, was not, strictly speaking, a Western invention. The Chinese had developed block printing long before Gutenberg devised the printing press. But "the earliest impulse to printing in China was not to diffuse knowledge, but to ensure religious or magical benefits from precise replication of a holy image or a holy text."[122] Thus, printing was not sufficient to bring about democracy any more than gunpowder was (another

Chinese invention). That an equality of conditions did not develop in the very place that first developed printing (and gunpowder) demonstrates as much.

Democratized man did not spring full-fledged from the teachings of Christ like Athena from the head of Zeus, and Tocqueville had no illusions about the egregious inequalities that Christianity accommodated for much of its history. The development of the equality of conditions that Tocqueville surveyed across the centuries that preceded his own was not precipitous. In time, it gathered momentum, as movements of this sort tend to do, but the social institutions and moral sentiments it moved against were so firmly entrenched that not only was a precipitate advance infeasible, but periodic retrogressions were unavoidable. Perhaps the most glaring of these, certainly in Tocqueville's own day, was slavery.

> Christianity had destroyed servitude; Christians of the sixteenth century reestablished it; they nevertheless accepted it only as an exception in their social system, and they took care to restrict it to a single one of the human races. They thus made a wound in humanity less large, but infinitely more difficult to heal.[123]

Tocqueville's writings on slavery make it clear just how odious he felt that institution to be, particularly in that land that so tellingly regarded it as peculiar.[124] He considered it to be "the greatest scourge of America,"[125] and "the most dreadful of all evils that threaten the future of the United States."[126] The sight of it not only filled him with horror and despair,[127] but moved humanity itself to "wail."[128] What made slavery so exceedingly execrable in America's case was that it was being sustained by an enlightened and Christian people who extolled so highly and guarded so jealously those inestimable goods that they denied their African brethren, liberty and the pursuit of happiness foremost among them. Tocqueville had no doubt that eradicating this scourge would require enormous effort and sacrifice and would engender "great misfortunes;" but he also had no doubt that in time, it would be eradicated: "in the midst of the democratic freedom and enlightenment of our age, it is not an institution that can endure."[129] The (re)introduction of chattel slavery into the West was a misstep along history's providential march; a regression that ineluctably would be corrected. That progressive march effaced the distance between man and man; it did not enlarge it. "Christianity destroyed slavery ... by asserting the rights of the slave."[130] The abrogation of those rights was an enormity that could not be countenanced indefinitely.

As with democracy, Tocqueville's relationship with Christianity was ambivalent. At some level, he never wholeheartedly embraced either. He could not dispel the unease that attended the sight of democracy's triumphant march across the ruins of the *ancien régime* nor could he dispel the internal doubt that triumphed over, or at least tempered, his religious convictions. But his reluctance to embrace the democratic revolution stemmed from a critical understanding of it whereas his reluctance to embrace Catholicism appears more to have been a personal crisis of faith.[131] Tocqueville espied the perils that reposed in the very heart of democracy; with respect to Christianity, Tocqueville found that the failings reposed in his own heart. Thus, while Tocqueville was highly critical of democracy, he seems to have accepted Christianity as unequivocally good, even if he found that his own want of goodness prevented him from devoting himself to it without equivocation.

That there is no analogous appraisal of Christianity in the work of an author who proclaimed himself to be the Antichrist[132] ought to come as no surprise. Much of Tocqueville's thought on the kinship between Christianity and democracy likely would have met Nietzsche's approval, not least the understanding that Christianity is the great source of modern morality—an insight that seems so evident it hardly merits mentioning but bears repeating in an age that endeavors so indefatigably to detach itself from its historical moorings in general and its religious ones in particular. But such concord pales before the much more substantial and ultimately insuperable discord that divided them on this score. The essential goodness of Christianity that, in Tocqueville's estimation, inhered in that "admirable moral system" could not be reconciled with Nietzsche's verdict that Christianity has been "the greatest misfortune of humanity so far."[133] The religion that earned Tocqueville's admiration was, for Nietzsche, an abomination.

Christianity constituted less the invention of new values than an inversion of old ones. On this question, Tocqueville and Nietzsche remain in agreement. As Tocqueville explained in a letter to Arthur de Gobineau, "Christianity did not exactly create new duties, or to put it in other terms, it did not establish new virtues; but it changed their relative position."[134] Such a sentiment, if not the tone of it, very well could have come from Nietzsche's own pen. Where the two sharply and irreparably part ways is with respect to the value of this reversal. For Tocqueville, Christianity's overturning of the pagan world was an extraordinary development. Christian virtue was something higher, much higher than "the rude and half-savage virtues" it replaced.[135] The Antichrist saw the matter antithetically.

> The whole labor of the ancient world *in vain*: I have no word to express my feelings about something so tremendous. And considering that its labor was a preliminary labor, that only the foundation for the labors of thousands of years had just then been laid with granite self-confidence—the whole *meaning* of the ancient world in vain! Wherefore Greeks? Wherefore Romans?
>
> Greeks! Romans! The nobility of instinct, the taste, the methodical research, the genius of organization and administration, the faith in, the *will* to, man's future, the great Yes to all things, become visible in the *imperium Romanum*,

visible for all the senses, the grand style no longer mere art but become reality, truth, *life*. And not buried overnight by a natural catastrophe, not trampled down by Teutons and other buffaloes, but ruined by cunning, stealthy, invisible, anemic vampires. Not vanquished—merely drained. Hidden vengefulness, petty envy become master. Everything miserable that suffers from itself, that is afflicted with bad feelings, the whole ghetto-world of the soul *on top* all at once.[136]

In Nietzsche's mind, Christianity's inversion of values constitutes "the highest of all conceivable corruptions,"[137] one that ruined man and weakened him,[138] and toppled the great cultures of antiquity, not by vanquishing them, but by sapping them.

Nietzsche's denunciation of Christianity pervades his corpus,[139] but his most thorough examination of the reversal of values that Christianity affected is found in *On the Genealogy of Morality*. There Nietzsche returned to the problem of morality, or more specifically, "the *origin* of our moral prejudices," a matter that received its first provisional treatment "in the collection of aphorisms that bears the title *Human, All-Too-Human. A Book for Free Spirits*." Even more germane to the matter at hand, Nietzsche set out to descry the origin of good and evil, a question that already occupied him in his youth. At the tender age of 13, Nietzsche "gave God credit for it and made him the *father* of evil." In the thirty years that elapsed between his "first philosophical essay" and one of his last, Nietzsche learned "to separate theological from moral prejudice and . . . no longer searched for the origin of evil *beyond* the world."

> Some training in history and philology, together with my innate fastidiousness with regard to all psychological problems, soon transformed my problem into another: under what conditions did man invent the value judgments good and evil? *and what value do they themselves have*? Have they up to now obstructed or promoted human flourishing? Are they a sign of dis-tress, poverty and the degeneration of life? Or, on the contrary, do they reveal the fullness, strength and will of life, its courage, its confidence, its future?[140]

From such inquiries, a new truth,[141] a decidedly unchristian truth,[142] was born.

In the first essay of the polemic, the aptly titled "'Good and Evil', 'Good and Bad'," Nietzsche delves into the heart—the heartlessness, he might say—of Christianity and there exposes the origin of good and evil. "The truth of the *first* inquiry is the birth of Christianity: the birth of Christianity out of the spirit of *ressentiment*, not, as people may believe, out of the 'spirit'."[143] That exposure rests on the postulation, perhaps pedestrian now, that there was nothing transcendent or eternal about the teachings of Christ, to say nothing of the teacher himself. "Verily, men gave themselves all their good and evil. Verily they did not take it, they did not find it, nor did it come to them as a voice from heaven."[144] Indeed, not only were Christian values not of divine origin, but they were in essence a reaction against an existing value system, originating not from up high, but in Nietzsche's estimation, from down low. What Christianity presupposed, what it required for its existence, was not a divine creator or the sacrifice of His only begotten son or the transubstantiation, but an enemy to oppose and a system of values to undo or redo. Christianity was born "out of the spirit of *ressentiment* . . . [it was] a countermovement by its very nature, the great rebellion against the dominion of *noble* values."[145]

The system of values against which Christianity rebelled exemplified what Nietzsche labeled "master morality." Its mode of valuation has been addressed above and need only be touched upon here. As conceived originally, good and bad were evaluations established by the ruling order out of "the pathos of nobility and distance . . . [and] the continuing and predominant feeling" that it experienced in relation to the lower orders over which it lorded.[146] The masters, brimming with strength and vigor and a thirst for life, felt themselves to be the noble, the good, the beautiful, the happy ones.[147] The concept of good then was conceived spontaneously by the ruling order and assigned to those things that reflected its own power. Thus, under the original conception, enemies were not considered bad, to say nothing of evil, so long as they were worthy enemies (in that they too teemed with vigor and valor). "How much respect a noble man has for his enemies!"[148] "In Homer, the Trojan and the Greek are both good."[149] The concept bad was formulated subsequently and, one might add, logically: what was not good was bad; what was not noble, ignoble. "Good and bad is for a long time the same thing as noble and base, master and slave."[150] All that was weak, craven, sick, crooked was held to be not good, that is, bad, by those who teemed with life and whom, as a result, life appeared to favor. In the context of Nietzsche's teaching, it bears stressing that in the aristocratic or master mode of valuation, the concept bad is a tangential or incidental invention. Good is the foundational and generative value and it is only because one inevitably encounters what is not good that its opposite value was fashioned. In the noble mode of valuation, the "negative concept 'low', 'common', 'bad' is only a pale contrast created after the event compared to its positive basic concept," that is, the good;[151] a mere "afterthought, an aside, a complementary color."[152]

Slave morality posits values in an antithetical manner. While it too juxtaposes an idea of the good with that which is not good so that nominally, the negative concepts of the respective moralities appear congruous if not synonymous, evil and bad are antagonistic values precisely because the concepts of good that they oppose are adverse to one another. What is good to the

Christian is contemptible to the noble and what is good to the noble is evil in the eyes of the Christian. Again, Christianity did not furnish new values so much as reverse old ones. Its creative act was not so much the invention of good and evil, but the inversion of good and bad that undergirded the value system it undertook to overturn. One might say Christianity is doubly derivative in that not only did it fail to invent new values, but the means it used to invert old ones had been appropriated from its monotheistic antecedents. But this lack of originality requires no apology, for it is thanks to those who glorified Christ's ascendance, not those complicit in his downfall, that the slave revolt in morality proved triumphant, and not for a people, but for all people—for humanity en masse.

The success of that revolt can be understood, in part, by the universality of its appeal. The pre-Christian world was a hierarchical one whereupon a very broad base there rested a (comparatively) very small elite.[153] The inversion of values signified an inversion of that hierarchy. The multitudes that for so long had been condemned by the ruling class, condemned to a life of hardship that they enjoyed no prospect of escaping, were now afforded a hope the likes of which had been unimaginable heretofore. Nietzsche surmised that "nothing, perhaps, is so wearying as the sight of a perpetual conqueror." For centuries, Rome had been just that. "[The] centuries long speechless hatred for Rome on the part of its wearied spectators, which extended as far as Rome ruled, at last discharged itself in *Christianity*."[154] Through a reversal of values, those once scorned by the ruling class would be favored in the eyes of the one true master, God. What is more, in those same eyes, the few whom fortune formerly favored would be scorned. Societal dregs rendered masters; aristocratic rulers reduced to misery—if not in this life, then in the one to come. For Nietzsche, this was "the most fatal seductive lie that has yet existed."[155] "Christianity owes its triumph to this miserable flattery of personal vanity: it was precisely all the failures, all the rebellious-minded, all the less favored, the whole scum and refuse of humanity who were thus won over to it. The 'salvation of the soul'—in plain language: 'the world revolves around me'."[156] To be sure, the reversal of values did not portend an overthrow of Rome then and there; there was no prospect that the meek would depose the ruling class and assume command of the empire. Rather, all hope was invested in the life to come. In the minds of early Christians, the world appeared "ripe for destruction."[157] The Last Judgment was imminent, and so too salvation. Immortality would be their reward.

In Nietzsche's reckoning, Christianity was not simply seditious, it was vindictive. And it is not only Christianity that this vindictiveness infects, but the moral system that was born from it, the very system that prevails to this day. Both are born from impotence; both slavish in their valuations of life; both punish those whom life has favored and call it justice; and both dream of leaving this world behind, whether through its destruction (Christianity) or correction (modern science). Nietzsche inveighed against the notion that Christianity is a religion of love. On the contrary, it was, from the start, a religion of revenge, or as Nietzsche put it, *ressentiment*. It sought not so much to redeem the pagan world as to undo it. "It avenged itself on Rome by dreaming of a last *judgment*."[158] Christianity counseled judge not, lest ye be judged, yet damned everything that was un-Christian. What the people wanted, and what Christianity promised them, was that which they lacked under the pre-Christian mode of valuation, namely power. "These weaklings—in fact *they*, too, want to be the powerful one day, this is beyond doubt, one day *their* 'kingdom' will come too."[159] To underscore just how vengeful and "unchristian" the spirit of Christianity is, Nietzsche adduces the words of two of Christianity's greatest apologists. Per Aquinas, in the heavenly kingdom, the blessed will have an opportunity to observe "the torment of the damned *so that they may even more thoroughly enjoy their blessedness.*" As for a jubilant Tertullian, he anticipates that his own joy will be roused when he casts his "*insatiable* gaze" upon those who denied Christ in this life—including not only the monarchs and governors who persecuted his followers, but also the poets, tragedians, and philosophers who simply declined to count themselves among them—flailing in the flames of eternal damnation.[160]

This hatred for one's enemies contrasts sharply with the reverence the noble feels for his. No doubt for each, the enemy is someone to be opposed and overcome. But whereas the Christian views his enemy as an antithesis of all that is good and holy (to such a degree that that enemy does not merely merit punishment, but *eternal* punishment), the noble sees his enemy as a reflection of what is good—a being who, like himself, has been naturally endowed with those qualities that make one good; that make one deserving of esteem. "The noble man . . . insists on having his enemy to himself, as a mark of distinction, indeed he will tolerate as enemies none other than such as have nothing to be despised and a *great deal* to be honored!"[161] The Christian, on the other hand, envisions a world that has been rid of enemies; a world where the wolf and lamb will lie down together.[162] In that vision, the wolf has ceased to be a wolf; it has been denatured. When the noble would opt for a world where wolves remain wolves, it is not first and foremost so that they may oppress lambs, but that they may find in it others like themselves—others whom nature has been good to, whom nature has turned out well. Though still enemies, they present the opportunity for the noble to further affirm their own nobility. The noble warrior longs for worthy competitors; for worthy enemies. A life without them is no life at all. For the noble, it is the unopposed life that is not worth living.

That, of course, is the very life that the Christian longs for; and not just the Christian, but all those who have come to power in the aftermath of the slave revolt in morality—that is, the people themselves. Whereas the master finds life to be good, the slave feels it to be bad; and it is bad because life has not been good—to him. Thus, while master morality is affirmational, slave morality is negational. It is hostile to life, which the slave views as having been hostile to him. Life becomes an enemy, and not the sort of enemy one esteems, but the sort that one despises. For the slave, life needs to be negated, escaped, corrected—however one wishes to qualify it, the slave is, at heart, a reactionary.

> The beginning of the slaves' revolt in morality occurs when *ressentiment* itself turns creative and gives birth to values: the *ressentiment* of those beings who, denied the proper response of action, compensate for it only with imaginary revenge. Whereas all noble morality grows out of a triumphant saying 'yes' to itself, slave morality says 'no' on principle to everything that is 'outside', 'other', 'non-self' : and *this* 'no' is its creative deed. This reversal of the evaluating glance—this *essential* orientation to the outside instead of back onto itself—is a feature of *ressentiment*: in order to come about, slave morality first has to have an opposing, external world, it needs, physiologically speaking, external stimuli in order to act at all,—its action is basically a reaction.[163]

By now it should be apparent just how different the concepts of good are in the respective modes of valuation. In an effort to overthrow his enemies through the only means at his disposal, the slave overturned the entire pagan world, rendering all that had been bad good and condemning all that had been good as evil. In the wake of this upheaval, he could be heard saying:

> Only those who suffer are good, only the poor, the powerless, the lowly are good; the suffering, the deprived, the sick, the ugly, are the only pious people, the only ones saved, salvation is for them alone, whereas you rich, the noble and powerful, you are eternally wicked, cruel, lustful, insatiate, godless, you will also be eternally wretched, cursed and damned![164]

In a world where the poor, the impotent, the lowly were the rule, though not the measure, and the powerful and privileged were the measure but not the rule, this inversion of values enjoyed an overtly democratic bent.

The slave revolt in morality then was not simply a revolt against the masters, but a revolt against nature, against life itself. A moral code that values weakness and sickness and devalues strength and health, amounts to a flagrant violation of the natural order. To elevate the common man above the noble was a perversion of the order of rank between man and man. To make the average person an exemplar and the repository of the highest values signified a diminution of all value. "Whatever can be common will never have much value."¹⁶⁵ To render "petty people's morality as the measure of things: this is the most disgusting degeneration culture has yet exhibited."¹⁶⁶ What Nietzsche found particularly execrable was not that the common man would invert values, but that he would posit himself as the standard of all values; that he would have the impudence to proclaim, "We good people—*we are the just.*"¹⁶⁷

> What really happens here is that the most conscious *conceit of being chosen* plays modesty: once and for all one has placed *oneself*, the "community," the "good and the just," on one side, on the side of "truth"—and the rest, "the world," on the other. This was the most disastrous kind of megalomania that has yet existed on earth: little miscarriages of prigs and liars began to claim for themselves the concepts of God, truth, light, spirit, love, wisdom, life—as synonymous for themselves, as it were, in order to define themselves against "the world": little superlative Jews, ripe for every kind of madhouse, turned all values around in their own image, just as if "the Christian" alone were the meaning, the salt, the measure, also the *Last Judgment*, of all the rest.¹⁶⁸

Though the Jews were the priestly people *par excellence*, it was for Christianity in particular that the full brunt of Nietzsche's animus was reserved. Mankind's "greatest misfortune,"¹⁶⁹ its "one immortal blemish" was, in his eyes, Christianity, not Judaism, and it was Christianity's "eternal indictment" that he avowed to "write on walls, wherever there are walls."¹⁷⁰ It was upon Christianity, not Judaism, that Nietzsche ultimately declared war and with which he spurned any rapprochement.

> I regard Christianity as the most fatal seductive lie that has yet existed, as the great unholy lie: I draw out the after-growth and sprouting of its ideal from beneath every form of disguise, I reject every compromise position with respect to it—I force a war against it.¹⁷¹

Still, that great misfortune was possible "only because a related, racially related kind of megalomania already existed in the world" and paved the way for it.¹⁷² The success of Christianity's slave revolt was predicated on a method of attack that already had been contrived; a method that entailed standing the natural order on its head and exalting those very qualities for which nature reserved no special place.

> When the oppressed, the downtrodden, the violated say to each other with the vindictive cunning of powerlessness: "Let us be different from evil people, let us be good! And a good person is anyone who does not rape, does not harm anyone, who does not attack, does not retaliate, who leaves the taking of revenge

to God, who keeps hidden as we do, avoids all evil and asks little from life in general, like us who are patient, humble and upright"—this means, if heard coolly and impartially, nothing more than: "We weak people are just weak; it is good to do nothing *for which we are not strong enough*"—but this grim state of affairs, this cleverness of the lowest rank which even insects possess (which play dead, in order not to "do too much" when in great danger), has, thanks to the counterfeiting and self-deception of powerlessness, clothed itself in the finery of self-denying, quiet, patient virtue, as though the weakness of the weak were itself—I mean its essence, its effect, its whole unique, unavoidable, irredeemable reality—a voluntary achievement, something wanted, chosen, a deed, an *accomplishment*.[173]

This approach affects a curious inversion, not only of the preexisting moral code but of nature itself. Slave morality's foundational "no" is a no to the very qualities to which life had said "yes"! Those qualities that nature had rewarded are repudiated by the slave. What by nature is good is rendered bad—evil, really—by the slave. The outcome is a reversal of the natural order; a turning upside down of natural hierarchies. One might imagine an inverted food chain in which prey are elevated to the top and predators relegated to the bottom. With the slave revolt in morality, the lamb acquires wings and ascends to heaven while the eagle has its wings clipped and is consigned to hell.

> There is nothing strange about the fact that lambs bear a grudge towards large birds of prey: but that is no reason to blame the large birds of prey for carrying off the little lambs. And if the lambs say to each other, "These birds of prey are evil; and whoever is least like a bird of prey and most like its opposite, a lamb—is good, isn't he?", then there is no reason to raise objections to this setting-up of an ideal beyond the fact that the birds of prey will view it somewhat derisively, and will perhaps say: "We don't bear any grudge at all towards these good lambs, in fact we love them, nothing is tastier than a tender lamb"—It is just as absurd to ask strength *not* to express itself as strength, *not* to be a desire to overthrow, crush, become master, to be a thirst for enemies, resistance and triumphs, as it is to ask weakness to express itself as strength.[174]

Rooted in *ressentiment*, this is precisely what slave morality demands. It demands that the strong, the healthy, the powerful, all that formerly had been good, renounce what had accounted for their goodness, and recasts all that heretofore had been bad—weakness, sickness, poverty, and the like—as being signs of strength. Under slave morality, the weak are good because they are not strong; they think themselves good because they have no claws.[175]

Those who cannot see past Nietzsche's celebration of cruelty do not, it seems, read Nietzsche well, if at all. That Nietzsche does celebrate cruelty is no secret. "No cruelty, no feast: that is what the oldest and longest period in human history teaches us—and punishment, too, has such very strong *festive* aspects!"[176] But Nietzsche's elevation (or perhaps restoration) of cruelty was not aimed at bringing about an age of unrestrained barbarism.[177] (Indeed, to the extent Nietzsche would not eradicate eagles (or lambs) from the world, the argument could be made that his future is less inhumane than the democratized one toward which humanity hastens, where eagles would have no place and only lambs would be allowed.) Cruelty was no end or good in itself. Rather, it constituted one of life's indispensable ingredients, without which life would become insipid. Much that is sublime and profound in the world owes its origins to the very qualities that modern man, taking his bearings from his Christian antecedent, endeavors to do away with. Nietzsche decried slave morality not because it aimed at eradicating cruelty (indeed, as Nietzsche would have it, its aim was not the eradication of cruelty, but its propagation—at least for the unelect—in perpetuity), but because it aimed at eradicating the very conditions that human greatness presupposes.

The result of all this was not simply that the way to greatness was foreclosed, but that the overall health of man declined. What adds insult to injury is that the decline was not in the natural order of things, but was effected, or rather self-inflicted, unnaturally. For Nietzsche, that is what slave morality emphatically is—unnatural, even anti-natural. It distorts and sins against reality. Nietzsche goes so far as to asseverate with respect to Christian morality and Christian theology, there is not "a single point of contact with reality."[178] Everything is imagined, and in such a way that reality, instead of being honored and reflected, is disparaged and inverted. The Christian God is understood not as something natural, but something beyond, something outside, indeed something opposed to, nature. "God as the declaration of war against life, against nature, against the will to live!"[179]

> This [Christian] *world of pure fiction* is vastly inferior to the world of dreams insofar as the latter *mirrors* reality, whereas the former falsifies it. Once the concept of "nature" had been invented as the opposite of "God," "natural" had to become a synonym of "reprehensible": this whole world of fiction is rooted in *hatred* of the natural (of reality!); it is the expression of a profound vexation at the sight of reality.[180]

The slave revolt devalued the natural world and erected a factitious one in its stead. Only by doing so could the retrograde and weak "call themselves 'the good'."[181] At heart, the man of *ressentiment* knows this not to be the case; that is, he agrees that what constitutes the noble's goodness is, in fact, good.

But because he was not commensurately gifted by nature, he maligns what he knows to be good and construes it as evil. With the old good disposed of, a new one is fabricated. And not just a new good, but a new world. Because the power that the slave knows in his heart to be good cannot be procured in this life, he posits a beyond in which it will be his. So as to elevate his standing in this life, weakness is mendaciously rendered "an *accomplishment*."[182] The result of all this dissembling is that sickness becomes more valued than health. "Christianity *needs* sickness just as Greek culture needs a superabundance of health."[183] In this manner the man of *ressentiment* distorts reality. His duplicity does justice neither to the world he condemns nor the one he sanctifies.

Perspectivist that he was, Nietzsche understood that the masters' worldview was not definitive; that they too distort reality. That is simply how humans—slaves and masters alike—get by in this world: they cannot do otherwise. But the masters' distortion of reality is comparatively much smaller. Or to frame that more positively, the masters are more truthful; their mode of valuation, more honest. "The 'well-born' *felt* they were 'the happy'; they did not need first of all to construct their happiness artificially by looking at their enemies, or in some cases by talking themselves into it, *lying themselves into it* (as all men of *ressentiment* are wont to do)."[184] Likewise, they do not covet what is not theirs and scorn it because it never will be theirs. They honor what they know and feel to be good and disdain what does not partake of that goodness, and they do so naturally. In doing so, they uphold the natural order that uplifted them, in contrast to the man of *ressentiment*, whose underhanded "twist[ing] of the concepts good and evil, true and false . . . imperil[s] life and slander[s] the world."[185]

> The active, aggressive, over-reaching man is still a hundred paces nearer to justice then the man who reacts; he simply does not need to place a false and prejudiced interpretation on the object of his attention, like the man who reacts does, has to do. In fact, this explains why the aggressive person, as the stronger, more courageous, nobler man, has always had a *clearer* eye, a *better* conscience on his side: on the other hand it is easy to guess who has the invention of 'bad conscience' on his conscience,—the man of *ressentiment*![186]

Nietzsche harbored no secret reverence for the slave revolt in morality, but he gave honor its due. A reversal of values that did not merely combat, but unequivocally and irreversibly overturned all the prodigious exploits of the pagan world, all the pomp and grandeur of Rome, was not to be taken lightly. There was something astounding at work here, and one glimpses the awe Nietzsche felt for it when he speaks of the true architects of the slave revolt in morality, the Jews. Nietzsche did not hesitate to provide the Jews with the dubious distinction of being "the *most catastrophic* people of world history,"[187] but it was only because of their genius and indomitability that such an "honor" could be bestowed. Their superlativeness cut both ways. "The Jews were a priestly nation of *ressentiment par excellence*, possessing an unparalleled genius for popular morality" and against whom "peoples with similar talents" paled in comparison.[188]

> Nothing that has been done on earth against "the noble," "the mighty," "the masters" and "the rulers," is worth mentioning compared with what *the Jews* have done against them: the Jews, that priestly people, which in the last resort was able to gain satisfaction from its enemies and conquerors only through a radical revaluation of their values, that is, through an act of *the most deliberate revenge*.[189]

While the slave revolt in morality—"a revolt which has two thousand years of history behind it and which has only been lost sight of because—it was victorious"[190]—begins with the Jew, it was Christianity, the "heir to this Jewish revaluation,"[191] that saw it through. "[Christianity] is *not* a counter-movement to the Jewish instinct, [but] is its very consequence, one inference more in its awe-inspiring logic."[192] Notwithstanding the anti-Jewish animus he episodically has unleashed across the past two millennia, the Christian is, in the end, "*the ultimate Jewish consequence.*"[193]

What began as a revolt of a particular people ended up as a reversal of values for all people. In the contest between Rome and Judea, "Rome has been defeated beyond all doubt."[194] The human race has been redeemed from the masters; "everything is being made appreciably Jewish, Christian or plebeian";[195] everything, in short, is being democratized. Again, that democratization was affected by Christianity, not Judaism. Christianity is democratic in essence in a manner that cannot be said of Judaism, which is the religion of a people (not all people), and a chosen people at that. This much could not be said of the Christians who were never a people strictly speaking, but rather were a motley amalgam of different peoples, albeit peoples of a similar stripe.

> The Christian movement, as a European movement, has been from the start a collective movement of dross and refuse elements of every kind . . . . It does *not* express the decline of a race, it is an aggregate of forms of decadence flocking together and seeking each other out from everywhere. It is *not*, as is supposed, the corruption of antiquity itself, of *noble* antiquity, that made Christianity possible. The scholarly idiocy which upholds such ideas even today cannot be contradicted harshly enough. At the very time when the sick, corrupt chandala strata in the whole *imperium* adopted Christianity, the *opposite type*, nobility, was

present in its most beautiful and most mature form. The great number became master; the democratism of the Christian instincts *triumphed*. Christianity was not "national," not a function of a race—it turned to every kind of man who was disinherited by life, it had its allies everywhere.[196]

Christianity's democratic essence is further revealed in its historical unfolding (as adumbrated by Nietzsche):

The Jews tried to prevail after they had lost two of their castes, that of the warrior and that of the peasant; in this sense they are the "castrated": they have the priests and then immediately the chandala—
   As is only fair, a break develops among them, a revolt of the chandala: the origin of Christianity.
   Because they knew the warrior only as their master, they brought into their religion enmity toward the noble, toward the exalted and proud, toward power, toward the ruling orders—they are pessimists from indignation—
   Thus they created an important new posture: the priest at the head of the chandala—against the noble orders—
   Christianity dew the ultimate conclusion of this movement: even in the Jewish priesthood it still sensed caste, the privileged, the noble—it abolished the priest—
   The Christian is the chandala who repudiates the priest—the chandala who redeems himself—
   That is why the French Revolution is the daughter and continuation of Christianity—its instincts are against caste, against the last privileges—[197]

Now would be a felicitous time to make that daughter's acquaintance.

THE FRENCH REVOLUTION

With the French Revolution, history's democratic forces came to a head. That is not to say that the movement of history reached its end, though for many at the time, events likely seemed to portend as much. Rather, the democratic currents that had coursed through the centuries had, by the closing decade of the eighteenth, gathered so much momentum that they simply no longer could be restrained. The fervor with which the Revolution was embraced not just by the popular mind, but by many of the West's most luminous ones is as telling an indication as any of just how far the democratization of man had advanced.[198]

Nietzsche did not devote much space to the Revolution, though the gravity of it clearly was not lost on him. His writings are littered with sundry reflections on the event, almost all of them animadversional.[199] For Nietzsche, the Revolution was a stepping-stone along the path to man's ultimate leveling. It was the "daughter and continuation of Christianity"; one more triumph of Judea over the classical ideal;[200] the denouement of an uncompromising faith in reason and equality. The confluence of those wellsprings of Western Civilization (Athens and Jerusalem) in the French Revolution was so remarkable and seemingly so well orchestrated that one might think the unfolding of the West has been the work of some divine dramaturge. On the face of it, the Revolution's hostility toward Christianity was inversely proportional to its reverence for reason. But the revolutionaries bastardized reason by idolizing it. And while the ferocity with which they assailed Christianity was rivaled by the fervency with which they celebrated reason, the Revolution was more religious than rational—its foundational principles owing more to the divine teachings they defiled than to the human faculty they deified. In this regard at least, the revolutionaries were the heralds of post-modernity, divorcing themselves vociferously from Christian theology whilst remaining faithfully wed to Christian morality. Such ironies may have been lost on the children of Rousseau, but not on Nietzsche, who could never be counted among them.

In contrast to the passing thoughts one finds dispersed throughout Nietzsche's writings, a substantial part of Tocqueville's work was devoted to the French Revolution. At some level, this could be attributed to the far more personal connection that bound Tocqueville to the upheaval, a connection that was not only national but familial. Born a year after Napoleon crowned himself emperor, Tocqueville was raised in the shadows of the Revolution. While he did not witness its terrors firsthand,[201] the ancestral ties that connected him to them were so numerous and perdurable that they could not but leave their impress upon him.

Tocqueville's great grandfather was Guillaume-Chrétien de Lamoignon de Malesherbes, the celebrated French statesman who, at the age of 71, voluntarily came out of retirement to defend King Louis XVI before the Convention. His efforts were in vain and almost certainly foreordained to be so. Within a year of the King's execution, *sans-culottes* descended upon Malesherbes's estate and arrested the aged statesman along with the other members of his family who happened to be there. Included among the arrestees were Louise, the youngest granddaughter of Malesherbes and her husband Hervé, future parents of Alexis. They were brought to Paris and summarily incarcerated in various prisons scattered throughout the city, only to be reunited in the Port-Libre. The reunion was short lived. Malesherbes saw his favored daughter and her husband, as well as a granddaughter and her husband, lose their heads to the same apparatus that was to claim his own on April 23, 1794. As if this were not enough, the Committee saw to it that Malesherbes' seventy-six-year-old sister and two of his secretaries were beheaded as well.[202] Hervé subsequently learned that his own execution was scheduled for 12 Thermidor (July 30, 1994), an end he narrowly escaped thanks to Robespierre's fall three days prior. All in all, Tocqueville's parents spent ten months in prison. Though they emerged with their heads, they did not do so unscathed: Herve's hair had gone white at the age of twenty-one and for the rest of his days, he established the habit of napping each afternoon between 3:00 and 4:00, thereby blocking out 3:30, "the exact time aristocrats were called before the revolutionary tribunal to receive their death sentences."[203] Louise's nerves had been shattered; her health would never fully recover.

The narrowness with which Alexis evaded oblivion was not lost on him. Just how indelibly the family scars were stamped upon his own soul is evinced by a letter written two years before his own death in which he recounted what constituted his earliest childhood memory.

> As though I were back there again now, I remember a certain evening in the chateau where my father was living at the time and where a large number of our close relatives had gathered for a family party. My mother, who had a strong, sweet voice, began to sing a song that was famous at the time of our civil disturbances and that told about the misfortunes of King Louis XVI and his death. When she stopped, everyone was crying, not so much over the many individual afflictions all had suffered, not even over the many relatives lost in the civil war and on the scaffold, but over the fate of this man who had died more than fifteen years before and whom most of those shedding tears for him had never seen. But this man had been the king.[204]

Without question, the Revolution that so ineffaceably scarred Tocqueville's family impacted the development of his own thought. But it did not predetermine it. To reduce a person's thinking to the times in which he thinks depreciates not only the value of the thought but that of the thinker as well. That humans are shaped by their surroundings does not entail that they are confined to them. A thinker's worth can be measured in no small part by his ability to transcend his age; by the extent to which he becomes timeless.[205] The abiding question that consumed Tocqueville was how might human grandeur be preserved in an age without any sense of grandeur? How might the craving for equality—the animating appetite of democratic man—be moderated in such a manner that the possibility of human greatness, of human distinction, that is, of human *in*equality, not be done away with? It was in this vein that Tocqueville approached one of the most prominent episodes in the protracted history of mankind's democratization. His thinking circumscribed the Revolution and not the Revolution his thinking. He approached it not as one of its victims motivated by a spirit of resentment, nor as one of its adulatory partisans studiously inattentive to its many miscarriages, but rather as one concerned about the dignity, not of Frenchmen or noblemen, but of all men.

> I hope I have written the present work without prejudice but I do not pretend to have written it without passion. It would hardly be possible for a Frenchman to feel nothing when he speaks of his country and ponders his times. I admit that in studying our old society in all its aspects, I have never entirely lost sight of our modern society. I wanted to discover not only what illness killed the patient, but how the patient could have been cured. I have acted like a doctor, dissecting every organ in order to discover the laws which govern the whole of life. My purpose has been to paint a picture both accurate and instructive.[206]

Tocqueville averred that the Revolution gave birth to modern society.[207] It signified a turning point beyond which there could be no going back; a fissure that cleaved history in two, severing a democratic future from an aristocratic past. About that future, Tocqueville divined three truths.

> The first is that today humanity is driven by an unknown force which we can hope to moderate, but not to defeat, which sometimes gently urges and sometimes shoves us towards the destruction of aristocracy. Second, of all forms of society, the one where aristocracy does not and cannot exist is just the one which will have the most difficulty escaping absolute government for long. The third truth, finally, is that nowhere does despotism produce such pernicious effects as in just this kind of society; for, more than any other kind of government, despotism favors the development of all the vices to which such societies are especially prone, and thus pushes them in the direction which they are inclined to go.[208]

The antidote to the democratic despotism that darkened Tocqueville's vision of the future was liberty, which Tocqueville essentially regarded as a good in itself.

> Liberty alone can effectively combat the natural vices of these kinds of societies and prevent them from sliding down the slippery slope where they find themselves. Only freedom can bring citizens out of the isolation in which the very independence of their circumstances has led them to live, can daily force them to mingle, to join together through the need to communicate with one another, persuade each other, and satisfy each other in the conduct of their common affairs. Only freedom can tear people from the worship of Mammon and the petty daily concerns of their personal affairs and teach them to always see and feel the nation above and beside them; only freedom can substitute higher and stronger passions for the love of material well-being, give rise to greater ambitions than

the acquisition of a fortune, and create the atmosphere which allows one to see and judge human vices and virtues.[209]

As Tocqueville reflected later in that work:

> I have often wondered where the source of this passion for political freedom is, which, in all times, has made men do the greatest things that humanity has accomplished, in what feelings it is rooted and nourishes itself. I see clearly that, when nations are badly led, they readily conceive the desire to govern themselves; but this kind of love of independence, which takes rise only from some particular and fleeting problems brought on by despotism, is never durable: it passes with the accident that gave birth to it; they seem to love freedom, but one finds they only hated the master. What peoples who are made for freedom hate, is the evil of subjection itself.
>
> I also do not think that true love of liberty was ever born just from the sight of the material goods that freedom produces; for this often succeeds in hiding it . . . . Men who prize only these kinds of goods have never enjoyed freedom for long.
>
> That which, in all times, has so strongly attached certain men's hearts to freedom, are its own attractions, its own peculiar charm, independent of its benefits; it is the pleasure of being able to speak, act, and breathe without constraint, under the government of God and the laws alone. Whoever seeks for anything from freedom but itself is made for slavery.[210]

The peculiar problem of democratic societies is that democratic peoples tend to value equality above liberty and as a result, find themselves well disposed toward despotism, insofar as the state alone has the ability to slake the people's thirst. Because the intensity of that thirst increases as democracy advances, the cost of slaking it, namely freedom itself, appears worth it. Such a state should not conjure up the terrors that frequently attend despotic regimes, particularly those of recent times. Despotism in the age of democracy would be, as Tocqueville characterized it, soft or mild (*despotisme doux*)—a sort of popular or elective despotism. The state will not seek to brutalize its people; there will be no labor camps, secret police, show trials, or summary executions. Rather, through an inordinate number of detailed and complex rules, the state will take great pains to regulate the lives of its citizens and will do so, professedly, in their interests. It will provide and care for the people; from harm it will keep them; and it will go to great lengths to render them happy. Indeed, as Tocqueville put it, one could liken it to paternal power, save for this one crucial difference: whereas a father prepares his children for adulthood, the state will seek to keep its citizens irrevocably fixed in childhood.[211] The state wants the people's unquestioning obedience and the best way to ensure this is not by forcing their allegiance, but by fostering their dependence. A people that extol equality above liberty can be wealthy, powerful, and durable, but they will never know greatness. "What will never exist in such societies are great citizens and above all a great people, and I am willing to state that the average level of hearts and minds will never cease to decline so long as equality and despotism are combined."[212]

For Tocqueville, what made the French Revolution so deserving of the study was not simply the well-known equalizing forces that propelled it, but the less appreciated but no less consequential centralizing forces that paved the way for it. The power of the former blinded people to the import of the latter and while the forces of equality carried the day because the perils of centralization were overlooked, the Revolution's success was at best dubious. There, in the inexorable advance of the French Revolution, Tocqueville discovered an enduring lesson for the democratic age and its devotees who reflexively and unremittingly clamor for more and more equality.

"In 1789 the French made the greatest effort ever undertaken by any people to disassociate themselves from their past, and to put an abyss between what they had been and what they wished to become."[213] Tocqueville was of the opinion that the French were "less successful in their unique enterprise" than is generally accepted. For while the French beheaded the king, depredated the church, and decimated the nobility, they failed to confront the beast that had been devouring the *ancien régime* from within for more than a century, namely the state itself. Thus, it was not long after the monarchy fell that the state, more absolute than ever, was resurrected under "the ruthless dictatorship of the Reign of Terror.... It was a totalitarian dictatorship... embracing every detail of public and private life. It was as though the Revolution had reacted violently against all that it had done in the last four years and had suddenly returned to the centralizing tradition of the old absolutism."[214] It is true that that exercise in totalitarianism was short lived and can be attributed in part to the excesses toward which revolutions naturally incline, but it is no less true that the absolutist tendencies of the French were deep-rooted and abiding. Thus, a decade after beheading their own king, the French eagerly kneeled before an emperor who possessed power far more plenary than what their king had ever enjoyed.[215]

On the face of it, these outcomes were inconsistent with the Revolution's purported aims. Those who commanded its first stages were devotees of the Enlightenment, committed to liberty and concerned more with elevating the many than tearing down the few. The ideals they embraced were antipathetic to the despotism into which the Revolution precipitously devolved, and the loftiness and liberality of soul that they exuded ensured that their deeds would not be blotted out by the crimes that they had—unwittingly, to be sure—set in motion. "The first stage of '89... was a time of youth, enthusiasm, pride, a time of generous and sincere emotions, whose memory, despite its mistakes, will always be preserved by humanity, and which, for a long time to come, will trouble the sleep of all those who wish to corrupt or enslave France."[216] The glory that Tocqueville gleaned in the Revolution—at least at its outset—cannot be squared with Nietzsche's characterization of it as a slave revolt.[217] But however noble the intentions of the first revolutionaries may have been,[218] their work quickly devolved into something more akin to Nietzsche's gruesome farce, a truth to which Tocqueville was not blind.[219]

In the end, the Revolution achieved far too little at far too high a cost. It is true that, as Tocqueville observed, "it entirely destroyed, or is in the process of destroying (because it is still in progress), everything that derived from aristocratic and feudal institutions in the old society, everything that was in some way connected to them, everything that bore, in the least degree, their smallest imprint." But seeing that those institutions were destined to perish (with or without a revolution), the destruction the Revolution wrought ultimately was for naught. "If it had not taken place, the old structure would nevertheless have collapsed."[220] Not only was the undertaking superfluous, it was self-defeating, in that the French, by eradicating all vestiges of hierarchy, made possible a tyranny that would have been far more difficult to establish in a world where that hierarchy remained. It is not the least irony of that epochal upheaval that as the French clamored for liberty without parallel, they paved the way for a despotism without precedent.

This calls attention to the senselessness and catastrophic futility of the Revolution. It destroyed a moribund feudal order that would have collapsed of its own accord[221] and did nothing to arrest a swelling central state that was, at least in principle, held in check by that feudal order. It aimed its attack on a devitalized foe, perhaps more symbolic than real, and gave no heed to the advance of a much more powerful and potentially pernicious oppressor. But imprudent though it may have been, it is little wonder that the Revolution behaved as it did, even if it veered so tragically from the script it was supposed to follow. For one, the feudal order had become intolerable. Tocqueville, his intrinsic sympathies for the aristocracy notwithstanding, was well aware that the French nobility had become odious in the eyes of the people. The nobles enjoyed all the privileges of their ancestors but no longer met their obligations to the people upon which the legitimacy of those privileges had rested. Thus, the French aristocrat naturally became the poster child of oppression. Meanwhile, the state—the real organ of oppression—escaped the people's ire because it oppressed indirectly, at one remove. Its agents were natural objects of resentment, but the state itself remained clandestine and faceless. What is more, not only did the state elude blame for society's ills, it also was viewed as the sole entity capable of remedying those ills. "It could promise much and give much."[222]

Tocqueville's research led him to the ostensibly paradoxical conclusion that the revolt against the feudal order broke out in the very country where feudalism had most receded. In France, serfdom had been abolished long before the Revolution, so long, in fact, that by 1789, virtually no vestiges of it were to be found anywhere in the country.[223] This was hardly the case in most of Europe at that time. One did not have to travel to tsarist Russia to reach the realm of serfdom. Throughout the Hapsburg Empire and much of Eastern Europe, peasants were attached to lands they did not own, where they labored under compulsion without any prospect of financial recompense.[224] Tocqueville devotes much of his comparative analysis to the situation in Germany where, at the time of the Revolution, peasants were proscribed from leaving the manor to which they belonged; could not rise in rank, change profession, or marry without their master's consent; and were subject to manorial justice, which watched over their private lives and punished with severity their intemperance and laziness.[225] It is true that the German peasant did not fare quite as poorly as his brethren to the east, especially in places like Poland and Russia where peasants could be bought and sold, thereby rendering their legal condition somewhat analogous to the chattel slaves of North America; but still, his condition bore far more in common with them than it did with the French peasant of his day.

By contrast, the French peasant was legally free. "[He] came and went, bought and sold, made contracts and worked as he wished."[226] What is more, not only had the peasant ceased to be a serf, but he had become a landowner. This state of affairs was not established by the Revolution but predated it. In his travels, Arthur Young, the English author and statistician, noted that half the land of France belonged to the peasants.[227] Such a state of affairs, which Young was astonished to discover, was inconceivable elsewhere. Even in England, where there had been no serfdom for centuries, the bulk of land was concentrated in the hands of a few thousand families.[228]

The increasing independence of the French peasant was accompanied by a general increase in prosperity during the eighteenth century. Population, wealth, and industry were all on the rise. Curiously then, the Revolution bent on destroying the old regime broke out in a place where the lowest orders were least oppressed and at a time when "public prosperity increased with a previously unprecedented speed."[229] Indeed, as Tocqueville points out, "the parts of France which were going to be the chief base of [the Revolution] were precisely those where progress was most apparent."[230] In brief, "the French found their position the more unbearable as it improved . . . . Feudalism in all its power never inspired as much hatred in the French than at the moment it was about to disappear." History may be "full of similar spectacles,"[231] but it is one that appears emblematic of the age of democracy. As Tocqueville observed elsewhere, "when inequality is the common law of a society, the strongest inequalities do not strike the eye; when everything is nearly on a level, the least of them wound it. That is why the desire for equality always becomes more insatiable as equality is greater."[232]

Still, one should not overestimate the condition of the French peasant nor, for that matter, the general living standards that prevailed in pre-Revolutionary France. While on the whole, the eighteenth century was marked by increased prosperity, in the years leading up to 1789, the French economy suffered a series of economic setbacks that in large part stemmed from a number of poor harvests (a cautionary reminder that the children of the Enlightenment were still the playthings of nature).[233] While it would be superficial to reduce the French Revolution to an economic conflict or class struggle, there can be no doubt that the economic crisis of 1789 was one of the principal factors igniting what the King initially mistook for a rebellion.[234] As for the French peasant, though in many ways his status had improved appreciably, the conditions under which he lived often remained miserable.[235] As Tocqueville spells out in one of the chapter titles of *The Old Regime and the Revolution*, in spite of the very real progress that had been made, "the condition of the French peasant was sometimes worse in the Eighteenth Century than it had been in the Thirteenth."[236] Tocqueville points to two interrelated factors that account for this apparent anomaly: the nobility's abandonment of the peasantry and the concomitant aggrandizement of the state.

As had been broached above, a healthy, well-constituted aristocracy cares for those lower orders that fall under its aegis. This was certainly the case with the French aristocracy prior to the eighteenth century. Tocqueville concedes that "the nobles had offensive privileges [and] they possessed burdensome rights, but they assured public order, dispensed justice, executed the law, came to the help of the weak, and ran public affairs." As a result, their rights seemed less burdensome and their privileges less offensive to the poor over whom they watched. By the time of the Revolution, across much of France the nobles had all but relinquished their duties, while jealously clinging to their rights and privileges. Feudalism was preserved as a civil institution while ceasing to be a political one.[237]

While it does not excuse their dereliction of duties, what the nobles really sought to leave behind was the countryside. The peasants tied to it were almost incidental casualties. Already, at the start of the seventeenth century, Henry IV complained that the nobles were deserting the country's rural areas. "By the middle of the eighteenth century, this desertion had become almost universal."[238] It was to the towns and cities in general, and Paris and Versailles in particular, that the nobles fled, having been enticed by the promise of power, prestige, and pomp that radiated from those places. In time, their exodus would prove ruinous not only to the peasantry but to the entire apparatus of the *ancien régime*.

Cut off from the nobility, the French peasant was left to his own devices, which—in the absence of the wealth, education, and resources with which their delinquent masters had been blessed—were decidedly limited. There was an almost tragic irony to his situation. He acquired liberties his ancestors had never known and had come to possess the very lands to which his ancestors had been bound, and yet his situation was often more pathetic than that of his antecedents. The fourteenth-century peasant was at once more oppressed and more cared for than his eighteenth-century counterpart: "The aristocracy that sometimes tyrannized him, never abandoned him."[239] As for the more liberated peasant of the eighteenth century, he "no longer suffered all the evils his ancestors had, but he endured many miseries his ancestors never had known."[240]

> They were free, they were landowners, and they remained almost as ignorant and often more miserable than their serf ancestors. They remained without technology in the midst of prodigies of the arts, and uncivilized in a world shining with enlightenment. While keeping the intelligence and shrewdness natural to their race, they had not learned how to make use of it; they could not even succeed at cultivating their land which was their only business. "I see under my own eyes the agriculture of the tenth century," [said] a celebrated English agronomist.[241]

It is little wonder that the peasantry, mired in "this abyss of poverty and isolation" and "kept there as if it were sealed and impenetrable,"[242] harbored so much animosity for the aristocracy.

In view of fashionable narratives and the ever waxing denunciation of existing inequalities, it is worth stressing that it was not poverty alone that gave rise to the peasant's rancor. The egregious disparities that separated a penurious peasantry from a prodigal aristocracy did not spark the Revolution. To put it in more contemporary terms, the root cause of the Revolution was not income inequality or the wealth gap. Rather, it was a nobility that concomitantly shirked its responsibilities and maintained its privileges that inflamed the enmity of the people. And the proof of this is that it was in those parts of France where the old regime was best preserved, particularly in the west, "that the flame of civil war was lit and fed and where the Revolution was longest and most violently resisted."[243] Where the countryside and the peasants who labored there had not been abandoned, the upper and lower classes stood together, not as revolutionaries, but as counterrevolutionaries.[244] There peasants fought beside nobles, not as unwilling participants, but as eager and often leading combatants, to preserve a stratified social order whose bottom rungs they were fated to occupy.²⁴⁵ As la *Guerre de Vendée* makes plain, misery and oppression need not go hand in hand with inequality.

There is another seemingly ironic lesson to be found in the War in the Vendée. The nobles who defended the monarchy at the end of the eighteenth century had resisted the encroachments of the monarchy in the previous century. Tocqueville points to the letter of an intendant who complains that the nobles of Anjou (a former province in western France) preferred living with their peasants and thereby refused to do their duty to the king. In doing so, they stood apart from their fellow aristocrats who deserted the countryside in droves and presaged the entrenched resistance to the Revolution by opposing that which paved the way for it: the state's centralization. For as Tocqueville noted with regard to the nobility's "abandonment of the countryside . . . the chief and permanent cause . . . was not the will of certain men, but the slow and constant actions of institutions." And the slow and constant actions of those vortiginous institutions was to draw people and power to Paris—the heart of the growing state. The nobility did not spontaneously vacate the countryside, but rather was encouraged to do so, both directly and indirectly: directly, insofar as the policy, at least since the time of Richelieu, was "to divide the nobility from the people and attract the nobles to court and into government service" with an eye to limiting their influence; indirectly, because "as the nobility lost its political rights" without acquiring new ones, and as local freedoms were appropriated by the state, "the emigration of the nobility increased: there was no longer any need to encourage them to leave; they no longer had any desire to stay home. Country life had become boring to them."²⁴⁶ While the nobles' departure from the countryside did much to set the stage for 1789, the more root cause was the growth of the central state, first because it precipitated the exodus of the nobles, and second because it did nothing to mitigate the misery that was left in their wake.

Here is an insight that adverts to the cornerstone of Tocqueville's thought. In the democratic age, few problems loomed larger than that of centralization,²⁴⁷ and one cannot appreciate his approach to the democratic revolution in general, and the French Revolution in particular, without coming to terms with his assessment of it. With regard to the French Revolution, Tocqueville proffered the then unpopular insights that centralization was a product of the old regime, not of the Revolution itself; that save for that centralization, the Revolution could not have advanced as it did; and that "the only part of the old regime's political constitution which survived the Revolution" was the institution of centralization.²⁴⁸ Those claims are not the mere speculations of a theoretically-inclined mind; they are, as Tocqueville demonstrates, amply borne out by the historical record.

At the heart of the old regime stood the Royal Council (*le counseil du roi*). This "uniquely powerful administrative body . . . decided all important matters and supervised lesser authorities. All roads led to the Royal Council, and from it came the impulses that guided everything."[249] Strictly speaking, the authority the Council enjoyed was delegated. All power inhered in the king. He alone decided, even when it was the Council that decreed. Louis XIV's dictum, *l'etat c'est moi*, was not mere hyperbole. But it was through the Royal Council and its agents—most notably the intendants—that the king ruled France.[250] The Council secretly determined taxes; organized the militia; controlled public works; administered charities; and maintained public order. In his research, Tocqueville happened upon a number of decrees that might be read as farce had they not been enacted in earnest—decrees that forced artisans to employ certain methods and manufacture certain products; prohibited specific crops from being sown on lands that the Council did not deem appropriate; and even required that vineyards be torn up for, in the Council's opinion, having been planted in the wrong soil.[251] Presumably, a defense for such decrees could be mounted, but setting that aside, what ought to command attention is the veritable ubiquity of the Royal Council: virtually no part of the *ancien régime* was out of its reach.

> Under the old regime as now, there was in France no city, town, or village, no tiny hospital, factory, convent, or college, which could have an independent will in its own affairs, or freely administer its own goods. Then, as today, the government kept the French under its tutelage and if the insolent word paternalism had not yet been invented, the reality already had been.[252]

That reality was reflected in the state's efforts to manage and micromanage more and more of the lives of its people, as the examples above attest. There is, Tocqueville perceptively avers, an instinct common to all governments that predisposes them "to want to run everything themselves."[253] In this regard, France was no exception, though the extent to which it got what it wanted on this score was, indeed, exceptional. Over time, as more and more power was appropriated from a pliant nobility, the state expanded its regulatory reach and perfected its regulatory art. "As [it] became more detailed, more extended, it also became more uniform and more knowledgeable. It moderated itself while succeeding in taking over everything; it oppressed less, while it controlled more."[254]

For Tocqueville, the expansion of the French state was premonitory, not only for the French but for all those who belong to the age of democracy. In that interminable age that was but dawning at the time of Tocqueville's birth, central authorities will control more but oppress less. They will be despotic, but their despotism will be soft and pleasing. The *ancien régime* patently was no democracy; one reasonably could rejoin that the character of centralization in eighteenth-century France is but a poor portent for what character the state will assume under a less stratified regime. But to reason thus is to ignore or distort what is central to Tocqueville's argument. The Revolution was directed against the aristocracy, not the central state. In fact, those who supported the Revolution favored centralization, albeit not always wittingly, just as those who favored centralization paved the way for and served to further the Revolution, again not always wittingly. There was a symbiotic relationship between the two—between the egalitarianism that the Revolution advanced and the centralization that the state embodied. As a rule, a central authority will prefer an egalitarian order to a hierarchical one for the following reason: the more the distance between man and man is effaced, the more alike people become, and the more alike people become, the easier they are to manage. Similarly, a democratic people will naturally prefer a centralized authority to a decentralized one, because in principle, a single authority with uniform rules is better suited to actualize what the people long for most: equality. Centralization and democracy go hand in hand in a manner that cannot be said of centralization and aristocracy. This claim is supported, not refuted, by the case of France, where democracy has fared much better under centralization than aristocracy had. As Tocqueville mused, "When a people has destroyed its aristocracy, it runs toward centralization as if self-impelled. It then requires far less effort to encourage it down the slope towards centralization than to hold it back. In such a nation's midst, all powers tend naturally towards unity, and it is only with great skill that one can succeed in holding them apart." Centralization facilitated the destruction of the *ancien régime* and "so naturally took its place" in the democratic regime that superseded it.[255]

The notion that a regime might impress its character upon its people (and vice versa) and, by doing so, distinguish them from other people enjoys little if any legitimacy in the age of democracy. No doubt the world is populated by leftists and rightists; globalists and nationalists; haves and have-nots; Asians and Africans; but these distinctions are incidental and do not bespeak different human types. To a common humanity all belong. That there might be a constitutional difference between, say, a tyrannical soul and an aristocratic one was an idea put forward not only by the antiquated thinkers of antiquity but by that anomalous thinker of modernity—Alexis de Tocqueville. While Tocqueville reduced the pluralism of classical thought to a dualism, he still held that people could be distinguished by their political or social orientation, not in the petty and partisan sense that polarizes the present, but in a more elemental and enduring manner.[256] Regimes with different constitutions yield souls with different constitutions. The distinction between individuals governed by a constitutional monarch and those who cow before an absolute one is not just outward but inward. So too with those who belong to a regime that pursues military glory and those attached to one that prizes commercial glory. With respect to Tocqueville's own countrymen, centralization had a profound effect on their character, one that accounted for their turbulent and ostensibly incoherent history wherein they impetuously clamored for liberty one moment and obsequiously bowed before an emperor the next.

For one, the growing centralization of the old regime resulted in a growing uniformity of the French people. This uniformity evolved naturally from the undermining of all local and provincial authorities and the ever-increasing encroachments of the Royal Council. At the center of the kingdom stood "a single body . . . which ruled public administration throughout the country"; a single minister directed almost all internal affairs; each province was ruled by a single official who was a stranger to the province he oversaw.[257] Is it any wonder that a people governed thus grew more and more alike? Tocqueville observed that the uniformity of the legislation to which the people were subject reflected the uniformity of the people themselves.

> As one descends the course of the eighteenth century, one sees an increasing number of edicts, royal declarations, decrees of the Council which apply the same rules, in the same way, to all parts of the empire. It was not only the government, but the governed, who conceived the ideas of such a general and uniform legislation, everywhere the same, the same for all; this idea is evident in all the projects for reform which follow one another during the thirty years preceding the outbreak of the Revolution. Two centuries before, the very substance of such ideas, if one can speak thus, would have been lacking.[258]

In the eighteenth century, the "substance of such ideas" was on hand because the aristocracy not only ceased to direct affairs but ceased to direct ideas as well. The conviction that all men are equal—one that would have found no footing in an aristocratic age, that is, in an age founded on the conceit that all men are *not* equal—met no resistance in an age when the aristocracy no longer governed. That is not to say that France prior to the Revolution approached anything akin to democracy. The distance between the upper and lower classes was chasmic. "But, at bottom, everyone above the masses resembled one another." While nobles and bourgeois still did not enjoy the same rights, "they had the same ideas, the same habits, the same tastes, were inclined to the same pleasures, read the same books, spoke the same language." They were "enlightened by the same sun . . . . [T]heir education had been equally theoretical and literary. Paris, [which] more and more became the only teacher of France, ended up giving the same shape and a similar way of thinking to all minds."[259]

Not the least consequential idea to permeate the intellective milieu was that of human equality. In the minds of the upper class that idea may have been merely abstract, but hindsight was hardly needed to see that what the privileged posited in theory the underprivileged would demand in fact.

In spite of the growing uniformity of the French people, they became more and more isolated from one another. This too was a factor that greatly contributed to the Revolution's outbreak and one that arose naturally from the centralization of the state. As the government became more and more centralized, it jealously guarded the powers it had accrued. Initially wary of free associations and assemblies, in time it became downright hostile to them.

> What characterized government in France was the violent hatred which the government felt for all those outside it, noble or bourgeois, who wanted to concern themselves with public affairs. The smallest independent body which seemed to want to come into being without its permission frightened the government; the tiniest free association, whatever its object, disturbed it; it only allowed those which it had arbitrarily created and governed to exist.[260]

Far from being some transient sentiment unique to the reign of Louis XIV, this mindset traverses much of French history. "During the whole course of the long history of the French monarchy, where so many remarkable rulers appear, some notable for their intelligence, others for their character, almost all for their courage, there is not a single one who makes an effort to bring the classes together and unite them in any way but in submission to an equal dependence." There is, as Tocqueville notes, one exception: "one alone [who] wanted to, and even wholeheartedly attempted to [bring the people together], and that one—who can fathom the judgments of God!—was Louis XVI."[261]

Before the aggrandizement of the state, which commenced most notably with Louis XIV, the people belonging to the different estates routinely were in close contact with each other. Nobles and peasants enjoyed an intimate relationship with one another, as the latter worked the lands of the former and the former dutifully watched over the latter. The following account of the Vendéan nobility is exceptional only because it is taken from the eighteenth century; in centuries prior, it would have reflected the rule. "They had grown up with their tenants under the same oak trees, shared the same country pastimes and had been suckled at the same breasts. These noblemen who hunted and drank with their peasants and tenants had already sown the seeds of egalitarian principles [long before the Revolution]."[262] Moreover, meetings of the Estates-General brought members of the different orders together. By the eighteenth century, the people were cut off from one another. The nobles had forsaken the peasants and had virtually no interaction with nor any understanding of them. As for the growing bourgeoisie, prior to the eve of the Revolution, the Estates-General had last met in 1614. Since then,

> the bourgeois and the noble no longer had contact with one another in public life. They no longer felt the need to come together and reach agreements; every day they were more independent of each other, but also more estranged from one another. In the eighteenth century this revolution was complete; these two never met except by chance in private life. The two classes were no longer merely rivals, they were enemies.[263]

By the time of the Revolution, the fissures that fractured France ran deep. Notwithstanding their increasing similitude, nobles scorned the bourgeois for their want of nobility, while the bourgeois resented the nobles for the privileges they themselves were not permitted to enjoy. The bourgeois did not want to do away with the nobility, so much as encourage it to shed its exclusivity so that they might join its ranks. Yet, it was with the people against the nobility that the bourgeois imprudently and fatefully sided.

This imprudence could be explained in part, and no doubt was exacerbated by, the upper classes' dissociation from the lower. On the whole, the wealthy few—nobles and bourgeois alike—were sympathetic to the people's plight. But having been cut off from them for so long, the proverbial haves had no real understanding of the have-nots—of their suffering, their longings, and, not least importantly, what they were capable of. Because the people had not appeared on the political scene for more than a century, the upper classes "ceased to believe they could ever mount the stage again."[264] Thus, it was with grievous naïveté that the well-intentioned upper classes paved the way to the scaffold and set the stage for their own downfall. In what amounted to a confessional and expiatory undertaking, the government publicly proclaimed its own missteps and professed that public distress had been aggravated by the greed of the rich.[265] For their part, nobles sincerely pitied the poor, while spurning them with no less sincerity. "The lower classes had already become an object of their sympathy, without ceasing to be the object of their disdain." The nobles referred to the plebeians whose cause they took up as "vile peasants[,] rough and ignorant beings, turbulent people and coarse and insubordinate characters."[266] None of this appeared imprudent because it was assumed on the part of the upper classes that the lower classes simply lacked the ability to comprehend. On this score, Tocqueville was reminded of "Mme Duchatelet, who according to Voltaire's secretary, felt no embarrassment at undressing in front of her servants, not considering it really proven that valets are men."[267] The posture of the nobles then was one of rank condescension; because the people were too stupid to help themselves, it was up to the nobles to help them. As 1789 approached, the elites—in one of those unconscious displays of imbecility so indicative of elites—invited the commoners to air their grievances. Instead of earning the respect and gratitude of the lower classes, they excited their envy and hatred. In this way, the upper classes actively sowed the seeds of their own demise. "The enthusiasm of the educated classes ended up setting afire and arming the angers and lusts of the masses."[268]

Again, all this was made possible by the educated classes' longstanding disconnect from and ignorance of the people they sought to help. Though the members of the nobility had ceased to govern long ago, they still thought they commanded because of the privileges they retained. "Since they still walked first in processions, they thought that they still led." But the reality was something different entirely: "no one followed them, they were alone, and when, finally, some came to overthrow them, the nobility could do nothing but flee." For their part, the bourgeois sided with the people against the nobility, proceeding on the misguided supposition that the uneducated masses would be manageable and could be employed to further their own interests. Again, the reality was altogether different. "Only after he had put arms in their hands did he realize that he had excited the passions of which he had no idea, passions that he was as powerless to contain as to direct, and of which he was going to become the victim after having been the promoter."[269] The pathetic miscalculation on the part of the elites betrays just how tremendous the rift between themselves and the masses had grown. As Tocqueville reflected,

> it is curious to see in what strange security those who occupied the upper and middle floors of the social edifice lived, at the very moment when the Revolution began, and to hear them talking innocently among themselves about the virtues of the people, of their mildness, their devotion, their innocent pleasures, when 1793 is already before them: a ridiculous and terrible sight![270]

Colored by the romanticized views then in vogue, the peasant assumed a similitude to Rousseau's noble savage, whose innate goodness and sympathy precluded him from doing any harm.

> It seemed as if the Jacquerie, the Maillotins, and the Sixteen had been completely forgotten, and that it was unknown that the French, who are the gentlest and even the most benevolent people in the world as long as they remain peacefully undisturbed, become the most barbarous nation on earth as soon as violent passions arouse them.[271]

If the superlativeness of French barbarism is open to dispute, the celerity with which that barbarism is stirred is not. After all, it was not with the Terror that the beheadings began, but with the Revolution itself.[272]

The dreadful violence that the Revolution unleashed was an unintended, albeit logical consequence of what was the tacit, if not official, policy of the state: "dividing people in order to govern them more absolutely."[273] Per the logic of the state, a factious public without any common interest to speak of is more tractable and less likely "to join in common resistance." That logic was reflected in a surreptitious report to the king issued by Turgot (the brilliant and short-lived comptroller-general of finances) and cited by Tocqueville:

> The nation ... is a society made up of different orders badly united, and of a people whose members have very few ties, where, by consequence, no one cares about anything but his own personal interests. Nowhere is any common interest visible. The villages, the towns have no more contact than do the regions of which they are part. They cannot even agree among themselves to undertake necessary public works. In this perpetual war of claims and counter-claims, His Majesty is obliged to decide everything by himself or through his delegates. They wait for your special orders in order to contribute to the public good, in order to respect someone else's rights, sometimes even to exercise their own.[274]

Herein lies one of the more pernicious effects of centralization, one that Tocqueville repeatedly returns to in his writings. As the administrative apparatus extended its reach and its direction of affairs became more absolute, the people withdrew into themselves and became more servile. Taking no part in governing the larger community to which they once belonged, their horizon contracted considerably. They took no interest in matters save for those that directly impacted them, their own weal being their sole concern. At the same time, they became increasingly dependent on the state. As society advanced, it "created new needs every minute, and every one of them was a new source of power for the central government; for only the government was in a position to satisfy them."[275] Bereft of the will and capacity to take charge of their own fates, people across France, regardless of rank, implored the state in their hours of need.[276]

The French monarchy serves as one of those admonitory lessons with which history is glutted, namely that one should be careful what one wishes for, for ultimately the state got what it wanted: a divided and dependent populace. But in so doing, it summoned its own destruction. By dividing the people, it fomented animosities between them. As would be made apparent in due course, it was much easier to divide the people than it was to unite them. When at last they did come together, they did so only "to tear each other apart."[277] Moreover, by supplanting Providence, the state assumed a part it ultimately could not play. It aimed to manage everything with the result that it was held accountable for everything it failed to manage, even those matters that were plainly beyond its control, including the weather.[278] In the end, the monarchy's undoing was its own doing.

Centralization, however, did not go as quietly as the monarchy. Though "centralization fell with absolute government,"[279] its death was short lived.

> Let us no longer be astonished at seeing with what marvelous ease centralization was reestablished in France at the beginning of this [nineteenth] century. The men of '89 had knocked down the building, but its foundations had remained in the very souls of its destroyers, and on those foundations it was possible to rebuild it again, and to construct it more solidly than ever.[280]

So long dependent on a central authority, the people quickly found that they were unprepared to live without it. While the Revolution was inspired by noble sentiments, those sentiments could not be sustained. The "disinterested beliefs and generous feelings which . . . motivated the educated classes and pointed them towards revolution" quickly gave way to the grievances and resentments of the crowd.[281] What animated those who were the architects of and principal actors in the first stage of the Revolution was a genuine devotion to both liberty and equality: "when [men] wanted to create not only democratic institutions, but free ones; when they sought not only to destroy privileges but to honor and recognize rights."[282] Inevitably, it would seem, these men were unseated and with them went the Revolution's nobler impulses. The longing for liberty gave way to implacable demands for equality. Instead of erecting institutions that were both democratic and free, the French wanted "to build a society where men were as alike, and conditions as equal, as humanity could admit." This comes as no surprise given that in the souls of the French, the passion for liberty was "more recent and less well-rooted" than "the violent and inextinguishable hatred of inequality."[283] Extolling equality far above liberty, the French "desire[d] nothing more than to become the equal servants of the master of the world,"[284] a desire that was sated with the rise of Bonaparte. But even before Napoleon crowned himself emperor, the French found themselves submitting to a central authority whose power—in terms of both its absoluteness and brutality—terribly exceeded what had been exercised by their late king.

> [A] stronger government, much more absolute than that which the Revolution had overthrown arose and concentrated all power in itself, suppressed all freedoms so dearly bought and put vain idols in their place. . . . [T]his government called the votes of electors who could neither inform themselves, nor organize, nor choose, "the sovereignty of the people."[285]

Thus, for example, the National Convention, which purported to embody the will of the people, came to power with a national voter turnout of roughly

15 percent[286]. That low turnout is explained in part by the revolutionaries already in power who controlled the press and excluded from legitimate candidacy those who did not support their agenda.[287] What is more, this National Convention was a shell, a hollow governing body that had been deprived of any legitimate authority by the Committee of Public Safety, which concentrated all power—legislative, executive, and judicial: the very definition of tyranny[288]—in itself.[289] For roughly a year, the Committee effectively and despotically ruled France, managing its war efforts, curtailing the people's freedoms, and issuing death sentences with reckless and terrifying abandon. A nation of nearly thirty million souls ruled by twelve—a paragon of centralization if ever there was one.[290]

Tocqueville's point is that that sort of centralization neither materialized nor ended with the Revolution. What made the systematic and centralized terror into which the Revolution devolved possible was that the French had long been accustomed to a central authority and were much better versed in being ruled than in ruling themselves. Robespierre's rise proceeded the fall of an absolute monarch and preceded the ascension of an emperor more absolute still. When, at last, the master—take your pick—did fall, "what was most substantial in his work remained; his government dead, his bureaucracy still lived and every time that [the French] have since tried to bring down absolute power, [they] have limited [themselves] to placing liberty's head on a servile body."[291] And therein lies the danger—one of many, to be sure—of centralization: it fosters a sense of dependency that proves much easier to implant than uproot. The French make this amply clear. At some level, the people of France were anything but servile, a verity learned quickly by the nations of Europe that gathered against them at the close of the eighteenth century and again at the start of the nineteenth. Yet, the very people who would "trouble the sleep of all those who [might] wish to corrupt or enslave [them],"[292] contented themselves time and time again by acquiescently surrendering their freedom to a central state. Having for so long been denied the opportunity to be free, the French were poorly schooled in the art of being free; not knowing what to do with it or how best to preserve it, they impetuously forsook the liberty that they had sacrificed so much to secure.

In the end, the French Revolution was an emphatically French affair.

> France alone could give birth to a revolution so sudden, so radical, so impetuous in its course, and yet so full of backtracking, of contradictory facts and contrary examples. Without the reasons which I have given, the French would never have made the Revolution, but it must be recognized that all these reasons together would not succeed in explaining such a revolution anywhere else but in France.[293]

Still, the fact that the French alone could have effected such a Revolution should not detract from its universality; nor does it refute the position that that paradigmatically democratic revolution had very ancient roots, stretching all the way back to Athens and Jerusalem and the twin faiths they bequeathed to posterity and to which posterity still pertinaciously clings: faith in human reason and human equality. One might liken those foundational revolutions to parents who not only birthed a democratic man but taught him to take his first tentative steps. By 1789, democratic man had learned to march with such formidable force that nothing could impede his path. That march is far from over. Democratic man presses onward, stumbling occasionally along the way. But with the French Revolution, it was made clear that the future would be his. The age of aristocracy had given way to that of democracy. In this new age, to what species valets belong is no longer open to question.

The French Revolution signifies a late and particularly prominent moment in mankind's democratic advancement. As such, it does much to illumine some of the aspects that the democratic revolution writ large portends. For while the Revolution was distinctly French, it also exhibited a number of features that are indicative of the democratic revolution in and of itself. Not the least of these concerns the centralization of the state, a problem to which Tocqueville devoted so much of his thinking, not only in *The Old Regime and the Revolution* but in *Democracy in America* as well. Though it bore a particularly French stripe, there were many aspects of the centralization that evolved under and outlived the old regime that were emblematic of centralization as such. The pernicious consequences of centralization—servility to the state, isolation from one's fellow man, disassociation from political life— are not peculiar to the French, but are characteristic of centralization as such, regardless of the nationality of the people who fall under its yoke. A specter haunts not just Europe, but the world over in the in the age of democracy— the specter of centralization.

It is a testament to the acuity of Tocqueville's mind that he not only was able to discern the centralizing forces that paved the way for, and were solidified further by, the Revolution, but was also able to apprehend what those forces augured in the age of democracy. Again, it was man's democratization, not that of the French, that ever remained Tocqueville's concern and in view of it, he drew lessons from the French Revolution that could be applied to the larger democratic one. Centralization is a problem not just for the French, but for the democratized, in whatever land they may find themselves. Likewise, the philosophical ideas that spawned and sustained the Revolution and the manner in which the Revolution behaved exhibited universal features (and dangers) that were not lost on Tocqueville.

Revolutions tend to be sired. It is no trifling attestation to the Great Man Theory that such momentous events often are traced back to a single author.

Even in the democratic age, when people are inclined to credit impersonal rather than personal forces for (mis)directing history, one finds that this approach to history has not been rejected outright. It is enough to note that even the Russian Revolution, heir to the French, was not without its father.²⁹⁴

As for the French Revolution, its paternity typically is traced back to that hopelessly romantic and delinquent father, Jean-Jacques Rousseau. Rousseau's impress on the French Revolution and, by extension, subsequent leftist upheavals, is not exactly a matter of conjecture. In 1794, at the height of revolutionary fervor, Rousseau's remains were disinterred from his modest grave in Ermeonville and transported to the Pantheon in Paris with all due pomp. A delegation from his native city carried a banner that felicitously captured the underlying sentiment: "Aristocratic Geneva proscribed him, a regenerated Geneva has avenged his memory."²⁹⁵ France of the *ancien régime* had treated Rousseau with no greater respect than had his native Geneva, exiling the philosopher in 1761 and ordering his books, *Emile* in particular, to be burned publicly. A France reborn, shorn of its ancient inequities, would honor in death the patron saint that had been profaned in life. These redemptive efforts did not require the Terror for their realization, but commenced at the outset of the Revolution, with pamphlets celebrating Rousseau's genius being distributed and popular appeals being made to commemorate the author of the *Social Contract*.

> In 1790, in a speech to the National Assembly supporting the idea of raising a statue to Rousseau, it was declared that "You should see in Jean-Jacques Rousseau . . . the precursor of our great Revolution; you should recall that he taught you how to form men for freedom, when you were on the eve of making the French a free people. The Social Contract has been for you the charter in which you have rediscovered the right usurped from the nation, and above all the imprescriptible right of sovereignty."²⁹⁶

Rousseau's ideas routinely were quoted in public and printed in newspapers; collections of his most memorable epigrams were published; and a pocket-sized edition of the *Social Contract* was issued to soldiers so that they could carry it with them into battle.²⁹⁷ At a time when the Church was being depredated and desecrated, this work served as a sort of secular bible. That Robespierre was rumored to have slept with a copy of the *Social Contract* under his pillow,²⁹⁸ further affirms the extent of Rousseau's influence on the unfolding of the French Revolution.

Still, though the title Father of the French Revolution is not undeserved, the procreative power needed to generate so prodigious an event cannot be generated by a single man. Himself a child of the Age of Reason, Rousseau became one of the leading figures of the Enlightenment. He belonged to a group of French intellectuals who called themselves *philosophes*, a group that included among its ranks some of the day's most eminent minds (Voltaire, Diderot, Condorcet, and Montesquieu, to name but a few). These children of the Enlightenment, in various and often conflicting ways, aimed to dispel the ignorance and superstition that had beset and retarded humankind since its infancy and engender a new age of progress where the old authorities would be displaced and new authorities would be grounded squarely in reason. These were, to speak anachronistically, public intellectuals who "did not see their mission as limited to the advancement of knowledge[, but rather] tried to influence things in a concrete way by appealing to public opinion and swaying it in the direction they wanted."[299] Had they limited their pursuits to those of the literary and philosophic varieties, their renown might not have been any less, but their influence would have been very different. Tocqueville observes that around the middle of the eighteenth century, men of letters in France began to involve themselves in public affairs in a manner that had been unknown in France formerly. "They constantly concerned themselves with topics related to government . . . every day . . . discussing the origin of societies and their original forms, the primordial rights of citizens and those of authority, the natural and artificial relations among men, the error or legitimacy of custom, the very principle of laws."[300] Their influence was all the more remarkable because their ideas were not merely read but applied. Those who conducted affairs took their bearing more or less directly from those who directed minds, putting in practice the "abstract principles" the latter put on paper.[301]

Though few of the *philosophes* were political theorists and despite the diversity of their views, they shared a common conceit regarding the improvement, if not perfection, of society. Tocqueville goes so far as to assert that it was the single idea of which the political philosophy of the eighteenth century consisted: "they all think that it would be good to substitute basic and simple principles, derived from reason and natural law, for the complicated and traditional customs which ruled the society of their times."[302] This was true not only of the *philosophes* in general but also of a less celebrated group of thinkers known as the *physiocrats*. Though their writings may have "contributed less to the coming of the Revolution," Tocqueville maintains "that it is in their writings above all that [one] can best study the Revolution's true nature."[303] The political solutions proffered by the physiocrats were much more concrete than the abstract and very general ideas of the *philosophes*.[304]

> All the institutions that the Revolution was going to permanently abolish had been the particular objects of the physiocrats' attacks; none had found grace in their eyes. On the contrary, all those which may pass for the Revolution's own work had been announced in advance and ardently recommended by them;

one could hardly cite a single one whose seed had not been sown in some of their writings; we find in the physiocrats all that is most substantial in the Revolution.[305]

That intransigently egalitarian temper so indicative of the times permeated the writings of the physiocrats. In them, one finds not only an uncompromising animosity against privilege, but a hatred of diversity as well: "they adore equality even in servitude." As a matter of principle, the physiocrats scorned the past—"an object of limitless contempt" in their eyes. While property rights were held to be sacrosanct, other civil liberties enjoyed a much more tenuous standing. Deliberative assemblies were viewed as pernicious and checks and balances as "a fatal idea in government."[306] That might seem incongruous for thinkers bent on combating the absolutism that inhered in the French monarchy, but one must recall that what was hated was the face of that authority, not its substance. As Tocqueville put it, for the physiocrats, "it was not a question of destroying absolute power but of converting it."[307] And the means for doing so would be the state, which

> was not only to rule the nation but to shape it in a certain way; it was for the state to form the citizen's mind according to a particular model set out in advance; its duty was to fill the citizen's head with certain ideas and to furnish his heart with certain feelings that it judged necessary. In reality, there were no limits to its rights, nor bounds to what it might do; it not only reformed men, it transformed them; perhaps it concerned the state alone to make different people out of them! "The state makes men whatever it wants," says Bodeau. This phrase sums up all their theories.
>
> This particular form of tyranny, which we call democratic despotism, of which the Middle Ages has no idea, was already familiar to the physiocrats. No more hierarchy within society, no more classes, no more fixed ranks; a people composed of almost identical and entirely equal individuals, this jumbled mass recognized as the sole legitimate sovereign, but carefully deprived of all the faculties which might permit it to direct and even to oversee its own government. Above society, a single official, charged with doing everything in its name, without consulting it. To control it, a public reason without means of expression; to stop it, revolutions not laws: in theory, a subordinate agent; in fact, a master.[308]

While the physiocrats' commitment to laissez faire principles would be found repugnant, there is much in their program to satisfy even the most devout socialist, as Tocqueville rightly saw.[309]

Again, on the face of it, it would seem odd to advance as the corrective to France's monarchical regime a state where power was increased and more narrowly concentrated, that is, to replace an absolute monarchy with a more absolute state. But the question was one of ends. Under the old system, power was used to preserve a stratified society grounded in longstanding traditions and inherited privileges. Under the new system, power will be used to undo those traditions and privileges so as to effect a society with no lasting stratifications to speak of. That the potential for abuse would be no smaller in the new system than it was in the old seems to have been of little concern to the physiocrats. Indeed, the only guarantee against the abuse of power that they put forward was public education. As François Quesnay, teacher of Turgot and one of the principal founders of the physiocratic school, put it, "despotism is impossible if the nation is enlightened."[310] The unflagging faith in reason as a panacea for societal ills is a conceit that is central not only to the Revolution, but to the Enlightenment and the modern project more broadly. It is a faith that, as Nietzsche showed, has a very ancient pedigree.

What is remarkable about the French Revolution in the context of man's millennial democratization is that in that pivotal upheaval, the West's foundational faiths—in reason as a corrective and in the equality of souls—are so wonderfully fused. The revolutionaries—those who unrelentingly propelled the Revolution forward to its tragic heights—presumably would be averse to conceding as much, if only because doing so would entail acknowledging their debt to the past when what they in fact wanted was to sever themselves irrevocably from it. But their aversion on this score is a blind spot, one that is common to all revolutionaries who are hellbent on starting anew. Societies are not remade overnight. No doubt revolutionary ideas can be novel and frequently are extreme, but as a rule, the fighting faiths of revolutionaries are not of their own making; they are, in a manner of speaking, handed to them. And the French Revolution makes this as plain as any. Certainly in the context of French history, overthrowing the monarchy and leveling the social order was at once novel and extreme. But one who deduces that the principles that precipitated that leveling were rooted in Robespierre or even the French Enlightenment digs superficially; just as one who maintains that the foundational faiths of the West are intrinsic to man *qua* man (so that the revolutionaries were merely appealing to human nature) thinks tendentiously. Both claims stem from a lack of the historical sense of which Nietzsche wrote. None of this is to gainsay the sincerity—or zealotry, as the case often was—with which the revolutionaries believed that they had dissociated themselves from the past, but, to paraphrase Horace, you can drive out history with a pike, but she will always come back.

Fanaticism tends to distort the truth rather than reveal it, though the ardency with which fanatics maintain their convictions readily leads people—including the fanatics themselves—to think otherwise. Again, there is no reason to question the sincerity with which the revolutionaries felt that they were starting afresh. In their minds, Year One was just that. But the fanaticism with which they executed their plan should not suggest that they succeeded—or that ever they could. Nor should it conceal the derivativeness of their ideals and the debt they owed to those distant and originary revolutionaries who laid the cornerstones of Western Civilization. This should be borne in mind especially in the case of Jerusalem, owing to the unbridled ire with which the revolutionaries attacked Christianity. "In France, Christianity was attacked with a kind of fury, without even any attempt to put another religion in its place."[311] But what they attacked was the face of Christianity, not its substance, for ultimately what the revolutionaries wanted was the very ideal that Christianity advanced: an equality of souls, albeit one before the state rather than God. To paraphrase Nietzsche, under the Revolution, Christian morality proved more perdurable than Christian dogma.[312]

None of this eluded Tocqueville who argues that the animus toward Christianity, though egregious, was not essential to the Revolution. "The war against religion was only an incident in the Revolution, one of its striking but fleeting aspects, a transitory product of the ideas, passions, and particular circumstances which preceded and prepared the Revolution, and not part of the Revolution's own spirit."[313] What the revolutionaries despised was not so much the religious teachings of the Church, but the political institution it had become.

> The priests were not hated because they claimed to regulate the affairs of the other world, but because they were landowners, lords, tithe collectors, and administrators in this one; not because the Church could not take its place in the new society that was being created, but because it occupied the strongest and most privileged place in the old society which was being ground into dust.[314]

In short, it was primarily an attack on privilege and not on religion.[315] In this regard, it was in keeping with "the particular circumstances which preceded and prepared the Revolution." The Church also constituted a symbol that ran counter to the ideas that were then *le dernier cri*. It was a pillar of the *ancien régime*; an outgrowth of privilege and bastion of tradition, that preserved and profited from existing hierarchies and recognized an authority superior to individual reason.[316] Moreover, as with the nobility, the Church appeared to have lost its way; to have abandoned its charge and grown corrupt, profiting from privileges it no longer had any legitimate claim to, if ever it did.[317] The "spectacle of so many abusive or ridiculous privileges," the persistence of "so many bizarre and irregular institutions . . . which seemed doomed to live forever after having lost their virtue" instilled in the people an irresistible yearning to wipe the slate clean; to destroy all that had rotted with age and to reorder society rationally so as to ensure that such rottenness would not recur. Because those who advanced such ideas were so utterly divorced from politics and devoid of practical experience in governing, they "didn't have any idea of the dangers which always accompany even the most necessary revolutions." As for the people themselves, who were no better versed in these matters and whose passions had been inflamed by the promise that their miseries would soon be allayed and their standing elevated, the imprudence of putting into practice the abstract theories then in vogue was lost on them.[318]

All of this helps to explain why in eighteenth-century France, "general and abstract theories of government" were so well received and blindly trusted,[319] but it does little to explain why such ideas found a receptive audience beyond its borders. Whatever shared history binds the peoples of Europe together, the fact remains that their respective histories are distinct and so too the peoples born (respectively) from them. There is a reason why the people of France are French and not Swiss or Dutch or Polish. Yet, across Europe, the ideas of the Revolution were widely and ardently embraced.[320] The reason already has been suggested: those ideas were not so much French as they were democratic, and they spoke to people wherever people had been democratized.[321] The French Revolution was but a part of a much larger one and it behaved accordingly.

Though it was unmistakably a political revolution, Tocqueville argued that it "acted like and began to look like a religious [one:]"

> Every political and civil revolution has taken place within the borders of a single country. The French Revolution did not have a territory of its own; further, to some extent its effect has been to erase all the old frontiers from the map. It has united or divided people despite their laws, traditions, characters, and languages, turning compatriots into enemies, and strangers into brothers; or rather it established, above all particular nationalities, a common intellectual homeland where men of all nations could become citizens.
>
> In all history you will not find a single political revolution which had this character. You will find it only in certain religious revolutions. The French revolution must be compared to a religious revolution, if you want to find an analogy to help in understanding it.
>
> Schiller justly remarks, in his history of the Thirty Years War, that the great Reformation of the sixteenth century brought together nations which hardly knew each other, and united them through their new feelings. Indeed Frenchmen fought Frenchmen while Englishmen came to their aid, and men born at the furthest extreme of the Baltic penetrated the heart of Germany in order to protect Germans whom they had never heard of before. All foreign wars took on something of the character of civil wars; in all civil wars foreigners appeared. Every country's old interests were forgotten for new interests; questions of territory gave way to questions of principle. All the rules of diplomacy were mixed up

and confused, to the great astonishment and dismay of the statesmen of the time. This is precisely what happened to Europe after 1789.[322]

The Revolution behaved in such a manner because there was something fundamentally religious about it. At least in their post-classical, post-pagan iterations, religions address man *qua* man. They do not restrict themselves to people of this era or inhabitants of that land, but touch upon all those who comprise, and ever have comprised, humanity. Christianity was the first to adopt this universal approach—or at least to do so successfully. Unlike the religions it superseded, it was not "particular to one people, to one form of government, to one social state, to one time or race," which is why, in part, it "conquered in so short a time a great part of the human race." Similarly, "the French Revolution operated, with respect to this world, in precisely the same manner that religious revolutions have acted with respect to the other world. It considered the citizen in an abstract manner, outside of any particular society, the same way that religion considers man in general, independently of time and place."[323] In this way, the revolutionaries, good Rousseauians that they were, viewed society everywhere as being nothing but a form of illegitimate bondage.[324] Man's natural state is equality and it is to that state that humans will return. And it is reason that not only permits man to see his natural right but to secure it (with a good dose of force, admittedly). Reason will dispel the error and deceit upon which all societies previously reposed and will restore to man the human equality that rightfully and naturally is his.

It is there in the French Revolution that those foundational revolutions of Western Civilization coalesce so marvelously. And it is only with such late-born children that such a coalescence is possible. As Tocqueville notes, neither the actions that were carried out during the Revolution nor the ideas proffered under it were without precedent. "In all eras, even in the High Middle Ages, there have been agitators who, in order to change particular customs, have invoked the general laws of human society, who attempted to oppose the natural rights of man to the constitution of their country."[325] What had changed by the eve of the Revolution was that the distance between man and man had been overcome—not entirely, to be sure, but substantially all the same. In this regard, one is able to perceive how the French Revolution was but a chapter in a much larger narrative, one that stretched back millennia. "The most extraordinary thing was not that the French Revolution did what it did, or that it came up with the ideas that it produced: the great novelty was that so many nations had reached a point where such practices were so effectively employed, and such principles so readily accepted."[326] The French Revolution did not precede man's democratization; it presupposed it.

NOTES

1. James Madison to W. T. Barry (August 4, 1822). James Madison, *Madison: Writings* (New York: Library of America, 1999), 790. Madison's prologue was a popular government governed by an ill-informed populace.
2. Tocqueville, *Old Regime*, 99.
3. François Furet, *Interpreting the French Revolution*, 2. "What sets the French Revolution apart is that it was not a transition but a beginning and a haunting vision of that beginning. Its historical importance lies in the one trait that was unique to it, especially since this 'unique' trait was to become universal: it was the first experiment with democracy." Ibid, 79.
4. In a celebrated passage, Lessing wonderfully sheds light on this disposition and by doing so, reveals how at odds this disposition is with the scientific (or scientistic) dogmas that hold sway today. "The worth of a man does not consist in the truth he possesses, or thinks he possesses, but in the pains he has taken to attain that truth. For his powers are extended not through possession but through the search for truth. In this alone his ever-growing perfection consists. Possession makes him lazy, indolent, and proud. If God held all truth in his right hand and in his left the everlasting striving after truth, so that I should always and everlastingly be mistaken and said to me, 'Choose,' with humility I would pick on the left hand and say, 'Father grant me that; absolute truth is for thee alone'." Gotthold Ephraim Lessing, *Anti-Goeze*, quoted in *Lessing's Theological Writings: Selections in Translation* (Stanford: Stanford University Press, 1957), 42–3. A related truth, also too little appreciated in the present age, was conveyed by Dostoevsky when he observed that "*happiness lies not in happiness but only in the attempt to achieve it.*" Fyodor Dostoevsky, *A Writer's Diary*, vol. 1, trans. Kenneth Lantz (Evanston, IL: Northwestern University Press, 1994), 335.
5. Jardin notes that Tocqueville controlled the "form and style" of his writing with "severe exaction." Jardin, *Tocqueville*, 483. Elsewhere he observes, "[Tocqueville's] preference for a 'classical' clarity of literary form, one that would express ideas elegantly and soberly, was a family heritage. Before the *Democracy* was published, the father and brothers of the young writer weighed every turn of phrase, down to individual words, and all three required the sort of exactness that gives Alexis's style, in places, a crystalline purity" (54).
6. Tocqueville, *Old Regime*, 85.
7. See Chapter Two, note 143 above. For criticisms leveled by later historians, see Richard Herr, *Tocqueville and the Old Regime* (Princeton: Princeton University Press, 1962), 120–5. For Tocqueville's "excessive reliance on an imperfect source," namely Louis-Marie Prudhomme's *Résumé général*, see Gannett, *Tocqueville Unveiled*, 124–5. Its defects aside, "*L'Ancien Régime et la Révolution* was at once recognized by the public as the best study that been written of pre-Revolutionary France. The century that has passed since it appeared has not seen its prestige shaken." Herr, *Tocqueville and the Old Regime*, 9. Another half century can be tacked on to Herr's estimation, as the publication of three new English translations of the work in the twenty-first century attests.

8. See, for example, Nietzsche, *Genealogy of Morality*, 33, as well as *Twilight of the Idols*, 552–3.

9. "I see only one man who experienced [the French Revolution] as it must be experienced, with *nausea*—Goethe." Nietzsche, *Twilight of the Idols*, 553.

10. Ibid.

11. Nietzsche, *Zarathustra*, 243.

12. "Socrates was the first who brought philosophy down from the heavens, placed it in cities, introduced it into families, and obliged it to examine into life and morals, and good and evil." Cicero, *Cicero's Tusculan Disputations: Also Treatises On the Nature of the Gods, and On the Commonwealth* (New York: Harpers and Brothers, 1877), 164.

13. Tocqueville, *Old Regime*, 97.

14. Ibid, 100: "Christianity conquered in a short time a great part of the human race, easily crossing the barriers that had halted the pagan religions. I do not think it is lacking respect for that holy religion to say that it owed its triumph in part to the fact that it, more than any other, was separate from all that might be particular to one people, to one form of government, to one social state, to one time or to one race."

15. "Religious skepticism was the most private of his contradictions. He disguised it as best he could. His wife did not know of it." Jardin, *Tocqueville*, 384. Shortly after Tocqueville's death, Gustave de Beaumont, Tocqueville's closest friend and traveling companion to America, remarked to Nassau Senior (another close friend of Tocqueville) "that the subject of religion was 'the only subject about which, during forty years of intimacy, we did not speak'" (Beaumont to Senior, conversation of August 1860). Quoted in Gannett, Jr., *Tocqueville Unveiled*, 217 n.3. Regarding Tocqueville's religious comportment at the time of his death and whether or not he found faith in his dying days, see Jardin, 528–31. Tocqueville had a crisis of faith, one he seemingly never recovered from fully, at the age of sixteen when he explored his father's library in Metz. He recounted the experience thirty-five years later in a letter to Madame Swetchine, a Russian mystic who lived in Paris: "I don't know if I've ever told you about an incident in my youth that marked me deeply for the rest of my life; how when I was enclosed in a kind of solitude during the years just before childhood, when I was prey to an insatiable curiosity whose only available satisfaction was a large library of books. I heaped pell-mell into my mind all sorts of notions and ideas which belong more properly to a more mature age. Until that time my life had passed enveloped in a faith that hadn't even allowed doubt to penetrate into my soul. Then doubt entered, or rather hurtled in with an incredible violence, not only doubt about one thing or another in particular, but an all-embracing doubt. All of a sudden I experienced the sensation people talk about who have been through an earthquake when, the ground shakes under their feet, as do the walls around them, the ceilings over their heads, the furniture beneath their hands, all of nature before their eyes. I was seized by the blackest melancholy, then by an extreme disgust with life—though I knew nothing of life—and was almost prostrated by agitation and terror at the sight of the road that remained for me to travel in this world. Strong passions drew me out of this state of despair; they turned me away from the sight of these intellectual ruins and led me toward tangible objects. But still, from time to time, these feelings experienced in my early youth . . . take possession of me again. Then once more I see the

world of ideas revolving and I am lost and bewildered in this universal motion that upsets and shakes all the truths on which I base my beliefs and my actions." Letter dated February 26, 1857, quoted in Jardin, *Tocqueville*, 61. See also Brogan, *Alexis de Tocqueville*, 49–56. Similar sentiments (and language) are conveyed in a letter penned by a much more youthful Tocqueville to Charles Stoffels (October 22, 1831). Tocqueville, *Selected Letters on Politics and Society*, 62–4.

16. Nietzsche, *Antichrist*, 656.

17. Tocqueville obviously was familiar with Plato and devoted some time to his writings, but he says virtually nothing about him and it is not clear how much of Plato's philosophy he grasped. As Brogan notes, Tocqueville respected Plato but was puzzled by him. Brogan, *Alexis de Tocqueville*, 321. In a letter to Kergolay (August 8, 1838), Tocqueville professes that "on the whole, I consider [Plato] a poor political theorist." Quoted in Lamberti, *Tocqueville and the Two Democracies*, 260, n. 95.

18. To say nothing of its Testament: "In the centuries of its foundation[, Christianity] perpetuated that unheard of philological farce concerning the Old Testament: I mean the attempt to pull the Old Testament from under the feet of the Jews with the assertion it contained nothing but Christian teaching and *belonged* to the Christians as the *true* people of Israel, the Jews being only usurpers." Nietzsche, *Daybreak*, 49.

19. Nietzsche, *Beyond Good and Evil*, 4. On Christianity's democratization of Platonism, see Pierre Hadot, *What is Ancient Philosophy?* (Cambridge, MA: Harvard University Press, 2002), 247–52.

20. Ibid: "How could such a disease infect Plato, the most beautiful outgrowth of antiquity? Did the evil Socrates corrupt him after all? was Socrates in fact the corrupter of youth? did he deserve his hemlock?" See also ibid, 103: "There is something in Plato's moral philosophy that does not really belong to him, but is there in spite of him, as it were: namely, the Socratism that he was really too noble for." As well as *Human, All Too Human*, 123–4: "With the Greeks everything goes quickly forward, but it likewise goes quickly downwards; the movement of the whole machine is so accelerated that a single stone thrown into its wheels makes it fly to pieces. Socrates, for example, was such a stone; in a single night the evolution of philosophic science, hitherto so wonderfully regular, if all too rapid, was destroyed. It is no idle question whether, if he had not come under the spell of Socrates, Plato might not have discovered an even higher type of philosophic man who is now lost to us for ever." For the novelty of Nietzsche's treatment of Socrates in the history of Western thought, see Werner J. Dannhauser, *Nietzsche's View of Socrates* (Ithaca, NY: Cornell University Press, 1974).

21. A rather damning indictment of democracy is put forward by Socrates in Book VIII of the *Republic*. As noted above, classical teleology lends itself to inegalitarianism for the very reason that not all human beings are equally capable of realizing the end toward which they are naturally directed. It is also worth noting that however democratic Socrates' dialogic approach may be, Socrates, as a rule, engaged the nobles of Athens, not the *demos*.

22. Nietzsche, *Birth of Tragedy*, § 11.

23. Pierre Hadot, *The Veil of Isis* (Cambridge, MA: Harvard University Press, 2006), 1.

24. Nietzsche, *Birth of Tragedy*, 63–4.
25. Nietzsche, *Genealogy of Morality*, 72.
26. "In a certain sense Euripides, too, was merely a mask; the deity who spoke out of him was not Dionysus nor Apollo, but an altogether newborn daemon called *Socrates*." Nietzsche, *Birth of Tragedy*, 60.
27. Ibid, 64.
28. Ibid, 62.
29. Nietzsche, *Twilight of the Idols*, 474–5. "Socrates is plebian; he is uneducated and also never went back and picked up his education lost in childhood. Further, he is, to be precise, ugly and as he himself said, he suffers the greatest from natural passions. Flat nose, thick lips, bulging eyes: Aristoxenus (whose father, Spintharus, was familiar with Socrates) reports he was prone to violent outbursts." Friedrich Nietzsche, *The Pre-Platonic Philosophers*, trans. Greg Whitlock (Urbana, IL: University of Illinois Press, 2001), 144.
30. Nietzsche, *Beyond Good and Evil*, 107.
31. Nietzsche, *Twilight of the Idols*, 475.
32. Ibid, 493.
33. Ibid, 479.
34. Ibid, 475–6.
35. Nietzsche, *Human, All Too Human*, 37. "All heroes treat one another as heroes, even when they are enemies; the bond which linked heroic warriors together was the unity of the code, which transcended tribal and even ethnic boundaries. This common feeling helps to explain why the *Iliad* displays practically no cultural differences between Greek and Asiatic, despite the obvious real disparities which must have existed." Donlan, *Aristocratic Ideal*, 14.
36. Nietzsche, *Birth of Tragedy*, 64.
37. Ibid, 65–6.
38. Ibid, 74–5.
39. "'Formerly, all the world was mad', say the most refined, and they blink." Nietzsche, *Zarathustra*, 130.
40. "What is it that common people take for knowledge? What do they mean when they want 'knowledge'? Nothing more than this: something strange is to be reduced to something *familiar*." Nietzsche, *Gay Science*, 300.
41. Plato, *Apology of Socrates*, in *Four Texts on Socrates*, trans. Thomas G. West and Grace Starry West (Ithaca, NY: Cornell University Press, 1995), 70 (21d).
42. See, for example, Nietzsche, *Human, All Too Human*, 16, 22; *Gay Science*, 171–2; *Beyond Good and Evil*, 7. Tocqueville also makes this point: "General ideas do not attest to the strength of human intelligence, but rather to its insufficiency, because there are no beings in nature exactly alike: no identical facts, no rules indiscriminately applicable in the same manner to several objects at once." *Democracy*, 411.
43. William Blake, *The Marriage of Heaven and Hell* (New York: Oxford University Press, 1975), xxii.
44. "Assuming, finally, that we succeeded in explaining our entire life of drives as the organization and outgrowth of one basic form of will (namely, of the will to

power, which is *my* claim); assuming we could trace all organic functions back to this will to power and find that it even solved the problem of procreation and nutrition (which is a single problem); then we will have earned the right to clearly designate *all* efficacious force as: *will to power*. The world seen from inside, the world determined and described with respect to its 'intelligible character'—would be just this 'will to power' and nothing else." Nietzsche, *Beyond Good and Evil*, 36.

45. Nietzsche, *Gay Science*, 291.

46. Nietzsche, *Birth of Tragedy*, 82.

47. Science in the context of antiquity should not be confused with its modern usage. "Science is a modern category, not an ancient one: there is no one term that is exactly equivalent to our 'science' in Greek. The terms *philosophia* (love of wisdom, philosophy), *episteme* (knowledge), *theoria* (contemplation, speculation) and *peri physeos historia* (inquiry concerning nature) are each used in particular contexts where the translation 'science' is natural and not too misleading." G.E.R. Lloyd, *Early Greek Science: Thales to Aristotle* (New York: W. W. Norton, 1970), preface. It is telling that the Greeks had no word for scientist, which was coined only in the nineteenth century, at a time when modern science's independence from philosophy had been firmly established.

48. Plato, *Phaedo*, 99d.

49. Nietzsche, *Human, All Too Human*, 15.

50. "Traditionally philosophy and science were not distinguished: natural science was one of the most important parts of philosophy. The great intellectual revolution of the seventeenth century which brought to light modern natural science was a revolution of a new philosophy *or* science against traditional (chiefly Aristotelean) philosophy *or* science." Strauss, "Introduction to History of Political Philosophy" in *Introduction to Political Philosophy*, 159.

51. For example, Newton's most celebrated work, itself one of the most celebrated works in the history of science, was entitled *Mathematical Principles of Natural Philosophy* [*Philosophiæ Naturalis Principia Mathematica*], not natural science.

52. Strauss, "An Epilogue" in *Introduction to Political Philosophy*, 128.

53. H. Floris Cohen, *The Scientific Revolution: A Historiographical Inquiry* (Chicago: University of Chicago Press, 1994), 167.

54. Nietzsche, *Birth of Tragedy*, 5.

55. Ibid, 4–5.

56. "The Great War was the psychological turning point . . . for modernism as a whole. The urge to create and the urge to destroy had changed places." Modris Eksteins, *Rites of Spring: The Great War and the Birth of the Modern Age* (New York: Houghton Mifflin Company, 2000), 328.

57. Nietzsche, *Birth of Tragedy*, 82.

58. "It is palpably obvious that chance was formerly the greatest of all discoverers and observers and the benevolent inspirer of those inventive ancients, and that more spirit, discipline and scientific imagination is employed in the most insignificant invention nowadays than the sum total available in whole eras past." Nietzsche, *Daybreak*, 26.

59. "Since Copernicus man has been rolling from the center toward *X*." Nietzsche, *Will to Power*, 8. To this cosmos-altering discovery, there can be added Darwin's "deadly" truth regarding "the lack of any cardinal distinction between man and animal." Nietzsche, "On the Uses and Disadvantages of History for Life," 112.

60. Nietzsche, *Birth of Tragedy*, 4.

61. The word *barbaros* (βάρβαρος) in Ancient Greek onomatopoetically evokes the sense of babbling. For a brief history of its usage and significance, see Thomas E. J. Weidemann, "Barbarian" in *Oxford Classical Dictionary*, 233.

62. Nietzsche, *Birth of Tragedy*, 7.

63. Ibid, 4.

64. Ibid, 7.

65. Ibid, 4.

66. Nietzsche, *Pre-Platonic Philosophers*, 8.

67. Plato, *Phaedo*, in *The Last Days of Socrates*, trans. Hugh Tredennick (New York: Penguin Books, 1987), 153 (96b).

68. Ibid, 154 (96c).

69. Ibid, 155–6 (97e–98b).

70. Incidentally, science returned to this understanding in its maturity, that is, after its divorce from natural philosophy. Ironically, it did so without shedding its Socratic faith.

71. "Socrates saw that the previous philosophers' accounts of things in terms of their components failed to explain human actions, because such accounts left no room for choice or purpose." Catherine Zuckert, *Plato's Philosophers: The Coherence of the Dialogues* (Chicago: University of Chicago Press, 2009), 185.

72. Nietzsche, *Pre-Platonic Philosophers*, 125–6.

73. Nietzsche, *Gay Science*, 168.

74. "When Socrates commands 'you' in applying the cave image, he marks the founding moment of Socratic-Platonic political philosophy, for his words forge his ultimate alliance, with the philosophers of the future. From our privileged late perspective, it is possible to see that alliance stretch across millennia as the long history of Platonic political philosophy . . . Socrates's going down aims to permanently alter philosophy's place in the city, to be the fountainhead of philosophy as socially responsible, philanthropic in a knowing way." Laurence Lampert, *How Philosophy Became Socratic: A Study of Plato's Protagoras, Charmides, and Republic* (Chicago: University of Chicago Press, 2010), 372–3.

75. Nietzsche, *Pre-Platonic Philosophers*, 143.

76. Ibid, 145.

77. Aristophanes, *The Clouds*, lines 156–68.

78. Heidegger effected a return to the pre-Socratics by devoting his meditations to Being and setting aside ethical considerations. In doing so, he produced what is arguably the most significant philosophic work of the twentieth century (*Being and Time*) and aligned himself with what was arguably the most execrable political movement of that, or perhaps, any century. It would seem that while a return to the pre-Socratics is not entirely cut off, once philosophy has been brought down from the heavens and into the city, in the city it should remain. Nietzsche grasped this lesson all too well, though his greatest student failed to appreciate it.

79. Nietzsche, *Pre-Platonic Philosophers*, 145.
80. "Every period of history, every culture, following this or that image of literary tradition, or emphasizing this or that aspect of the many sides of his character, has made up its own Socrates, seeing in him every time an ideal or a symbol as variable as are the possible interpretations." Mario Montuori, *Socrates: Physiology of a Myth* (Amsterdam: J.C. Gieben, 1981), 6.
81. Ibid, 145.
82. On Spartan education, see Rahe, *Republics Ancient and Modern* vol. 1, 125–71.
83. To appreciate the scale and consequence of the Socratic revolution, it merits pointing out that a moral order grounded in custom and tradition (as opposed to reason and knowledge) was not simply indicative of the Greeks or of aristocratic communities, but was the way of pre-Socratic peoples the world over. "Nietzsche argues that the passion for knowledge has not always been held in such high esteem. For the longest time, during the prehistory of man, the various peoples of the earth were governed by what Nietzsche calls the 'morality of morals,' which is to say, a morality of strict obedience and custom. The nature of the good and the nature of justice were defined by traditional ways of thinking and acting, not by the dictates of reason. People knew what was right and what was wrong as if by instinct and did not need to look at any higher standard for guidance. They would have viewed the modern habit of thought which seeks to understand every idea and action in terms of some ultimate rationale, some universal principle, as a kind of irreverence and even sacrilege. Among such peoples the quest for universal truths as a source of guidance was largely irrelevant because the typical individual was wholly defined by a heritage he never questions." Detwiler, *Nietzsche and the Politics of Aristocratic Radicalism*, 73–4.
84. Nietzsche, *Birth of Tragedy*, 66.
85. Nietzsche, *Daybreak*, #544. "It was Socrates who discovered the antithetical magic, that of cause and effect, of ground and consequence: and we modern men are so accustomed to and brought up in the necessity of logic that it lies on our palate as the normal taste" (217–8).
86. Nietzsche, *Twilight of the Idols*, 478.
87. See Book III of the *Republic*, where Socrates cuts the Homeric heroes—Achilles in particular—down to size.
88. Nietzsche, *Pre-Platonic Philosophers*, 145.
89. Ibid.
90. Ibid, 146.
91. Plato, *Apology*, 38a.
92. Ibid, *Pre-Platonic Philosophers*, 145 [emphasis added].
93. Nietzsche, *Birth of Tragedy*, 66.
94. Nietzsche, *Human, All Too Human*, 123.
95. Nietzsche, *Beyond Good and Evil*, 107.
96. Nietzsche, *The Twilight of Idols*, 478.
97. Ibid, 479.
98. Nietzsche, *Genealogy of Morality*, 19.
99. Plato, *Apology*, 31a-b.
100. Nietzsche, *Daybreak*, 219–20.

101. Nietzsche, *Pre-Platonic Philosophers*, 145–6.

102. The classic affirmation of this view is Plato's *Republic*. See also Strauss, *Natural Right and History*, chap. 4: "Since the classics viewed moral and political matters in the light of man's perfection, they were not egalitarians. Not all men are equally equipped by nature for progress toward perfection, or not all 'natures' are 'good natures'. While all men, i.e., all normal men, have the capacity for virtue, some need guidance by others, whereas others do not at all or to a much lesser degree . . . . Since men are then unequal in regard to human perfection, i.e., in the decisive respect, equal rights for all appeared to the classics as most unjust. They contended that some men are by nature superior to others and therefore, according to natural right, the rulers of others" (134–5).

103. Tocqueville, *Democracy*, 413.

104. Nietzsche, *Antichrist*, 619.

105. Tocqueville to Arthur de Gobineau, September 5, 1843 in *The European Revolution and Correspondence with Gobineau,* ed. and trans. John Lukacs (Garden City, New York: Doubleday Anchor Books, 1959), 193. On the transformative impact that Christianity had on almsgiving in the ancient world, see Peter Brown, *The Ransom of the Soul: Afterlife and Wealth in Early Western Christianity* (Cambridge, MA: Harvard University Press, 2015), Chapter 3. "The notion of civic euergetism had always assumed a strictly civic (one might say almost political) model of society. The wealthy were expected to spend their money on their city and on the comfort and entertainment of their fellow citizens—and on those only . . . . Poverty, in itself, gave no entitlement. Those who received benefits from the wealthy received them not because they were poor but because they were citizens.

"For Christian bishops such as Augustine to preach in favor of giving alms to the poor was to do far more than stir the wealthy to occasional acts of charity and compassion. It was to undermine the traditional model of society that had directed their giving habits up to this time. Civic notables were challenged to abandon the notion of citizen entitlement. They were urged to look beyond their fellow citizens and to switch their giving toward the gray immensity of poverty in their city and in the countryside around them.

"Altogether, to accept Christian preaching was to make a major shift in one's image of society. In terms of the social imagination, it involved nothing less than moving from a closed universe to an open one   The duty of the Christian preacher was to urge the rich no longer to spend their money on their beloved, well-known city, but to lose it, almost heedlessly, in the faceless mass of the poor. Only that utterly counterfactual gesture—a gesture that owed nothing to the claims of one's hometown or of one's fellow citizens—would earn the rich 'treasure in heaven'" (86–7).

106. Nietzsche, *Human, All Too Human*, 332.

107. "It is certainly not an overstatement to say that no one has ever spoken so greatly and so nobly of what a philosopher is as Nietzsche." Leo Strauss, "An Introduction to Heideggerian Existentialism" in *The Rebirth of Classical Political Rationalism: An Introduction to the Thought of Leo Strauss* (Chicago: University of Chicago Press, 1989), 40.

108. See, for example, Tocqueville to Gobineau, September 5, 1843 in *Correspondence with Gobineau*, 190–5.

109. Nietzsche, *Antichrist*, 656.

110. Tocqueville to Gobineau, September 5, 1843 in *Correspondence with Gobineau*, 192.

111. Compare Tocqueville's letter to Gobineau, October 2, 1843 in *Correspondence with Gobineau*, 205 with Nietzsche, *Antichrist*, 44–6.

112. Tocqueville to Gobineau, October 2, 1843 in *Correspondence with Gobineau*, 208.

113. Tocqueville to Gobineau, September 5, 1843 in ibid, 191–2.

114. Nietzsche, *Antichrist*, 634.

115. *Romans* 10:12.

116. *Acts* 17:26.

117. *Galatians* 3:28.

118. "These elementary truths of our faith seem commonplace today—though we neglect their implications all too often. It is difficult for us to imagine the disturbance they created in the soul of man in the ancient world. At the first tidings of them humanity was lifted on a wave of hope . . . . It became conscious of deliverance. To begin with, needless to say, it was not an external deliverance—not that social liberation which was to come, for instance, with the abolition of slavery. That liberation . . . was brought about slowly but surely under the influence of the Christian idea of man. 'God', says Origen . . . 'made all men in his own image, he molded them one by one'. But from the outset that idea had produced a more profound effect. Through it, man was freed, in his own eyes, from the ontological slavery with which Fate burdened him. The stars, in their unalterable courses, did not, after all, implacably control our destinies. Man, every man, no matter who, had a direct link with the Creator, the Ruler of the stars themselves. And lo, the countless Powers—gods, spirits, demons—who pinioned human life in the net of their tyrannical wills, weighing upon the soul with all their terrors, now crumbled into dust . . . . It was no longer a small and select company that, thanks to some secret means of escape, could break the charmed circle: it was mankind as a whole . . . . No more circle! No more blind destiny! No more Moira! No more Fate! Transcendent God, God the 'friend of men', revealed in Jesus, opened for all a way that nothing would ever bar again. Hence that intense feeling of gladness and of radiant newness to be found everywhere in early Christian writings." Henri de Lubac, *The Drama of Atheist Humanism* (San Francisco: Ignatius Press, 1998), 21–3.

119. On the concord between monotheism and democracy, see Tocqueville, *Democracy*, 420: "Men who are alike and equal readily conceive the notion of a single God imposing the same rules on each of them and granting them future happiness at the same price. The idea of the unity of the human race constantly leads them back to the idea of the unity of the Creator, whereas on the contrary, men very separate from one another and very unalike willingly come to make as many divinities as there are peoples, castes, classes, and families, and to trace a thousand particular paths for going to Heaven." On the question of monotheism failing to precipitate man's democratization, consider Tocqueville's reflections on Islam. "Mohammed had not only religious doctrines descend from Heaven and placed in the Koran, but political maxims, civil

and criminal laws, and scientific theories. The Gospels, in contrast, speak only of the general relations of men to God and among themselves. Outside of that they teach nothing and oblige nothing to be believed. That alone, among a thousand other reasons, is enough to show that the first of these two religions cannot dominate for long in enlightened and democratic times, whereas the second is destined to reign in these centuries as in all the others." Ibid, 419–20. "The great vice of Islam, the real cause of its political inferiority, lies neither in its dogma nor even in its morality, but in its habit of confusing the spiritual with the temporal, the religious law with the secular law. The Koran is Bible and Code in one—it is the word of the Prophet that takes the place of law. Ordinances and customs are therefore consecrated to eternity by religion, and because of that fact alone every Mussulman civilization is necessarily stationary." Anatole Leroy-Beaulieu, *L'Empire des tzars et les Russes*, quoted in Gaetano Mosca, *The Ruling Class*, trans. Hannah D. Kahn (New York: McGraw Hill, 1939), 140. For a brief and insightful look at the decline of the Arabic world, see Hillel Ofek, "Why the Arabic World Turned Away from Science," *The New Atlantis* (Winter 2011): 3–23.

120. Tocqueville, *Democracy*, 11.

121. Ibid, 5–6.

122. Daniel J. Boorstin, *The Discoverers: A History of Man's Search to Know His World and Himself* (New York: Random House, 1985), 498.

123. Tocqueville, *Democracy*, 326–7.

124. Thomas Sowell, *Black Rednecks and White Liberals* (New York: Encounter Books, 2005), 127.

125. Tocqueville to Edward Vernon Childe, April 2, 1857 in *Tocqueville on America after 1840: Letters and Other Writings* ed. and trans. Aurelian Craiutu and Jeremy Jennings (New York: Cambridge University Press, 2009), 224.

126. Tocqueville, *Democracy*, 326.

127. Tocqueville to Theodore Sedgwick, April 13, 1857 in *Tocqueville on America After 1840*, 226.

128. Ibid, Tocqueville to Jared Sparks, October 13, 1840, 53.

129. Tocqueville, *Democracy*, 348. To the extent that slavery endures in the twenty-first century, it does so predominantly in undemocratic and unenlightened places and moreover, does so not as an institution, but as a crime—fittingly—against humanity.

130. Ibid, 334.

131. See note 15 above.

132. Nietzsche, *Ecce Homo*, 263.

133. Nietzsche, *Twilight of the Idols*, 552.

134. Tocqueville to Gobineau, September 5, 1843 in *Correspondence with Gobineau*, 191.

135. Ibid, 191.

136. Nietzsche, *Antichrist*, 560–1.

137. Ibid, 655.

138. Nietzsche, *Twilight of the Idols*, 502–3.

139. Amongst his major works, the notable exception is *The Birth of Tragedy*: "Profound, hostile silence about Christianity throughout the book." Nietzsche, *Ecce Homo*, 271.

140. Nietzsche, *Genealogy of Morality*, 4–5.
141. Nietzsche, *Ecce Homo*, 312.
142. Nietzsche, *Genealogy of Morals*, 11.
143. Nietzsche, *Ecce Homo*, 312.
144. Nietzsche, *Zarathustra*, 171.
145. Nietzsche, *Ecce Homo*, 312.
146. Ibid, *Genealogy of Morality*, 12.
147. Ibid, 20.
148. Ibid, 22. Dannhauser suggests that, not without ambiguity, for Nietzsche, Socrates constituted such an enemy, that is, an enemy worthy of being one. Dannhauser, *Nietzsche's View of Socrates*, 63. Tellingly, in a fragment drafted in 1875, Nietzsche confessed that "Socrates . . . is so close to me that almost always I fight against him." Quoted in Walter Kaufmann, "Nietzsche's Admiration for Socrates," *Journal of the History of Ideas* 9, no. 4 (1948): 479.
149. Nietzsche, *Human, All Too Human*, 37.
150. Ibid.
151. Nietzsche, *Genealogy of Morality*, 20.
152. Ibid, 22.
153. This is true even of democratic Athens, which was but a part of the "aristocracy of masters" that was emblematic of the ancient world, to employ Tocqueville's apt characterization. Tocqueville, *Democracy*, 413.
154. Nietzsche, *Daybreak*, 42–3.
155. Nietzsche, *Will to Power*, 117.
156. Nietzsche, *Antichrist*, 619.
157. Nietzsche, *Daybreak*, 43.
158. Ibid.
159. Nietzsche, *Genealogy of Morality*, 29.
160. Ibid, 30–1.
161. Ibid, 22.
162. Isaiah 11:6.
163. Nietzsche, *Genealogy of Morality*, 20.
164. Ibid, 17.
165. Nietzsche, *Beyond Good and Evil*, 40.
166. Nietzsche, *Will to Power*, 117.
167. Nietzsche, *Genealogy of Morality*, 28.
168. Nietzsche, *Antichrist*, 621–2.
169. Ibid, 634.
170. Ibid, 656.
171. Nietzsche, *Will to Power*, 117.
172. Nietzsche, *Antichrist*, 622.
173. Nietzsche, *Genealogy of Morality*, 26–7.
174. Ibid, 25–6.
175. Nietzsche, *Zarathustra*, 230.
176. Nietzsche, *Genealogy of Morality*, 43.
177. See, for example, André Comte-Sponville, "The Brute, the Sophist, and the Aesthete: 'Art in the Service of Illusion,'" in *Why We are not Nietzscheans*

(Chicago: University of Chicago Press, 1997), 21–69. Comte-Sponville employs the fashionable, but superficial, technique of selecting random quotes to support his charge that "Nietzsche is one of the rare philosophers, the only one perhaps . . . who . . . *nearly systematically*, advocated force against law, violence or cruelty against gentleness, war against peace" 31 [emphasis added]. The carelessness of his approach is made plain when he cites the little old woman in *Thus Spoke Zarathustra* as being an expositor for Nietzsche's position on women, an approach that amounts to arguing that Euthyphro is the expositor of Plato's position on piety. More broadly, the problem with Comte-Sponville's approach is that Nietzsche said a lot and a lot of what he said is contradictory. Thus, for example, in the writings of a philosopher who "nearly systematically . . . advocated violence or cruelty against gentleness," one finds the following: "It is not impossible to imagine society *so conscious of its power* that it could allow itself the noblest luxury available to it—that of letting its malefactors go *unpunished*. 'What do I care about my parasites', it could say, 'let them live and flourish: I am strong enough for all that' . . . . Justice, which began by saying 'Everything can be paid off, everything must be paid off ', ends by turning a blind eye and letting off those unable to pay—it ends, like every good thing on earth, by *sublimating itself*. The self-sublimation of justice: we know what a nice name it gives itself—*mercy*; it remains, of course, the prerogative of the most powerful man, better still, his way of being beyond the law." Nietzsche, *Genealogy of Morality*, 47–8. As Kurt Tucholsky, the German satirist, quipped, "Who cannot claim [Nietzsche] for their own? Tell me what you need and I will supply you with a Nietzsche citation . . . for Germany and against Germany; for peace and against peace; for literature and against literature—whatever you want." Quoted in Steven E. Aschheim, *The Nietzsche Legacy in Germany: 1890-1990* (Berkeley: University of California Press, 1992), 274. To a much narrower degree, Tocqueville fits this mold as well. "Tocqueville's works could be quoted as authority by men who stood for, or thought they stood for, opposing political or intellectual alternatives." Drescher, *Dilemmas of Democracy*, 252. See also Aurelian Craiutu, "Tocqueville's Paradoxical Moderation," *The Review of Politics* 67, no. 4 (Autumn 2005): 601–6. For a sustained criticism of the "many Tocquevilles" thesis famously advanced by Robert Nisbet ("Many Tocquevilles," *American Scholar* 46, no. 1 (Winter 1977): 59–75), see Matthew J. Mancini, "Too Many Tocquevilles: The Fable of Tocqueville's American Reception," *Journal of the History of Ideas* 69, no. 2 (April 2008): 245–68: "In truth, there aren't that many Tocquevilles. He was a great political thinker who investigated the links among democracy, revolution, mores, and culture, and the great shift from aristocratic to democratic regimes. Only by abandoning the self-indulgent approach of considering his works in light of immediate concerns, investigating the undeniable historical record, and adhering to basic standards of evidence and argument can the field [of Tocqueville studies] hope to attain the rigor that its subject deserves" (268). To the ambiguity of his writings, Tocqueville was hardly oblivious. "I please many people of conflicting opinions, not because they understand me, but because they find in my work, by considering it only from a single side, arguments favorable to their passion of the moment" (Tocqueville to Eugène Stoffels, February 21, 1835). Tocqueville, *Selected Letters on Politics and Society*, 99–100.

178. Nietzsche, *Antichrist*, 581.
179. Ibid, 585.
180. Ibid, 582.
181. Ibid, 583–4.
182. Nietzsche, *Genealogy of Morality*, 27.
183. Nietzsche, *Antichrist*, 632.
184. Nietzsche, *Genealogy of Morality*, 21.
185. Nietzsche, *Antichrist*, 594.
186. Nietzsche, *Genealogy of Morality*, 49.
187. Nietzsche, *Antichrist*, 593.
188. Nietzsche, *Genealogy of Morality*, 32.
189. Ibid, 17.
190. Ibid, 18.
191. Ibid, 17.
192. Nietzsche, *Antichrist*, 592.
193. Ibid, 593.
194. Ibid, 489.
195. Nietzsche, *Genealogy of Morality*, 19.
196. Nietzsche, *Antichrist*, 633–4.
197. Nietzsche, *Will to Power*, 111. This verity was not lost on Tocqueville. As Lamberti points out, "In the final analysis, Tocqueville was willing to accept the moral content of the French Revolution because he saw it as a consequence of the Christian revolution." Lamberti, *Tocqueville and the Two Democracies*, 161.
198. Hegel may be the most celebrated and towering example. Though not blind to the bloodshed that it unleashed, the Revolution remained, in Hegel's mind, "a glorious mental dawn. All thinking beings shared in the jubilation of this epoch. Emotions of a lofty character stirred men's minds at that time; a spiritual enthusiasm thrilled through the world, as if the reconciliation between the divine and the secular was now first accomplished." G. W. F. Hegel, *Philosophy of History*, trans. J. Sibree (Mineola, NY: Dover, 1956), 447. That sense of jubilation is echoed in Wordsworth's *The French Revolution as It Appeared to Enthusiasts*, where the Revolution also is likened to a new dawn. While Wordsworth eventually changed his tune on the French Revolution, his Romantic compatriots Shelly and Bryon remained supportive to the end. To this cursory and desultory list of supporters, one might add the names of Kant, Herder, Paine, Jefferson, and Condorcet (until, of course, the Revolution consumed him).
199. "As Nietzsche saw it, the only good that came out of the French Revolution was Napoleon, who embodied the elitist ideals of antiquity in modern garb." Graeme Garrard, "Nietzsche for and against the Enlightenment," *The Review of Politics* 70, No. 4 (Fall, 2008): 602.
200. Nietzsche, *Genealogy of Morality*, 33.
201. In Tocqueville's mind, this "historical distance" would prove an asset in his efforts to comprehend the Revolution as it permitted him to grasp what eluded the gaze of "contemporary observer[s], even one with such evident political sagacity and skills [as Burke]." Gannett, *Tocqueville Unveiled*, 63. As Tocqueville opined in

The Old Regime and the Revolution, "today we are situated at just the right place to best see and judge this great thing [the French Revolution]. We are far enough from the Revolution to feel only faintly the passions of those who made it, but we are close enough to understand and empathize with the spirit that led them to it. Soon this will be impossible, for great revolutions which succeed make the causes which produced them disappear, and thus become incomprehensible because of their own success" (95).

202. For an account of Malesherbes' arrest and execution, see Simon Schama, *Citizens: A Chronicle of the French Revolution* (New York: Alfred A. Knopf, 1989), 822–7.

203. Joseph Epstein, *Alexis de Tocqueville: Democracy's Guide* (New York: Harper Collins, 2006), 10.

204. Alexis de Tocqueville to Lady Theresa Lewis (May 6, 1857), quoted in Jardin, *Tocqueville,* 38.

205. "What does a philosopher demand of himself first and last? To overcome his time in himself, to become 'timeless'. With what must he therefore engage in the hardest combat? With whatever marks him as a child of his time. Well, then! I am, no less than Wagner, a child of this time; that is, a decadent: but I comprehended this, I resisted it. The philosopher in me resisted." Friedrich Nietzsche, *The Case of Wagner* in *Basic Writings of Nietzsche,* 611. Drochon, who seeks to rescue Nietzsche's political philosophy from the legions of scholars who are bent on democratizing and depoliticizing him, immures Nietzsche in his time and as a result, de-philosophizes him. Far from being timeless, Nietzsche's political philosophy becomes hopelessly timebound. As Drochon writes in the conclusion of *Nietzsche's Great Politics,* "the very thesis of this book . . . [is] that Nietzsche's political thought can *only* be *properly* understood in its nineteenth-century context" (181) [emphasis added]. If that were true, Nietzsche would have no political philosophy, or at least one neither worth his salt nor his readers' time. A better way to approach Nietzsche's political philosophy is not to view him as an armchair commentator on the politics of his day, but as a peerless philosopher on the human condition—that is, on the politics of every day. His meditations on the state, aristocracy, democracy, religion, culture, morality, and man (from first to last to over)—to list but a few of the intrinsically political matters that his mind embraced—are not simply outgrowths of or responses to nineteenth century politics, but well from something much deeper and touch upon many things much broader. If, as Drochon argues, Nietzsche dreamt of a unified Europe "to serve as a geopolitical counterweight to Russia and the British Empire" (2), one would be forced to conclude that that dream, along with that Empire, set long ago. But that conclusion would be patently wrong, though only because the premise is. This is not to say that Nietzsche's thought can be divorced entirely from his time. The heralding of God's death, for example, presupposed that the earth be unchained from its sun (*Gay Science* "The Madman"), that is, it presupposed the Scientific Revolution. But as with all great philosophers, Nietzsche's reflections are not the mere products of his day. No one reasonably could contend that Plato's political thought only can be properly understood in its fourth century (BC) context. One who wishes to rescue Nietzsche's political philosophy from those who would seek to domesticate and thereby efface it should extend him the same courtesy and do him, and his readers, the same justice.

206. Tocqueville, *Old Regime*, 86. "De Tocqueville's luminous account, *The Old Regime and the Revolution*, the product of his own archival research, provided cool reason where before there had been the burning quarrels of partisanship." Schama, *Citizens*, xiii.
207. Tocqueville, *Old Regime*, 86.
208. Ibid, 87.
209. Ibid, 88.
210. Ibid, 216–7.
211. Tocqueville, *Democracy*, 663.
212. Tocqueville, *Old Regime*, 88.
213. Ibid, 83.
214. Christopher Dawson, *The Gods of Revolution* (New York: New York University Press, 1972), 92.
215. "On May 18, 1804, after a decisive plebiscite, Napoleon was made hereditary emperor of the French and on December 2 staged his coronation. (The vote in the plebiscite was 3.6 million for, 2,569 against.)" Terry Pinkard, *Hegel: A Biography* (New York: Cambridge University Press, 2001), 194. Napoleon's nephew, Charles Louis Napoléon Bonaparte (Napoleon III), would receive similar support from the French half a century later. After successfully staging a coup, "a plebiscite on December 12, 1851 approved Louis Napoleon's destruction of parliamentary government by seven and a half million to six hundred thousand votes." Herr, *Tocqueville and the Old Regime*, 16.
216. Tocqueville, *Old Regime*, 85. This sentiment was echoed by Madame de Stael: "Never has French society been more brilliant and at the same time more serious. It was the last time, alas! that the French spirit showed itself in all its luster. It was the last time, and in many respects also the first that Parisian society could give an idea of that intellectual intercourse which is the noblest enjoyment of which human nature is capable. Those who have lived at that time cannot help recognizing that nowhere at any time had they seen so much life and intellect so that one can judge by the number of men of talent which the circumstances of that time produced what the French would be, if they were called to take part in public affairs under a wise and sincere form of government." Quoted in Dawson, *The Gods of Revolution*, 62–3.
217. Nietzsche, *Beyond Good and Evil*, 45.
218. In a letter dated November 29, 1856, Gobineau, echoing a number of Tocqueville's own views, calls into question Tocqueville's admiration for the incipient phase of the Revolution. "I confess that I see something very vile in this assembly [The Constituent Assembly of 1789] which applauded the first violences, the mad comedy of the capture of the Bastille, the first massacres, the burning of the castles. Simply because they did not see that it was all of their own making and that their own heads would soon be cut off, do you think that these wrongs done may be qualified by saying that these were generous mistakes? Why *generous?*" *Correspondence with Gobineau*, 300–1.
219. On this score, the more prophetic, or perhaps profound, view belonged to Nietzsche who understood that as a rule, political revolutions that aim at the "overturning of all social orders" are doomed to fail. "The experiences of history have taught us, unfortunately, that every such revolution brings about the resurrection of

the most savage energies in the shape of the long-buried dreadfulness and excesses of the most distant ages." Nietzsche, *Human, All Too Human*, 169. On this understanding, the Terror was not an aberration or betrayal of '89, but its logical consequence. Whereas Tocqueville would celebrate the spirit of '89, Nietzsche would "strangle the Revolution at birth [so as] to make it not happen." Ibid, 367. That being said, Tocqueville was no revolutionary and harbored a deep-seated distaste for revolutions. "Family memories and education impressed upon his mind an ineradicable horror of the revolutionary spirit." Lamberti, *Tocqueville and the Two Democracies*, 4. As Tocqueville remarked in a letter to Eugène Stoffels (October 5, 1836): "I do not think that in France there is a man who is less revolutionary than I, nor one who has a more profound hatred for what is called the revolutionary spirit." *Selected Letters on Politics and Society*, 113.

220. Tocqueville, *Old Regime*, 106.

221. "Modern France was special not because it had gone from an absolute monarchy to a representative régime or from a world of noble privilege to a bourgeois society. After all, the rest of Europe went through the same process without a revolution and without Jacobins, even though events in France may have hastened that evolution here and there and spawned some imitators." Furet, *Interpreting the French Revolution*, 79.

222. Tocqueville, *Old Regime*, 84.

223. Tocqueville excepts "one or two of the recently conquered eastern provinces" where "the last vestiges of serfdom remained." By way of contrast, "from the thirteenth century serfdom was no longer to be found in Normandy." Ibid, 112. "Early in the fourteenth century King Phillip the Fair of France freed the serfs on the royal domain, and in 1315 his son Louis X ordered the liberation of all serfs 'on fair and suitable conditions'. Gradually, from the twelfth to the sixteenth century, at different times in divers [sic] countries west of the Elbe, serfdom gave place to peasant proprietorship; the feudal manor broke up into small estates, and the peasantry rose in the thirteenth century to a degree of freedom and prosperity it had not known for a thousand years." Will Durant, *The Age of Faith: A History of Medieval Civilization from Constantine to Dante—A.D. 325-1300* (New York: Simon and Schuster, 1950), 644-5.

224. "In Eastern Europe the peasantry had sunk into serfdom which in the eighteenth century was still expanding in Russia, though in the Habsburg Empire the government was trying to restrain it. The peasant, with the usual exceptions, worked under the direction of the lord, often as much as six days a week, without wages, under a system of compulsion that could be forced by flogging or imprisonment. Though lacking secure tenure of any particular piece of land, he was attached to the estate; that is, the purchaser or seller of the land bought or sold the village and its inhabitants as well." Palmer, *World of the French Revolution*, 21.

225. Tocqueville, *Old Regime*, 111.

226. Ibid, 112.

227. Ibid, 113.

228. Palmer, *World of the French Revolution*, 15.

229. Tocqueville, *Old Regime*, 220.

230. Ibid, 221–2.
231. Ibid, 222–3.
232. Tocqueville, *Democracy*, 513.
233. "[B]etween the 1730's and around 1770, the French economy made rapid and sustained advances with good harvests, a rising population, rising prices and expanding overseas trade. Between 1770 and 1778 this prosperous time came to an end and there was no recovery made over the next decade. On the contrary, difficulties continued, with wild, short-term fluctuations, and this period culminated with the truly catastrophic harvest of 1788. The most spectacular result was a swift and steady rise in the price of grain over subsequent months, a rise which reached its highest point on 14 July 1789." William Doyle, *Origins of the French Revolution* (New York: Oxford University Press, 1988), 31.
234. "The King had been out all day hunting. Returning tired, he went to bed early and was awakened by the news of the fall of the Bastille. 'Is it a rebellion'? he is said to have asked the Duc de La Rochefoucauld-Liancourt, the Grand Master of the Wardrobe. 'No, Sire', the Duke replied emphatically, 'It is a revolution.'" Christopher Hibbert, *The Days of the French Revolution* (New York: Quill, 1981), 87.
235. "Economic conditions were unfavorable to the maintenance of either patience or order. Long term trends had for years been unfavorable to the laboring classes. The ratios between farm prices and rents had worsened for the peasants since 1770. Wage earners both in towns and country suffered from the fact that, since 1740, wages had risen only about 22 percent as against a 65 percent rise in prices. The immediate short-run situation was very bad. The harvest of 1788 had been poor throughout Western Europe. The price of grain rose continually until by July of 1789 it took over half a worker's daily wage simply to buy bread for an average family, when it was obtainable at all. Here was one of the great ironies of history. The mass of the French people, through the action of impersonal forces, had enjoyed relatively favorable economic conditions under an inferior king, Louis XV. Under Louis XVI, his more admirable successor, they sank into privation." Palmer, *World of the French Revolution*, 57.
236. Tocqueville, *Old Regime*, 180.
237. Ibid, 117–8.
238. Ibid, 180.
239. Ibid, 182.
240. Ibid, 183.
241. Ibid, 189.
242. Ibid.
243. Ibid, 222.
244. "In that rural world [of the Vendée] the local nobility seems to have been more residential and less bitterly resented than in other parts of France. Violent riots had been few and far between in 1789. Because of the relative isolation of the villages from each other, the Church and its curates exercised a disproportionately more influential role. They baptized, married and buried; gave education to the children; helped the infirm and destitute; and on Sundays provided the only place where inhabitants could recognize in each other their shared sense of community." Schama, *Citizens*, 694–5.

245. The causes of the counter-revolution in western France are enormously complex and little agreed upon by scholars. As Alfred Cobban observed, "The difficulty for historians has not been the absence of plausible explanations for the revolt of the Vendee, nor of evidence with which to support them, but rather the superfluity of explanations and the attempt to single one prime cause out of so many while disproving all the others." Alfred, Cobban, "Review of *The Vendée: A Sociological Analysis of the Counterrevolution of 1793*, by Charles Tilly," *History and Theory* 5, no. 2 (1966): 198. For an approach that de-emphasizes the political motivations and highlights economic and demographic ones, see Charles Tilly, *The Vendée: A Sociological Analysis of the Counterrevolution of 1793* (Cambridge, MA: Harvard University Press, 1968). François Furet argues that "the mainspring of the Vendéen revolt was religious, and not social or simply political: just as the nobles appeared as latecomers on the scene, royalism came only second, in the wake of the call to God and the Catholic tradition." François Furet, *Revolutionary France: 1770-1880*, trans. Antonia Nevil (Cambridge, MA: Blackwell, 1992), 125. Furet's verdict is echoed by Jacques Godechot: "From the outset . . . the war of the Vendée took on a dual aspect: on the one hand it was a peasant insurrection—the peasants exceedingly indifferent to the form of the government, wanted their religion, 'good priests', and above all, no militia, no drawing lots. On the other hand, it was a counter-revolutionary movement: the nobles wanted to take advantage of the peasant revolt in order 'to restore the throne and altar', according to the formula which they employed at that time." Jacques Godechot, *The Counter-Revolution Doctrine and Action: 1789–1804* (Princeton: Princeton University Press, 1981), 213.

246. Tocqueville, *Old Regime*, 181–2.

247. Contrary to Seymour Drescher's claim, "the problem of centralization did not move to the center of Tocqueville's conception of the democratic state" only after the first volume of *Democracy in America* was published. Seymour Drescher, "Tocqueville's Two Democracies," *Journal of the History of Ideas* 25 (1964): 212. That problem and the specter of soft despotism was on Tocqueville's mind *before* he journeyed to America, as his letter of April 21, 1830 to Charles Stoffels attests. As Aurelian Craiutu, referencing this letter, notes: "In 1830, a year before embarking for America, he [Tocqueville] spoke of the reign of individualism and the state as a second Providence, endowed with an immense new power. He also understood that the advance of civilization would bring forth a public administration that becomes not only more centralized, but also more inquisitive and minute, by interfering to a greater extent in private concerns and regulating more undertakings than ever before. This was the new soft despotism which Tocqueville described in *Democracy in America*, but whose first sketch appears in the letter to Stoffels." Aurelian Craiutu, "Tocqueville and the Political Thought of the French Doctrinaires (Guizot, Royer-Collard, Rémusat)," *History of Political Thought* 20, no. 3 (1999): 476–7. See also Robert T. Gannett, Jr., *Tocqueville Unveiled*, 6.

248. Tocqueville, *Old Regime*, 118.

249. Ibid, 119.

250. "The Marquis d'Argenson tells us, in his memoirs that one day Mr. Law said to him: 'I would never have believed what I saw when I was controller of finance.

Know that the kingdom of France is ruled by thirty intendants. You have neither a parlement, nor estates, nor governors; it is thirty subordinate officials, detached for duty in the provinces, on whom the happiness or misfortune of those provinces, their prosperity or their poverty, depend." Ibid, 120.

251. Ibid, 124.
252. Ibid, 131.
253. Ibid, 136.
254. Ibid, 137.
255. Ibid, 137–8.
256. On this score see Pierre Manent, "Democratic Man, Aristocratic Man and Man Simply: Some Remarks on an Equivocation in Tocqueville's Thought" in *Modern Liberty and its Discontents*, trans. Daniel J. Mahoney (Lanham, MD: Rowman and Littlefield, 1998), 68: "One might suggest that, by defining aristocracy and democracy as 'regimes of humanity' rather than as political regimes, Tocqueville only recovers the original Greek meaning of the notion of regime and moreover the meaning of politics. For Aristotle, as well as for Plato and Thucydides, there corresponds to each regime a human 'type', and, in this sense, a 'distinct humanity'. But besides the fact that the Tocquevillean regimes correspond only partially to part of the 'Greek' regimes, one consideration obliges us to distinguish them rigorously. The Greek regimes are affected by an essentially 'cyclical' history, a history that is circumscribed and regulated by *nature*.

"In contrast, Tocquevillean democracy bears or implies a process, an *indefinite history*."

257. Tocqueville, *Old Regime*, 135.
258. Ibid, 149.
259. Ibid, 151–2.
260. Ibid, 139–40.
261. Ibid, 170.
262. Marquise de la Rochejaquelein, quoted in Michael Ross, *Banners of the King: The War of the Vendee 1793–1794* (New York: Hippocrene Books, 1975), 21.
263. Tocqueville, *Old Regime*, 155.
264. Ibid, 225.
265. On the burdensome feudal obligations that the poor bore the brunt of, see Doyle, *On the Origins of the French Revolution*, 195–8. By way of illustration: "In 1777, when a humble farm servant might only earn 60 livres in a year, Charles-Eugène-Gabriel La Croix Castries, a well-connected future Marshal of France, paid 770,000 livres for a package of feudal rights over a swathe of the Cévennes hills near Nîmes. For that sum he obtained the right to dues on crops across fifty parishes, to tolls on local bridges, a mining monopoly, and even the right to charge for seigneurial courts in litigation. He had no difficulty in subletting the rights to collect these dues to eager middlemen, confident that there were fat profits to be made. For the poor cottager or sharecropper, the weight of rents, dues, tithes and taxes, was so heavy that even fertile and well-stocked farms only yielded enough for a bare subsistence to those who worked them." David Andress, *The Terror: The Merciless War for Freedom in Revolutionary France* (New York: Farrar, Straus and Giroux, 2005), 22.

266. Tocqueville, *Old Regime*, 228.
267. Ibid, 227.
268. Ibid, 230.
269. Ibid, 191.
270. Ibid, 190.
271. Ibid, 229.
272. Andress, *Terror*, 4–5.
273. Tocqueville, *Old Regime*, 191.
274. Ibid, 170.
275. Ibid, 137.
276. This want of initiative is wonderfully illustrated by an example that Tocqueville provides in his notes: "This extinction of all local public life had gone beyond anything that we can imagine. One of the roads which led from Maine to Normandy was impassible. Who asked for it to be repaired? The Generality of Touraine, through which it passed? The province of Normandy or that of Maine, so interested in the cattle trade, which followed this road? Some canton finally, especially harmed by the bad state of this road? The generality, the province, the cantons are without voice. It is necessary for the merchants who use the road and who get bogged down in it to themselves attract the central government's attention. They write to Paris to the controller-general, and ask him to come to their aid." Ibid, 282.
277. Ibid, 171.
278. Ibid, 145.
279. Ibid, *Old Regime*, 245.
280. Ibid, 145.
281. Ibid, 230.
282. Ibid, 85.
283. Ibid, 244.
284. Ibid, 85.
285. Ibid, 85–6.
286. Malcolm Crook, *Elections in the French Revolution* (New York: Cambridge University Press, 1996), 85.
287. Ibid, 94. See also Andress, *Terror*, 55: "Declared candidacy or canvassing was officially prohibited; electors were supposed to be free to judge in their own minds which worthy individuals to nominate. The Jacobins, however, had begun to drop heavy hints about the kinds of individuals to avoid, and even in some areas bent the law by suggesting names to favour through papers and pamphlets. Those who were interested in the electoral process were in any case those likely to take an activist view of the Revolution—as with every election from this point on, only a minority of those eligible troubled to take part, and thus inclined the result towards radicalism."
288. James Madison, *Federalist* No. 47, in the *Federalist Papers*, 269.
289. Furet, *Revolutionary France*, 134.
290. For an account of The Committee of Public Safety at its height, see R. R. Palmer, *Twelve who Ruled: The Year of the Terror in the French Revolution* (Princeton: Princeton University Press, 1989).
291. Tocqueville, *Old Regime*, 245.

292. Ibid, 85.
293. Ibid, 247.
294. See Chapter One, note 130 above.
295. Damrosch, *Rousseau*, 493.
296. James Miller, *Rousseau: Dreamer of Democracy* (New Haven: Yale University Press, 1984), 139.
297. Ibid, 143.
298. Ruth Scurr, *Fatal Purity: Robespierre and the French Revolution* (New York: Henry Holt and Company, 2007), 231.
299. Pierre Force, "Philosophes" in *Encyclopedia of Political Theory* edited by Mark Bevir (Los Angeles: Sage Publications, 2010), 1039.
300. Tocqueville, *Old Regime*, 195.
301. Ibid, 200.
302. Ibid, 196.
303. Ibid, 209.
304. Of course, the abstractness and generality of those ideas did not prevent people from attempting to apply them concretely. Their failure to appreciate the practical inapplicability of such ideas suggests that their grasp of them was perilously flawed. As Rousseau remarked of his own *Social Contract*, "Those who boast that they fully understand it are brighter than I am." Quoted in Damrosch, *Rousseau*, 476.
305. Tocqueville, *Old Regime*, 209–10.
306. Ibid, 210.
307. Ibid, 212.
308. Ibid, 212–3.
309. "We believe that the destructive theories which are known in our days under the name of *socialism* are of recent origin; this is a mistake: these theories were contemporary with the first physiocrats." Ibid, 213. Tocqueville's criticism of socialism was principled and unstinting. See, for example, his speech to the Constituent Assembly on September 12, 1848, quoted in *The New Individualist Review* (Indianapolis: Liberty Fund, 1981), 60–5. "AND AFTER this great Revolution, is the result to be that society which the socialists offer us, a formal, regimented and closed society where the State has charge of all, where the individual counts for nothing, where the community masses to itself all power, all life, where the end assigned to man is solely his material welfare—this society where the very air is stifling and where light barely penetrates? Is it to be for this society of bees and beavers, for this society, more for skilled animals than for free and civilized men, that the French Revolution took place? Is it for this that so many great men died on the field of battle and on the gallows, that so much noble blood watered the earth? Is it for this that so many passions were inflamed, that so much genius, so much virtue walked the earth?" (62). On the growing prominence of the problem of socialism in Tocqueville's thought, see Drescher, *Dilemmas of Democracy*, chap. 7.
310. François Quesnay, *Maximes générales de gouvernement économique d'un royaume agricole* quoted in Tocqueville, *Old Regime*, 210.
311. Tocqueville, *Old Regime*, 203.

312. Nietzsche, *Genealogy of Morality*, 119. Hence, the enduring faith of atheistic socialists in a this-worldly beyond. Nietzsche, *Twilight of the Idols*, 534–5.

313. Tocqueville, *Old Regime*, 96.

314. Ibid, 97.

315. As Tocqueville observed in his notes, "The property that [the revolutionaries] seized violently [from the clergy] was booty from the ancient world, the destruction of one feudal edifice . . . . They robbed an aristocratic property to pay religiously a democratic debt." Quoted in Gannett, *Tocqueville Unveiled*, 63.

316. Tocqueville, *Old Regime*, 204.

317. "We know that clerical lords enjoyed the same advantages [as the French nobility]; for the Church, which had a different origin, a different purpose, and a different nature than feudalism, had nevertheless finally become deeply enmeshed with it. Even if it was never entirely incorporated into that foreign body, it had penetrated so deeply within it, that it was as if it was encrusted there. Thus bishops, canons, and abbots possessed fiefs or subfiefs in virtue of their ecclesiastical functions; the convent usually had the lordship of the village in which it was situated. The Church had serfs in the one part of France where they still existed; it employed the corvée, levied dues on fairs and markets, had its oven, its mill, its winepress, its stud bull. More than any else in the world, the French clergy possessed the right to collect tithes." Ibid, 116.

318. Ibid, 196–7.

319. Ibid, 197.

320. R. R. Palmer, *The Age of Democratic Revolution: The Struggle* vol. II (Princeton: Princeton University Press, 1964).

321. Again, it is worth stressing that those longings belonged to democratic man and not to man simply, as the events that unfolded in the Vendée make plain.

322. Tocqueville, *Old Regime*, 99.

323. Ibid, 100.

324. Rousseau, *Social Contract*, 163–4.

325. Tocqueville, *Old Regime*, 101.

326. Ibid.

Chapter 4

Democratic Man

As history demonstrates time and time again, reports of its death tend to be greatly exaggerated. History did not end with the collapse of the *ancién regime*, any more than it did with the collapse of the Soviet one. Nor for that matter did mankind's democratization. But the French Revolution marks a watershed all the same. History may not have come to an end, but the *ancien régime* incontestably did. The event signifies an epochal rift separating an ineludible democratic future from an irretrievable aristocratic past. The ever latent and episodically open conflict between aristocratic and democratic man had for all intents and purposes been settled. The reign of the few was over; that of the many had only begun. So total was the triumph of democratic man that the mere survival of aristocratic man would become doubtful. This is not meant to imply that democratic peoples carried out a concerted effort to extirpate their erstwhile masters (though in many cases they did). But as time would show, it is in the nature of the democratic majority to expand its ranks inexorably until all rank is abolished. If aristocracies rigorously circumscribe themselves, its members jealously guarding their privileges and excluding from their orbit all those whom nature has not privileged, democracies swell unremittingly, either passively absorbing all who dwell beyond it or actively overcoming all who dare to oppose it. "With us or against us!—there can be no alternative." Difference was a thing of the past; homogeneity was the way of the future. It is time to understand in whose hands man's fate now lies.

The French Revolution was brought about by democratic man, not vice versa. Were it not for the advent of this particular human type, the Revolution would not have been possible. If, in a manner of speaking, the Revolution helped make the world safe for democracy, it did so—to echo Tocqueville's stance—unnecessarily. The ascendancy of democratic man had all but been destined and it had been destined before the Bastille fell. The force of those two earlier revolutions intensified over the centuries giving rise to a particular human type, namely the democratic one. Faith in himself—in the power of his own reason and intrinsic worth—would become a constituent attribute of this new being. But as often happens with spreading faiths, the teachings of those responsible for fathering them largely had been perverted. Equality without God supersedes equality before God and the primary aim of reason is no longer to master nature within but to do so without. Though to be fair, in the democratic mind, these signify progressions, not perversions. It is in keeping with the character of this human type to spurn all wisdom that he has not discovered himself.

It comes then as little surprise that democratic man tends to be so lacking in self-awareness. If he is not denigrating the past, he is apt to ignore it outright. Where he comes from and how he got here tend to be matters of scant concern, especially when compared to the far more pressing question of where he is heading. The golden age lies before him, not behind.[1] Democratic man is intensely "futural." In his mind, the future assumes a hitherto unknown prominence at the expense of the past and often the present as well. One might say that democratic man is particularly inclined to flout the Delphic command ("know thyself"), one because it is ancient and two because it is a command. To honor the injunction inscribed at the temple's entrance requires an awareness of one's origins, of one's essence, which leaves democratic man remarkably unfit for such an undertaking. (That he disdains essences, especially with regard to himself, does not help matters. In the present day, that disdain is amply displayed in the widespread penchant to choose and change one's identity.[2] Of course, an identity that is freely chosen and changed is not much of an identity, an irony that appears largely lost on those who celebrate such freedom. A square that might become a circle is not much of either—or perhaps anything, for that matter.) Notwithstanding the considerable amount of time and resources that are devoted to analyzing the psyche and inflating the self in the modern age, democratic man grows increasingly less aware of who he is.

Symptomatic of this waning awareness is democratic man's willful disregard for his past. The very idea that his animating faiths might owe something to two figures whose hours upon the stage expired over two millennia ago likely would be received with derision. Of Socrates, his knowledge is lacking; at Christ, he scoffs with diminishing decorum. His debt to both is not simply denied, it is unknown. If the remoteness of those figures excuses democratic man's ignorance of them, that excuse becomes less compelling in the case of those modern thinkers who were instrumental in accelerating the march of democracy, and of whom democratic man is no less ignorant. History may have been given its democratic bent in Athens and Jerusalem, but disciples—albeit frequently unconscious ones (unconscious of their discipleship, that is)—were needed to advance it.

A preponderance of those unwitting disciples belongs to modernity, surveyed in some detail above. Though they sought to curtail the influence of Socrates and Christ, they wound up promoting it, at least with respect to the democratization of humanity, a process that progressed precipitously on their watch thanks to their exaltation of human reason and equality. That is not meant to imply that the movement was seamless; that no quarrel exists between the ancients and the moderns. The moderns' denunciation of the ancients for concerning themselves with imagined republics and principalities that never were nor, as the moderns averred, ever could be was itself not imagined, though arguably misguided. Classical thought's inability to stem the savagery that riddles history convinced the moderns that ancient wisdom was but folly. It would be better to accept the baseness of man and endeavor to contain it, rather than strive to correct it. If the ancients aspired to elevate man, the moderns sought to domesticate him. But although the moderns repudiated the ancients in no uncertain terms, they did not do so outright. Indeed, they embraced, almost reflexively, the two most fateful teachings to have emerged from antiquity: the primacy of reason over instinct and the inborn equality of all human beings. Small wonder then that the diminution of the human spirit followed. Inborn equality and irremediable baseness make for a sorry mix. Reason, that saving grace, would be utilized not to elevate man, but to tame him.

With regard to the foundation of modernity, few thinkers enjoy a more prominent place than René Descartes. Generally credited with begetting modern philosophy, Descartes also played a decisive part in shaping the character of democratic man, a role that was not lost on Tocqueville. Reflecting on the philosophic method of an inveterately unphilosophic people, Tocqueville observed that "America is . . . the one country in the world where the precepts of Descartes are least studied and best followed." This in spite of the fact that "Americans do not read Descartes' works" and no civilized people "are less occupied with philosophy than they."[3] How to reconcile this ostensible incongruity?

Being free from "the spirit of system, from the yoke of habits, from family maxims, from class opinions, and, up to a certain point, from national prejudices,"[4] and having forsaken "the traditions of class, profession, and family,"[5] "each American calls only on the individual effort of his reason."[6] Beholding the world like little Cartesians, they accept nothing as given and place trust only in "their own reason as the most visible and closest source of truth." As though they too were contemplating a ball of wax before the fire, "each withdraws narrowly into himself and claims to judge the world from there." A mind thus fashioned presumes that "everything in the world is explicable and nothing exceeds the bounds of intelligence." Indeed, it goes so far as to deny what it cannot comprehend.[7]

It is true that there was something unique about the American experience, which should caution one against conflating the American mind with the democratic mind as such. But the American perspective, to say nothing of America itself, served as a sort of exemplar, in which features that would be common to all peoples in the age of democracy might be discerned. As Tocqueville understood it, America was the one country in the world where the democratic revolution seemed "nearly to have attained its natural limits." He crossed the Atlantic to see "an image of democracy itself" and survey a land that displayed "the results of the democratic revolution" without having suffered the revolution itself.[8] America may have been the one country where the precepts of Descartes were best followed (and least studied), but an adherence to those precepts was not unique to America; it was part and parcel of the democratic perspective. The philosophic method, devised by Descartes and employed by luminaries such as Voltaire, was not strictly French, nor European for that matter. Rather, it was, in essence, democratic. Thus Tocqueville found on the other side of the Atlantic a people born democratic[9] who applied the method without ever having studied it. It was as if "they [had] found it in themselves." But on his side of the pond, where people were not born democratic but were increasingly becoming so, the method found minds no less receptive to it. "The same method was established and vulgarized in Europe only as conditions there became more equal and men more alike."[10]

This intrinsically democratic method could be established only once man had been sufficiently democratized, "when people were beginning to be equal and resemble each other."[11] But once established, it effectively assured that the democratization of man would proceed apace. While Descartes formalized this method, its underlying principle preceded him. First used to call into question matters of faith (Luther and Calvin) and later applied to the natural sciences and "philosophy properly so-called" (Bacon and Descartes), it was only a matter of time before the "objects of all beliefs" were subject to "the individual examination of each man."[12] As more and more minds adopted this approach, society teetered and all but collapsed during the Revolution. "It is not because the French changed their ancient beliefs and modified their ancient mores that they turned the world upside down; it is because they were the first to generalize and to bring to light a philosophic method with whose aid one could readily attack all ancient things and open the way to all new ones."[13]

This sort of attack was superfluous in the New World, where there were no ancient institutions to overturn. What is more, it was "religion that gave birth to the Anglo-American societies." Christianity tempered any revolutionary longings and greatly limited the scope of matters to which this philosophic approach could be applied. "The Americans having accepted the principal dogmas of the Christian religion without examination, are obliged to receive in the same manner a great number of moral truths that flow from them and depend on them. That restricts the actions of individual analysis within narrow limits and spares from it several of the most important human opinions."[14] While the unique circumstances of America's birth allowed its people to escape the pangs that beset the French (and other Europeans) in their democratic rearing, it is worth noting that whenever and wherever democracy is firmly established, upheavals of the sort that the French Revolution exemplified will become a thing of the past. The material progress that democracy promises, the likes of which earlier ages scarcely could have dreamt, as well as the outward agitation of its people and their ever-renewed infatuation with novelties, belies the stagnation that will come to typify the age of democracy. Rather than be perennially or periodically upheaved, society will drift restlessly toward a terminus whose perils the people will be blissfully oblivious to. The denouement of that democratic drift, which Nietzsche and Tocqueville each prevised in his own way, will be examined below.

The Americans proved to be unwittingly good Cartesians in another manner, one that was bound intimately to the first. It was not only the method that so forcefully appealed to the democratic mind, but the objective as well. Descartes provided philosophy with a new raison d'être, one that served to free modern thought from its classical moorings. For the ancients, what distinguishes man from beast is reason or understanding so that it is in keeping with human nature and the natural order to which humans belong for man to develop his understanding more fully. Philosophy is man's highest calling because by virtue of it, humans come closest to realizing the end toward which they naturally are directed. Because of the strict demands that such a calling makes, the life of the mind was reserved for the few, but those capable of answering it understood that philosophy was good intrinsically, as a way of life that accorded most with nature, yielding a proper ordering of the human soul and, by virtue of that, supreme health and happiness. In a manner of speaking, philosophy was its own reward.[15]

The teleological principles upon which the classical understanding of philosophy reposes largely had been disposed of by the time Descartes composed his *Discourse*. This was in no small part a logical if not inevitable consequence of the Copernican revolution. With the realization that man enjoyed, no cosmologically privileged place came the awareness that nature provided no meaningful standards by which to guide him. The nihilistic overtones found in the opening of Nietzsche's *On Truth and Lie in the Extra Moral Sense* likely would have shocked the sensibilities of those early modern thinkers, but for all intents and purposes, the trajectory from Copernicus's discovery to Nietzsche's is not difficult to trace. Still, unlike their late- and postmodern successors, the early moderns held on to the conceit that human nature was fixed. The earth may have been freed from its moorings but in the minds of those thinkers, man was not yet metaphysically free. The second wave of modernity would be needed to wipe the slate clean.[16] But while the early moderns preserved a conception of human nature, they radically reconceived man's relation to nature. In their eyes, through which—on this score at least—all good moderns see, nature ceases to specify ends toward which human beings are salubriously impelled. The good life is no longer the life in accordance with nature—with man's higher nature—but a life in opposition to nature, for which man's baser nature is eminently well suited. It is on the overcoming of nature, not the fulfillment of it, that man's happiness depends. Descartes did as much as anyone to propagate this quintessentially modern view.

> I have never entertained any pretensions about the products of my thinking. When the result of the application of my methods was merely my own satisfaction concerning some speculative questions, or perhaps the regulation of my own behavior by the principles which it showed me, I did not feel obliged to write of them. For when it comes to morals, everyone is so convinced of his own good sense that there might be as many reformers as individuals if others than those whom God has established as sovereigns over his peoples, or to whom he has given enough grace and zeal to be prophets, were permitted to attempt reforms. So even though my speculations pleased me very much, I believed that other persons had their own speculations which perhaps pleased them even more. As soon, however, as I had achieved some general notions about physics, and when, testing them in various critical problems, I noticed how far they might lead and how they differed from the principles accepted up to this time, I thought that I could not keep them hidden without gravely sinning against the rule that obliges us to promote as far as possible the general good of mankind. For they have satisfied me that it is possible to reach knowledge that will be of much utility in this life; and that instead of the speculative philosophy now taught in the schools we can find a practical one by which knowing the nature and behavior of fire, water, air, stars, the heavens, and all the other bodies which surround us, as well as we now understand the different skills of our workers, we can employ these entities for all the purposes for which they are suited and so make ourselves masters and possessors of nature.[17]

A century and a half before the democratic tide swept across Europe, while Christendom was being rent by sectarian strife, Descartes furnished the philosophic foundations for modern natural science upon which the success of that science, and of democracy as well, so squarely rests.

The Americans had no greater knowledge of the aims of Descartes' philosophical project than they did its methods, but that did not prevent them from realizing that project with staggering celerity. Like many before him (and after), Tocqueville was struck by the natural features of the New World. The "vast wilderness" of the Mississippi Valley was, in his eyes, "the most magnificent dwelling that God has ever prepared for the habitation of man."[18] With its coasts, "so well prepared for commerce and industry," extensive rivers, "green and moist solitudes, and boundless fields that the plowshare of the laborer has not yet turned," the continent as a whole appeared to have been fashioned by Providence for the purpose of establishing a great nation.[19] Tocqueville appreciated just how much America owed to its location. Not only did the land teem with natural resources, "offer[ing] inexhaustible nourishment for industry and work,"[20] so that "human industry can spread without bounds,"[21] but its cartographic isolation allowed its people to live without fear of invasion. With a largely uninhabited world to the north and a largely undeveloped one to the south, hemmed in by the Atlantic to the east and the Pacific to the west, Tocqueville remarked that "the Union is almost as isolated in the world as if it found itself confined on all sides by the ocean."[22] But this irenic setting did not ensure prosperity. If the land conduced to the founding of a great nation, it hardly guaranteed one. What was of greater importance than the physical makeup of America was the mental makeup of its people. At odds with many thinkers, past, present, and—no doubt—future, Tocqueville maintained that a country's fate is not determined by its geography. As he flatly states, "physical causes . . . do not influence the destiny of nations as much as one supposes."[23]

Tocqueville found that evidence supporting his position was not in short supply. For one, "the immense wilderness" upon which adventurers from the Old World happened had not been "entirely deprived of the presence of man" prior to their arrival.[24] But "although the vast country . . . was inhabited by numerous tribes of natives, one can just say that at the period of discovery it still formed only a wilderness. The Indians occupied it, but they did not possess it. It is by agriculture that man appropriates soil, and the first inhabitants of North America lived from products of the hunt."[25] As Tocqueville saw it, the natives had been dealt an unkind hand. Having fashioned the land for the establishment of a great civilization, "Providence . . . seemed to have given them a short lease on it; they were there, in a way, *only in the meantime.*"[26] Their salvation came down to the tragic choice of war or civilization: "they had to destroy the Europeans or become their equals."[27] It was tragic because whatever their choice, ruin was their ineluctable lot. Tocqueville's esteem for America's natives was sincere and considerable, as was his commiseration for their unenviable fate. But his lofty sentiments did not prevent him from seeing the simple and disconcerting truth that the natives' way of life could not be countenanced by civilization's advance. To wish away their decimation, as is so fashionable today, is to wish away so many of the privileges that those who rail against the white man's iniquity undeniably take for granted. But all that aside, the natives' existence makes plane that the establishment of America depended far more on the character of its inhabitants than it did on the character of the land they inhabited.

This point is further corroborated by contrasting America's fate with that of the lands to America's north and south. To the south—the West Indies and later the shores of South America—Europeans happened upon a paradisiacal world that contrasted sharply with what they discovered in North America, where "everything . . . was grave, serious, [and] solemn." Dazzled by the splendor they took in, "they believed themselves transported to the fabulous regions that poets had celebrated . . . . All that was offered to view seemed prepared for the needs of man or calculated for his pleasures."[28] The North American wilderness appeared infecund in comparison. Yet, despite its inexhaustible fertility, South America labored in vain to

> support democracy. If, for peoples to be happy, it were enough to have been placed in a corner of the universe and to be able to spread at will over uninhabited lands, the Spanish of South and southern America would not have to complain of their lot. And if they did not enjoy the same happiness as did the inhabitants of the United States, they ought at least to have made themselves envied by the peoples of Europe. There are nevertheless no nations on earth more miserable than those of South America.[29]

To the north, and to his delight, Tocqueville found Frenchmen, who displayed the trappings of European enlightenment and civilization. Yet, although they shared far more in common with the Anglo-Americans than they did with the native ones, and notwithstanding that they had equal access to nature's plenitude, he found "the French population of Canada pressed into a space too narrow for it,"[30] "the debris of an old people lost in the midst of the flood of a new nation."[31] Lest one contend that "the rigors of the climate"[32] precluded the French from achieving in Canada what the Americans achieved in the United States, Tocqueville reminds his native readers that "there was a time when we as well could have created a great French Nation in the American wilderness."[33] But in the wildernesses of the New World, neither the French[34] nor the Spanish nor the natives both north and south of the equator managed to establish a nation that even remotely rivaled America. Geography cannot explain away America's exceptionalism.

While the Americans owed much to the soil that supports them,[35] they owed far more to what those who appropriated the soil brought with them. One of the many remarkable things about America's genesis is that it is so well known. In that land that God had held in reserve for a late-born people,[36] "democracy such as antiquity had not dared to dream of sprang full-grown and fully armed from the midst of the old feudal society."[37] Nations are like individuals in that so much of their character is established when they are young. "Peoples always feel [the effects] of their origins. The circumstances that accompanied their birth and served to develop them influence the entire course of the rest of their lives."[38] The problem for those who wish to comprehend a people's character is that the origins of that people are shrouded in remote and unrecorded times. But in the case of America, that problem does not prevail. "America is the only country where one has been able to witness the natural and tranquil developments of a society."[39] America's birth is Tocqueville's point of departure and its centrality to *Democracy in America* would be difficult to overstate. Indeed, it is "the key to almost the whole work."[40] In Tocqueville's view, what was central to America's point of departure was that in spite of the manifold differences that characterized "the emigrants who came at different periods to occupy the territory that today covers the American Union," they shared among themselves "common features" and "all found themselves in an analogous situation."[41] Those features included a common heritage; shared language; democratic birth; widespread enlightenment; similar education (particularly of the political stripe); and, not least importantly, the incorporation of "two perfectly distinct elements that elsewhere have often made war with each other," namely the *spirit of religion* and the *spirit of freedom*.[42]

This last point is of paramount importance and modern detractors of religion who still prejudicially champion humanity's democratization would do well to pay heed. Tocqueville, whose own people were no strangers to religious discord, was awestruck by the Americans' ability to wed so peaceably their religious faiths and political freedoms. To Tocqueville, what was so incredible was not that they tolerated each other, but that their relationship was symbiotic; these two forces, which historically had been so antagonistic and mutually destructive, lent support to one another so that each was stronger in the company of the other than either would be on its own.

> Far from harming each other, these two tendencies, apparently so opposed, advance in accord and seem to lend each other a mutual support.
>
> Religion sees in civil freedom a noble exercise of the faculties of man; in the political world, a field left by the creator to the efforts of intelligence. Free and powerful in its sphere, satisfied with the place that is reserved for it, it knows that its empire is all the better established when it reigns by its own strength alone and dominates over hearts without support.
>
> Freedom sees in religion the companion of its struggle and its triumphs, the cradle of its infancy, the divine source of its rights. It considers religion as the

safeguard of mores; and mores as the guarantee of laws and the pledge of its own duration.[43]

This delicate union, which seemed miraculous to the young Frenchman and appears pernicious to so many enlightened minds today,[44] was preserved with relative ease because its establishment was coeval with America's. The marriage of those typically combative forces permitted the fledgling nation not only to survive the precarious incunabulum that attends the birth of all nations, but, in time, to distinguish itself in ways that few, if any, nations ever have.

While the emigrants' "common features" were essential to the success of their undertaking, no less important was the "analogous situation" in which they found themselves. In the American wilderness, the Europeans were afforded a chance to start anew in a manner that simply was not possible in the long-settled territories of the Old World. They were not presumptuous enough to reconstruct time so that it began with them, but they did in effect build civilization from the ground up. They had, as it were, returned to the state of nature and promptly compacted to extricate themselves from it.[45] The leap of faith this venture necessitated is difficult to fathom, all the more so because of the venture's unequivocal success. But as Tocqueville notes, those who make such leaps tend not to be among the prosperous and powerful. In their shared poverty and misfortune, they were equals and thus "had no idea of any superiority whatsoever of some over others." Even those emigrants who did have such an idea—for it so "happened that on several occasions great lords came to America as a consequence of political or religious quarrels"—promptly realized that it was not profitable to establish a hierarchy of ranks; indeed, not only was it not profitable, but it was not possible. The stubbornness of that untamed and rebellious land required constant effort to cultivate.[46] The result was that "American soil absolutely repelled territorial aristocracy." In this manner, "all the new European colonies contained, if not the development, at least the seed of a complete democracy."[47]

> Americans had the chance of birth working for them: their fathers had long since brought equality of conditions and of intelligence onto the soil they inhabited, from which the democratic republic would one day issue as from its natural source. This is still not all; with a republican social state, they willed to their descendants the most appropriate habits, ideas, and mores to make a republic flourish. When I think about what this original fact produced, it seems to me that I see the whole destiny of America contained in the first Puritan who landed on its shores, like the whole human race in the first man.[48]

All of this helps to account for America's success and explain why her people, so unversed in philosophy, advanced the modern project with such indefatigable gumption. As argued above, that project is intrinsically democratic. And so too were those who founded America. Enlightened and late born, unbound by the strictures of class and far removed from the divisions that sundered the Old World, the Americans were well suited to advance the modern project, even if they had little conscious understanding of what that project was. That project would advance on its own accord with the birth of a democratic people. For at bottom, the modern project is a reflection or expression of the democratic soul; it is designed to secure the (democratic) soul's desiderata. Thus, good, albeit unwitting Cartesians that they were, the Americans utilized their individual reason to navigate the New World and conquer it. By marginalizing human distinctions, reason leveled the playing field and helped make the world—new and old—safe and comfortable for democracy. With America's founding, modern man made tremendous strides toward attaining his grandest ambition: bringing heaven down to earth and enjoying the fruits of the life to come here and now.

If so brazen an ambition would have been thought a profanation by early Americans, whose religiosity was much more deep-seated than late ones, it did not prevent them from advancing toward it. As Tocqueville observed, the Americans' eschatological longings reflected a peculiar amalgamation of spiritual and material concerns.

> Men sacrifice their friends, their family, and their native country to a religious opinion; one can believe them to be absorbed in the pursuit of the intellectual good that they have come to buy at such a high price. One nevertheless sees them seeking with an almost equal ardor material wealth and moral satisfactions, heaven in the other world and well being and freedom in this one.[49]

While "the situation of the Americans is . . . entirely exceptional,"[50] their desire for material well-being was anything but. This desire is not an elemental part of human nature, any more than is the desire for equality (or freedom for that matter).[51] But it is an elemental part of democratic human nature, that is, the nature of democratic man. "Among all the passions that equality gives birth to or favors, there is one that it renders particularly keen and that it sets in the hearts of all men at the same time: the love of well-being. The taste for well-being forms the salient and indelible feature of democratic ages."[52] It bears repeating that Tocqueville came to America to ponder the future, not of America so much, but of democracy. There he beheld much that was exceptional, but none of that prevented him from seeing what he had set out to find: the rule.

In the age of democracy, there was nothing remarkable about the love of well-being, even if there was something remarkable about the conspicuity of that love in America. "Cupidity is always breathless [in America], and the human mind, distracted at every moment from pleasures of the imagination and works of intellect, gets carried away only in the pursuit of wealth."[53] The cupidity that Tocqueville beheld had an aim ulterior to the one that was advocated explicitly by early modern thinkers such as Locke. Tocqueville knew of no country "where the love of money holds a larger place in the heart of man" than it did in America.[54] This love resulted less from the desire for comfort than it did for distinction.

> The prestige that attached to old things having disappeared, birth, condition, and profession no longer distinguish men or hardly distinguish them; there remains scarcely anything but money that creates very visible differences between them and that can set off some from their peers. The distinction that arises from wealth is increased by the disappearance and diminution of all others.[55]

The craving for wealth that was so prominently on display in America is, if not an explicit aim of the modern project, an unavoidable consequence of it.[56] As the distance between man and man is (a)bridged, individuals will seek to distinguish themselves by what few legitimate means remain available, few of which are more effective than amassing and displaying wealth. Aristocratic man was distinguished by his nature; he remained noble in the absence of wealth. Democratic man has no natural distinctions; in the absence of artificial ones, such as wealth, nothing sets him apart. Hence, the change in values that attended the transition from an aristocratic age to a democratic one. What was considered "servile cupidity" in the age of aristocracy is considered "noble and estimable ambition" in the age of democracy.[57]

The seeds of the modern project may have been sown in the Old World, but it was the soil of the New that proved most propitious for their germination and propagation. There nature retreated before man's advance, leaving in its wake opportunities that were not available, or even imaginable, in the world that had been left behind.

> Europe is much occupied with the wilderness of America, but the Americans themselves scarcely think of it. The marvels of inanimate nature find them insensible, and they so to speak perceive the admirable forests that surround them only at the moment at which they fall by their strokes. Their eyes are filled with another spectacle. The American people sees itself advance across this wilderness, draining swamps, straightening rivers, peopling the solitude, and subduing nature. This magnificent image of themselves is not offered only now and then to the imagination of the Americans; one can say that it follows each of them in the least of his actions as in his principal ones, and that it is always there, dangling before his intellect.[58]

This intellect exhibited an unmistakably democratic bent. As Tocqueville observed, in America "the purely practical part of the sciences is cultivated admirably, and people attend carefully to the theoretical portion immediately necessary to application . . . but there is almost no one in the United States who gives himself over to the essentially theoretical and abstract portion of human knowledge."[59] This utilitarian approach was integral to the modern project and reflects the disconnect between aristocratic and democratic science—the former giving precedence to the pleasures of the mind, the latter to those of the body.

> Most men who compose [democratic] nations are very eager for present material enjoyments; as they are always discontented with the position they occupy and always free to leave it, they dream only of the means of changing their fortune or of increasing it. For minds so disposed, every new method that leads to wealth by a shorter path, every machine that shortens work, every instrument that diminishes the costs of production, every discovery that facilitates pleasures and augments them seems to be the most magnificent effort of human intelligence. It is principally in this way that democratic people apply themselves to the sciences, understand them, and honor them.[60]

By spurning purely "abstract notions . . . whose application is not known or is very distant"[61] and by "demand[ing] of science only its particular applications to the arts and the means of rendering life easy"[62] the Americans demonstrated what wonderfully effective and dedicated Cartesians they were.

On Nietzsche, none of this was lost. Though he never stepped foot off the Continent and though he had exceedingly little to say about the country that so captivated Tocqueville, Nietzsche grasped the central problems that absorbed Tocqueville during his peregrination of America. Tocqueville had to traverse the Atlantic to behold the democratic future; Nietzsche divined it from the confines of his impenetrable solitude.[63]

While Nietzsche paid the Americans virtually no heed, he apprehended, with perhaps greater profundity than any before—and arguably since—the human type that modernity would beget. One did not need to study a nation of unconscious Cartesians, a nation founded on "reflection and choice" rather than "accident and force,"[64] to appreciate the procreative part that Descartes played in generating this new age and in spawning the human type to whom it would belong. The authority of reason is, after all, one of the quiddities of modernity[65] and reason's command owes much to the "father of rationalism," as Nietzsche well understood. This does not contravene Nietzsche's point regarding Socrates's turn to reason and his vortical effect on the course of so-called world history. To be sure, the Cartesian revolution would not have been conceivable had the Socratic one not preceded it. But Descartes' method was qualitatively different insofar as he took up "the ancient theological problem of 'faith' and 'knowledge'—or, more clearly, of instinct and reason" and resolved it by siding unequivocally with the latter. "The question of whether, with respect to the value of things, the instincts deserve more authority than reason (reason wants some ground or 'what for?', some purpose or utility behind our values and actions)—this is the same old moral problem that first emerged in the person of Socrates."[66] By elevating the role of reason and, in the process, attenuating the instincts of Greek nobility ("Rationality *against* instinct. Rationality at any price"[67]), Socrates proved himself to be "an instrument of disintegration." But that "superior dialectician" having "initially sided with reason," realized in the end that the instincts must receive "their fair dues, *along with* reason—we have to follow our instincts but persuade reason to come to their aid with good motives."[68] Reason could not do away with instinct. At bottom, there was an irrational element to all moral judgments, for as Socrates descried, his own reasoning, far from being autonomous, "was in the service of his own instincts."[69] It was Descartes "who granted authority to reason alone."[70]

The democratizing impact of reason has been addressed above. Reason allowed the lower orders to become ascendant; to level the playing field of a world in which they were so manifestly disadvantaged. Reason smiles on all alike. "It is no respecter of persons. Nothing is more democratic than logic, that is, *compelling* agreement by force of reasons."[71] It is hardly any wonder then, that in a democratic age—"in the age of *suffrage universel*, i.e., when everyone may sit in judgment on everyone and everything"[72] and when the people want to do "away with all masters"[73]—reason would assume such prominence, and Descartes, "the father of rationalism (and consequently grandfather of the Revolution)"[74] who posited that no authority should escape the tribunal of reason, would enjoy such a privileged position (even if only implicitly so).[75]

The overthrowing of old authorities does not result in an age without authority, but in an age with new ones. The deposition of the old masters—Aristotle, the Church, God, et al.—made way for the coronation of a new one, namely reason, or more to the point, science. The ubiquitous faith in science in the age of democracy presents a curious spectacle, in that on the whole, the mysteries of science are as inscrutable to the average person today as were those of the Church to the average person of an earlier day. Part of what accounts for this is that to reap the benefits of science, there is no need to have any command of it. One might say the same of the Church, but the authority of the Church could not survive its own internal schisms, to say nothing of the external discoveries that became increasingly difficult to square with Biblical teaching.[76] Moreover, modern science caters to the masses more effectively.

Pleasures of the mind or spirit are inaccessible to those who are not intellectually or spiritually inclined, but those of the body are available to all who are corporally predisposed, that is, to all. Even the critic of science is thankful for and does not hesitate to avail himself of the blessings that modern science bestows (in medicine, technology, communications, transportation, and so forth). Thus it is not simply the promise of science, but its success in making good on it that renders its authority acceptable to those who are reluctant to abide any authority in which they do not play a part. The promise of science—"as little pain as possible, as long life as possible"—is not unlike that of the Church it superseded. "Thus it is a kind of eternal bliss, though a very modest kind in comparison with the promises of religions."[77]

The promise of modern science betrays a lack of objectivity and a tendentious attachment to this world instead of the sedulous detachment upon which its adverted objectivity is purported to rest. The moderns may have sought to sever all roots from their antiquated antecedents, but in many cases, they simply did not dig deep enough. This is not to discount their daring, to say nothing of their genius; nevertheless, the worldview upheld by the early moderns still rests on the cornerstones that were first set in Athens and Jerusalem two millennia prior. This is reflected not simply in the democratic character of modernity—"the *democratic* movement is the heir to Christianity"[78]—but in that of modern science as well, whose democratic and, one might add, Socratic bent is unmistakable. Though thinkers like Descartes and Bacon may have afforded science its distinctly modern direction, science's "archetype and progenitor" remains that figure in whom the conviction that nature is decipherable and reason could serve as a catholicon[79] first came to light.

> Our whole modern world is caught in the net of Alexandrian culture, and the highest ideal it knows is *theoretical man*, equipped with the highest powers of understanding and working in the service of science, whose archetype and progenitor is Socrates. The original aim of all our means of education is to achieve this ideal; every other form of existence has to fight its way up alongside it, as something permitted but not intended.[80]

Socrates bequeathed to man "a profound *delusion*" that to this day "belongs inseparably to science," namely "the imperturbable belief that thought, as it follows the thread of causality, reaches down into the deepest abysses of being, and that it is capable, not simply of understanding existence, but even of *correcting* it."[81] The "spirit of science" appealed to a particular human type, one that judged life and found it wanting. "Wherever [Socratism] directs its probing gaze, it sees lack of insight and the power of delusion, and it concludes from this lack that what exists is inwardly wrong and objectionable."[82] Socratism was a tool of dissolution, a symptom of degeneration.[83] Those who were strong and healthy, on whom life shone favorably, knew nothing of what Socrates took to be his duty and what all modern science has as its objective: correcting existence.[84]

Socrates's progenitorial role in the evolution of science ought not to diminish just how far modern science has strayed from its ancestral beginnings. That children follow paths different from the ones their fathers have set them on is a truism that needs no substantiation. It is one thing to harbor faith in the explicability of nature and in knowledge as a panacea and something else to strive at "establishing the slavery of nature" as modern science does.[85] While Socratism rests on the conviction that existence is perverse and reprehensible, what Socrates ultimately found wanting was not so much nature, but human nature. His task was how to improve man, not nature, and even if he signified a symptom of degeneration when measured against the paragons of the Homeric age and those for whom such paragons still counted as heroes, it cannot be overlooked that his concern remained something from which science turned its investigative gaze the very moment it became modern, namely virtue.[86] In doing so, the moderns lowered the aim of philosophy, sacrificing nobility for efficiency. This utter disregard for the character of man makes plain how *un*Socratic science has become. Preoccupied only with remedying nature's defects, the moderns tacitly, and sometimes not so tacitly, sanctioned the defects of man.

The lowering of philosophy's aims—its transformation from being a way of life set on ennobling man to a mode of thought designed to ease his lot—was possible only after the democratization of man had advanced far enough along. Socrates may have sown the seeds of that democratization, but as noted above, he was no apostle of democracy. Much as Athenian democracy offends modern democratic sensibilities, so too does Socratic thought. At heart, there is something inescapably inegalitarian about it. It preserves what, as a rule, democratized man finds intolerable—an order of rank. Only after that subsequent and more overtly democratic revolution took place did the concern for the common man gain sway. It was not so much Socratism that paved the way for nature's enslavement, but Platonism for the people.

No one reasonably could contend that Christianity was indifferent to man's character. That ever has been, at some level, its chief concern. But Nietzsche's point is that the human type that Christianity concerned itself with—that it, in a manner of speaking, deified—was abject. Christianity was possible only after the "noble type" had declined and "the rabble gained prominence."[87] The advent of Christianity heralded the decline of the classical world. Its triumph signified an inversion and "revaluation of all the values of antiquity."[88] Under this new specter of that paradoxical formula "god on the cross" the noble were rendered evil and all those who heretofore had been found ignoble were made good. In short, Christianity was a slave rebellion, "a rebellion of everything that crawls on the ground against that which has height: the evangel of the 'lowly' *makes* low."[89]

Like Socrates, the Christian found life wanting, but unlike Socrates, he did so not because man was deficient in virtue or wisdom but because life had been unfair. It was the "violated, oppressed, suffering, unfree . . . [those] who [were] uncertain of themselves and weary" upon whom Christianity—or more broadly speaking, slave morality—depended for its success. Suspicious of "the whole condition of man" and hostile to "the virtues of the powerful," the oppressed esteemed those

> qualities that serve to alleviate existence for suffering people . . .: pity, the obliging, helpful hand, the warm heart, patience, industriousness, humility, and friendliness receive full honors here since these are the most useful qualities and practically the only way of holding up under the pressure of existence. Slave morality is essentially a morality of utility.[90]

What the Christian wants—and this is true of modern man in general regardless of whether his faith is in God or the absence of God and, strictly speaking, is *not* true of Socratism—is a remedy to the hardships of life, to the iniquities and inequities of existence. What he wants above all is *to abolish suffering*."[91]

> Anyone who probes the conscience of today's European will have to extract the very same imperative from a thousand moral folds and hiding places, the imperative of herd timidity: "we want the day to come when there is *nothing more to fear!*" The day to come—the will and way *to that day* is now called "progress" everywhere in Europe.[92]

As originally envisioned, progress would be realized in the life to come. But it was only a matter of time before the rewards of the next life were demanded in this one. Faith in Christianity's eschatological promises could not be sustained. And the wherefore was not that natural science had confounded Christian eschatology and made faith in the coming life all but impossible, but that those teachings—or more specifically, Christian morality itself—hastened the devitalization of Christian faith. "Christianity *as a dogma* was destroyed by its own morality."[93]

> You see what it was that really triumphed over the Christian God: Christian morality itself, the concept of truthfulness that was understood ever more rigorously, the father confessor's refinement of the Christian conscience, translated and sublimated, into a scientific conscience, into intellectual cleanliness at any price. Looking at nature as if it were proof of the goodness and governance of a god; interpreting history in honor of some divine reason, as a continual

testimony of a moral world order and ultimate moral purpose; interpreting one's own experiences as pious people have long enough interpreted theirs, as if everything were providential, a hint designed and ordained for the sake of the salvation of the soul—that is *all* over now, that has man's conscience *against* it, that is considered indecent and dishonest by every more refined conscience—mendaciousness, feminism, weakness and cowardice.[94]

It was this "sense of truthfulness developed highly by Christianity" that ultimately spelled Christianity's end.[95] Christianity may have been Platonism for the people, but in this regard at least, there was something positively un-Platonic about it insofar as it espoused a will to truth without embracing the need for noble lies.[96] This "discipline in truth-telling . . . finally forbids itself the *lie entailed in belief in God.*"[97] Essentially, it was this sublimated sense of truthfulness, of intellectual cleanliness at any price, and not natural science, that spelled Christianity's undoing. Modern science was not so much the repudiation of Christian morality as it was its derivation. Thus, one could discover and promulgate truths that did irreparable damage to Christian theology and still profess to be a good Christian. What is more, one could, in good faith, attempt to reconcile those truths and the spirit of Christianity. It is true that in the end, Christian dogma could not withstand the advance of science, but ostensibly, Christian morality was none the worse for it. What Nietzsche had said of the falseness of the Christian vis-à-vis the Jew[98] is no less salient with respect to the modern scientist vis-à-vis the Christian: the contemporary scientist can feel anti-Christian without realizing that he himself is the ultimate Christian consequence.

Nietzsche harbored an abiding appreciation for modern science,[99] but that appreciation did not cloud his awareness that ultimately science rested on the self-defeating values he sought to overcome. Science was not a negation of the ascetic ideal that had brought about the degeneration of man, but rather the "*most recent and noble manifestation*" of it.[100] Indeed, it was modern science, more so than the ideal from which it was born, that cosmically decentered and displaced man and so effectively expedited the advent of nihilism.[101]

> Has not man's self-deprecation, his *will* to self-deprecation, been unstoppably on the increase since Copernicus? Gone, alas, is his faith in his dignity, uniqueness, irreplaceableness in the rank-ordering of beings,—he has become *animal*, literally, unqualifiedly and unreservedly an animal, man who in his earlier faiths was almost God ("child of God," "man of God") . . . . Since Copernicus, man seems to have been on a downward path—now he seems to be rolling faster and faster away from the center—where to? into nothingness? into the "piercing sensation of his nothingness?"—Well! That would be the straight path—to the *old* ideal?[102]

When it comes to man's self-belittlement, modern science has been remarkably compelling. But it also has been remarkably inattentive to the nihilism it has engendered. This ought to come as no surprise, seeing that it is incapable of restoring the faiths it has destroyed, to say nothing of begetting new ones to replace them. By its very nature, science is beholden to ideals it did not—and cannot—create. "Science itself never creates values."[103] "Strictly speaking, there is no 'presuppositionless' knowledge, the thought of such a thing is unthinkable, paralogical: a philosophy, a 'faith' always has to be there first, for knowledge to win from it a direction, a meaning, a limit, a method, a *right* to exist."[104] And the faith to which modern science remains wed, in spite of its pretensions to objectivity and contempt for the past, is the faith that Socrates bequeathed to posterity, a faith that Plato set down and refined and Christianity popularized for mass consumption.

On this note, at the end of section 24 of the Third Essay of *On the Genealogy of Morality*, Nietzsche counsels his readers to consult section 344 of *The Gay Science*, or "better still, the whole fifth book of that work, similarly the preface to *Daybreak*."[105] Space does not permit that preferred content be included here, but it is worth quoting section 344—"*How we, too, are still pious*"—at some length for the light it sheds on a matter that remains so obstinately obscured.

> We see that science also rests on a faith; there simply is no science "without presuppositions." The question whether *truth* is needed must not only have been affirmed in advance, but affirmed to such a degree that the principle, the faith, the conviction finds expression: "*Nothing* is needed *more* than truth, and in relation to it everything else has only second-rate value."

Whence "this unconditional will to truth," to "truth at any price[?]" What is particularly peculiar and illuminating about it is that life itself aims "at semblance, meaning error, deception, simulation, delusion, self-delusion;" that is, as Nietzsche remarks elsewhere, life requires falsification—or to put it differently, untruth is a necessary condition of life (*Beyond Good and Evil* #4). It follows, then, that the

> "Will to truth" . . . might be a concealed will to death.
>
> Thus the question "Why science?" leads back to the moral problem: *Why have morality at all* when life, nature, and history are "not moral"? No doubt, those who are truthful in that audacious and ultimate sense that is presupposed by the faith in science thus *affirm another world* than the world of life, nature, and history; and insofar as they affirm this "other world"—look, must they not by the same token negate its counterpart, this world, our world?—But you will have gathered what I am driving at, namely, that it is still a *metaphysical faith*

upon which our faith in science rests—that even we seekers after knowledge today, we godless anti-metaphysicians still take our fire, too, from the flame lit by a faith that is thousands of years old, that Christian faith which was also the faith of Plato, that God is the truth, that truth is divine—But what if this should become more and more incredible, if nothing should prove to be divine any more unless it were error, blindness, the lie—if God himself should prove to be our most enduring lie?[106]

Notwithstanding the many faiths that have withered before its advance, science's faith in that old ideal remains unwavering, and not because it has been validated, but because it has been unexamined. The questionability of truth—of the will to and value of it—is not simply unresolved; it has yet to be firmly faced. What also remains insufficiently questioned and further demonstrates modern science's faith in the old ideal is the goodness of its goal. In effect, that goal is to abolish adversity; or to put it differently, correct existence. But the biases of modern science are no less on display when one considers not just its foundations or its aims, but the manner in which it goes about measuring reality. This is well illustrated with that branch of modern science whose success has made it the envy of all other sciences: physics.

> Now it is beginning to dawn on maybe five or six brains that physics too is only an interpretation and arrangement of the world (according to ourselves! if I may say so) and *not* an explanation of the world. But to the extent that physics rests on belief in the senses, it passes for more, and will continue to pass for more, namely for an explanation, for a long time to come. It has our eyes and our fingers as its allies, it has visual evidence and tangibility as its allies. This helped it to enchant, persuade, *convince* an age with a basically plebeian taste—indeed, it instinctively follows the canon of truth of the eternally popular sensualism. What is plain, what "explains?" Only what can be seen and felt—this is as far as any problem has to be pursued.[107]

This "plebeian" way of beholding the world is contrasted with "the strong attraction of the Platonic way of thinking," which was "a *noble* way of thinking" for the very reason that it did not depend on the support of everyone's fingers and eyes. It signified a resistance to this plebian empiricism that presupposed an ability to master one's senses.[108] One might say that with that nobler way of thinking, it was mind that triumphed over matter and not matter over mind.

Modern physics' democratic proclivities are evident in the order that it imposes on the natural world. Nature's conformity, which modern "physicists are so proud of," is no matter of fact, no text, but is merely an interpretation that betrays "the democratic instincts of the modern soul!"

"Everywhere, equality before the law—in this respect, nature is no different and no better off than we are": a lovely case of ulterior motivation; and it serves once more to disguise the plebeian antagonism against all privilege and autocracy together with a second and more refined atheism. "*Ni Dieu, ni maître*" [neither God nor master]—you want this too: and therefore "hurray for the laws of nature!"—right?[109]

One could, as Nietzsche does, posit that it is not order, but a lack of order—an eternal chaos[110]—that characterizes the cosmos. "Somebody with an opposite intention and mode of interpretation could come along and be able to read from the same nature, and with reference to the same set of appearances, a tyrannically ruthless and pitiless execution of power claims."[111] At the very least, in an age that denies God's omnipotence and not infrequently, outright denies God, one should "beware of saying there are laws in nature. There are only necessities: there is nobody who commands, nobody who obeys, nobody who trespasses."[112] But verbal misuses aside, Nietzsche's point is that modern physics has not espied the character of the world so much as interpreted it in a manner that conforms to the biases of the interpreters and the prevailing predilections of the day. Seeing flux and chaos where the modern physicist imposes rule and order would be inconsistent with the central aim of modern science: mastering and possessing nature. What is more, a cosmos "governed" by an inexorable will to power would be antipathetic to the democratic proclivities that pervade modernity.[113] In the end, science does not discern the nature of reality, so much as try to interpret and make sense of it. If science is the effort to humanize the external world,[114] then modern science has taken as its measure for the anthropomorphization of nature not *Homo sapiens*, but *Homo democroticus*.

Modern science's democratic bent can be observed in another field, one that compelled a change in human posture no less radical than the change precipitated by Copernicus: evolutionary biology and more specifically, Darwinism. In his own day, Nietzsche had been suspected of supporting that school of thought.[115] It is a charge that endures,[116] and one need only peruse the prologue of *Zarathustra* to appreciate why. But it is a claim that is not fit to survive scrutiny. Nietzsche's opposition to Darwinism was in keeping with his opposition to Christianity, for reasons that on the face of it will seem incoherent: both prioritized the weak above the strong. But how can that be said of a theory whose central tenet has been distilled into the dictum—however tautological and "regrettable"[117]—survival of the fittest? An answer can be deduced from the fact that this theory, which proved so fatal to Christian dogma, turned out not to be inconsistent with Christian morality.[118]

Nietzsche's philosophy permits no such reconciliation. His understanding of the fundamental character of all life is anti-Christian, anti-democratic, and decidedly anti-Darwinian.[119] Life is not defined by the struggle for existence, that is, preservation, but by the struggle for, or rather will to, power. "Life itself is will to power—self-preservation is only one of the indirect and most frequent *consequences* of this."[120] As Zarathustra declaims to those who are wisest:

> Test in all seriousness whether I have crawled into the very heart of life and into the very roots of its heart.
> Where I found the living, there I found the will to power; and even in the will of those who serve I found the will to be master.
> [As life itself confided,] "the truth was hit not by him who shot at it with the word of the 'will to existence': that will does not exist. For, what does not exist cannot will; but what is in existence, how could that still want existence? Only where there is life is there also will: not will to life but—thus I teach you—will to power."[121]

This is not a mere matter of semantics. Nietzsche's own musings on human "evolution" are antithetical to Darwin's, a verity that has not prevented scholars from trying to adapt the one to the other.[122] When surveying the human race, Nietzsche beholds "the reverse of the struggle for existence as taught by Darwin's school"—"on top and surviving everywhere" he finds "those who compromise life and the value of life."[123] Higher types will, from time to time, arise, but the species does not rise with them nor in their wake. "The level of the species is *not* raised." It is precisely the stronger, the exceptions, who do not survive.[124] "The higher type represents an incomparably greater complexity—a greater sum of coordinated elements: so its disintegration is also incomparably more likely. The 'genius' is the sublimest machine there is—consequently the most fragile." What is more, the traits that constitute the higher types are not transmittable. "The brief spell of beauty, of genius, of Caesar is *sui generis*: such things are not inherited."[125] The outcome is the opposite of what Darwin's school postulates: "The species do not grow in perfection: the weak prevail over the strong again and again, for they are the great majority."[126] The struggle of life results in "the inevitable dominion of the average, even the sub-average types." Their dominion is not an indication of their strength so much as their ability to persist and multiply. Through "their numbers, their shrewdness, their cunning," the lower type preponderates.[127] It is the lower type that possesses greater spirit, that is, "care, patience, cunning, simulation, self-control and everything that is mimicry."[128] And as evinced by the slave revolt in morality with its inversion of values, "cunning often prevails over strength."[129] As a result, it is specious to infer from their preponderance that the extant human type signifies a stronger or higher breed. Indeed, Nietzsche goes so far as to assert that the notion "that *species* represent any progress is the most unreasonable assertion in the world." The school of Darwin has been deluded everywhere and to such an extent that Nietzsche cannot help but wonder how its adherents "can be so blind as to see so badly at *this* point."[130]

The answer lies in the biases of modern science. Darwinists see so badly at this point because they survey life through democratic eyes, but as a more impartial observer would admit, life is not democratic. A nobler science would not regard the instinct of self-preservation as decisive[131] nor would it prioritize the powers of adaptation. Instead, greater prominence would be given to those beings who fashioned the world; those to whom the world adapted, rather than those who adapted to it. But in Darwinism, one would be hard pressed to find anything noble.

> The democratic idiosyncrasy of being against everything that dominates and wants to dominate, the modern *misarchism* (to coin a bad word for a bad thing) has gradually shaped and dressed itself up as intellectual, most intellectual, so much so that it already, today, little by little penetrates the strictest, seemingly most objective sciences, and is *allowed* to do so; indeed, I think it has already become master of the whole of physiology and biology, to their detriment, naturally, by spiriting away their basic concept, that of actual *activity*. On the other hand, the pressure of this idiosyncrasy forces "adaptation" into the foreground, which is a second-rate activity, just a reactivity, indeed life itself has been defined as an increasingly efficient inner adaptation to external circumstances (Herbert Spencer). But this is to misunderstand the essence of life, its *will to power*, we overlook the prime importance that the spontaneous, aggressive, expansive, re-interpreting, re-directing and formative forces have, which "adaptation" follows only when they have had their effect; in the organism itself, the dominant role of these highest functionaries, in whom the life-will is active and manifests itself, is denied.[132]

That the slave revolt in morality impacted not just morals and values, but the strictest and most objective sciences as well attests to its astounding success. It is thanks to the ascension of the herd that the values that sustain it not only have affected those sciences but have done so surreptitiously, so that their practitioners and those who accept their discoveries as dogma can preserve the fiction that those sciences are indeed objective. As if the only way to see the world is one that explains *their* triumph and what is more, interprets it as progress, as evolution! A democratized science for a democratized world. But prioritizing the desire for self-preservation is itself a symptom of decline, "the symptom of a condition of distress, of a limitation of the fundamental instinct of life which aims at *the expansion of power* and, wishing for that, frequently risks and even sacrifices self-preservation." Thus, for example,

Spinoza not only "considered the instinct of self-preservation decisive," but *had* to see it that way, owing to the fragility of his own health.[133] The perennial precariousness of his existence brought with it the consuming desire to preserve it.[134] Nietzsche maintains that it was probably due to the origins of most natural scientists that this Spinozistic dogma was able to gain such a foothold among them.

> In this respect they belong to the "common people"; their ancestors were poor and undistinguished people who knew the difficulties of survival only too well at firsthand. The whole of English Darwinism breathes something like the musty air of English overpopulation, like the smell of the distress and overcrowding of small people. But a natural scientist should come out of his human nook; and in nature it is not conditions of distress that are *dominant* but overflow and squandering, even to the point of absurdity. The struggle for existence is only an *exception*, a temporary restriction of the will of life. The great and small struggle always revolves around superiority, around growth and expansion, around power—in accordance with the will to power which is the will of life.[135]

If the outcome of democratizing science was that thinking merely lost its prior charm or that, as Tocqueville put it, science devoted itself to the pleasures of the body rather than those of the mind, one might find little cause for concern. But insofar as science has become the predominant mode of apprehension in which humanity has placed its ultimate trust—upon which its very salvation now depends—the fate of man cannot be disjoined from it. What is at stake is not simply the manner in which man interprets the character of the world, but rather the very character of man himself. The former ever reflects something of the latter. Again, Darwinism could become gospel only in an age where a certain human type had become preponderant. But because it is gospel, it brooks no alternatives. And to the extent that it conveys a sense of progress (the value-neutrality of the word "evolution" is dubious at best),[136] it posits as the consummation of existence this particular species of man, namely the democratic one.

> Summit and target of the world-process! Meaning and solution of all the riddles of evolution come to light in modern man, the ripest fruit of the tree of knowledge!—that I call an ecstatic feeling of pride; it is by this sign that one can recognize the first-born of all ages, even though they may have also come last. Contemplation of history has never flown so far, not even in dreams; for now the history of mankind is only the continuation of the history of animals and plants; even in the profoundest depths of the sea the universal historian still finds traces of himself as living slime; gazing in amazement, as at a miracle, at the tremendous course mankind has already run, his gaze trembles at that even

more astonishing miracle, modern man himself, who is capable of surveying this course. He stands high and proud upon the pyramid of the world-process; as he lays the keystone of his knowledge at the top of it he seems to call out to nature all around him: "We have reached the goal, we are the goal, we are nature perfected."[137]

Endowed with a Darwinian perspective of life, man takes as the apogee of the evolutionary process "the ultramodern, humble moral weakling who 'no longer bites.'"[138] Those who do bite; who call into question man's democratization; who oppose ridding the world of inequality, strife, suffering, and the like, are atavisms in need of correction or, that failing, eradication. Because nobility in some form or another presupposes inequality—an order of rank—the triumph of the modern, democratic spirit augurs a de-nobling and diminution of the human spirit. It portends superintending over humanity a homogeneity that will allow no space for the richness and grandeur that once pervaded it.

This prospect does not stem from Darwinism so much as the hegemony of modern science more broadly. Not just evolutionary biology, but "*all* science . . . is nowadays seeking to talk man out of his former self-respect as though this were nothing but a bizarre piece of self-conceit."[139] It would be fatuous to exonerate science on the grounds that science merely sets the record straight; that it is nothing more than a method for apprehending the nature of existence; and that if the fact of the matter is that man's respect for himself is nothing but a piece of bizarre conceit, then man should be disabused or at any rate, science should not be rebuked for disabusing him. But that itself is a bizarre conceit that bespeaks the hegemony of the scientific mindset. Science enjoys no privileged insight into the character of being. It interprets the natural world and does so only after that world has been falsified. The "falsification of the world through numbers"[140] is a *pre*scientific phenomenon. Science "depends on presuppositions with which nothing in the real world corresponds"—number, identity, thing-hood.[141] All these "things" are constructs. Insofar as science purports to disclose the nature of reality based on these constructs, it shows itself to be naïve, if not dishonest. But what troubles Nietzsche is not that science's understanding of the world is false, but that it is superficial and stupid. And that stupidity and superficiality, Nietzsche contends with customary acridity, reflect the disposition of those who treat science as gospel—the too-easily satisfied members of "the spiritual middle class," who "never catch sight of really great problems and question marks" and lack the courage to plumb reality to its abysmal depths. Science then, particularly in its materialistic and mechanistic guise, is a prejudice, the prejudice of those who want to master the world "completely and forever with the aid of our square little reason" and reduce it "to a mere exercise for a calculator and an indoor diversion for mathematicians." But this degradation of existence is an offense, not only to existence, but to those minds whose vistas are not so narrowly circumscribed.

> Above all, one should not wish to divest existence of its *rich ambiguity*: that is a dictate of good taste, gentlemen, the taste of reverence for everything that lies beyond your horizon. That the only justifiable interpretation of the world should be one in which *you* are justified because one can continue to work and do research scientifically in *your* sense (you really mean, mechanistically?)—an interpretation that permits counting, calculating, weighing, seeing, and touching, and nothing more—that is a crudity and naïveté, assuming that it is not a mental illness, an idiocy.
>
> Would it be rather probable that, conversely, precisely the most superficial and external aspect of existence—what is most apparent, its skin and sensualization—would be grasped first—and might even be the only thing that allowed itself to be grasped? A "scientific" interpretation of the world, as you understand it, might therefore still be one of the *most stupid* of all possible interpretations of the world, meaning that it would be one of the poorest in meaning. This thought is intended for the ears and consciences of our mechanists who nowadays like to pass as philosophers and insist that mechanics is the doctrine of the first and last laws on which all existence must be based as on a ground floor. But an essentially mechanistic world would be an essentially *meaningless* world. Assuming that one estimated the *value* of a piece of music according to how much of it could be counted, calculated, and expressed in formulas: how absurd would such a "scientific" estimation of music be! What would one have comprehended, understood, grasped of it? Nothing, really nothing of what is "music" in it![142]

Modern man has reached a juncture where he takes himself to be the pinnacle of progress and regards the scientific understanding of the world as being true as such.[143] To put it more Nietzscheanly, a degenerate human type is held to be the highest and a meaningless interpretation of the world is considered the only authoritative one. The fate of man now lies in the hands of a being who longs above all else for a life without suffering and privation, without struggle and distinction, and who increasingly acquires the means for securing what he wants. Man's salvation portends his ruin.

That ruin is revealed in Zarathustra's vision of the last man, whose time draws near and whose day will be interminable. The spirit—or spiritlessness—of those who comprise this shepherdless herd is captured well by Leo Strauss: "The last man, the lowest and most decayed man, the herd man without any ideals and aspirations, but well fed, well clothed, well housed, well medicated by ordinary physicians and by psychiatrists is Marx's man of the future seen from an anti-Marxist point of view."[144] The age of the last man is the logical if not ineludible denouement of the modern longing. What the last man has, modern man wants. Far from being superlatively contemptible, as Zarathustra would have it, modern man finds the last man commendable—or at least his state enviable. This suggests, as Nietzsche recognized, that modern man is not the last—"Alas, the time is coming when man will no longer shoot the arrow of his longing beyond man, and the string of his bow will have forgotten how to whir!"[145]—but toward that end he hastens and draws ever closer.

The triumph of the modern longing would signify a flattening of the human spirit to the point of dissolution. Man, who once prided himself on having been made in the likeness of God, will, in the aftermath of His death, possess wants little different from those of an ass. Inasmuch as he will have conquered scarcity, he will, of course, be more efficacious in securing what he wants, but his highest desires will not be substantively different from those of brutes.[146] The flattening of the soul portends as much. Brutes do not have higher wants and, on account of orders of rank being anathema to them, neither will last men.[147] "Everybody wants the same, everybody is the same."[148] There will be no more exceptions. For Nietzsche, who maintained that the species has not progressed and, qua species, could not progress, the measure of man was to be found in those extraordinary individuals—the exceptions to the rule—whose possibility will be precluded in the age of the last man. When that age arrives, man would be, in Nietzsche's eyes, deserving of destruction.[149]

While Tocqueville likely would have found such pronouncements deplorable, he shared the apprehensions that gave rise to them. The "religious dread" that inspired him to weigh the fate of man whose democratization was a fait accompli should not be conflated with the nausea that afflicted Nietzsche,[150] but ultimately they had the same origin, namely the "mediocratization" of man:

> The *total degeneration of humanity* down to what today's socialist fools and nitwits see as their "man of the future"—as their ideal!—this degeneration and diminution of humanity into the perfect herd animal (or, as they say, into man in a "free society"), this brutalizing process of turning humanity into stunted little animals with equal rights and equal claims is no doubt *possible*! Anyone who has ever thought this possibility through to the end knows one more disgust than other men.[151]

Tocqueville, who shared Nietzsche's uncanny prognosticatory powers, likewise divined the prospect of man's animalization. What was to be feared most in the democratic age was that man would become small. In a passage that has a strikingly Nietzschean ring to it, Tocqueville wrote:

> I avow that for democratic societies I dread the audacity much less than the mediocrity of desires; what seems to me most to be feared is that in the midst of the small incessant occupations of private life, ambition will lose its spark and its greatness; that human passions will be appeased and debased at the same time, so that each day the aspect of the social body becomes more tranquil and less lofty.[152]

The problem is, as Tocqueville understood it, that democratic man *is* small. He can, in effect, not be otherwise. In no small part, it is his passion for equality that accounts for this. It is mistaken to believe that the principal and continuous object of democratic man's desire is freedom. What he esteems above all else is equality.[153] It is this ardent, "eternal" love for equality that touches upon the heart of democratic man. Indeed, this love is so unappeasable that, as Tocqueville incisively noted, democratic man would prefer to be equal and unfree than free and unequal.[154]

The passion for equality need not be depraved, as both Tocqueville and Nietzsche acknowledge. In the words of the former, there exists "a manly and legitimate passion for equality that incites men to want all to be strong and esteemed. This passion tends to elevate the small to the rank of the great."[155] In Nietzsche's words: *"Two kinds of equality*—The thirst for equality can express itself either as a desire to draw everyone down to oneself (through diminishing them, spying on them, tripping them up) or to raise oneself and everyone else up (through recognizing their virtues, helping them, rejoicing in their success)."[156] But this sublimated passion for equality is largely incompatible with the spirit of democracy, for it requires accepting that people are *not* equal; that some are great and some, presumably most, are not. One could contend that the manly and legitimate passion for equality can be reconciled with the democratic hostility toward rank on the understanding that the order of rank will become moot once the small are elevated to the level of the great. But this prospect is implausible. For one, the arduousness that the ascent to greatness demands is distasteful to the children of modernity, who have been reared on stories of the life to come in the here and now (or not too far off)— a life of ease and plenty, not one of hardship and austerity. The one of least resistance is the preferred path, and when it comes to spreading equality, it is easier to level than elevate. But even setting aside people's "propensity for laziness,"[157] inequality still would persist because there are some qualities that cannot be promoted to parity, perhaps none of greater consequence than those pertaining to the human intellect. "Intellectual inequality comes directly from God, and man cannot prevent it from existing always."[158] So long as there are great minds, there will be small ones, for "it is impossible, whatever one does, to raise the enlightenment of the people above a certain level."[159]

It is conceivable that a democratic people could countenance, and even celebrate, the gulf between man and man and glory in the greatness of mankind's paragons, thereby, as Nietzsche suggests, making themselves great. But again, that prospect appears dubious if not delusional.[160] To frame it in a contemporary light, equality of opportunity yields an inequality of outcomes that proves increasingly insufferable for democratic man, for the reason that, as Tocqueville so perspicaciously exposed, the desire for equality is uncompromising and "always becomes more insatiable as equality is greater."[161] Hence, the unlikelihood of reconciling the noble passion for equality with the spirit of democracy and the readiness with which that spirit embraces the degraded passion for equality.

> One must not conceal from oneself that democratic institutions develop the sentiment of envy in the human heart to a very high degree. It is not so much because they offer to each the means of becoming equal to others, but because these means constantly fail those who employ them. Democratic institutions awaken and flatter the passion for equality without ever being able to satisfy it entirely. Every day this complete equality eludes the hands of the people at the moment when they believe they have seized it, and it flees, as Pascal said, in an eternal flight; the people become heated in the search for this good, all the more precious as it is near enough to be known, far enough not to be tasted. The chance of succeeding stirs them, the uncertainty of success irritates them; they are agitated, they are wearied, they are embittered. All that surpasses them, in whatever place, then appears to them as an obstacle to their desires, and there is no superiority so legitimate that the sight of it does not tire their eyes.[162]

If intellectual equality cannot be achieved by elevating intellects, it can by leveling them. This is done by denying that any veritable inequality exists. In part, this explains why the Americans were such committed unconscious Cartesians. As Tocqueville observed, "having become nearly all the same, they all see each other from very close, and, not perceiving in anyone among themselves incontestable signs of greatness and superiority, are constantly led back to their own reason as the most visible and closest source of truth."[163] The result is that no man is wise enough to be another man's authority. This is not to suggest that all minds are equal in all respects or that there are no authorities. The modern world teems with experts of various stripes, whom democratic peoples, in good Baconian fashion, commend.[164] But in matters pertaining to how one *ought* to live, each believes himself to be his own best judge and that no man is so superior in reason that he can serve as a guide for the opinions of others.

It might seem that what ought to follow is a terrific diversity of thought the likes of which the world has never before known, but the reality is just the opposite: mass conformity on a scale never before seen. The leveling of intellects does not annul all authority, so much as it gives way to a new one. In aristocratic times, ideas were directed by great men, by either superior individuals or the reigning class. "As citizens become more equal and alike, the penchant of each to believe blindly a certain man or class diminishes. The disposition to believe the mass is augmented, and more and more it is opinion that leads the world."[165] The reason for this is perfectly logical. Because democratic man feels with pride that he is the equal of each of his neighbors, he infers, reasonably enough, that when all have the same enlightenment, truth will be found on the side of the greatest number. "It is the theory of equality applied to intellects."[166] As a result, public opinion enjoys "a singular power among democratic peoples, the very idea of which aristocratic nations could not conceive. It does not persuade one of its beliefs, it imposes them and makes them penetrate souls by a sort of immense pressure of minds on the intellect of each."[167] In this fashion, "the majority draws a formidable circle around thought." One is free to think what one wants inside those limits, but woe to him who dares to stray beyond those boundaries. "It is not that he has to fear an auto-da-fé, but he is the butt of mortifications of all kinds and persecutions every day. A political career is closed to him: he has offended the only power that has the capacity to open it up. Everything is refused to him, even glory."[168] The democratization of man constitutes an overturning of the aristocratic and, one might contend, natural order. In the age of democracy, great minds are subject to lesser ones.

Tocqueville attributes the absence of great statesmen in America to this overturning. That absence, as Tocqueville readily acknowledged, is not complete. America had the good fortune of being founded by distinguished statesmen, though tellingly, their distinction becomes less evident the further democracy advances.[169] At the time of America's founding, great intellects were able to direct lesser ones. "The celebrated men of this period, associating freely in the movement of minds, had a greatness that was proper to them; they spread their brilliance over the nation and did not borrow [their brilliance] from it."[170] It is a testament to the people's prudence that they recognized the wisdom of those celebrated men and placed their confidence in them. But in the age of democracy, such a state was something of an anomaly, a transitory moment that ran counter to the spirit of the times and hence, could not be sustained. In democracy's natural evolution, the despotism of the majority is "always growing."[171] This evolutionary anomaly can be attributed to the unique circumstances that were favorable to it, namely "the ruin of the first confederation which made the people fear they would fall into anarchy."[172] But once those fears subsided, the majority could reclaim its authority and refuse to abide those who would seek to limit it. And so the fall of the Federalists, whose "moral power was very extensive" and who "counted in their ranks almost all the great men the War of Independence had given birth to," was predestined, precisely because they were the party that wanted to restrict popular power. "[They] struggled against the irresistible inclination of their century and of their country."[173] They could not survive the Republican alluvion.[174]

The tyranny of the majority is one of the defining features of the democratic age. As the demise of the Federalists suggests, one either must defer to or be undone by it. "It is of the very essence of democratic government that the empire of the majority is absolute; for in democracies, outside the majority, there is nothing that resists it."[175] Undemocratic despotism—the preferred form that prevailed throughout history and does so in many parts of the world to this day—is but a crude arrangement that, not for lack of trying or severity, fails to subdue its subjects as effectively and comprehensively as democratic or majoritarian despotisms do. "Chains and executioners are the coarse instruments that tyranny formerly employed; but in our day civilization has perfected even despotism itself which seemed, indeed, to have nothing more to learn."[176]

The majority's absolute empire is grounded in a popular sovereignty that loosely can be likened to Rousseau's general will. While popular sovereignty in America's expansive democratic republic permits a degree of faction that never would be tolerated in the much smaller and more homogenous republic that Rousseau envisioned and moreover, legitimates an alienation of the will that Rousseau maintained was illegitimate, it nonetheless shares these principal features: it is general,[177] it enjoys a presumptive infallibility,[178] and it compels those who defy it to get on board (or go under).[179] Unlike the general will, the popular sovereignty that prevails in the age of democracy is established inadvertently. When all intellects have been leveled, the logical inference is that "there is more wisdom and enlightenment in many men united than in one alone."[180] Might does not make right, but majorities do. Not simply does the majority possess greater wisdom, but greater worth as well. This too follows from the leveling consequences that attend the democratization of man. When an equivalent value is ascribed to each individual, it follows that the greater value will inhere on the side of the greater number. Thus, "the moral empire of the majority is also founded on the principle that the interests of the greatest number ought to be preferred to those of the few."[181] But however arithmetically sound the foundations of this empire may be, it remains absolute and absolutism should not become less alarming the more popular it becomes. As Tocqueville put it, "when I feel the hand of power weighing on my brow, it matters little to know who oppresses me, and I am no more disposed to put my head in the yoke because a million arms present it to me."[182] Without genuine freedom of thought, the human mind—and humanity with it—cannot but atrophy. That absence of this freedom was prominently on display when

Tocqueville toured the United States. As he trenchantly remarked, "I do not know any country where, in general, less independence of mind and genuine freedom of discussion reign than in America."[183] To adduce countries where there might exist a greater lack would do little to contravene Tocqueville's point, particularly in this age of deplatforming, cancel culture, and political correctness, which grows increasingly intractable, illiberal, and, in a word, tyrannical. "A new face for servitude" appears in the age of democracy; it may bare the face of the people themselves, but all the same, it "is something to cause profound reflection by those who see in the freedom of the intellect something holy and who hate not only the despot but despotism."[184]

In the democratic future, Tocqueville beheld another face for servitude, what he baptized soft or mild despotism. If the tyranny of the majority is primarily a tyranny of the mind, mild despotism is more a tyranny of the body—the former an intellectual despotism, the latter a political one. They are not competing forms of despotism, but remarkably symbiotic ones. Both are peculiar to the age of democracy. And both, owing to their formidable reach, would have been the envy of all erstwhile despots.

As "a new political science is needed for a world altogether new,"[185] a new understanding is needed for a form of despotism that finds no analog in the annals of history. Tocqueville had no doubt that should "absolute power come to be established anew among the democratic peoples of Europe . . . it would take a new form and that it would show itself with features unknown to our fathers."[186] Without recourse to precedent—"the old words despotism and tyranny are not suitable"—he labored to delineate what as yet had no name.

> I want to imagine with what new features despotism could be produced in the world: I see an innumerable crowd of like and equal men who revolve on themselves without repose, procuring the small and vulgar pleasures with which they fill their souls. Each of them, withdrawn and apart, is like a stranger to the destiny of all the others: his children and his particular friends form the whole human species for him; as for dwelling with his fellow citizens, he is beside them, but he does not see them; he touches them and does not feel them; he exists only for himself and for himself alone, and if a family still remains for him, one can at least say that he no longer has a native country.
>
> Above these, an immense tutelary power is elevated, which alone takes charge of assuring their enjoyments and watching over their fate. It is absolute, detailed, regular, far-seeing, and mild. It would resemble paternal power, if, like that, it had for its object to prepare men for manhood; but on the contrary, it seeks only to keep them fixed irrevocably in childhood; it likes citizens to enjoy themselves provided that they think only of enjoying themselves. It willingly works for their happiness; but it wants to be the unique agent and sole arbiter of that; it provides for their security, foresees and secures their needs, facilitates

their pleasures, conducts their principal affairs, directs their industry, regulates their estates, divides their inheritances; can it not take away from them entirely the trouble of thinking and the pain of living?

It is the mildness and solicitude of this new form of despotism that renders it so insidious. In its traditional guise, despotism did not dissemble. An agreeable despotism was a contradiction in terms. But that is precisely what mild despotism is—agreeable. But as Tocqueville warns his readers, a despotism does not become less despotic the more gratifying it becomes.

So it is that every day it [democratic despotism] renders the employment of free will less useful and more rare; it confines the action of the will in a smaller space and little by little steals the very use of free will from each citizen. Equality has prepared men for all these things: it has disposed them to tolerate them and often even to regard them as a benefit.

Thus, after taking each individual in its powerful hands and kneading him as it likes, the sovereign extends its arms over society as a whole; it covers its surface with a network of small, complicated, painstaking uniform rules through which the most original minds and the most vigorous souls cannot clear a way to surpass the crowd; it does not break wills, but it softens them, bends them, and directs them; it rarely forces one to act, but it constantly opposes itself to one's acting; it does not destroy, it prevents things from being born; it does not tyrannize, it hinders, compromises, enervates, extinguishes, dazes, and finally reduces each nation to being nothing more than a herd of timid industrious animals of the government is the shepherd.[187]

The aggrandizement of the state looms large in Tocqueville's thought. It is a prominent theme in his earliest writings and arguably the principal theme of his last, and hence appears a more pressing and abiding issue than the more well-known problem of majority tyranny. Indeed, for Tocqueville, the state may signify the central peril in the democratic future.

A number of factors in the age of democracy lend themselves to the establishment of mild despotism. For one, there is the sheer enormity of the state. Its scope portends to be total: no part of the political and social milieu will lie beyond it. The art of administrative centralization—not to be confused with governmental centralization[188]—will be further and further perfected so that no citizen will be able to evade the yoke of the central state, which will seek to govern every aspect of life.[189] In earlier times, no sovereign could have stretched its regulatory reach so far, and not because the modern state depends on technologies that heretofore were inconceivable, but because the fabric of humanity and the character of man are substantively different today from what they were throughout history.

In past centuries, one never saw a sovereign so absolute and so powerful that it undertook to administer all parts of a great empire by itself without the assistance of secondary powers; there was none who attempted to subjugate all its subjects without distinction to the details of a uniform rule, nor one that descended to the side of each of them to lord it over him and lead him. The idea of such an undertaking had never presented itself to the human mind and if any man had happened to conceive of it, the insufficiency of enlightenment, the imperfection of administrative proceedings, *and above all the natural obstacles that inequality of conditions gave rise to* would soon have stopped him in the execution of such a vast design.[190]

What the democratization of man promised was the elevation and liberation of the lower orders; ironically, what it presages is the debasement and servitude of all.

What substantiates Tocqueville's concern is not that the prospect itself is so ominous—one could imagine any number of malefic futures that would not merit much reflection—but that the conditions for its actualization are so propitious. And, to repeat, it is not so much the character of the modern state that renders those conditions so propitious, but that of modern man. "Despotism, which is dangerous in all times . . . is particularly to be feared in democratic centuries."[191] Tocqueville was convinced that "no nations are more at risk of falling under the yoke of administrative centralization than those whose social state is democratic."[192] What renders democratic peoples singularly susceptible to the establishment of despotism is that "in centuries of equality all men are independent of one another, isolated and weak."[193] This is a natural, and, it would seem, ineluctable consequence of man's democratization. As people become more and more equal; as the intermediary powers between citizen and state are abolished; as familial ties are attenuated and religion loses its "empire over souls,"[194] each person becomes detached and "occupied with himself alone."[195] Democratic man, who feels himself the equal of any of his neighbors in isolation, "is overwhelmed by his own insignificance and weakness"[196] when he considers his place in the larger whole of which he constitutes an inappreciable part. The awareness of his own insignificance and the realization that all others are equal and hence, equally insignificant, impels those in the age of democracy to deny the influence of great individuals on the course of history and give all credit to very general ideas and impersonal forces, whether it be "the nature of races, the physical constitution of the country or the spirit of civilization,"[197] so that "humanity always seems to run by itself."[198] This perspective denies not only great individuals but whole peoples the ability to shape their destinies, leaving them subject "either to an inflexible providence or a sort of blind fatality."[199] In an age when aristocratic virtue, which once gave an extraordinary strength to individual resistance, is no more; when towns and provinces have lost their distinctive qualities and have become habituated to obeying the same laws so that "it is no more difficult to oppress them all together than to oppress one of them separately"; when consanguineous ties, which bound families together (both intra- and intergenerationally), have deteriorated, leaving each individual to himself; "when nothing can be encountered old enough so that one fears to destroy it, nor nothing be conceived so new that one cannot dare it"; in short, when each citizen is "equally powerless, equally poor, equally isolated," what good can one effect by pitting "his individual weakness [against] the organized force of the government?"[200]

The degradation of man and the aggrandizement of the state go hand in hand. As individuals grow more diminutive and disconnected, they become less capable of fulfilling their own needs and increasingly turn to the state to fulfill those needs for them. Affairs that once fell under the purview of families and communities become matters for the state to handle once familial and communal bonds deteriorate and dissolve. Democratic man's desires may be less lofty than those of his aristocratic predecessors, but they are no less pressing. Indeed, given their material bent and the hydra-like quality that material desires possess, wants tend to multiply more readily and demand more—and more immediate—satisfaction in the age of democracy.[201] As people shrink into themselves, becoming more isolated and vulnerable, they depend more and more upon the state to indulge their ever-expanding needs, which they no longer can satisfy on their own.

> It results from the very constitution of democratic nations and their needs that the power of the sovereign must be more uniform, more centralized, more extended, more penetrating, and more powerful in them than elsewhere. Society there is naturally more active and stronger, the individual more subordinated and weaker: the one does more, the other less; that is mandatory.[202]

Thus, it is not simply that the more democratized people become, the less capable they are of resisting a perpetually expanding state, but that their very existence becomes more and more contingent upon such a state. Democratic man requires a paternalistic state to sustain him much as aristocratic man required a servile class upon which to prop himself. Without it, he is nothing. What renders democratic man's dependence on the state all the more inescapable is that he does not just need the state, he idolizes it. It is the guarantor of all he holds dear, including that which he holds most dear: equality.

On the face of it, there is something incongruous about democratic man's refusal to bow before a master and the eagerness with which he prostrates himself before the state. In part, this is explained by the confluence of democratic man's pride in his own independence and the inflated sense of confidence he maintains vis-a-vis his own neighbors on the one hand, and the awareness of his own limitations and hence the limitations of all those around him on the other. Unable to expect any succor from his equals "since they are all impotent and cold . . . he naturally turns his regard to the immense being that rises alone in the midst of universal debasement. His needs and above all his desires constantly lead him back toward [the state] and in the end he views it as the unique and necessary support for individual weakness."[203]

The democratic state atones for democratic man's lack. In a world where each is isolated and weak, it alone rises above the undifferentiated crowd and in so doing, secures the admiration of the people. This is in keeping with the manner in which democratic man extols public opinion. While the opinion of no individual is privileged, that of the majority is authoritative. Similarly, while the authority of no individual (over another) is legitimate, that of the state (over all) is inviolable. In an age of equals, legitimacy—whether of opinion or power—rests on numbers or, more to the point, magnitudes. Where one finds the majority, there one finds right (which is not to say one finds it in the right). And so democratic man sees no incongruity between the pride he takes in his own autonomy and his utter subservience to a central state to which he accords "no limits" and which he firmly believes has the "right to take each citizen by the hand and lead him."[204]

This mass voluntary servitude is unique to the democratic age. In earlier times, when people were radically unalike, the idea of a central authority to which all equally were beholden was unworkable in practice and untenable in theory. When people are radically alike, it is unreasonable that the rule that applies to one should not equally apply to all. So deep-rooted and widespread is this conceit in the age of democracy that it has become axiomatic. People who are polarized on any number of political questions will find themselves in agreement on this very one. Among his own people, who at the time were more democratically advanced than any other people of Europe, Tocqueville observed that even those parties that "make war on each other most roughly do not fail to agree on this [one] point," namely "that the government ought to be acting constantly and to take everything in hand" and this in spite of the fact that most acknowledge "that government acts badly!" "The unity, ubiquity, and omnipotence of the social power, the uniformity of its rule, form the salient feature characterizing all newly born political systems of our day. One finds them at the foundation of the most bizarre utopias. The human mind pursues these images even when it dreams."[205]

These democratic dreams are rooted in the principal passion of democratic man—the passion for equality, which "holds a greater place in the human heart each day."[206] What Hobbes had said of the desire for power could be said of democratic man's passion for equality: it ceaseth only in death—of the individual or, should such a thing be possible, of inequality itself. So unslakable is this thirst for equality that the more it is quenched, the stronger it grows.

> The hatred that men bear for privilege is increased as privileges become rarer and less great, so that one would say that democratic passions are more inflamed in the very times in which they find the least nourishment.... When all conditions are unequal, there is no inequality great enough to offend the eye, whereas the smallest dissimilarity appears shocking in the midst of general uniformity; the sight of it becomes more intolerable as uniformity is more complete. It is therefore natural that the love of equality grows constantly with equality itself; in satisfying it, one develops it."[207]

Thus, it is the natural inclination of democratic "minds and hearts" to favor the general accretion of power in the central state. Because the state is "above all citizens and uncontested, it does not excite the envy of any of them and each believes he deprives his equals of all the prerogatives he concedes to it."[208] Democratic man's hatred of privilege is so inexorable, his longing for equality so ingrained, and both so conducive to the aggrandizement of the state, that it allows "the science of despotism" to be reduced to a single principle: "The first and in a way the only necessary condition for arriving at centralizing public power in a democratic society is to love equality or to make it believed [that one does]."[209]

Nietzsche's own meditations on the modern state, though more elliptical and scattered, are, on the whole, consistent with Tocqueville's.[210] The modern state—that "coldest of all cold monsters"—caters to the people's philistine inclinations in *its* interest. It hangs "a sword and a hundred appetites" over the people and in exchange for their adoration "will give [them] everything." Mendaciously it proclaims, "I, the state, am the people," but a people precedes the state and its ways and customs—what make it a people—run counter to the interests of the state. It was creators and lawgivers, not the state, who founded peoples, who "hung a faith and love over them," and thereby "served life." "Every people speaks its tongue of good and evil, which the neighbor does not understand." Every people has "invented its own language of customs and rights." But the state is a "confusion of tongues of good and evil."[211] In the democratic bedlam that overspreads the modern state, values are confounded and corrupted. The state itself possesses no higher value; its greatest ambition is its own growth and perpetuation, again, for its own sake, not the people's. It wants nothing more than to be "the most important beast on earth."[212] To that end, it tyrannizes the people, but in a manner that is consistent with the spirit of the age; that is, it tyrannizes democratically or as Tocqueville would have it, softly. It does not demand the people's fidelity, but rather, by glutting them with superfluities that they increasingly cannot do without, nurtures their dependence; superfluities that do not elevate life, but stifle and degrade it. "State I call it where all drink poison, the good and the wicked; state, where all lose themselves, the good and the wicked; state, where the slow suicide of all is called 'life'."[213]

The new idol is the epithet Zarathustra gives to the modern state and it is no mere rhetorical flourish. In his third *Untimely Meditation*, Nietzsche posits that the dissolution of the Church gave way to the modern state and that the state "wants men to render it the same idolatry they formerly rendered the church."[214] But this new idol is, in Nietzsche's view, inferior to the old.

> Let us not forget what a church is, as opposed to any "state." A church is above all a structure for ruling that secures a higher rank for the *more spiritual* human beings and that *believes* in the power of spirituality to the extent of forbidding itself the use of all cruder instruments of force; and on this score alone, the church is under all circumstances a *nobler* institution than the state.[215]

In the end, Nietzsche condemns the modern state because it heralds the diminution of man. As "the highest goal of mankind," the state signifies "a relapse not into paganism but into stupidity."[216] The aims of the state and the loftier aspirations of man are incompatible. "Culture and state—one should not deceive oneself about this—are antagonists."[217] That the state counts itself a benefactor of culture, or as it more commonly is referred to today, "the arts," should not blind one to the fact that "it furthers culture in order to further itself and cannot conceive of a goal higher than its own welfare and continued existence. What the money-makers really want when they ceaselessly demand instruction and education is in the last resort precisely money."[218] As humans devote ever more attention to political affairs, they forfeit the capacity to create anything that transcends the trivialities that are indicative of day-to-day politics.

> In the end, no one can spend more than he has: that is true of the individual, it is true of a people. If one spends oneself for power, for power politics, for economics, world trade, parliamentarianism, and military interests—if one spends in *this* direction the quantum of understanding, seriousness, will and self-overcoming which one represents, then it will be lacking for the other direction.[219]

Nietzsche surveyed his age and found his contemporaries spent. It was not that energy was in short supply. He understood, as did Tocqueville,[220] that modernity is afflicted by an excess of energy; by a continuous and frenetic ferment. "Haste and hurry [are] now universal."[221] Rather, modern man expends the greatest quantum of his energy on matters that do not merit it; he employs his loftier capacities to sate his baser appetites.

> To make society safe against thieves and fireproof and endlessly amenable to every kind of trade and traffic, and to transform the state into a kind of providence in both the good and the bad sense—these are lower, mediocre and in no way indispensable goals which ought not to be pursued by means of the highest instruments *which in any way exist*—instruments which ought to be saved up for the highest and rarest objectives! Our age may talk about economy but it is in fact a squanderer: it squanders the most precious thing there is, the spirit.[222]

The prioritizing of security and material comfort brings with it a neglect of the human soul, a neglect that is reflected in modern man's inability to distinguish higher from lower. A person who is occupied with keeping abreast of the affairs of the day is a person who pays no heed to the enduring questions that have occupied the noblest minds for millennia. Is it any wonder then that "one no longer has the slightest notion how different the seriousness of philosophy is from the seriousness of a newspaper[?]" Modern man has not only "lost the last remnant of a philosophical mode of thinking, but of a religious one as well and in their place [has] acquired not even optimism, but journalism, the spirit and spiritlessness of our day and our daily papers."[223]

While the specter of the modern state did not loom as large in Nietzsche's thought as it did in Tocqueville's, there can be no doubt that in his own way, Nietzsche apprehended the danger that the modern state poses and that his apprehension is consistent with Tocqueville's own ruminations on the matter.[224] Part of what explains the state's less prominent place in Nietzsche's philosophy is that in some ways the new idol was a matter of tangential concern. The rise of the state was a symptom of man's decline, not the cause: to relieve the symptoms without remedying the disease would be pointless. For Tocqueville, that disease was, in a manner of speaking, inoperable. Because the metastasis of democracy could not be reversed, the democratic distemper could only be palliated, not cured. To this end, Tocqueville devoted himself to educating his contemporaries, and more importantly, his posterity, about the dangers that inhered in humanity's democratization, the mild despotism of a ubiquitous central state not least among them. A people enlightened on this score would stand a better chance of resisting the encroachments of the state and preserving what Tocqueville reckoned an unqualified good—not human equality, but liberty. For Nietzsche, the problem was not the democratic state, but democratic man. So long as democratic values prevailed; so long as slave morality went uncontested, it was futile to forewarn the people about the dangers that lay ahead in the democratic future for in their minds, they were goals to be sought, not pitfalls to be avoided. That futility was immediately made clear to Zarathustra when the people of Motley Cow rejoiced rather than recoiled at the prospect of becoming last men. In an age that belongs to aspiring last persons, salvation could not be secured through the education of the people, only through their overcoming.

The remedies that Tocqueville and Nietzsche proffered are irreconcilable, that much is plain. All the same, there exists a profound concord not only between their diagnoses, but their prognoses as well. Among the many "diverse features" that Tocqueville divines in the democratic future, "the most general and most striking . . . [is] that almost all prominent points are worn down to make a place for something middling that is at once less high and less low, less brilliant and less obscure than what used to be seen in the world." Saddened and chilled by "the spectacle of this universal uniformity," Tocqueville's only solace, one to which Nietzsche had no recourse, was that God wills such a future for man. What appears decadence in Tocqueville eyes is progress in God's; what pains the former pleases the latter. "Equality is perhaps less elevated; but it is more just, and its justice makes for its greatness and its beauty."[225] But while the democratization of humanity is foreordained, it remains to be seen whether it will lead to "freedom or servitude, to enlightenment or barbarism, to prosperity or misery."[226] Should it be the latter, can one really find solace in the idea that equality in misery, servitude, and barbarism is more just? Can one really glean in such an outcome greatness and beauty?[227]

Perhaps Spinozans and God might answer affirmatively, but Tocqueville was neither. Nor, for that matter, was he a fatalist. This allowed him to maintain some hope that the democratic future would not be bereft of freedom and enlightenment. "Providence has not created the human race either entirely independent or perfectly slave. It traces, it is true, a fatal circle around each man that he cannot leave; but within its vast limits man is powerful and free; so too with peoples." Be that as it may, it is toward servitude, not liberty, that democratized man inclines. Having squandered that independence of spirit that distinguished him from all other beings, man will lose "little by little the faculty of thinking, feeling, and acting by [himself], and thus . . . gradually [fall] below the level of humanity."[228] It is this denouement that Tocqueville dreaded most.

> If citizens continue to confine themselves more and more narrowly in the circle of small domestic interests, there to become agitated without rest, one can apprehend that in the end they will become almost inaccessible to those great and powerful public emotions that trouble peoples, but develop and renew them.

When I see property become so mobile and the love of property so anxious and ardent, I cannot prevent myself from fearing that men will arrive at the point of looking on every new theory as a peril, every innovation as a distressing trouble, every social progress as a first step toward revolution, and that they will altogether refuse to move for fear that they will be carried away. I tremble, I confess, that they will finally allow themselves to be so much possessed by a relaxed love of present enjoyments that interest in their own future and that of their descendants will disappear, and they will rather follow the course of their destiny weakly than make a sudden and energetic effort when needed to redress it.

People believe that the new societies are going to change face daily, and I am afraid that in the end they will be too unchangeably fixed in the same institutions, the same prejudices, the same mores, so that the human race will stop and limit itself; that the mind will fold and refold around itself eternally without producing new ideas, that man will exhaust himself in small, solitary, sterile motions, and that, while constantly moving, humanity will no longer advance.[229]

What is this dread if not the dread of the last man, of that man "who makes everything small . . . [and whose] race is as ineradicable as the flea-beetle?"[230] It was not dread that consumed Nietzsche, but nausea—"nausea over man, over 'the rabble' was always his greatest danger."[231] It was the overall degeneration of man, his animalization into the dwarf animal of equal rights and claims, that induced Nietzsche's nausea, but also inspired his task.[232] That task was the overcoming not just of the ideal that has heretofore held sway, "but also [of] those things *which had to arise from it*, [of] the great nausea, the will to nothingness, [of] nihilism."[233]

What is disquieting is not simply that nihilism—that "uncanniest of all guests"—stands at the door,[234] but that man seems to take no notice; that he is not in the least disquieted by the fact that he inhabits an age in which "*the highest values devalue themselves*"; an age in which "the aim is lacking [and] 'why'? finds no answer."[235] "The most universal sign of the modern age [is that] man has lost *dignity* in his own eyes to an incredible extent."[236] But in an age where "haste is universal because everyone is in flight from himself";[237] where "the objective of all human arrangements is through distracting one's thoughts to cease *to be aware* of life";[238] where "work and industry . . . rage like an epidemic . . . [and] the time for thinking and quietness in thinking are lacking,"[239] what hope remains that man will weigh, with due gravity, the crisis of his age and find a way to think through it, to think beyond it? If man's greatest events are not his loudest but his stillest hours so that inaudibly the world revolves, is not man, in this time of epidemical sound and fury, rapidly approaching an age when the world will cease to revolve?

NOTES

1. "The imagination of the poets placed the Golden Age in the cradle of mankind, in the ignorance and brutality of early times. It is rather the Iron Age that should be relegated there. The Golden Age of the species is not behind us, it is before us. It will be found in the perfection of the social order. Our fathers have not seen it; our children will one day attain it. It is up to us to clear the way for them." Henri de Saint-Simon, *The Reorganization of European Society*, quoted in Frederic Ewen, *Imagination: The Creative Genius of Europe from Waterloo (1815) to the Revolution of 1848* (New York: New York University Press, 2004), 153.

2. This penchant—or "cocky faith," as Nietzsche puts it—flourishes in democratic times. In such times, "the individual becomes convinced that he can do just about everything and *can manage almost any role*, and everybody experiments with himself, improvises, makes new experiments, enjoys his experiments; and all nature ceases and becomes art." This freedom is not, in Nietzsche's view, something to celebrate. Richard Rorty miserably misreads (or misconstrues) Nietzsche when he writes that for Nietzsche, "there is *nothing* more powerful or important than self-redescription." Richard Rorty, *Contingency, Irony, and Solidarity* (New York: Cambridge University Press, 1999), 99 [italic in the original]. One thing more important for Nietzsche (and no doubt there are many things more important), is creating, not on a petty individual scale, but on a grand societal one. What the preponderance of these actors in democratic times precludes is a higher type; the "great 'architects,'" as Nietzsche qualifies them. "The strength to build becomes paralyzed; the courage to make plans that encompass the distant future is discouraged; those with a genius for organization become scarce: who would still dare to undertake projects that would require thousands of years for their completion? For what is dying out is the fundamental faith that would enable us to calculate, to promise, to anticipate the future in plans of such scope, and to sacrifice the future to them—namely, the faith that man has value and meaning only insofar as he is *a stone in a great edifice*; and to that end he must be *solid* first of all, a 'stone'—and above all not an actor!" Nietzsche, *Gay Science* (#356) 302–3. Tocqueville was not oblivious to, nor untroubled by, this restive paralysis that afflicted those in the age of democracy. See, for example, *Democracy*, "Why the Americans Show Themselves so Restive in the Midst of Their Well-Being," 511–4.

3. Tocqueville, *Democracy*, 403.
4. Ibid.
5. Ibid, 413.
6. Ibid. 403.
7. Ibid, 404. "It seems that nothing exists for modern men beyond what can be seen and touched; or at least, even if they admit theoretically that something more may exist, they immediately declare it not merely unknown but unknowable, which absolves them from having to think about it." René Guénon, *Crisis of the Modern World*, 83.
8. Tocqueville, *Democracy*, 12–3.
9. "The great advantage of the Americans is to have arrived at democracy without having to suffer democratic revolutions, and to be born equal instead of becoming so." Ibid, 485.

10. Ibid, 404.
11. Ibid, 405.
12. Ibid, 404–5.
13. Ibid, 405.
14. Ibid, 406.
15. This is a central argument of Plato's *Republic*.
16. Rousseau set that wave in motion when he posited that what defines humans essentially is their undefinedness. With his teaching on free will and perfectibility, Rousseau furnished a firm foundation to support the seemingly limitless plasticity of man.
17. René Descartes, *Discourse on Method*, 39–40.
18. Tocqueville, *Democracy*, 21.
19. Ibid, 268.
20. Ibid, 293.
21. Ibid, 160.
22. Ibid.
23. Ibid, 293.
24. Ibid, 23.
25. Ibid, 26–7. See also Tocqueville, *Memoir on Pauperism*, 40–1. The first inhabitants presumably did live from products of the hunt, but the inhabitants the Europeans encountered were not the first, a fact studiously ignored by those who consider Native Americans to be virginal autochthons. Nor for that matter were they without agriculture. See, for example, Charles Mann, *1491: New Revelations of the Americas Before Columbus* (New York: Alfred A. Knopf, 2005).
26. Tocqueville, *Democracy*, 27.
27. Ibid, 212–3.
28. Ibid, 22.
29. Ibid, 293. On the difficulty of sustaining democracy in Latin America, see Francis Fukuyama, *The Origins of Political Order: From Prehuman Times to the French Revolution* (New York: Farrar, Straus and Giroux, 2011), 355–72: "Although democracy has roots going back to the first postindependence regimes in the early 1800s, not a single regime in Latin America has had a continuous history of democratic government" (357).
30. Tocqueville, *Democracy*, 293.
31. Ibid., 392.
32. Ibid, 160.
33. Ibid, 391. That time survived into the early nineteenth century when Napoleon, following the French debacle at St. Domingue, forsook his "plan for an expanded French presence in the Western Hemisphere" and unloaded his transatlantic assets. Napoleon's "North American dream" effectively came to an end with his memorable declamation: "Damn sugar, damn coffee, damn colonies!" Christopher Blackburn, "Bonaparte, Napoleon" in *The Louisiana Purchase: A Historical and Geographical Encyclopedia*, ed. Junius P. Rodriguez (Santa Barbara: ABC-CLIO, 2002), 44–5.
34. On some thoughts why the French proved so ineffectual in their colonial endeavors, see Alexis de Tocqueville, "Some Ideas about what Prevents the French

from Having Good Colonies," in *Writings on Empire and Slavery*, ed. and trans. Jennifer Pitts (Baltimore: Johns Hopkins University Press, 2001), 1–4.

35. Tocqueville, *Democracy*, 267.
36. Ibid, 268.
37. Ibid, 35.
38. Ibid, 28.
39. Ibid.
40. Ibid, 29. And not just the whole work. Just how vital it was in Tocqueville's mind to plumb the historical record can be gathered from the following: "The search for origins even drove Tocqueville in 1833 . . . to travel to England for the first time to explore the American starting point. This growing stress on point of departure would become even more striking in the 1850s as Tocqueville planned *The Old Regime*. His initial interest was to write about Napoleon and his Empire, but he soon realized that such a project required treatment of the causes and course of the Revolution itself. Tocqueville found himself looking at the old regime in order to uncover the roots of the events of 1789 and after. *The Old Regime and the Revolution* was itself testimony to the importance for Tocqueville of the point of departure and historical circumstances." James T. Schleifer, *Tocqueville* (Medford, MA: Polity, 2018), 25–6. As Furet noted, "Tocqueville's attachment to history did not spring from a love of the past but from his sensitivity to the present"—and, one might add, the future. Furet, *Interpreting the French Revolution*, 132.
41. Tocqueville, *Democracy*, 29.
42. Ibid, 43.
43. Ibid, 43–4.
44. Those minds would include not only the new atheists who vociferously denounce religion as a rule (e.g., Richard Dawkins, Daniel Dennett, etc.), but also those who demand an ever-stricter separation of church and state (e.g., Robert Boston, Frank Lambert, Jay Wexler, etc.). On America's deep-rooted religiosity see Samuel P. Huntington, *Who are We?: The Challenges to America's National Identity* (New York: Simon and Schuster, 2004), Chapter 5.
45. The Mayflower Compact serves as fine a real-world illustration of a social contract as any. On this score, see Hannah Arendt, *On Revolution* (New York: Penguin Books, 1990), 167: "The really astounding fact in the whole story [of the Mayflower Compact] is that their obvious fear of one another was accompanied by the no less obvious confidence they had in their own power, granted and confirmed by no one and as yet unsupported by any means of violence, to combine themselves together into a 'civil Body Politick' which, held together solely by the strength of mutual promise 'in the Presence of God and one another', supposedly was powerful enough to 'enact, constitute, and frame' all necessary laws and instruments of government."
46. On the colonists' "termitelike" relationship with the forest and the "arboricide" that they committed in the name of progress, see J. C. Furnas, *The Americans: A Social History of the United States 1587–1914* (London: Longman, 1970), 28–35.
47. Tocqueville, *Democracy*, 29–30.
48. Ibid, 266–7.
49. Ibid, 43.

50. Ibid, 430.

51. On the question of freedom, see Orlando Paterson, *Freedom: Freedom in the Making of Western Culture* (New York: Basic Books, 1991), x: "For most of human history, and for nearly all of the non-Western world prior to Western contact, freedom was, and for many remains, anything but an obvious or desirable goal. . . ."

"Indeed, non-Western people have thought so little about freedom that most human languages did not possess a word for the concept before contact with the West."

52. Tocqueville, *Democracy*, 422. Reflecting on the middle class of his native France, Tocqueville found it to be "moderate in all things except in its love for ease and comfort." Tocqueville, *The Recollections of Alexis de Tocqueville*, trans. Alexander Teixeira de Mattos (New York: Columbia University Press, 1949), 3.

53. Tocqueville, *Democracy*, 429.

54. Ibid, 50.

55. Ibid, 587–8.

56. On the modern unleashing of the acquisitive and appetitive spirit, see David Wootton, *Power, Pleasure, and Profit*.

57. Tocqueville, *Democracy*, 594.

58. Ibid, 461.

59. Ibid, 434.

60. Ibid, 436–7.

61. Ibid, 433.

62. Ibid, 429.

63. While Nietzsche did not need to avail himself of it, he appeared to appreciate the merits of Tocqueville's approach. See Nietzsche, *Human, All Too Human*, 382–3: "*On the study of the body politic*—The worst ill-fortune for him who nowadays wants to study economics and politics in Europe, and especially in Germany, lies in the fact that, instead of exemplifying the *rule*, conditions actually obtaining exemplify the *exception* or *transitional* and *terminal* states. For this reason one has to see past the immediate factual data and to direct one's eyes, for example, to North America—where one can still *see* and seek out the inaugural and normal motions of the body politic, if only one *wants* to—whereas in Germany, this can be done only through arduous historical study or, as aforesaid, with a telescope." As for the unsparing solitude in which his life passed, Nietzsche's personal correspondence is littered with references to it. Here suffice it quote but one: "I feel *condemned* to my solitude and fortress. There is no choice any more. The unusual and difficult task which commands me to go on living commands me to avoid people and to bind myself to no one any more." Nietzsche to Malwida von Meysenbug (May 12, 1887), *Selected Letters of Friedrich Nietzsche*, 266.

64. Alexander Hamilton, *Federalist* No. 1, in *Federalist Papers*, 1.

65. Nietzsche, *Will to Power*, 42.

66. Nietzsche, *Beyond Good and Evil*, 80.

67. Nietzsche, *Ecce Homo*, 271.

68. Nietzsche, *Beyond Good and Evil*, 80–1.

69. Laurence Lampert, *Nietzsche's Task: An Interpretation of Beyond Good and Evil* (New Haven: Yale University Press, 2001), 158.

70. Nietzsche, *Beyond Good and Evil*, 81.
71. Nietzsche, *Gay Science*, 291.
72. Nietzsche, *Will to Power*, 458.
73. Nietzsche, *Beyond Good and Evil*, 93.
74. Ibid, 81.
75. "The general character and disposition of the Rationalist are, I think, difficult to identify. At bottom he stands (he always stands) for independence of mind on all occasions, for thought free from obligation to any authority save the authority of 'reason'. His circumstances in the modern world have made him contentious: he is the enemy of authority, of prejudice, of the merely traditional, customary or habitual. His mental attitude is at once skeptical and optimistic: skeptical, because there is no opinion, no habit, no belief, nothing so firmly rooted or so widely held that he hesitates to question it and to judge it by what he calls his 'reason'; optimistic, because the Rationalist never doubts the power of his 'reason (when properly applied) to determine the worth of a thing, the truth of an opinion or the propriety of an action. Moreover, he is fortified by a belief in a reason' common to all mankind, a common power of rational consideration, which is the ground and inspiration of argument: set up on his door is the precept of Parmenides–judge by rational argument. But besides this, which gives the Rationalist a touch of intellectual equalitarianism, he is something also of an individualist, finding it difficult to believe that anyone who can think honestly and clearly will think differently from himself." Michael Oakeshott, *Rationalism in Politics* (Indianapolis: Liberty Press, 1991), 5–6.
76. To Copernicus's fatal find, one could add the fateful discoveries of Columbus and Darwin.
77. Nietzsche, *Human, All too Human*, 69. See also *Gay Science*, 85–6.
78. Nietzsche, *Beyond Good and Evil*, 90.
79. Nietzsche, *Birth of Tragedy*, 82.
80. Ibid, 86.
81. Ibid, 73.
82. Ibid, 66.
83. Nietzsche, *Twilight of the Idols*, 474; *Ecce Homo*, 272.
84. Nietzsche, *Birth of Tragedy*, 66.
85. Nietzsche, *Will to Power*, 500.
86. Plato, *Apology*, 31b.
87. Nietzsche, *Beyond Good and Evil*, 47.
88. Ibid, 44.
89. Nietzsche, *Antichrist*, 620.
90. Nietzsche, *Beyond Good and Evil*, 157.
91. Ibid, 116.
92. Ibid, 89.
93. Nietzsche, *Genealogy of Morality*, 119.
94. Nietzsche, *Gay Science*, 307.
95. Nietzsche, *Will to Power*, 7.
96. See Laurence Lampert, *Nietzsche and Modern Times: A Study of Bacon, Descartes and Nietzsche* (New Haven: Yale University Press, 1993), 356.

97. Nietzsche, *Genealogy of Morality*, 118–9.
98. Nietzsche, *Antichrist*, 593.
99. This is perhaps most evident in the works of his middle period (*Human, All Too Human, Daybreak*, and the first four parts of *The Gay Science*), where a number of positive pronouncements on modern science can be found. But though Nietzsche is more openly critical of science in his later works, he never abjured his appreciation for it. See, for example, *Antichrist*, 627–9. In many ways, Nietzsche's criticism was directed more at scientism than at science. "Science, [Nietzsche] argues, provides neither an ultimate description of the world nor a description of the world as it is in itself. It is therefore not a practice to which all others are secondary and inferior. He does not object to science itself (see, for example, 'Long live physics!' GS, 335) but rather to an interpretation which refuses to acknowledge that science is itself an interpretation in the sense that it provides a revisable description of a part of the world which is no more real than any other. The problem has been that the methods of science have been assumed to be better than any others, and its objects have been considered to be more real or ultimate than anything else." Alexander Nehamas, *Life as Literature* (Cambridge, MA: Harvard University Press, 2002), 65.
100. Nietzsche, *Genealogy of Morality*, 110.
101. Nietzsche, *Will to Power*, 8.
102. Nietzsche, *Genealogy of Morality*, 115.
103. Ibid, 113.
104. Ibid, 112.
105. Ibid, 113.
106. Nietzsche, *Gay Science*, 280–3.
107. Nietzsche, *Beyond Good and Evil*, 15. See note 7 above.
108. Ibid, 15.
109. Ibid, 22.
110. Nietzsche, *The Gay Science*, 168.
111. Nietzsche, *Beyond Good and Evil*, 22.
112. Nietzsche, *The Gay Science*, 168.
113. Nietzsche, *Beyond Good and Evil*, 22.
114. Nietzsche, *The Gay Science*, 172–3.
115. Nietzsche, *Ecce Homo*, 261.
116. See, for example, Robin Small, "What Nietzsche Did During the Science Wars," in *Nietzsche and the Sciences*, ed. Thomas H. Brobjer and Gregory Moore (Burlington, VT: Ashgate, 2004), 155–70; John Richardson, *Nietzsche's New Darwinism* (Oxford: Oxford University Press, 2004).
117. Gavin de Beer, "Charles Robert Darwin," in *Dictionary of Scientific Biography*, vol. 3, ed. Charles Gillispie (New York: Scribner, 1971), 573.
118. Nietzsche, *The Will to Power*, 239–40. In Daniel Dennett's claim that Darwin's idea of evolution bears "an unmistakable likeness to universal acid[, in that] it eats through just about every traditional concept" one finds hyperbole and naïveté in equal measure. Daniel C. Dennett, *Darwin's Dangerous Idea: Evolution and the Meanings of Life* (New York: Simon and Schuster, 1995), 63.

119. For a sound assessment of Nietzsche's critique of Darwin, see Lewis Call "Anti-Darwin, Anti Spencer: Friedrich Nietzsche's Critique of Darwin and 'Darwinism,'" *History of Science* 36 (1998): 1–22.

120. Nietzsche, *Beyond Good and Evil*, 15.

121. Nietzsche, *Zarathustra*, 226–7.

122. It is illuminating that attempts to reconcile Nietzsche with Darwin or tease out Nietzsche's latent Darwinism require that Nietzsche be corrected. John Richardson illustrates this as well as anyone. A mere two pages into his well-reviewed *Nietzsche's New Darwinism*, Richardson makes his position plain: "By analyzing these similarities and differences with Darwinism, we can answer some of the pressing interpretive problems that arise over Nietzsche. These problems include certain obtrusively apparent *flaws* in his overall position—ways it *repels* us, whether as false or contradictory, as bad or silly. For each of those four topic areas [biology, metaethics, ethics-politics, and aesthetics] I'll stress a different such problem, and try to show that his neo-Darwinism gives Nietzsche a way to answer it. These problems will be, I hope, some of the objections or suspicions that most incline or dispose us against him" [emphases in the original]. Richardson, and he is not alone, possesses the uncanny ability to understand Nietzsche's own thought better than Nietzsche himself did. Thus, Richardson—and thanks to him, his readers too—"can conclude that Nietzsche has drawn the wrong lessons from his own central thoughts," regarding those "political lessons that we abhor." If Nietzsche only comprehended just how Darwinian his thought really was, he would not have proffered so many unpalatable teachings! Were Nietzsche to return—eternally or otherwise—and happen upon Richardson's work, the very safe money has it that he would find himself tickled, not corrected. Richardson, *Nietzsche's New Darwinism*, 4–5, 217.

123. Nietzsche, *Will to Power*, 365.

124. "Man—even the mediocre specimen—is in a sense more powerful than other species; but Nietzsche has little thought of power over others, and mankind as a whole does not represent to his mind an advance over other animals, any more than reptiles seem to him 'superior' to fish. He has in mind the 'fortunate accidents'—Socrates or Caesar, Leonardo or Goethe: men whose 'power' gives them no advantage in any 'struggle for existence'—men who, even if they outlive Mozart, Keats, or Shelley, either leave no children, or in any case no heirs. Yet these men represent the 'power' for which all beings strive—for the basic drive, says Nietzsche, is not the will to preserve life but the will to power—and it should be clear how remote Nietzsche's 'power' is from Darwin's 'fitness'." Kaufmann, *Nietzsche*, 329.

125. Nietzsche, *Will to Power*, 363.

126. Nietzsche, *Twilight of the Idols*, 523.

127. Nietzsche, *Will to Power*, 364–5.

128. Nietzsche, *Twilight of the Idols*, 523.

129. Nietzsche, *The Will to Power*, 362.

130. Ibid, 365.

131. Nietzsche, *Gay Science*, 291–2.

132. Nietzsche, *Genealogy of Morality*, 52.

133. "Spinoza was never in robust health. He suffered from a respiratory ailment for most of his life . . . and his thinness and pallor . . . were no doubt a reflection

of this." Stephen Nadler, *Spinoza: A Life* (Cambridge: Cambridge University Press, 2001), 155.

134. Hardly the epitome of health, Nietzsche's own life undercuts this argument. On Nietzsche's own overcoming, see especially, *Ecce Homo*, as well as the preface to *The Gay Science*.

135. Nietzsche, *Gay Science*, 291–2.

136. "Many modern scientists are reluctant to concede that Darwin was a progressionist, because they themselves reject progress as being too value-laden, and there is a temptation to assume that the founder of the movement shared our own perception of the theory." Peter J. Bowler, *Evolution: The History of an Idea* (Berkeley: University of California Press, 2003), 146. Proof, if ever it were needed, that the commitment to being objective does not guarantee objectivity. Darwin himself was rather unambiguous on this score, as his peroration to *On the Origin of Species* makes plain: "And as natural selection works solely by and for the good of each being, all corporeal and mental endowments will tend to progress towards perfection." Charles Darwin, *The Origin of Species*, vol. 2 (New York: D. Appleton and Co., 1896), 428.

137. Nietzsche, "On the Uses and Disadvantages of History for Life," 107–8.

138. Nietzsche, *Genealogy of Morality*, 8.

139. Ibid, 115.

140. Nietzsche, *Beyond Good and Evil*, 7.

141. Nietzsche, *Human, All Too Human*, 16, 22.

142. Nietzsche, *Gay Science*, 334–6.

143. The irony of the materialists' pride was not lost on Tocqueville. "There are many things that offend me in the materialists. Their doctrines appear to me pernicious and their haughtiness revolts me. If their system could be of some utility to man, it seems that it would be in giving him a modest idea of himself. But they do not make anyone see that this should be so; and when they believe they have sufficiently established that they are only brutes, they show themselves as proud as if they had demonstrated they were gods." Tocqueville, *Democracy*, 519.

144. Strauss, "Three Waves," 97.

145. Nietzsche, *Zarathustra*, 129.

146. On the constitutional difference in wants—in the nature of wants—between man and brute, see Strauss, *Natural Right and History*, 126–7.

147. "In the ensuing vacuum [resulting from God's death], European humanity is confronted with two possibilities, descending toward the last man or ascending toward the... *Übermensch*. The former is a rejection of the existing rank order of the passions; the latter the establishment of a new discipline." Confronted with this choice, there can be little doubt which will hold the (much) greater appeal. "The easiest and in a sense most likely is a democratic possibility in which all internal discipline or hierarchy within the self dissolves, and we simply wander this way and that satisfying our momentary desires." Gillespie, *Nietzsche's Final Teaching*, 32–3, 47.

148. Nietzsche, *Zarathustra*, 130.

149. See, for example, *Will to Power*, 544:

"The *greatest* of struggles: for this a new weapon is needed."

"The hammer: to provoke a fearful decision, to confront Europe with the consequences: whether its will 'wills' destruction."

"Prevention of reduction to mediocrity. Rather destruction!"

150. For one, Tocqueville had recourse to something Nietzsche did not—[his] faith. On this note, see Joshua Mitchell, *The Fragility of Freedom: Tocqueville on Religion, Democracy, and the American Future* (Chicago: University of Chicago Press,), 99–101.

151. Nietzsche, *Beyond Good and Evil*, 92.

152. Tocqueville, *Democracy*, 604. As Tocqueville, reflecting on audacity's decline in the age of democracy, noted, "At each instant citizens fall under the control of the public administration; they are brought insensibly and almost without their knowing it to sacrifice new parts of their individual independence to it every day, and the same men who from time to time overturn a throne and ride roughshod over kings bend more and more without resistance to the slightest will of a clerk." Ibid, 659.

153. "In the formulation 'liberty is equal for all', which essentially distills the definition of democratic liberty, the predicate is *stronger* than the noun. The extension of liberty to all members of the social body changes its meaning. The center of gravity of the social mechanism tips to the side of equality. To affirm the equal liberty of all citizens amounts to affirming equality first." Manent, *Tocqueville and the Nature of Democracy*, 23.

154. Tocqueville, *Democracy*, 52.

155. Ibid.

156. Nietzsche, *Human All too Human*, 136.

157. Nietzsche, "Schopenhauer as Educator" in *Untimely Meditations*, 127.

158. Tocqueville, *Democracy*, 51. See also ibid, 513: "Whatever the people's efforts, it will not succeed in making conditions perfectly equal within itself; and if it had the misfortune to reach this absolute and complete leveling, the inequality of intellects would still remain, which, coming directly from God, will always escape the laws."

159. Ibid, 188.

160. That dubiety is substantiated by the rise and fall of the Federalists, who "wanted to restrict popular power" and were, as a result, "always in a minority." What allowed them "to direct affairs" at the time of the founding was the widespread fear of disorder that the confederal misadventure engendered. But that fear was fated to be a "passing disposition"—and so too the deference that was accorded the few who would dare to restrict the power of the many. Ibid, 168.

161. Ibid, 513.

162. Ibid, 189.

163. Ibid, 404.

164. Ibid, 436–7.

165. Ibid, 409.

166. Ibid, 236.

167. Ibid, 409.

168. Ibid, 244.

169. The recent fall of George Washington, literal in some cases, attests as much. Soo Kim, "George Washington Statue in Portland Toppled, Covered in Burning U.S. Flag," *Newsweek*, June 19, 2020, https://www.newsweek.com/george-washington-statue-portland-toppled-covered-burning-us-flag-1512075.

170. Tocqueville, *Democracy*, 246.
171. Ibid.
172. Ibid, 168.
173. Ibid.
174. Though the defeat of the Federalists was inevitable and, when the time came, resounding, Tocqueville recognized that their efforts were not for naught. "The coming of the Federalists to power is, in my opinion, one of the most fortunate events that accompanies the birth of the great American Union. The Federalists struggled against the irresistible inclination of their century and of their country. Whatever their goodness or vice, their theories were wrong in being inapplicable in their entirety to the society they wanted to rule; what happened under Jefferson would therefore have happened sooner or later. But their government at least left the new republic time to settle in and afterwards permitted it to bear without inconvenience the rapid development of the doctrines they had combated. Moreover, a large number of their principles were in the end introduced under the creed of their adversaries; and the federal constitution, which still subsists in our time, is a lasting monument to their patriotism and their wisdom" (*Democracy*, 168–9). Given the numerous ways in which the fledgling nation had been blessed, both territorially and with respect to the character of those who peopled it, it is no small praise for Tocqueville to have considered the coming to power of the Federalists as one of the most fortunate events to accompany the birth of the union.
175. Ibid, 235.
176. Ibid, 244.
177. Rousseau, *Social Contract*, 180.
178. Ibid, 182.
179. Ibid, 175.
180. Tocqueville, *Democracy*, 236.
181. Ibid, 237.
182. Ibid, 410.
183. Ibid, 244.
184. Ibid, 410.
185. Ibid, 7.
186. Ibid, 299.
187. Ibid, 662–3.
188. Governmental centralization pertains to "certain interests [that] are common to all parts of the nation," for example, general tax laws and foreign affairs. Administrative centralization pertains to those "interests [that] are special to certain parts of the nation, such as, for example, the undertakings of the township." The difference obtains in the areas that are covered, not the manner in which they are covered. Both administrative and governmental centralization "concentrate the power to direct" the pertinent interests "in the same place or in the same hand." Ibid, 82.
189. Ibid, 654–5.
190. Ibid, 661–2 [emphasis added].
191. Ibid, 486. This point, so central to Tocqueville, is reiterated elsewhere in his disquisition on democracy, e.g., 666.
192. Ibid, 91.
193. Ibid, 413.

194. Ibid, 299.
195. Ibid, 419.
196. Ibid, 409.
197. Ibid, 470.
198. Ibid, 413.
199. Ibid, 471.
200. Ibid, 300–1.

201. "[T]he more needs a man has, the greater the likelihood that he will lack something, and thereby be unhappy; modern civilization aims at creating more and more artificial needs, and . . . it will always create more needs than it can satisfy, for once one has started on this path, it is very hard to stop, and, indeed, there is no reason for stopping at any particular point. It was no hardship for men to do without things that did not exist and of which they had never dreamed; now, on the contrary, they are bound to suffer if they lack these things, since they have become accustomed to consider them as necessities, with the result that they have, in fact, really become necessary to them. Therefore men struggle in every possible way to obtain the means of procuring material satisfactions, the only ones that they are capable of appreciating: they are interested only in 'making money', because it is money that enables them to obtain these things, the more of which they have, the more they wish to have, as they go on discovering fresh needs; and this passion becomes for them the sole end in life." René Guénon, *Crisis of the Modern World*, 93.

202. Tocqueville, *Democracy*, 666.
203. Ibid, 644.
204. Ibid, 641.
205. Ibid, 642.
206. Ibid, 479.
207. Ibid, 644–5.
208. Ibid, 645.

209. Ibid, 650. Here, a curious and unintended circularity to modern thought can be detected. The absolute authority championed by Hobbes was found unpalatable by his successors and in an effort to palliate his teaching, they proffered a limited, divided government in place of Hobbes's unlimited, indivisible one. But in the end, it is unlimited government that proves more satisfactory precisely because it is better suited to sate the desires of the people, the longing for equality chief among them.

210. Interestingly, not only does Nietzsche descry the specter of despotism lurking in the future state (particularly in its socialistic guise), but he also perceives in it a form of despotism that "outbids all the despotisms of the past." Nietzsche, *Human, All Too Human*, 173.

211. Nietzsche, *Zarathustra*, 160–1.
212. Ibid, 244.
213. Ibid, 161.
214. Nietzsche, "Schopenhauer as Educator," 150.
215. Nietzsche, *Gay Science*, 313.
216. Nietzsche, "Schopenhauer as Educator," 148.
217. Nietzsche, *Twilight of the Idols*, 509.

218. Nietzsche, "Schopenhauer as Educator," 174.
219. Nietzsche, *Twilight of the Idols*, 508–9.
220. See, for example, Tocqueville, *Democracy*, 587–8.
221. Nietzsche "Schopenhauer as Educator," 148.
222. Nietzsche, *Daybreak*, 180.
223. Nietzsche, "Schopenhauer as Educator," 147.
224. See, for example, Nietzsche, *Human, All too Human*, 112–3: "*Genius incompatible with the ideal state*—The socialists desire to create a comfortable life for as many as possible. If the enduring homeland of the comfortable life, the perfect state, were really to be attained, then this comfortable life would destroy the soil out of which great intellect and the powerful individual in general grows: by which I mean great energy. If this state is achieved mankind would have become too feeble still to be able to produce the genius . . . . The state is a prudent institution for the protection of individuals against one another: if it is completed and perfected too far it will in the end enfeeble the individual and, indeed, dissolve him—that is to say, thwart the original purpose of the state in the most thorough way possible."
225. Tocqueville, *Democracy*, 674–5.
226. Ibid, 676.
227. Paul Franco finds Tocqueville's "beautiful conclusion . . . not entirely satisfying," albeit for somewhat different reasons. See Franco, "Tocqueville and Nietzsche on the Problem of Human Greatness in Democracy," 454. That grounds for pessimism outweigh those for optimism is wonderfully suggested by Aurelian Craiutu and Jeremy Jennings when, based on Tocqueville's post-1840 correspondence with his friends across the pond, they speculate what a third volume of *Democracy in America* might look like. Craiutu and Jennings, "The Third Democracy."
228. Tocqueville, *Democracy*, 665.
229. Ibid, 616–7.
230. Nietzsche, *Zarathustra*, 129. As Franco notes, "Tocqueville's chilling portrayal of a gentle administrative despotism in which each nation becomes 'no more than a flock of timid and hardworking animals with the government as its shepherd' lacks nothing of Nietzsche's nihilistic portrait of the 'last man' except perhaps the blinking." Franco, "Tocqueville and Nietzsche on the Problem of Human Greatness in Democracy," 449.
231. Nietzsche, *Ecce Homo*, 234.
232. Nietzsche, *Beyond Good and Evil*, 92.
233. Nietzsche, *Genealogy of Morality*, 66.
234. Nietzsche, *Will to Power*, 7.
235. Ibid, 9.
236. Ibid, 16.
237. Nietzsche, "Schopenhauer as Educator," 158.
238. Ibid, 154.
239. Nietzsche, *Human, All Too Human*, 132.

Conclusion

"Where are we going? No one can say."[1] Pretensions to the contrary notwithstanding, for finite and fallible beings such as man, the future must always, to some degree, remain impenetrable. That does not discourage humans from striving to comprehend the incomprehensible. Indeed, the attempt—and temptation—may be elemental to their nature. Suspended between beast and god, prophesying may be as innate to man as it is unfathomable for those he has dominion over and unnecessary for those who have dominion over him. The sense of certainty enjoyed by those above and below—the latter from perfect ignorance, the former from perfect knowledge—consistently eludes man, in defiance of his best efforts. If the criterion of a true prophet is whether or not his word proves true,[2] then it is safe to say that throughout history false prophets have preponderated.

In spite of the often prophetic character of their ruminations, Nietzsche and Tocqueville were no prophets. Or rather, to the extent that they might be counted ones, they were antidotes to the prophets of modernity and hence, in a manner of speaking, anti-prophets. They were not mouthpieces of God any more than they were apostles of Reason or Science or Progress. They labored to forestall an end foretold, in one variation or another, by so many modern prophets. What is more, they sought not only to avert this or that denouement but any denouement. In doing so, they granted humans a sense of freedom, responsibility, and purpose that had been denied to them by so many pseudoscientific seers (Marx foremost among them) who enslaved humanity to a historical process that—such prophesiers heralded without irony—would result in its liberation. For Nietzsche and Tocqueville, humans were the agents of their destiny, not the mere playthings of it. "In human beings," Nietzsche mused, "*creature* and *creator* are combined."[3] While freedom may not be given to the former, to the latter it is integral. But the creator in man grows weak and does so because the creature in him grows strong. As a consequence, man's horizons contract.

> We often look back with condescension at the short life expectancies of people in the past—twenty-five, thirty, or thirty-five years—and proudly compare them with the doubling and tripling of life-expectancies over the course of the last few generations. In doing this, and because we are so shortsighted, we completely overlook the fact that in this same period we have shortened life tremendously. What does it mean to double or triple the life expectancy of one's physical existence when eternity has been lost? That still amounts to nothing.[4]

What vistas lie before those who have eternities with which to play![5]

As man's horizons narrow, so too does that fatal circle of which Tocqueville wrote, wherein humans are powerful and free and beyond which they are neither.[6] That too results from the creature in man becoming ascendant; from the ascension of democratic man, whose passions, ambitions, and imagination are small. As the fatal circle around man shrinks and man too with it, the day approaches when humans will be deprived—when they will deprive themselves—of mobility. What will follow is not man's annihilation, but his stagnation—an interminable stagnation of the sort that filled Tocqueville and Nietzsche with such profound dismay.

Presumably, that end is some ways off; the fatal circle has not caved in on man and the creative chaos has not been snuffed out of him. But although man remains free to chart his own course, the paths before him appear to be rather limited. In effect, Tocqueville and Nietzsche each reduce those paths to two: one leads to prosperity, enlightenment, and freedom; the other, to misery, barbarism, and servitude.[7] Or as Nietzsche would have it, the future belongs either to the last man or to the overman.

While Nietzsche's path to the overman and Tocqueville's path to freedom diverge sharply and irreconcilably, the paths to the last man and to equality in misery, barbarism, and servitude are ultimately one and the same. It is to this end that humanity triumphantly hastens. And therein lies the danger that both Nietzsche and Tocqueville espied with such prodigious perspicuity and trepidation. What filled their souls with dread fills democratic man's with delight. With the reins squarely in democratic man's hands, there is little to stop him from driving mankind off a precipice into a cavernous vacuity that will permit no escape. Nietzsche and Tocqueville sought to redirect or at least slow man's course and in this too they distinguish themselves from the prophets of modernity. Whereas Hegel and Marx foretold an end that had been all but fated, Nietzsche and Tocqueville foreshadowed an end that at all costs must be averted.

For Tocqueville, the key was to moderate democracy; for Nietzsche, to overcome it. Of the two, Tocqueville's approach appears the more prudent, palatable, and attainable. There is, according to Tocqueville, no prospect of "reconstructing an aristocratic society."[8] The future belongs to democratic man and what defines him most essentially is his passion for equality, a passion that is "ardent, insatiable, eternal, invincible." He will brook "poverty, enslavement and barbarism," but will never countenance aristocracy.[9] The providential march of history has delivered man's fate to the people and no people, left to its own devices, "has created an aristocracy at its heart."[10] But while going back is an impossibility, Tocqueville saw a way forward, one that would evade the dehumanizing denouement that distressed him so acutely. In America, he beheld a democracy that was moderated, not just in principle, but in fact. The Americans demonstrated that the democratization of humanity need not reduce man to misery, barbarism, and servitude. What allowed the American people to repel the worst excesses of democracy were a number of features that were woven into the fabric of their souls—individually and collectively. Chief among them were associational life and the art of self-government; the role of the family in general and the guiding role of women in particular; and last, but certainly not least, religion. Taken separately, each of these fosters in the democratic soul sentiments that are wholly contrary to the "dangerous instincts" that the principle of equality introduces (e.g., petty self-interest and an intemperate love of material pleasures)[11] and moreover establishes a bulwark against the despotism that menaces peoples in the age of democracy. Upon finding all these qualities reposing in a single people, Tocqueville was impelled to write the following:

> One of the happiest consequences of the absence of government (when a people is so fortunate as to be able to get on without it, a rare thing) is the development of individual power which never fails to result. Each man learns to think, to act for himself, without counting on the aid of an outside power which, however vigilant one suppose it, is never able to respond to all social needs. The man, thus accustomed to seeking for his well-being only from his own efforts, rises in his own opinion, as in the estimation of others, his spirit expands and grows strong at the same time.... But we must repeat, there are few peoples who are . . . able to get on without government. Such a state of affairs has never been possible except at the two extremities of civilization. Savage man, having only physical needs to satisfy, also counts only on himself; for a civilized man to do as much, he must have reached that social state where his intelligence permits him to perceive clearly what is useful, and where his passions do not prevent his executing it.[12]

Tocqueville may have found America's men unrefined,[13] its women unattractive,[14] and the lot of them horrid musicians,[15] but he had no illusions about which extremity of civilization they belonged to.

Early nineteenth-century America afforded Tocqueville some hope with respect to humanity's democratic future, but there can be little doubt that a visit to twenty-first-century America would dash those hopes considerably, if not entirely. Although many of the features that Tocqueville so greatly admired endure to this day, on the whole, they have not exactly fared well since he ventured across the pond. The ramparts that protect democracy from itself—from its worst impulses—have suffered a withering assault, especially of late.[16] Upon their ruins, materialism, conformism, and statism ascend to ever new heights. Once democratic man's baser instincts are let loose, there is little that can arrest their advance. This perhaps is the principal failing of the democratic palliatives that Tocqueville proffers. It is not that they are ineffective, but that they ultimately do nothing to dispel the pernicious proclivities that inhere in the democratic soul. At most, they check those tendencies, but they do not correct them. As a result, there is something tenuous about their place in a democratic society. Like the Federalists who "struggled against the irresistible inclination of their century and of their country,"[17] it would seem that in the end, such mitigatory dams and dikes are unable to withstand the inundatory tides of democracy. In the wake of their erosion, mankind will be drowned in shallow waters.[18]

Upon reflection, then, tempering the democratic spirit is not enough; what is needed is its overcoming. This was Nietzsche's understanding and his task. So long as democracy prevails, the decline of man and rise of the last man rise are inescapable. Democratic man proves to be the ebb of this great flood that is life, for he is incapable of creating anything beyond himself.[19] In his mind, he is an evolutionary apex, the consummation of history. In his hostility to all overcoming, he proves himself hostile to life, for that is what life is—overcoming. Nietzsche's task was to revaluate those values that were so inimical to life and thereby redeem man from the decadent nihilism that democratic man naïvely ushers in. He aimed to "translate humanity back into nature,"[20] an aim antithetical to the quintessentially modern ambition to conquer nature and, as it were, translate man out of it. This meant honoring life for what it is essentially—will to power—and embracing all the suffering, hardship, and inequality that naturally attend it and without which there can be no lasting greatness and meaningful growth. It also meant overcoming the spirit of revenge, which Nietzsche believed to be the latent and animating spirit of democracy[21] and the subject of man's best reflection so far.[22] That overcoming is embodied in Nietzsche's teaching on the eternal return—the "highest formula of affirmation that is at all attainable"[23] and "the ideal of the most high-spirited, vital, world-affirming individual, who has learned not just to accept and go along with what was and what is, but who wants it again *just as it was and is* through all eternity, insatiably shouting da capo not just to himself but to the whole play and performance."[24] This teaching is reserved for the philosopher of the future, whose "soul . . . has the longest ladder and reaches down deepest";[25] "the man of the most comprehensive responsibility, whose conscience bears the weight of the overall development of humanity."[26] This philosopher of the future, this "redeeming man of great love and contempt"[27] will create values, new values, ones that, while anathema to the spirit of democracy, will conduce to the affirmation of life and cultivation of the species.

That teaching cannot be reconciled with democratic values, a verity that continues to elude those who tendentiously labor to do just that. But Nietzsche's task is, by his own admission, "insane."[28] It hinges on the future coming of *his* philosophical legislators and commanders, of the *Übermensch*, of "the Roman Caesar with the soul of Christ,"[29] of which there is, to put it mildly, hardly any guarantee. Thus, those who, in reading Nietzsche and Tocqueville, apprehend the magnitude of the crisis to which they point and grasp something of the dread that so deeply disquieted them, are confronted with a seemingly hopeless alternative: either the apparently futile task of moderating democracy or the ostensibly impossible task of overcoming it. Those who would lose heart in the face of this alternative would do well to keep in mind that the solution to any problem presupposes an awareness of the problem. If there is to be any prospect of turning away that uncanniest of guests, that awareness must be preserved, particularly in the age of democracy, whose partisans remain studiously and insouciantly inattentive to the crisis of their age. In the minds of such partisans, "the cure for the evils of democracy is more democracy."[30] For those who think it folly to administer as a cure for a disease the disease itself, the real danger at this juncture is not despair, but resignation.

Among Nietzsche and Tocqueville's many virtues, it is not their least that while providing ample reasons to despair, they encourage their readers—by the lives they led no less than the ideas they left behind—not to succumb to it.

NOTES

1. Tocqueville, *Democracy*, 6.
2. Deuteronomy 18:22.
3. Nietzsche, *Beyond Good and Evil*, 117.
4. Imhof, *Lost Worlds*, 171.
5. Tocqueville maintains that "belief in an immaterial and immortal principle . . . is . . . necessary to the greatness of man." *Democracy*, 520.
6. Tocqueville, *Democracy*, 665.
7. Ibid, 676.
8. Ibid, 666.
9. Ibid, 482.

10. Ibid, 383.
11. Ibid, 419.
12. Quoted in George Wilson Pierson, *Tocqueville in America* (Baltimore: Johns Hopkins University Press, 1996), 382–3.
13. Ibid, 70.
14. Ibid, 320.
15. Ibid, 142–3.
16. While the extent of the damage, as well as the reasons for and impacts of it, are open to debate, it has been well established that extensive damage has occurred. Literature on these topics abounds. By way of cursory evidence, see, for example, Joint Economic Committee, "What We Do Together: The State of Associational Life in America," *Social Capital Project Report* No. 1–17 (May 2017): https://www.jec.senate.gov/public/vendor/_skins/jec2018/images/social_capital_project/051517/what-we-do-together.pdf; Kay S. Hymowitz, "Alone: The Decline of the Family has Unleashed an Epidemic of Loneliness," *City Journal*, Spring 2019, https://www.city-journal.org/decline-of-family-loneliness-epidemic; Pew Research Center, "In U.S., Decline of Christianity Continues at Rapid Pace," October 17, 2019, https://www.pewforum.org/2019/10/17/in-u-s-decline-of-christianity-continues-at-rapid-pace/.
17. Tocqueville, *Democracy*, 168.
18. "Thus all this past is abandoned: for one day the rabble might become master and drown all time in shallow waters." Nietzsche, *Zarathustra*, 314.
19. Ibid, *Zarathustra*, 124.
20. Nietzsche, *Beyond Good and Evil*, 123.
21. Nietzsche, *Zarathustra*, 211–14.
22. Ibid, 252.
23. Nietzsche, *Ecce Homo*, 295.
24. Nietzsche, *Beyond Good and Evil*, 50–1.
25. Nietzsche, *Zarathustra*, 320.
26. Nietzsche, *Beyond Good and Evil*, 54.
27. Nietzsche, *Genealogy of Morality*, 66.
28. Nietzsche, *Beyond Good and Evil*, 123.
29. Nietzsche, *Will to Power*, 513.
30. H. L. Mencken, *Notes on Democracy* (New York: Dissident Books, 2009), 29.

Bibliography

Andress, David. *The Terror: The Merciless War for Freedom in Revolutionary France*. New York: Farrar, Straus and Giroux, 2005.
Ansell-Pearson, Keith. *An Introduction to Nietzsche as Political Thinker*. New York: Cambridge University Press, 1994.
Appel, Frederick. *Nietzsche Contra Democracy*. Ithaca, NY: Cornell University Press, 1999.
Appiah, Kwame Anthony. *The Lies that Bind: Rethinking Identity*. New York: Liveright Publishing, 2018.
Arendt, Hannah. *On Revolution*. New York: Penguin Books, 1990.
Ariès, Philippe. *Western Attitudes toward Death from the Middle Ages to the Present*. Translated by Patricia Ranum. Baltimore, MD: Johns Hopkins University Press, 1975.
Aristophanes. *The Clouds*. In *Four Texts on Socrates*. Translated by Thomas G. West, and Grace Starry West. Ithaca, NY: Cornell University Press, 1995.
Aristotle. *The Complete Works of Aristotle*. 2 vols. Edited by Jonathan Barnes. Princeton, NJ: Princeton University Press, 1995.
_____. *The Politics*. Translated by Carnes Lord. Chicago, IL: University of Chicago Press, 1985.
Aron, Raymond. *Main Currents in Sociological Thought*. 2 vols. New Brunswick, NJ: Transaction Publishers, 1998.
Aschheim, Steven E. *The Nietzsche Legacy in Germany: 1890–1990*. Berkeley, CA: University of California Press, 1992.
Bacon, Francis. *Essays, Advancement of Learning, New Atlantis, and Other Pieces*. Edited by R. F. Jones. New York: Odyssey Press, 1937.
Bakhtin, Mikhail. *Problems of Dostoevsky's Poetics*. Translated by Caryl Emerson. Minneapolis, MN: University of Minnesota Press, 1984.
Ball, Walter William Rouse. *A Short Account of the History of Mathematics*. London: Macmillan and Co., 1908.

Barzun, Jacques. *From Dawn to Decadence: 1500 to the Present: 500 Years of Western Cultural Life.* New York: Harper Collins, 2000.
Becker, Jasper. *Hungry Ghosts: Mao's Secret Famine.* New York: The Free Press, 1996.
Beer, Gavin de. "Charles Robert Darwin." In *Dictionary of Scientific Biography.* 16 vols. Edited by Charles Gillispie, 3:565–76. New York: Scribner, 1971.
Blackburn, Christopher. "Bonaparte, Napoleon." In *The Louisiana Purchase: A Historical and Geographical Encyclopedia,* edited by Junius P. Rodriguez, 43–45. Santa Barbara, CA: ABC-CLIO, 2002.
Blake, William. *The Marriage of Heaven and Hell.* New York: Oxford University Press, 1975.
Bloch, Marc. *French Rural History: An Essay on its Basic Characteristics.* Translated by Janet Sondeheimer. Berkeley, CA: University of California Press, 1956.
Bloom, Allan. *The Closing of the American Mind.* New York: Simon and Schuster, 1987.
_____. *Giants and Dwarfs: Essays 1960–1990.* New York: Simon and Schuster, 1990.
_____. "Rousseau's Critique of Liberal Constitutionalism." In *The Legacy of Rousseau,* edited by Clifford Orwin, and Nathan Tarcov, 143–67. Chicago, IL: University of Chicago Press, 1997.
Boesche, Roger. "Hedonism and Nihilism: The Predictions of Tocqueville and Nietzsche." In *Tocqueville's Road Map: Methodology, Liberalism, Revolution, and Despotism,* 127–47. Lanham, MD: Lexington Books, 2006.
Bolkestein, H. "The Exposure of Children at Athens and the ἐγχυτρίστριαι." *Classical Philology* 17, no. 3 (1922): 222–39.
Boorstin, Daniel J. *The Discoverers: A History of Man's Search to Know his World and Himself.* New York: Random House, 1983.
Bowler, Peter J. *Evolution: The History of an Idea.* Berkeley, CA: University of California Press, 2003.
Brobjer, Thomas H. "Nietzsche's Magnum Opus." *History of European Ideas* 32, no. 3 (2006): 278–94.
Brogan, Hugh. *Alexis de Tocqueville: A Life.* New Haven, CT: Yale University Press, 2007.
Brown, Peter. *The Ransom of the Soul: Afterlife and Wealth in Early Western Christianity.* Cambridge, MA: Harvard University Press, 2015.
Call, Lewis. "Anti-Darwin, Anti Spencer: Friedrich Nietzsche's Critique of Darwin and 'Darwinism.'" *History of Science* 36 (1998): 1–22.
Cassier, Ernst. *Kant's Life and Thought.* New Haven, CT: Yale University Press, 1981.
_____. *Rousseau, Kant, Goethe: Two Essays.* Princeton, NJ: Princeton University Press, 1970.
Cate, Curtis. *Friedrich Nietzsche.* London: Hutchinson, 2002.
Ceaser, James W. *Liberal Democracy and Political Science.* Baltimore, MD: Johns Hopkins University Press, 1990.

Cicero. *Cicero's Tusculan Disputations: Also Treatises on the Nature of the Gods, and on the Commonwealth*. New York: Harpers and Brothers, 1877.

Cobban, Alfred. Review of *The Vendée: A Sociological Analysis of the Counterrevolution of 1793*, by Charles Tilly. *History and Theory* 5, no. 2 (1966): 198–201.

Cohen, H. Floris. *The Scientific Revolution: A Historiographical Inquiry*. Chicago, IL: University of Chicago Press, 1994.

Compton, Todd M. *Victim of the Muses: Poet as Scapegoat, Warrior and Hero in Greco-Roman and Indo-European Myth and History*. Washington, DC: Center for Hellenic Studies, 2006.

Connolly, William E. *Identity/Difference: Democratic Negotiations of Political Paradox*. Minneapolis, MN: University of Minnesota Press, 2002.

Copleston, Fredrick. *A History of Philosophy*. 11 vols. Garden City, NY: Image Books, 1964.

Craiutu, Aurelian. "Tocqueville's Paradoxical Moderation." *The Review of Politics* 67, no. 4 (Autumn 2005): 599–629.

———. "Tocqueville and the Political Thought of the French Doctrinaires (Guizot, Royer-Collard, Rémusat)." *History of Political Thought* 20, no. 3 (1999): 456–93.

Craiutu, Aurelian, and Jerry Jennings. "The Third *Democracy*: Tocqueville's Views of America after 1840." In *Tocqueville on America After 1840: Letters and Other Writings*. Edited and translated by Aurelian Craiutu and Jeremy Jennings, 1–39. New York: Cambridge University Press, 2009.

Crook, Malcolm. *Elections in the French Revolution*. New York: Cambridge University Press, 1996.

Dalrymple, Theodore. *In Praise of Prejudice: The Necessity of Preconceived Ideas*. New York: Encounter Books, 2007.

Damrosch, Leo. *Jean-Jacques Rousseau: Restless Genius*. New York: Houghton Mifflin Harcourt, 2005.

Dannhauser, Werner J. *Nietzsche's View of Socrates*. Ithaca, NY: Cornell University Press, 1974.

Darwin, Charles. *The Origin of Species*. 2 vols. New York: D. Appleton and Co., 1896.

Daston, Lorraine. "When Science went Modern." *The Hedgehog Review* 18, no. 3 (Fall 2016). https://hedgehogreview.com/issues/the-cultural-contradictions-of-modern-science/articles/when-science-went-modern.

Dawson, Christopher. *The Gods of Revolution*. New York: New York University Press, 1972.

Dennett, Daniel C. *Darwin's Dangerous Idea: Evolution and the Meanings of Life*. New York: Simon and Schuster, 1995.

Descartes, René. *Discourse on Method*. Translated by Laurence J. Lafleur. New York: Macmillan, 1956.

Detwiler, Bruce. *Nietzsche and the Politics of Aristocratic Radicalism*. Chicago, IL: University of Chicago Press, 1990.

Donlan, Walter. *The Aristocratic Ideal and Selected Papers*. Wauconda, IL: Bolchazy-Carducci Publishers, 1999.

Dostoevsky, Fyodor. *A Writer's Diary*. 2 vols. Translated by Kenneth Lantz. Evanston, IL: Northwestern University Press, 1994.

Doyle, William. *Origins of the French Revolution*. New York: Oxford University Press, 1988.
Drescher, Seymour. *Dilemmas of Democracy: Tocqueville and Modernization*. Pittsburgh, PA: University of Pittsburgh Press, 1968.
———. "Tocqueville's Two Democracies." *Journal of the History of Ideas* 25, no. 2 (1964): 201–16.
Drochon, Hugo. *Nietzsche's Great Politics*. Princeton, NJ: Princeton University Press, 2016.
Durant, Will. *The Story of Civilization*. 11 vols. New York: Simon and Schuster, 1950.
Edelstein, Ludwig. *The Idea of Progress in Classical Antiquity*. Baltimore, MD: Johns Hopkins University Press, 1967.
Eksteins. Modris. *Rites of Spring: The Great War and the Birth of the Modern Age*. New York: Houghton Mifflin Company, 2000.
Engels, Friedrich. *Socialism: Utopian and Scientific*. Translated by Edward Aveling. New York: Cosimo, 2008.
Epstein, Joseph. *Alexis de Tocqueville: Democracy's Guide*. New York: Harper Collins, 2006.
Else, Gerald F. *Aristotle's Poetics: The Argument*. Cambridge, MA: Harvard University Press, 1957.
Ewen, Frederic. *Imagination: The Creative Genius of Europe from Waterloo (1815) to the Revolution of 1848*. New York: New York University Press, 2004.
Febvre, Lucien, and Henri-Jean Martin. *The Coming of the Book: The Impact of Printing: 1450–1800*. London: NLB, 1976.
Finley, M. I. *The World of Odysseus*. New York: The New York Review of Books, 2002.
Force, Pierre. "Philosophes." In *Encyclopedia of Political Theory*. 3 vols. Edited by Mark Bevir, 3:1039. Los Angeles, CA: Sage Publications, 2010.
Foresman, Galen E. "Hell as Punishment: Pitfalls for the Pit." In *The Concept of Hell*, edited by Robert Arp, and Benjamin McCraw, 83–98. New York: Palgrave Macmillan, 2015.
Franco, Paul. "Tocqueville and Nietzsche on the Problem of Human Greatness in Democracy." *The Review of Politics* 76, no. 3 (2014): 439–67.
Frankfort, Henri, and Henrietta A. *The Intellectual Adventure of Ancient Man*. Chicago, IL: University of Chicago Press, 1977.
Fukuyama, Francis. "At the 'End of History' Still Stands Democracy." *The Wall Street Journal*, June 6, 2014. https://www.wsj.com/articles/at-the-end-of-history-still-stands-democracy-1402080661.
———. "The End of History?" *The National Interest* 16 (Summer 1989): 3–18.
———. *The End of History and the Last Man*. New York: Harper Perennial, 1993.
———. *Identity: The Demand for Dignity and the Politics of Resentment*. New York: Farrar, Straus and Giroux, 2018.
———. *The Origins of Political Order: From Prehuman Times to the French Revolution*. New York: Farrar, Straus and Giroux, 2011.
———. *Our Posthuman Future: Consequences of the Biotechnology Revolution*. New York: Farrar, Straus and Giroux, 2002.

Furet, François. "The Intellectual Origins of Tocqueville's Thought." *The Tocqueville Review* 7 (1985/1986): 117–29.

———. *Interpreting the French Revolution*. New York: Cambridge University Press, 1986.

———. *Revolutionary France: 1770–1880*. Translated by Antonia Nevil. Cambridge, MA: Blackwell, 1992.

Furnas, J. C. *The Americans: A Social History of the United States 1587–1914*. London: Longman, 1970.

Gannett, Jr., Robert T. *Tocqueville Unveiled: The Historian and his Sources for the Old Regime and the Revolution*. Chicago, IL: University of Chicago Press, 2003.

Garrard, Graeme. "Nietzsche for and against the Enlightenment." *The Review of Politics* 70, no. 4 (Fall 2008): 595–608.

Gibbons, Edward. *Decline and Fall of the Roman Empire*. 6 vols. New York: Alfred A. Knopf, 1993.

Gillespie, Michael Allen. *Nietzsche's Final Teaching*. Chicago, IL: University of Chicago Press, 2017.

Godechot, Jacques. *The Counter-Revolution Doctrine and Action: 1789–1804*. Translated by Salvator Attanasio. Princeton, NJ: Princeton University Press, 1981.

Grant, Edward. *The Foundations of Modern Science in the Middle Ages: Their Religious, Institutional, and Intellectual Contexts*. New York: Cambridge University Press, 1998.

Greenblatt, Stephen. *The Swerve: How the World Became Modern*. New York: W. W. Norton, 2011.

Guénon, René. *Crisis of the Modern World*. Hillsdale, NY: Sophia Perennis, 2004.

Hadot, Pierre. *The Veil of Isis*. Translated by Michael Chase. Cambridge, MA: Harvard University Press, 2006.

———. *What is Ancient Philosophy?* Cambridge, MA: Harvard University Press, 2002.

Hamilton, Alexander, John Jay, and James Madison. *The Federalist Papers*. Edited by Clinton Rossiter. New York: Mentor, 1999.

———. *Hamilton: Writings*. New York: The Library of America, 2001.

Hanson, J. W. *Universalism: The Prevailing Doctrine of the Christian Church during its First 500 Years*. Boston, MA: Universalist Publishing House, 1899.

Hassner, Pierre. "Georg W. F. Hegel." *History of Political Philosophy*. Edited by Leo Strauss, and Joseph Cropsey. Chicago, IL: University of Chicago Press, 1987.

Hatab, Lawrence J. *A Nietzschean Defense of Democracy*. Chicago, IL: Open Court, 1995.

Hegel, Georg Wilhelm Friedrich. *Lectures on the Philosophy of World History. Volume 1: Manuscripts of the Introduction and the Lectures of 1822–3*. Edited and translated by Robert F. Brown, and Peter C. Hodgson with the assistance of William G. Geuss. Oxford: Oxford University Press, 2011.

———. *Phenomenology of Spirit*. Translated by A. V. Miller. New York: Oxford University Press, 1977.

———. *The Philosophy of History*. Translated by J. Sebree. Mineola, NY: Dover, 1956.

———. *The Philosophy of Right*. Translated by T. M. Knox. New York: Oxford University Press, 1967.
Herodotus. *The Histories*. Translated by Aubrey de Sélincourt. New York: Penguin, 1996.
Herr, Richard. *Tocqueville and the Old Regime*. Princeton, NJ: Princeton University Press, 1962.
Hess, Moses. *Moses Hess: The Holy History of Mankind and Other Writings*. Edited and translated by Shlomo Avineri. New York: Cambridge University Press, 2004.
Hesiod. *The Works and Days; Theogony; The Shield of Herakles*. Translated by Richard Lattimore. Ann Arbor, MI: University of Michigan Press, 1991.
Hibbert, Christopher. *The Days of the French Revolution*. New York: Harper Perennial, 1999.
Hobbes, Thomas. *On the Citizen*. Edited and translated by Richard Tuck, and Michael Silverthorne. New York: Cambridge University Press, 1998.
———. *The Elements of Law in Three-Text Edition of Thomas Hobbes's Political Theory*. Edited by Deborah Baumgolden. New York: Cambridge, 2017.
———. *Leviathan*. Edited by David Johnston. New York: W.W. Norton, 2020.
Hollander, Paul. *The End of Commitment: Intellectuals, Revolutionaries, and Political Morality in the Twentieth Century*. Chicago, IL: Ivan R. Dee, 2006.
———. *From Benito Mussolini to Hugo Chavez: Intellectuals and a Century of Political Hero Worship*. Cambridge: Cambridge University Press, 2016.
Hollingdale, R. J. *Nietzsche: The Man and his Philosophy*. New York: Cambridge University Press, 1999.
Honig, Bonnie. *Political Theory and the Displacement of Politics*. Ithaca, NY: Cornell University Press, 1992.
Hook, La Rue van. "The Exposure of Infants at Athens." *Transactions and Proceedings of the American Philological Association* 51 (1920): 134–45.
Hornblower, Simon, and Anthony Spawforth, eds. *The Oxford Classical Dictionary*. 3rd ed. New York: Oxford University Press, 1996.
Huntington, Samuel P. *Who are We?: The Challenges to America's National Identity*. New York: Simon and Schuster, 2004.
Huxley, Aldous Huxley. *The Doors of Perception and Heaven and Hell*. New York: Harper and Row, 1990.
———. *Grey Eminence*. London: Vintage Books, 2005.
———. *Huxley and God: Essays on Religious Experience*. New York: Crossroad Publishing, 2003.
Huyler, Jerome. *Locke in America: The Moral Philosophy of the Founding Era*. Lawrence, KS: University of Kansas Press, 1995.
Hymowitz, Kay S. "Alone: The Decline of the Family has Unleashed an Epidemic of Loneliness." *City Journal*, Spring 2019. https://www.city-journal.org/decline-of-family-loneliness-epidemic.
Imhof, Arthur E. *Lost Worlds: How Our European Ancestors Coped with Everyday Life and Why Life Is So Hard Today*. Charlottesville, VA: The University of Virginia Press, 1996.

Jaki, Stanley L. *Angels, Apes, and Men.* Peru, IL: Sherwood Sugden and Company, 1990.
Jardin, André. *Tocqueville: A Biography.* Translated by L. Davis. New York: Farrar Straus Grioux, 1988.
Johnson, Paul. *Modern Times: The World from the Twenties to the Eighties.* New York: Harper and Row, 1985.
Johnston, David. "Hobbes's Mortalism." *History of Political Thought* 10, no. 4 (1989): 647–63.
Joint Economic Committee. "What We Do Together: The State of Associational Life in America." *Social Capital Project Report* No. 1–17 (May 2017): https://www.jec.senate.gov/public/vendor/_skins/jec2018/images/social_capital_project/051517/what-we-do-together.pdf.
Kant, Immanuel. *Critique of Practical Reason.* Translated by Thomas Kingsmill Abbott. Mineola, NY: Dover Publications, 2004.
———. *Critique of Pure Reason.* Translated by Norman Kemp Smith. New York: Bedford/St. Martin's, 1965.
———. *Groundwork of the Metaphysics of Morals.* Translated by H. J. Paton. New York: Harper and Row, 1964.
———. *Kant: Political Writings.* Edited by H. S. Reiss. Translated by H. B. Nisbet. New York: Cambridge University Press, 1991.
———. *Prolegomena to any Future Metaphysics.* New York: Macmillan Publishing Co., 1987.
———. "On a Supposed Right to Lie because of Philanthropic Concerns." In *Grounding for the Metaphysics of Morals.* Translated by James W. Ellington. Indianapolis, IN: Hackett Publishing, 1993.
Kaufmann, Walter. "Nietzsche's Admiration for Socrates." *Journal of the History of Ideas* 9, no. 4 (1948): 472–91.
———. *Nietzsche: Philosopher, Psychologist, Antichrist.* Princeton, NJ: Princeton University Press, 1974.
Kemiläinen, Aira. "The Idea of Patriotism During the First Years of the French Revolution." *History of European Ideas* 11, no. 1–6 (1989): 11–19.
Kierkegaard, Søren. *Fear and Trembling.* Translated by Alastair Hannay. New York: Penguin Books, 1985.
Kim, Soo. "George Washington Statue in Portland Toppled, Covered in Burning U.S. Flag." *Newsweek*, June 19, 2020. https://www.newsweek.com/george-washington-statue-portland-toppled-covered-burning-us-flag-1512075.
Kojève, Alexandre. *Introduction to the Reading of Hegel: Lectures on the Phenomenology of Spirit.* Ithaca, NY: Cornell University Press, 1980.
Krass, Peter. *Ignorance, Confidence, and Filthy Rich Friends: The Business Adventures of Mark Twain, Chronic Speculator and Entrepreneur.* Hoboken, NJ: John Wiley and Sons, 2007.
Krell, David Farrell, and Donald Bates. *The Good European: Nietzsche's Work Sites in Word and Image.* Chicago, IL: University of Chicago Press, 1999.
Lamberti, Jean-Claude. *Tocqueville and the Two Democracies.* Translated by Arthur Goldhammer. Cambridge, MA: Harvard University Press, 1989.

Lampert, Laurence. *How Philosophy Became Socratic: A Study of Plato's Protagoras, Charmides, and Republic*. Chicago, IL: University of Chicago Press, 2010.

———. *Nietzsche and Modern Times*. New Haven, CT: Yale University Press, 1995.

———. *Nietzsche's Task: An Interpretation of Beyond Good and Evil*. New Haven, CT: Yale University Press, 2001.

Laslett, Peter. *The World We Have Lost: England Before the Industrial Age*. New York: Charles Scribner's Sons, 1965.

Lawler, Peter Augustine. *Democracy and its Friendly Critics*. Lanham, MD: Lexington Books, 2004.

———. *The Restless Mind: Alexis de Tocqueville on the Origin and Perpetuation of Human Liberty*. Lanham, MD: Rowman and Littlefield, 1993.

Lessing, Gotthold Ephraim. *Lessing's Theological Writings: Selections in Translation*. Stanford, CA: Stanford University Press, 1957.

Lilla, Mark. *The Reckless Mind: Intellectuals in Politics*. New York: New York Review of Books, 2016.

Lincoln, Abraham. *Abraham Lincoln: Great Speeches*. Mineola, NY: Dover Publications, 1991.

Lloyd, G. E. R. *Early Greek Science: Thales to Aristotle*. New York: W. W. Norton, 1974.

Locke, John. *An Essay Concerning Human Understanding*. London: William Baynes and Son, 1823.

———. *Two Treatises of Government*. Edited by Peter Laslett. New York: Cambridge University Press, 2003.

Löwith, Karl. *Nietzsche's Philosophy of the Eternal Recurrence of the Same*. Translated by J. Harvey Lomax. Berkeley, CA: University of California Press, 1997.

Lubac, Henri de. *The Drama of Atheist Humanism*. San Francisco, CA: Ignatius, 1998.

Lutz, Donald S. *The Origins of American Constitutionalism*. Baton Rouge, LA: Louisiana University State Press, 1988.

Machiavelli, Niccolò. *Discourses on Livy*. Translated by Harvey C. Mansfield, and Nathan Tarcov. Chicago, IL: Chicago University Press, 2009.

———. *The Prince*. Translated by Harvey Mansfield. Chicago, IL: University of Chicago Press, 1988.

Madison, James. *Madison: Writings*. New York: Library of America, 1999.

Mahoney, Daniel J. "A Noble and Generous Soul." *The Claremont Review of Books* VII, no. 3 (Summer 2007). http://www.claremont.org/publications/crb/id.1398/article_detail.asp.

Mancini, Matthew J. "Too Many Tocquevilles: The Fable of Tocqueville's American Reception." *Journal of the History of Ideas* 69, no. 2 (April 2008): 245–68.

Robert Nisbet. "Many Tocquevilles." *American Scholar* 46 (1976–77): 59–75.

Manent, Pierre. *An Intellectual History of Liberalism*. Translated by Rebecca Balinski. Princeton, NJ: Princeton University Press, 1994.

———. *Modern Liberty and its Discontents*. Edited and translated by Daniel J. Mahoney, and Paul Seaton. Lanham, MD: Rowman and Littlefield, 1998.

———. *Tocqueville and the Nature of Democracy*. Translated by John Waggoner. Lanham, MD: Rowman and Littlefield, 1991.

———. "Tocqueville, Political Philosopher." *The Cambridge Companion to Tocqueville*. New York: Cambridge University Press, 2006.

Manion, Clarence E. *The Key to Peace*. Chicago, IL: The Heritage Foundation, 1951.

Mann, Charles. *1491: New Revelations of the Americas before Columbus*. New York: Alfred A. Knopf, 2005.

Mansfield, Harvey C. *Machiavelli's Virtue*. Chicago, IL: University of Chicago Press, 1996.

Marx, Karl. *Karl Marx: Selected Writings*. Edited by David McLellan. New York: Oxford University Press, 1984.

Mencken, H. L. *Notes on Democracy*. New York: Dissident Books, 2009.

Millett, Paul. "Aristotle and Slavery in Athens." *Greece & Rome* 54, no. 2 (2007): 178–209.

Miller, James. *Rousseau: Dreamer of Democracy*. New Haven, CT: Yale University Press, 1984.

Mises, Ludwig von. *Liberalism*. Indianapolis, IN: Liberty Fund, 2005.

Mitchell, Joshua. *The Fragility of Freed: Tocqueville on Religion, Democracy, and the American Future*. Chicago, IL: University of Chicago Press, 1995.

Montaigne, Michel de. *Essays*. Translated by Donald M. Frame. Stanford, CA: Stanford University Press, 1981.

Montuori, Mario. *Socrates: Physiology of a Myth*. Amsterdam: J.C. Gieben, 1981.

Mosca, Gaetano. *The Ruling Class*. New York, McGraw Hill, 1939.

Nadler, Stephen. *Spinoza: A Life*. Cambridge: Cambridge University Press, 2001.

Nehamas, Alexander. *Life as Literature*. Cambridge, MA: Harvard University Press, 2002.

Nietzsche, Friedrich. *Basic Writings of Nietzsche*. Translated by Walter Kaufmann. New York: Modern Library, 2000.

———. *Beyond Good and Evil*. Translated by Judith Norman. New York: Cambridge University Press, 2014.

———. *The Birth of Tragedy and the Case of Wagner*. Translated by Ronald Speirs. New York: Cambridge University Press, 2004.

———. *Daybreak*. Translated by R. J. Hollingdale. New York: Cambridge University Press, 1997.

———. *The Gay Science*. Translated by Walter Kaufmann. New York: Vintage Books, 1974.

———. *Human, All Too Human*. Translated by R. J. Hollingdale. New York: Cambridge University Press, 2000.

———. *On the Genealogy of Morals and Ecce Homo*. Translated by Carol Diethe. New York: Cambridge University Press, 2017.

———. *The Portable Nietzsche*. Translated by Walter Kaufmann. New York: Penguin Books, 1982.

_____. *Prefaces to Unwritten Works*. Translated and edited by Michael W. Grenke. South Bend, IN: St. Augustine Press, 2005.
_____. *The Pre-Platonic Philosophers*. Translated by Greg Whitlock. Urbana, IL: University of Illinois Press, 2001.
_____. *Selected Letters of Friedrich Nietzsche*. Edited and translated by Christopher Middleton. Indianapolis, IN: Hackett Publishing Company, 1996.
_____. *Untimely Meditations*. Translated by R. J. Hollingdale. New York: Cambridge University Press, 1997.
_____. *The Will to Power*. Edited by Walter Kaufmann. Translated by Walter Kaufmann, and R. J. Hollingdale. New York: Vintage Books, 1968.
Nisbet, Robert. "Many Tocquevilles." *American Scholar* 46, no. 1 (Winter 1977): 59–75.
Oakeshott, Michael. *Rationalism in Politics*. Indianapolis, IN: Liberty Press, 1991.
O'Brien, Connor Cruise. *The Suspecting Glance*. London: Faber and Faber, 1972.
Owen, David. "Nietzsche, Ethical Agency and the Problem of Democracy." In *Nietzsche, Power, and Politics: Rethinking Nietzsche's Legacy for Political Thought*, edited by Herman W. Siemens, and Vasti Roodt, 143–67. Berlin: De Gruyter, 2008.
_____. *Nietzsche, Politics, and Modernity: A Critique of Liberal Reason*. London: Sage Publications, 1995.
Palmer, R. R. *Twelve who Ruled: The Year of the Terror in the French Revolution*. Princeton, NJ: Princeton University Press, 1989.
_____. *The World of the French Revolution*. New York: Harper and Row, 1971.
Pangle, Thomas. "Nihilism and Modern Democracy in the Thought of Nietzsche." In *The Crisis of Liberal Democracy: A Straussian Perspective*, edited by Kenneth L. Deutsch, and Walter Soffer, 180–211. Albany, NY: State University of New York Press, 1987.
_____. *The Spirit of Modern Republicanism: The Moral Vision of the American Founders and the Philosophy of Locke*. Chicago, IL: University of Chicago Press, 1988.
_____. "The 'Warrior Spirit' as an Inlet to the Political Philosophy of Nietzsche's Zarathustra." *Nietzsche-Studien: Internationales Jahrbuch für die Nietzsche-Forschung* 15 (1986): 140–79.
Pascal, Blaise. *Pensées*. Translated by A. J. Krailsheimer. New York: Penguin, 1995.
Patterson, Cynthia. "'Not Worth the Rearing': The Causes of Infant Exposure in Ancient Greece." *Transactions of the American Philological Association* 115 (1985): 103–23.
Patterson, Orlando. *Freedom: Freedom in the Making of Western Culture*. New York: Basic Books, 1991.
Patton, Paul. "Nietzsche, Genealogy, and Justice." In *Nietzsche and Political Thought*, edited by Keith Ansell-Pearson, 7–22. London: Bloomsbury, 2013.
Peters, Edward. *Europe and the Middle Ages*. Upper Saddle River, NJ: Prentice Hall, 1996.
Pew Research Center. "In U.S., Decline of Christianity Continues at Rapid Pace." October 17, 2019. https://www.pewforum.org/2019/10/17/in-u-s-decline-of-christianity-continues-at-rapid-pace/.

Pierson, George Wilson. *Tocqueville in America*. New York: Oxford University Press, 1938.
Pinkard, Terry. *Hegel: A Biography*. New York: Cambridge University Press, 2001.
Plato. *Apology of Socrates*. In *Four Texts on Socrates*. Translated by Thomas G. West, and Grace Starry West. Ithaca, NY: Cornell University Press, 1995.
———. *Phaedo*. In *The Last Days of Socrates*. Translated by Hugh Tredennick. New York: Penguin Books, 1987.
———. *The Republic*. Translated by Allan Bloom. New York: Basic Books, 1991.
Plumer, Brad. "Humans are Speeding Extinction and Altering the Natural World at an 'Unprecedented' Pace." *The New York Times*, May 6, 2019. https://www.nytimes.com/2019/05/06/climate/biodiversity-extinction-united-nations.html.
Plutarch. *Plutarch's Lives*. 2 vols. Translated by John Dryden. New York: Modern Library, 1992.
Pocock, J. G. A. *The Machiavellian Moment*. Princeton, NJ: Princeton University Press, 1975.
Pope, Alexander. *The Poems of Alexander Pope: A One-Volume Edition of the Twickenham Text with Selected Annotations*. Edited by John Butt. New Haven, CT: Yale University Press, 1963.
Rahe, Paul. *Republics Ancient and Modern*. 3 vols. Chapel Hill, NC: The University of North Carolina Press, 1994.
Ramsey, Lydia, and Samantha Lee. "Humans Share Almost All of Our DNA with Cats, Cattle and Mice." *The Independent*, April 6, 2018, https://www.independent.co.uk/news/science/human-dna-share-cats-cattle-mice-same-genetics-code-a8292111.html.
Reade, Arthur, ed. *Study and Stimulants: Or, the Use of Intoxicants and Narcotics in Relation to Intellectual Life, as Illustrated by Personal Communications on the Subject, from Men of Letters and of Science*. London: Simpkin, Marshall, and Co., 1883.
Richardson, John. *Nietzsche's New Darwinism*. Oxford: Oxford University Press, 2004.
Riché, Pierre. *Daily Life in the World of Charlemagne*. Philadelphia, PA: University of Pennsylvania Press, 1978.
Robinson, James Harvey. *New History: Essays Illustrating the Modern Historical Outlook*. New York: The Macmillan Company, 1912.
Robinson, Joan. *Freedom and Necessity: An Introduction to the Study of Society*. New York: Pantheon Books, 1970.
Rorty, Richard. *Contingency, Irony, and Solidarity*. New York: Cambridge University Press, 1999.
Rosen, Stanley. *G.W.F. Hegel: An Introduction to the Science of Wisdom*. South Bend, IN: St. Augustine Press, 2000.
———. *The Mask of Enlightenment: Nietzsche's Zarathustra*. New York: Cambridge University Press, 1995.
———. *Plato's Republic: A Study*. New Haven, CT: Yale University Press, 2005.
Ross, Michael. *Banners of the King: The War of the Vendee 1793–4*. New York: Hippocrene Books, 1975.

Rousseau, Jean Jacques. *The Collected Writings of Jean-Jacques Rousseau (Volume 11): The Plan for Perpetual Peace, on the Government of Poland, and Other Writings on History and Politics*. Edited by Christopher Kelly. Translated by Christopher Kelly, and Judith Bush. Lebanon, NH: University Press of New England, 2005.

———. *The Confessions and Correspondence Including the Letters to Malesherbes*. Translated by Christopher Kelley. Dartmouth: Dartmouth University Press, 1995.

———. *Emile: Or on Education*. Translated by Allan Bloom. New York: Basic Books, 1979.

———. *The First and Second Discourses*. Translated by Roger D. Masters, and Judith R. Masters. New York: St. Martin's, 1969.

———. *The Reveries of the Solitary Walker*. Translated by Peter France. New York: Penguin, 1979.

———. *The Major Political Writings of Jean-Jacques Rousseau*. Translated and edited by John T. Scott. Chicago, IL: Chicago University Press, 2012.

Schama, Simon. *Citizens: A Chronicle of the French Revolution*. New York: Alfred A. Knopf, 1991.

Schleifer, James T. *The Making of Tocqueville's Democracy in America*. Indianapolis, IN: The Liberty Fund, 2000.

———. *Tocqueville*. Medford, MA: Polity, 2018.

Schrift, Alan, ed. *Why Nietzsche Still? Reflections on Drama, Culture, and Politics*. Berkley, CA: University of California Press, 2000.

Scott, John T. "Introduction." In *The Major Political Writings of Jean-Jacques Rousseau: The Two Discourses and the Social Contract*. Translated and edited by John T. Scott, xiii–xliv. Chicago, IL: University of Chicago Press, 2012.

Scruton, Roger. "The Great Swindle." *Aeon*, December 17, 2012. https://aeon.co/essays/a-cult-of-fakery-has-taken-over-what-s-left-of-high-culture.

Scurr, Ruth. *Fatal Purity: Robespierre and the French Revolution*. New York: Henry Holt and Company, 2007.

Siedentop, Larry. *Inventing the Individual: The Origins of Western Liberalism*. Cambridge, MA: Harvard University Press, 2015.

Silk, M. S., and J. P. Stern. *Nietzsche on Tragedy*. New York: Cambridge University Press, 1981.

Skinner, Quentin. *Machiavelli*. New York: Hill and Wang, 1981.

Slack, Paul. *The Impact of Plague in Tudor and Stuart England*. New York: Oxford University Press, 2003.

Small, Robin. "What Nietzsche Did During the Science Wars." In *Nietzsche and the Sciences*, edited by Thomas H. Brobjer, and Gregory Moore, 155–170. Burlington, VT: Ashgate, 2004.

Sowell, Thomas. *Black Rednecks and White Liberals*. New York: Encounter Books, 2005.

Starr, Chester G. *The Ancient Greeks*. New York: Oxford University Press, 1979.

———. *The Aristocratic Temper of Greek Civilization*. New York: Oxford University Press, 1992.

Storey, Benjamin. "Tocqueville on Technology." *The New Atlantis*, Fall 2013. https://www.thenewatlantis.com/publications/tocqueville-on-technology.

Strauss, Leo. *The City and Man*. Chicago, IL: University of Chicago Press, 1978.
———. *An Introduction to Political Philosophy*. Edited by Hilail Gildin. Detroit: Wayne State University Press, 1989.
———. *Natural Right and History*. Chicago, IL: University of Chicago Press, 1965.
———. *The Political Philosophy of Hobbes: Its Genesis and Basis*. Chicago, IL: University of Chicago Press, 1996.
———. *The Rebirth of Classical Political Rationalism*. Chicago, IL: University of Chicago Press, 1989.
———. *Studies in Platonic Political Philosophy*. Chicago, IL: University of Chicago Press, 1983.
———. *Thoughts on Machiavelli*. Chicago, IL: University of Chicago Press, 1995.
Strong, Tracy B. *Friedrich Nietzsche and the Politics of Transfiguration*. Champaign, IL: University of Illinois Press, 1999.
Stuurman, Siep. *The Invention of Humanity: Equality and Cultural Difference in World History*. Cambridge, MA: Harvard University Press, 2017.
Tocqueville, Alexis de. *Democracy in America*. Translated by Harvey C. Mansfield, and Delba Winthrop. Chicago, IL: University of Chicago Press, 2000.
———. *The European Revolution and Correspondence with Gobineau*. Edited and translated by John Lukacs. Garden City, NY: Doubleday Anchor Books, 1959.
———. *Journeys to England and Ireland*. Edited by J. P. Mayer. Translated by George Lawrence, and J. P. Mayer. New Haven, CT: Yale University Press, 1958.
———. *Memoir on Pauperism*. Translated by Seymour Drescher. Chicago, IL: Ivan R. Dee, 1997.
———. *The Old Regime and the Revolution*. Edited by François Furet, and Françoise Mélonio. Translated by Alan S. Kahan. Chicago, IL: University of Chicago Press, 1998.
———. "Political and Social Condition of France." *London and Westminster Review* 3, no. 1 (April 1836): 137–69.
———. *Recollections*. Edited by J. P. Mayer. Translated by Alexander Teixeira de Mattos. New York: Columbia University Press, 1949.
———. *Tocqueville on America after 1840: Letters and Other Writings*. Edited and translated by Aurelian Craiutu, and Jerry Jennings. New York: Cambridge University Press, 2009.
———. *The Tocqueville Reader: A life in Letters and Politics*. Edited by Olivier Zunz, and Alan S. Kahan. Malden, MA: Blackwell, 2002.
———. *Selected Letters on Politics and Society*. Edited by Roger Boesche. Translated by Roger Boesche, and James Toupin. Berkeley, CA: University of California Press, 1985.
———. *Writings of Empire and Slavery*. Edited and translated by Jennifer Pitts. Baltimore, MD: Johns Hopkins University Press, 2001.
Tevenar, Gudrun von. "Nietzsche on Nausea." *Journal of Nietzsche Studies* 50, no. 1 (2019): 58–78.
Trotsky, Leon. *Literature and Revolution*. New York: Russell and Russell, 1957.

Varden, Helga. "Kant and Lying to the Murderer at the Door...One More Time: Kant's Legal Philosophy and Lies to Murderers and Nazis." *Journal of Social Philosophy* 41, no. 4 (Winter 2010): 403–21.

Vincent, Ken R. "The Salvation Conspiracy: How Hell Became Eternal." *The Universalist Herald* (July/August 2006). https://christianuniversalist.org/resources/articles/salvation-conspiracy/.

Voltaire. *Voltaire in his Letters: Being a Selection from his Correspondence*. Translated by S. G. Tallentyre. New York: G. P. Putnam's Sons, 1919.

Warren, Mark. *Nietzsche and Political Thought*. Cambridge, MA: The MIT Press, 1998.

Watson, James E. M., Danielle F. Shanahan, Moreno Di Marco, James Allan, William F. Laurance, Eric W. Sanderson, Brendan Mackey, and Oscar Venter. "Catastrophic Declines in Wilderness Areas Undermine Global Environment Targets." *Current Biology* 26, no. 21 (2016): 2929–34.

Westermann, William Linn. *The Slave Systems of Greek and Roman Antiquity*. Philadelphia, PA: The American Philosophical Society, 1984.

Williams, Raymond. *Keywords: A Vocabulary of Culture and Society*. New York: Oxford University Press, 1985.

Wills, Garry. *Inventing America: Jefferson's Declaration of Independence*. New York: Vintage Books, 1979.

Wolf, Maryann. *Reader Come Back: The Reading Brain in a Digital World*. New York: Harper Collins, 2018.

Wootton, David. *The Invention of Science: A New History of the Scientific Revolution*. New York: HarperCollins, 2015.

———. *Power, Pleasure, and Profit: Insatiable Appetites from Machiavelli to Madison*. Cambridge, MA: Harvard University Press, 2018.

Zuckert, Catherine. *Plato's Philosophers: The Coherence of the Dialogues*. Chicago, IL: University of Chicago Press, 2009.

Index

Archimedes, 121
Arendt, Hannah, 278n45
Aristophanes, 162, 164
Aristotle, 14, 17, 19, 31, 44, 54, 62, 71n11, 163, 248

Bacon, Francis, 120, 158, 238, 249
Blake, William, 157
Bloch, Marc, 145n140, 147n148, 147n157
Bloom, Allan, 78n114, 136n35
Bonaparte, Napoleon, 186, 225n199, 227n215, 277n33, 278n40
Brogan, Hugh, 145–47n142

Calvin, John, 85n213, 238
Ceaser, James, 144n130
Cicero, 73n27, 214n12
Columbus, Christopher, 16, 280n76
Copernicus, 93, 218n59, 239, 252, 255, 280n76

Dalrymple, Theodore, 70n2
Darwin, Charles (and Darwinism), 47, 110, 218n59, 255–59, 281n18, 282n122, 282n124, 283n136
Dennett, Daniel, 281n118
Descartes, René, 30, 120, 158, 237–41, 247–49

Dostoevsky, Fyodor, 8n6, 213n4
Drescher, Seymour, 144n131, 147n148, 148n158, 148n162, 224n177, 230n247
Drochon, Hugo, 133n24, 134n26, 226n205

Engels, Friedrich, 81n177
Euripides, 138, 153–54, 216n26

Foucault, Michel, 138n61
Fukuyama, Francis, 1, 277n29
Furet, François, 141n102, 213n3, 228n221, 230n245, 278n40

Gillespie, Michael Allen, 88n224, 136n37, 139n61, 283n147
Guénon, René, 140n84, 276n7, 286n201

Hamilton, Alexander, 20, 135n34
Hegel, Georg Wilhelm Friedrich, 25, 54–61, 68, 81n170, 83n194, 84n202, 88n224, 96–99, 225n198, 290
Heidegger, Martin, 218n78
Hobbes, Thomas, 4, 18–29, 31–34, 38, 42–44, 56, 72–73nn25–26, 74n51, 76n86, 77nn89–90, 79n134, 99, 158, 270, 289n209
Huxley, Aldous, 3, 13, 70–71n6

Kant, Immanuel, 21–22, 25–26,
    41, 43–55, 79n131, 80n150,
    80nn153–54, 80n161, 82n180,
    83n194, 165–66, 225n198
Kaufmann, Walter, 133–34n26,
    282n124
Kierkegaard, Søren, 79n135
Kojève, Alexandre, 82n186

Lamberti, Jean-Claude, 133n14,
    225n197
Lampert, Laurence, 218n74
Lessing, Gotthold Ephraim, 213n4
Lincoln, Abraham, 5
Locke, John, 24–35, 38, 43–44, 56,
    75n70, 79n134, 84n201, 99, 246
Louis XIII, 3
Louis XIV, 196, 199
Louis XV, 229n235
Louis XVI, 186–87, 199, 229n235
Lubac, Henri de, 221n118
Luther, Martin, 238

Machiavelli, Niccolò, 16–19, 21, 32, 42,
    72n20, 75n69, 84n201, 150
Madison, James, 81n179, 135n34,
    213n1
Manent, Pierre, 77n108, 84n203,
    136n40, 231n256, 284n153
Marx, Karl, 25, 30, 54–56, 84n202,
    87nn221–22, 141n99, 143n121,
    146n142, 260, 289–90
Mises, Ludwig von, 75n67
Montaigne, Michel de, 83n196

Nehamas, Alexander, 281n99

Oakeshott, Michael, 280n75

Pascal, Blaise, 120, 135n30,
    143nn114–15, 263
Plato, 13–15, 17, 19, 26, 31, 44, 61–62,
    71n14, 75n55, 153–54, 157, 167,
    215n17, 215n20, 224, 226n205,
    231n256, 252–54
Plutarch, 83n196, 121

Quesnay, François, 209

Richardson, John, 282n122
Robespierre, Maximilien, 78n130, 187,
    204, 206, 209
Rorty, Richard, 276n2
Rousseau, Jean-Jacques, 20, 25, 31–46,
    48, 53, 77n98, 77nn108–9, 78n117,
    79n131, 84n202, 98–100, 135n30,
    135n34, 166, 186, 201, 206, 212,
    233n304, 265, 277n16

Saint-Simon, Henri de, 276n1
Schleifer, James, 132n14, 278n40
Socrates, 19, 47, 55, 82n182, 125,
    151–71, 214n12, 215nn20–21,
    216n26, 216n29, 218n71, 218n74,
    219n80, 219n85, 219n87, 223n148,
    236–37, 247–53, 282n124
Spencer, Herbert, 13, 110, 257
Spinoza, Baruch, 258, 282n133
Strauss, Leo, 17, 23, 36, 77n89, 83n198,
    84n201, 135n27, 217n50, 220n102,
    220n107, 260–61

Trotsky, Leon, 54
Turgot, Anne Robert Jacques, 202, 209
Twain, Mark, 1, 7n2, 8n3

Voltaire, 37, 207, 238

About the Author

David A. Eisenberg is an associate professor of political science at Eureka College. Prior to relocating to the cornfields of Central Illinois, he taught amid the skyscrapers of Midtown Manhattan at Baruch College, City University of New York, and was an associate director for academic affairs at Columbia University. He earned his MA and PhD from Claremont Graduate University and BA from Trinity College (Hartford, CT). His writings have appeared in a variety of online and print publications. Unable to grasp both, he prefers to maintain a handle on reality than on Twitter.

www.ingramcontent.com/pod-product-compliance
Lightning Source LLC
Chambersburg PA
CBHW021345300426
44114CB00012B/1088